MW00609292

900
LETTERS

DB BROWN, PHD

900 LETTERS

MARRIAGE, MOVIES, AND THE MARIANAS

Epigraph Books
Rhinebeck, New York

Paperback ISBN: 978-1-954744-78-3
Hardcover ISBN: 978-1-954744-79-0
eBook ISBN: 978-1-954744-80-6

Library of Congress Control Number: 2022909240

Photos on pages 119 and 220 courtesy of U.S. Army Signal Corps.

Book and cover design by Colin Rolfe

Epigraph Books
22 East Market Street, Suite 304
Rhinebeck, NY 12572
(845) 876-4861
epigraphps.com

CONTENTS

INTRODUCTION

There were over six million marriages in the United States during World War II, 1.7 million in 1944 alone. Six million love stories, each unique, each special, all of them taking place against a backdrop of terrible world conflict. Because of the war, many couples were separated for long periods of time and communicated with each other by writing letters. World War II ended more than seventy-five years ago, but fortunately many of these letters have survived and provide vivid and moving glimpses of those times.

In 1942, Harvey and Betty met at a USO dance in Beverly Hills. He was in training with the Army. She worked at a record store near several major motion picture studios. Harvey soon left California for continued training on the East Coast, and the two didn't see each other again until they became engaged on the Fourth of July in 1944. They were married that November, and the following Spring he was sent to Guam, where he served until the end of the war.

From April 1942 until January 1946, Betty and Harvey were together for only a few months, but they wrote to each other often, eventually almost daily. Through their correspondence, they got to know one another, became close, and eventually made plans to spend their lives together. They wrote long letters, a lost art these days. Of course, they shared feelings about their growing relationship, but they also described their daily lives, and their real-time observations about wartime America in the 1940s. Harvey wrote about his life in the Army, his daily routine, the bases where he served, his time overseas in Guam. Betty described life in Hollywood, the movies being produced, the music being performed and recorded, the effects of the war on families left at home. Betty saved their letters, some 900 of them, and she noted in one of them, "...maybe someone should write a book about our story...." Little did she know.

1

THE DANCE

It was Sunday, April 19, 1942. Betty Lundin didn't have to work at the music store. It had been a reasonably cool night, the temperature dropping to the low 40's, but during the day it got up to 91, the hottest day in Southern California since early November. She had breakfast with her parents and read the newspaper with her cup of coffee. The headlines and front-page stories were about the surprise American bombing raid on Tokyo the day before. The *Los Angeles Times*, along with papers across the country, contained accounts of Japanese reactions to the attack, but details of the bombing run, later known as "the Doolittle Raid," didn't come out until sometime later.

Betty was trying to help with the war effort. She was involved with various USO activities in Southern California and had been volunteering at weekly Sunday night dances at American Legion Post #253 in Beverly Hills. The next dance was that evening, and Betty and her friend Virjeanne took the streetcar over to the Post's clubhouse on Robertson Avenue. Many of the servicemen at the dance were stationed at nearby Clover Field in Culver City. At some point in the evening, Harvey Brown, a soldier from Pittsburgh, asked Betty to dance...

2

HARVEY

J. Harvey Brown Jr., the son of J. Harvey Brown and Elsie Mae Bell, was born in Pittsburgh, Pennsylvania on January 24, 1918. He was an only child.

The Brown family had lived in the vicinity of Pittsburgh since the beginning of the nineteenth century. Harvey's great-great grandfather, John Wesley Brown, was born there in about 1802 and had been a policeman as a young man, reputedly the first officer to patrol Pittsburgh's Second Avenue at night with a lantern and mace. By 1850, he was working as a shoemaker and was living with his family on North Alley in Allegheny City (then a separate town but currently the "North Side" of the City of Pittsburgh).

Harvey's great grandfather, Abraham Moore Brown, was born in Pittsburgh in 1831, and as a boy had driven mules on the old Pennsylvania Canal. In 1850, he was working as a carpenter and, shortly after that, began working on the railroad, building bridges on the new Fort Wayne line. After moving to Lima, Ohio, and living there for a few years, Abraham moved his family back to Pennsylvania and took a job as the yardmaster for the Cleveland and Pittsburg Railroad in McClure Township on the Ohio River just south of Pittsburgh. When the Civil War broke out, Abraham was the conductor of a Union hospital train, carrying wounded soldiers back from Chattanooga, Tennessee. He was in Chattanooga during the Battle of Lookout Mountain, and while there, he operated a restaurant for the soldiers. After the war, he ran the first freight train between Pittsburgh and Steubenville, Ohio. In 1877, Abraham was working as a weighmaster, and his family was living near the Union Depot in Pittsburgh. There were major railroad riots that summer, and Abraham's house, near the center of the riot area, was burned down. For the remainder of their lives, Abraham and his wife Margaret ran restaurants and boarding houses catering to Pittsburgh railroad workers.

Harvey's grandfather, Lee Harvey Brown, was born in McClure township in 1870. He worked as a yard clerk for the Pittsburgh, Cincinnati, and St. Louis Railroad, and later as a flagman at Union Station for the Pennsylvania Railroad. Harvey's father, Harvey Sr., was born in Pittsburgh in 1894 and married Elsie Bell in 1916. The Bell ancestors were originally from the village of Ballywalter in Northern Ireland. Shortly after his marriage to Elsie, John (also known as "Harvey") found work at a local meat packing plant and for a number of years was a salesman for an auto parts company.

In 1918, the year of Harvey's birth, an epidemic of "Spanish" influenza broke out. It was called the "most devastating outbreak of infectious disease in human history." As I write this in 2020 during the current COVID-19 pandemic, it is easy to understand the terror of that period. Between 1918 and 1920, fifty million lives were lost worldwide, with the death toll in the US exceeding 675,000. Pennsylvania was one of the hardest hit states in the country, and the three largest cities in the state—Philadelphia, Pittsburgh, and Scranton—were particularly affected. In Philadelphia, over seven hundred people died on October 16th alone. In Pittsburgh, there were approximately fifty thousand cases of influenza, and the city had the highest mortality rate in the country. The epidemic erupted during the final stages of World War I, with the flu spreading globally due to soldiers living in cramped quarters around the world. When the war ended (the Armistice was signed in November), people gathered in large celebrations all over the United States, causing the disease to spread even further. This was a frightening time to be raising small children, but the Browns were fortunate, and Harvey didn't become ill.

Harvey didn't like to be called "John" as schoolmates had teased him about the lyrics from the old song ("John Brown's body lies a moulderin' in the grave . . ."), so he went by his middle name. The Browns attended the Episcopal Church on Ellsworth Avenue, and Harvey served as an altar boy and sang in the choir. He studied Business Administration for a semester at Duquesne University before transferring to the University of Pittsburgh, where he pursued a degree in Mechanical Engineering. He took his Pitt classes at night, while working full-time for the Duquesne Light Company as a Mechanical and Design Draftsman, working with steam boiler and piping equipment.

On December 7, 1941, the Japanese attacked Pearl Harbor, and on the seventeenth, needing only thirty credits to graduate from Pitt, Harvey quit school and enlisted in the Army. He enlisted in Pittsburgh and was sent to the New Cumberland Army Depot, near Harrisburg, for processing. During the war, 90 percent of all new recruits from Pennsylvania were processed at the New Cumberland Reception Center. Because of his background, he was assigned to the Army Corps of Engineers and went to the Air Corps Technical School at Keesler Field in Biloxi, Mississippi, for his basic training. After completing the airplane mechanics course in Biloxi in April 1942, he was sent to the Douglas Aircraft Mechanic School in Santa Monica, California, for additional training. Douglas was part of the Boeing-Vega-Douglas (BVD) consortium and produced the B-17 Flying Fortress at their facility adjacent to Clover Field in Santa Monica (now Santa Monica Airport). Harvey's coursework at Douglas included instruction in airfield camouflage:

> With World War II raging in Europe, Douglas realized well before Pearl Harbor that his plant was a sitting duck for an air attack. He didn't wait for the government to protect him; he took the controls. Douglas asked his chief engineer and test pilot, Frank Collbohm, and a renowned architect, H. Roy Kelley, to devise a way to camouflage the plant. [Later, Collbohm would found Rand Corp. and Kelley would design its headquarters.] Together with Warner Bros. studio set designers, they made the plant and airstrip disappear—at least from the air.
>
> Almost 5 million square feet of chicken wire, stretched across 400 tall poles, canopied the terminal, hangers, assorted buildings, and parking lots. Atop the mesh stood lightweight, wood-frame houses with attached garages, fences, clotheslines, even "trees" made of twisted wire and chicken feathers spray-painted to look like leaves. Tanker trucks spewed green paint on the runway [of the aircraft plant] to simulate a field of grass. Streets and sidewalks were painted on the covering to blend into the adjacent Sunset Park neighborhood of modest homes that housed the Douglas employees.
>
> The tallest hanger was made to look like a gently sloping hillside neighborhood. Designers even matched up the painted streets with the real ones. When they were done, some pilots in the area landed at nearby airstrips instead, protesting that someone had moved the field. Douglas adapted. When planes were due, he stationed men at each end of the runway to wave red flags like matadors. Eventually signalmen were replaced with white markers painted on the hillsides.

The façade was such a success that Warner Bros. replicated it, fearing that its motion picture studio looked like an aircraft plant from the air.

Harvey's troop train arrived in Los Angeles from Biloxi on Wednesday, April 15, 1942, and years later, he recalled that first day in California. "I didn't see much of Los Angeles itself while I was there, but I sure remember standing around in Union Station with a couple of barracks boys on the ground beside me. We had just arrived and had been formed into a column of twos to wait for transportation to Santa Monica. When the streetcars arrived, we loaded up and started the long ride out to the Edgewater Hotel." The Edgewater was at 1711 Ocean Front, not far from the Santa Monica Pier, and like most hotels and apartment buildings, had been converted into housing for troops. Four days later, along with some buddies from the 415th Technical School Squadron, he took a streetcar to Robertson Avenue in Beverly Hills and went to a USO dance at the American Legion Post clubhouse—where he met, and danced with, Betty Lundin.

BETTY

Elizabeth Mae Lundin, known as "Betty," was born in Los Angeles on December 16, 1920. Her paternal grandparents were born in Sweden, and her mother's family was primarily from England and Ireland.

Betty's father, Perle Rudolph Lundin, was born in Paxton, Illinois, a town with many recent immigrants from Sweden. (In Swedish, "Perle" is an affectionate form of "Per.") His parents had met and married in Paxton, but both had come from the vicinity of Jönköping, a fairly large Swedish city. For generations, most of Perle's ancestors on both sides had worked at small farms near Jönköping, but in the early eighteenth century a few of them had been gunsmiths at the factory located near the Husqvarna waterfall. A factory still exists at the site, but in recent times Husqvarna is best known for the production of quality tools, lawnmowers, chain saws, and motorcycles—not gun barrels.

In his early twenties, Perle moved to Chicago and found work as a clerk at the Illinois Steel Corporation. When war broke out, he enlisted in the army and spent his time in the service working on military aircraft. The loud noise of the engines permanently damaged his hearing.

Betty Lundin's mother, Maeblossom Elizabeth Prior, was born in Chicago in 1894. Her family was from England on her father's side and primarily from Northern Ireland on her mother's. Her grandfather, Cornelius Winter Prior, had immigrated with his family in 1844 and, after working for several years as a farmer in Pennsylvania, had opened a series of daguerreotype and photography studios in Illinois and Nashville, Tennessee. Interestingly, in 1856 he had a studio in Freeport, Illinois, two blocks from that year's Lincoln-Douglas debate.

Maeblossom was working as a stenographer for the telephone company when she met and married Perle Lundin. They moved to California shortly thereafter.

When Betty was born in 1920, her parents had recently moved to the town of Venice in Southern California, and for the first seven years of her life, she lived almost directly across the street from a circus. Her father had found work at a paint store on Adams Boulevard, and the family lived near an area known as Barnes City, named after the traveling circus that had set up winter quarters there in 1914. In 1919, the owner of the circus, Al Barnes, bought a ranch between Venice and Culver City and established the site as the permanent home of the circus. Barnes City consisted of only a few square city blocks, but the impact on the residential area on all sides was dramatic. There were complaints about the smell, the roaring of lions, and the "braying" of elephants—and there was even a suggestion that the circus had brought the dreaded "Spanish flu" to the community in 1919.

Barnes boasted that he had more performing animals than all other circuses combined, and his star attraction was an elephant named Tusco. While the circus was on tour in the Northwest in 1922, Tusco broke loose in the town of Sedro-Wooley, Washington. Before being contained, the elephant "ran amuck," knocking down fences and telephone poles and completely demolishing a Model T Ford. The aftermath amounted to $20,000 in damages but terrific publicity for the circus. In 1923, Barnes opened a combination zoo and roadside attraction on his grounds, complete with sideshow acts. In 1927, Barnes City was annexed to the city of Los Angeles, and in that same year Barnes sold his property to a developer and moved his circus to Baldwin Park.

In about 1929, Betty's father left his job at the paint store and began working as a bond clerk in the office of the City Treasurer of Los Angeles, a position he held for the next twenty years. Betty graduated from Venice High School and then studied for two years at Santa Monica City College. During that time, she started working at Edmund Stella's Music Store on the corner of Main Street and Venice Boulevard in Culver City. In addition to record albums, Stella's carried pianos and other musical instruments, radios, and sheet music. There was also a service department that repaired musical instruments and radios. Culver City was at the epicenter of America's booming movie industry and was billed in 1937 as "Where 'Hollywood' Movies Are Made." In fact, Stella's store was only a few blocks away from four major movie studios: Metro-Goldwyn-Mayer Studio, Selznick International Pictures, Hal Roach Studios, and 20th Century-Fox Studios. An exciting environment for a teenage girl in the late 1930s.

By August of 1941, Betty was active with the USO, both directly as the Junior President of the Santa Monica chapter, and indirectly through work with Job's Daughters during her student days at Santa Monica City College. In early November, there was a Job's Daughters dance party: "Girls, here is your chance to jive to THE best records with your favorite beau at a 'Backwards Sport Dance', 3236 McManus Avenue, Friday, Nov. 7, 8 to 12:00, 25 cents couple, 15 cents stag." The dance was only a few blocks from the music store where Betty worked.

The attack on Pearl Harbor was a month later.

Betty was still working at Stella's Music Store when the US was attacked on December 7th, and she continued to volunteer with various local USO programs. She volunteered at gatherings held in Santa Monica at the Miramar Hotel, and she served as a "hostess" at the Sunday dances held at the American Legion Post in Beverly Hills.

Betty's USO ID, September 1943

4

FORT BELVOIR
TO PATTERSON
TO MIDDLETOWN

During an intermission at that first dance in Beverly Hills, Harvey and Betty sat on the hood of a car in the parking lot and chatted. They found they had many mutual interests like "big band" music (Harry James, etc.) and movies. Betty told him that Judy Garland was filming a new picture that week, *For Me and My Gal*, at MGM Studios a few blocks from the record store where she worked. At the end of the evening, they took the streetcar to Betty's neighborhood and they walked to her front door. They agreed to see each other again, and "when I went down to the 'trolley' that night after leaving your house, I felt like I had suddenly come out of the rain and into the sunshine." Two days later, Harvey wrote his first letter to her, not knowing it was the beginning of a several-hundred-letter correspondence:

Dear Betty:

Pardon me for using this rather antiquated stationary, but it is all that is available at the moment.

I wanted very much to make use of your address and come out to see you this week, but it doesn't look as if that will be possible. We are changing hotels tomorrow and we have already changed schools today so you can imagine the mess that things are in here. Our new hotel will probably be within a mile of the present one, so if you are agreeable I'll take a rain check on that get-together until later.

I'm planning on going out to the famous "Rosenkrantz" American Legion Post again next Sunday night, and I'm sure looking forward to seeing you there. Maybe there will be a Cadillac for us to sit on this time.

Looking forward to Sunday,
Harvey

The next day, Harvey's group moved to the Santa Monica Athletic Club on Ocean Front, at the base of the Santa Monica Pier. His unit stayed at SMAC for the duration of their schooling at Douglas Aircraft, and he and Betty saw each other several times. They went to at least one more of the Sunday USO dances in Beverly Hills. They danced to the music of Harry James and his Orchestra at the Palladium in Hollywood, and Harvey had a chance to chat with Mickey Serima, a friend from Pittsburgh who was playing percussion in the orchestra. They also saw Jan Savitt and his jazz band at Casa Mañana on Washington Boulevard in Culver City. Savitt's band was called the Top Hatters, and he would later say "we played thirty-one consecutive one-nighters all the way out to Hollywood. We did all the big ballrooms, and we did some of the theaters—you know, a week at the theaters here and there. And we did the Panther Room in Chicago, and all the big places. And we ended up in Hollywood where we played at the Casa Mañana." He later toured twice with Frank Sinatra, who served as a pallbearer when Savitt passed away in 1948.

While in California Harvey met Betty's mother and father, as well as her brother, Rod, and enjoyed sitting with them in front of their fireplace in Culver City.

Harvey left Santa Monica on May 11th, and he and Betty were in regular contact from then on. Only his letters from the next couple of years survive, not hers, but it is clear that both of them wrote regularly. His notes on postcards, sent after he left California, are very brief, but the postmarks trace the route of his troop train as he headed east: Tucson, El Paso, Houston, Biloxi, Pensacola, Jacksonville, and finally, Savannah. During the Houston stop, twenty of Harvey's buddies got off the train and boarded a bus for Galveston. "It was plenty tough to see them go. Keep your eye on the Air Corps.!!" From Pensacola on Wednesday, he wrote "I'm almost at the end of my trip. I should pull into Savannah about noon tomorrow, and I'll sure be glad to get off this train. All this riding gets you down. I still like California better than Florida!" Upon completion of the course at Douglas Aircraft, he had been assigned to the 301st Bombardment Squadron, stationed at Savannah's Hunter Field. He joined his unit there on May 22nd and took over his duties as an Airplane Mechanic. He immediately wrote to Betty: "How are you doing, chum? Are you still gladdening the hearts of the Army at the U.S.O.? I hope so because you were certainly cut out for that heart gladdening stuff. Take it from me, I know!

"Savannah is sure a different place from Venice or Santa Monica. The air base itself is swell, but the city is strictly on the sour side. Soldiers are thought to be slightly beneath the average citizen, and people seem to find it rather hard to be nice to us. One thing I regret (from my time in California) was that the Navy lived in your neighborhood, and not the Army. I just got this far when your letter came with the two sticks of gum! They only made me more determined to go back to California someday when this mess is all cleaned up. By the way, I've been trying to get hold of that record 'Octaroon,' but I'm still trying, so don't give up. I'm afraid that by now, I've said so much about that record that no matter how good it is, you'll be disappointed. Oh yes, I heard Harry James' 'Flight of the Bumblebee' the other day and it really is a knockout. Have you heard it? Well, I'll let you take over with the pen. My address will be on the envelope. Give my best to your mother and father and tell Rod to 'keep 'em jumpin'.'" Harvey and Betty both loved music and movies. Harvey's mention of recordings by Artie Shaw and Harry James set the tone for hundreds of letters over the next three-and-a-half years. He was able to find a copy of "Octoroon" and sent it to her. "I'm rather anxious to hear whether or not you got that record in good condition. It was packed in enough cardboard to fill a whole house, but even so I was still worried about it reaching you in good condition and not broken. I sure hope you like it. As you know it's one of my favorite recordings by one of my favorite bands. The woman in the music store had to send to Atlanta, Ga. for the record, and it was just luck that they happened to have one." Savannah was about nine hundred miles from Pittsburgh, and Harvey hoped to get a ten-day furlough so he could visit with his family. "I think I'll fly home in order to have as much time there as possible. I'd like you to see Pittsburgh, not only because it's a pretty nice place, but also because it's my hometown. Everyone does an awful lot of kidding about the smoke and dirt there, but really after living there a while, it kind of gets in your blood. I'll admit that California is a lot prettier than Pittsburgh, but I'd take Pittsburgh every time.

"A squadron of eighteen bombers just flew in so I guess we'll be getting called up to the field to look after them. There are more darn planes here now than I've ever seen."

Harvey started a letter on the 23rd but had to stop when he went on duty. The next morning, he continued writing: "I'm pretty tired. We pulled an inspection on one of our dive bombers last night, and that's a tough job. I'm sorry I'm not there (in California) to make some sort of retribution for the time I failed to 'get off at Main St.' At least we were able to get out to Casa Mañana to see Jan Savitt, even though the date was a little late. The next time I come to town, we'll paint the town a brighter shade than we were able to do the first time. Have you heard that new song of Glenn Miller's – 'Knit One, Perl Two'? There have been a pile of write-ups about it but as yet I haven't heard it. It's supposed to be a sure hit."

Betty was sending Harvey picture postcards, and he shared some of them with his friends. "All the boys that came here from California always gather around to see them, and they always have a big discussion about the good times we had there, and it always ends up by almost everyone wishing that they were back out there again."

Harvey applied for Officer Candidate School, and on July 8th he had an interview with the Officers Board of Review concerning his application: "... although I don't as yet know their decision, I feel fairly certain that I will be given a favorable grade. If that's so, I will be leaving in about a month or so for a three-month course on how to be an officer, etc. The Ordnance Division is the branch that I applied for, and they have schools in Aberdeen, Maryland and one in California, beside several others. Either Maryland or California would be fine for me. Maryland is next door to Pennsylvania and, of course,

Harvey (front row) at OCS graduation at Fort Belvoir, Virginia, Oct. 1942

California would be a lot closer to Venice than Georgia. This is going to be cut short because we've got to stand retreat in a few minutes and since we've just gotten a new commanding officer, we don't dare cross him up the first time he sees us!"

Harvey was still at Hunter Field at the end of July. "Last Wednesday, the temperature was 115 degrees on the runway, and that is a little too warm to suit me. Yesterday, we had a storm of almost hurricane proportion, and that helped to cool things off. Boy, I never saw wind and rain like that before in my life. There were several planes on the field partially disassembled when the storm hit and some of the lighter aluminum parts were blown clear out of sight. They haven't found them yet."

Harvey was still a mechanic, but he now was in charge of a crew. "I have a plane of my own to look after. I get to go up in it in the gunner's cockpit which is an awful lot of fun when we go on practice bombing raids out over the Atlantic Ocean. As far as getting to be a flying officer or bombardier, as you say, I don't think I'll be able to do that. The officer's school that I've chosen is the Ordnance School, and I don't think there will be any flying connected with that. My first choice was to be an officer in the Air Force, but the interviewing officer told me that my education and experience better suited me for the Ordnance Department. I would like to stay in the Air Force, but it looks as if there is nothing I can do about it. The interviewing officer gave me a 95.33% on my interview, so all I have to do now is wait until I am called. I'm glad you like 'Octaroon.' Those records you wrote about are new to me – I haven't heard any of them, but I'll make it a point to watch for them. Have you heard 'The Pennsylvania Polka'? Of course, I'm just a little prejudiced, but really it is good (Andrews Sisters.)"

On July 27th, he sent a telegram: "Leaving Savannah for Engineers School at Fort Belvoir Virginia August third. Will write soon, Love, Harvey." He was promoted to corporal just before leaving Savannah.

On Wednesday, Harvey wrote from the George Mason Hotel in Alexandria, Virginia. "Just a short note to let you know that I'm here in Alexandria and all ready to start school tomorrow morning at Fort Belvoir (8 miles south of here). I got here at 1:00 this afternoon, and another fellow and I are going to share a room here at the George Mason tonight. He's from my squadron back at Hunter Field, and we expect to go through school together. Everyone I've talked to so far seems to think that this course is a h___ of a tough one, but you know me...!" And a couple of days later: "Well, I'm finally settled here at Fort Belvoir and from the looks of things it's going to be pretty tough sailing for the next three months. The discipline is very strict, the academic studies are tough, and the drilling has to be 'just so.' The officers here keep one eye on us at all times and we have to perform everything to the letter at all times. Of course, that sort of procedure is to be expected and I don't think I'll have much trouble getting along okay. At least I hope not. The idea of this strict discipline seems to be to force out any weaklings who can't take it, and believe you me, that won't apply to me. I can take all that they dish out. The men here all seem to be first class fellows. Everything else, including food and accommodations, is right up to par. The Post here is really pretty, with lots of grass and trees all over the place. It is the nicest place I've been so far.... with the exception of California, of course.

"You can't imagine how glad I was to get the news that I was finally going to be on my way to officer's school. I had worked on it for a long time, and it was a big load off my mind when my orders finally came through. Now that I'm here I can see what a tough job I put myself in for."

There was evidently a gap between letters from Betty, but one arrived on August 21st and Harvey was delighted: "I was sure glad to have your letter. I could stand one every day! I'm going on my third week here at Fort Belvoir, and I must be getting in the groove because things don't seem nearly so tough now as they did when I first got here. I'm getting along fine with all my studies, but I'm having a little trouble with my practical work such as tearing down the different weapons – rifles, pistols, machine guns, howitzers, etc. Being in the Air Corps I never had any experience at that sort of stuff, but I'm catching on quick. It won't be long until I'm just as good as the rest. Mother and Dad are coming down this weekend (it's only 230 miles) so you can imagine how excited I am right now. Just about this time tomorrow night I'll be actually talking to them in person again for the first time in over eight months. I'm doubly glad that they are coming because I'm almost certain that I won't get a leave after school is over. Unless they can come down again while I'm here, this will no doubt be the last time I'll see them until after the war. I don't like to think of it that way, but facts are facts."

When Harvey wrote to Betty on September 7th, he had been at Fort Belvoir for a month. Betty had asked about local USO activities. "I haven't been to the U.S.O. since I came to Fort Belvoir. I don't even know where it is. Not that I don't want to go, because I like them very much, but the truth of the matter is, we just don't have the time. We have free time from supper time on Saturday night until 2200 o'clock (10:00 p.m.) on Sunday night, but we usually have enough studying to amply fill up that time. Last weekend (Labor Day), my folks were down again, and I couldn't do any studying then. I had a lot of fun while they were here. They are two really swell people. Incidentally, I told them all about you and after my description, they are really anxious to meet you. It would have been perfect if you could have been here then, we could have done Washington D.C. Have you by any chance heard the 'Pennsylvania Polka' yet? If you haven't got it, let me know and I'll send you one. Things here are still pretty stiff, but I'm getting more or less on the beam as time goes on. The studies aren't too tough, but they shove it at us so fast that it's a little hard to grasp. We are studying a wide variety of subjects and soon as we finish one, we get another. Right now, we have a new one, camouflage, and it's one of the most intriguing things I've ever studied. I've never before seen so many different ways of deceiving people. Then, of course, we study the firing of all the different sizes of weapons. The only ones we haven't had so far are the anti-tank guns and the howitzers. p.s. I am doing my best for an assignment on the West Coast!"

On Friday, September 25th, Harvey's unit had a fifteen-mile march under light combat packs. They carried rifles, bayonets, canteens, and cartridge belts—and on their backs they had light packs containing raincoats, mess equipment, and emergency first aid kits. On Saturday, they had a twenty-mile march under a full field pack, which contained a blanket, half a tent, poles and pegs for the tent, a change of underwear, an extra pair of socks, toilet articles and mess equipment. They also carried a rifle, a bayonet, a cartridge belt, and a first aid kit. On both marches, they carried gas masks. "I feel like a perambulatory hardware counter with all that stuff hanging on me. I'm just a wee bit tired tonight but the only thing that bothers me at all is the ankle I broke playing football in high school. If it doesn't get me down, I'll be o.k. tomorrow too.

"Thanks a million for sending me that copy of the Pennsylvania Polka. You ought to hear the fellow at the chapel playing it on the Hammond Electric.... wow! Most of those new pieces that you mention are new to me. I haven't heard 'Our Own U.S.A.' yet, but I'll listen for it. We have a radio in our Day Room, but the only time I hear it is when I go in to look at the bulletin board. Today, I've finished the second day in the eighth week of the course, so that leaves me a little less than five weeks to go. The time is passing amazingly fast, probably because we are kept so busy all the time, but it can't go too fast to suit me. I'm anxious to get those gold bars on my shoulders so that I'll be in a position to ask for a furlough. My folks have been down twice but it's still not the same as having some time at home. It's been over nine months now since I was at home, and the urge to get back for a while is getting pretty strong. Maybe I'll be able to make it after I graduate."

When Harvey wrote to Betty on October 22nd, he was within a week of graduating from Officer Candidate School at Fort Belvoir. "We graduate on the 28th, which is just six days away and it's really been a scramble getting my exams all polished off and getting my clothes all measured and tailored. What a mess! My new uniform came back from the tailors last night and it fits me like a dream. I really feel like an officer when I've got it on. As soon as I wear it officially and can get a couple of snaps taken, I'll send you one. I'm enclosing one that Mother and Dad took when they were down here about a month ago, and you'll notice that I'm leaning on my car. It's the one I bought about five months before enlisting and is now being used by Mother and Dad. It certainly was good to drive it again. *[Note: Harvey's car was a 1941 Chevrolet five passenger coupe.]* Herewith find notice that I formally invite you to attend my graduation. Although your being there is an impossibility, I want you to know that the spirit is there." He followed up with a post card a couple of days later. "The letter I promised is still not on its way and probably won't be until I get to my next assignment. I've seen quite a bit of Washington, but I prefer Dayton or Venice. Remember me to everyone."

On October 27th, Harvey received orders to report to Patterson Field in Ohio following the OCS graduation the next day. His friend Ralph Haver was also assigned to Patterson Field, and they were given ten days to make the trip. At the awards ceremony at Fort Belvoir on the 28th, Harvey received a

letter from Brigadier General Crawford, officially promoting him to Second
Lieutenant:

> 1. The Secretary of War has directed me to inform you that the President
> has appointed and commissioned you a temporary Second Lieutenant,
> Army of the United States, effective this date, in the grade shown in the
> address above.
>
> 2. This commission to continue in force during the pleasure of the
> President of the United States for the time being, and for the duration
> of the present emergency and six months thereafter unless sooner
> terminated.
>
> 3. There is enclosed herewith a form for oath of office which you are
> requested to execute and return. The execution and return of the required
> oath of office constitute an acceptance of your appointment. No other
> evidence of acceptance is required. This letter should be retained by you
> as evidence of your appointment. R.C. Crawford, Brigadier General, U.S.
> Army, Commandant

"I wish you could have seen our graduation. It was short and sweet but very
solemn and impressive. The commanding general of the Corps of Engineers
gave a very inspiring talk about us as men, gentlemen, and officers, and what
would be expected of us. The band played the Star-Spangled Banner and chills
just raced up and down my spine (remember how we talked about that?). The
ball we were given was swell. Everything was strictly formal."

At Patterson, Harvey was assigned to the 912th Air Force Engineering
Headquarters Co. Two weeks after arriving, life finally settled down enough
for Harvey to send off a proper letter to Betty. "I've been waiting until I finally
got settled here and could send you the address that I think will be fairly
permanent. At least for the next several months. You'll notice my station
assignment (Patterson Field, Ohio) on the envelope, but since I'm living in
a room off the Post, mail will get to me much faster if you send it to me at
this address in Osborn, Ohio. Osborn is a little town of four or five thousand
people, located about ten miles north of Dayton and just about a mile from
Patterson Field. I'm really lucky to get a room here because the housing problem is terrific." Harvey had found a room at 25 Davis Drive, and his roommate was Ralph Haver, also from Fort Belvoir. Ralph was from Pasadena, and
the two enjoyed talking about the places Harvey had seen during his stay in

California. "With two big airfields within five miles of each other (Wright and Patterson), there are more people around than there are places for them to stay. A large percentage of the personnel at these fields is civilian workers, and that makes the problem even more acute.

"My own work is pretty indefinite as yet because the company I've been assigned to has been just newly activated. Our whole personnel is 12 officers and 15 enlisted men. Around the first of the month we will get some 200 men fresh from a reception center and that's when our work will really begin. Our company is supposed to be highly technical, and each man should be a specialist in his own field, so considering the fact that we will have to give the new men their basic training too, you can see what a job we have on our hands. I'm being sent to a camouflage school here at Patterson Field and with that plus the training I got at Fort Belvoir, I ought to be pretty good at it. I imagine that camouflage will probably be my chief duty. I'm sure glad that I was given a ten day leave after graduation because it was just what I needed to give me back my old pep. I spent most of my time running around seeing friends and relatives, but I did manage to have a little time to myself. It was wonderful to sleep in my old bed again for the first time in almost eleven months. But to tell the truth, I was glad to get back to work again. This Army sort of gets in your blood, just like smoking cigarettes.... once a man starts, it's hard to stop."

Harvey didn't want Betty to think that the West Coast had a monopoly on movie stars. "First of all, I ran into Jane Withers in a little joint in Dayton last week. She's doing a show here in town and she was probably doing a little "slumming" between shows. And then we have another star here... Clark Gable, in person. He's here after finishing Officers School in Florida. I don't imagine he will stay very long because of some pretty confidential rumors that I have been hearing. It seems that his presence 'across the pond' would be quite a morale builder. I'm inclined to agree." Clark Gable had joined the Army Air Corps after his wife, Carole Lombard, died in a plane crash in February 1942; during the war, he flew combat missions in Europe. Jane Withers was a sixteen-year-old actress who had just filmed *Johnny Doughboy* and was appearing at the Colonial Theater in Dayton as part of a six-week tour; she was accompanied by her mother.

Harvey and Ralph were assigned to a suite in the Bachelor Officers Quarters (BOQ), and they moved there from Davis Drive at the beginning of January 1943. Both were granted furloughs over the holidays, and Harvey took Ralph home with him to Pittsburgh. "I came back from my leave last night, and as usual, I need another leave to rest up. We had the best time possible in Pittsburgh, and my roommate is anxious to go back again. Mother and Dad were awfully glad to see us and took us all over the place, showing us off. A good part of the time was spent in seeing relatives but the rest of the time we really went places and did things. On New Year's Eve, we went to Bill Green's Casino which is one of the nicest places there. We had a good time and really gave 1943 a good push down the runway."

As usual, Harvey mentioned music and movies. "The piece that has been running incessantly through my head lately is 'As Long as You're Not in Love with Anyone Else' but I can't for the life of me think whose recording it was that I heard. It might have been Dinah Shore's, but I'm not sure. It sure is swell, anyway. I've seen 'For Me and My Gal' and like it a lot. Be sure not to miss 'Stand by for Action' with Bob Taylor and Charles Laughton." *For Me and My Gal* starred Gene Kelly, Judy Garland, and George Murphy—and Kelly won an Oscar for Best Actor. Both of these pictures were filmed at the MGM Studios on Washington Boulevard in Culver City—less than a mile from the record store where Betty worked! She always let Harvey know of interesting records that came into Stella's. "Most of the songs that you mention in your letters are entirely new to me. I never hear them until a week or two after I read about them in one of your letters. I'm crazy about 'Why Don't You Fall in Love with Me?'. Also, 'I Had the Craziest Dream.' Keep me informed, I like it.

"There is a chance that I may be sent to camouflage school at Fort Belvoir for a two-week course. My chief duties here are with the camouflage platoon of our company, and any extra training I pick up will come in handy. I'm rather anxious to go, but I can't tell for sure yet that I'll get the assignment. There is a class starting on the 17th, but that class is full, so the earliest possible class I can make starts around the 1st of February. I'd come back here after the course is finished."

Harvey was kept busy at Patterson Field and wasn't able to write again for over a month. "We have been the busiest little beavers you have ever seen these past three or four weeks, and I've barely been able to keep in touch with my parents. We have been building barracks for our men and just last week we managed to move into them. These aren't regular Army barracks but prefabricated 'hutments' which are a little smaller and have only one story. They aren't bad, though, nice, and comfortable and a relief from the ordinary type of barracks. Now we are building shelving and coat racks and a few other things to make the insides more home-like. We got orders this morning that we are to build another of these hutments for a new bunch of men that will be coming in soon, so I guess it won't be long before we get 'on the ball' again. The weather here has been really swell the past couple of days, but today is a little cooler and the paper says it will be down to zero by tonight. Believe it or not, we haven't gotten all of our new men yet. We're just marking time without getting much done as far as training is concerned. We have only 71 so far with about 200 more yet to come. At this rate we'll still be here in 1950! If something doesn't happen soon, I'm going to try to get transferred to an outfit that has possibilities of going places. I haven't had much time for music lately, except for a piano concert by Roslyn Tureck…have you ever heard of her?" Roslyn Tureck, a Julliard graduate, was widely considered one of the country's best pianists. Harvey attended her concert at the Dayton Art Institute on February 4th. Three days after sending that last letter, Harvey sent a telegram saying he had been accepted to the camouflage school at Fort Belvoir, and he was on his way.

Harvey didn't get to the 2-week camouflage course at Fort Belvoir until February 27th; he was assigned quarters in the BOQ, and on the 1st, he reported to the Instructional Aids Department (in Building 202) where he was issued textbooks on:

> Organization and Tactics (Anti-Aircraft Artillery)
> Camouflage
> Tactics and Technique (Field Artillery)
> Advanced Maps and Aerial Photo Reading
> Protective Measures
> Role of Aerial Photography
> Protective Concealment
> Material for Protective Concealment
> Civilian Defense

Upon his return to Patterson Field, Harvey was issued his field gear:

> Gas mask
> 10 tent pins
> 2 tents, shelter, halves
> First-aid packet
> Canvas dispatch case
> Canvas field bag

Pistol belt
2 wool blankets
M-1910 Canteen
Dismounted canteen cover
Aluminum cup
Double web magazine pocket
Pouch for first aid packet
Waterproof bedding roll
Liner and bands

On April 1st, Harvey wrote again from Patterson Field. "We really are plenty busy now. Last Saturday night, we received a shipment of 132 new men and that brings us to a total of 228 and that's a few more than we should have. But that's ok because we'll probably drop a few as we get along with our training. From now on we'll really have our hands full. This last bunch of men came in from Jefferson Barracks, Missouri, and although they aren't exactly brain trusts, I think they'll develop into a swell bunch. This all boils down to—in about three months we'll be all trained and ready to go anywhere the Army feels like sending us. Boy, that'll be the day. It'll be the end to about a year and a half of fooling around over here trying to get fitted out for duty on the other side. We are going to have a hard time getting used to being so busy, but it'll be a big relief to get my hands dirty for a change."

Betty had written that she was going to hear Benny Goodman and wished Harvey could go with her. "It sure would be swell to go over to the Palladium to hear Benny Goodman with you. I don't think I'll ever forget the good time I had the last time I was there. I haven't seen Harry James since, but I never hear one of his recordings but what I think of that special night that we saw him in person. And another good time we had was in Culver City at the Casa Mañana when Jan Savitts was there. Of course, the dances at the little place in Beverly Hills were swell too, but those others stand out as being pretty special, don't you think? Be sure to write and tell me all about the new U.S.O. in Culver City."

Three weeks later, Harvey received orders to report to Olmsted Field in Middletown, Pennsylvania, where he would be a Camouflage Instructor with the Engineering Section. "I wanted to let you know that I'm moving again. Yes, and there's a slight chance that I'll come to the west coast. I was offered a chance to take a job as a camouflage instructor, and I took it more as a means to an end than a desire for the job. It means a quick promotion (I hope) and a move out of the 912th which I'm afraid has become stagnant for the duration. I know I won't be too crazy about this instruction business, but I'll do a lot of traveling and my experience will put me in demand as an officer in a Camouflage Battalion. These battalions are hot after officers and also they are outfits which quickly go overseas. The move will take place sometime next week so as soon as I find out the details, I'll let you know. Are you hoping as much as I am that I'll be sent somewhere near Venice?"

Harvey reported for duty in Middletown on May 4th and was immediately sent for a few days to the bases at Tobyhanna, Pennsylvania and Fort Dix, New Jersey. He was scheduled for projects at both airfields and was sent early in order to make observations and preliminary plans. On the 10th, he sent a postcard to Betty: "This is just a card to let you know that I haven't dropped clear out of sight. I'm in Tobyhanna, Pa. for a week or so and we expect to go to Middletown from here. So far no word on coming to California, but still hoping."

It had been a year since Betty and Harvey had seen each other.

5

CAMOUFLAGE

Instead of being sent to California, Harvey had been assigned to Air Service Command—Middletown Air Depot Control Area Command (MADCAC) at Olmsted Army Airfield in Middletown, Pennsylvania, near Harrisburg. He was serving as the Assistant Camouflage Officer at the base. As I write this in 2020, much of the Olmsted airfield has been incorporated into Harrisburg International Airport. However, during World War II, reconnaissance and transport units were being formed and organized at the base and were then reassigned to training bases around the country. "Do you realize that it's over a year now since I last saw you. Your letters are so swell that sometimes it doesn't seem that long but at other times it seems like decades. I wish I knew when this Army is going to get some sense and send me back to California. Right now, I'm back at Middletown, Penna. but either tomorrow or Tuesday I'm going back to Tobyhanna, Pa. for about ten days. From there, I expect to go to someplace in North Carolina but I'm not sure. Tobyhanna is a swell place in the summertime with oodles and oodles of mountain air, lots of trees and trout streams, etc. I won't have too much to do up there so maybe I'll have a chance to enjoy myself for a change.

"One nice part of this job is that I travel on a 'per diem' basis which means that I get six dollars a day for expenses for all the time I'm away from my home base which is Middletown. Now maybe for the first time in my life I can begin to save a little money. I've never been able to do it before, either in civil life, or since I've been in the Army. I've done quite a bit of flying since getting into this camouflage business. The only way you can judge the effectiveness of a camouflage installation is to view it from the air and that doesn't make me mad at all. Yesterday, I was up for about an hour and a half with Colonel Cressy from Tobyhanna. He's a swell fellow and is darned cooperative with the camouflage program." Two days after sending this letter, Harvey was ordered back to Tobyhanna to provide camouflage instruction for the Air Service Command troops stationed there.

It was hot in Tobyhanna that June, and though the temperature didn't get much over 90 degrees, it was very humid. The men were uncomfortable in their required khakis. There really wasn't much for Harvey to do during this visit, but he was trying to keep busy. "This Tuesday, one of the outfits here is going out on bivouac and I'm going with them to make sure that they keep themselves and their equipment well-hidden while they are there. They are going to use a good area with lots of trees etc. so it won't be too hard a job for me.

"I went to Scranton last night (about 25 miles north of here) and saw 'Crash Dive' with Tyrone Power. It's not bad but it is a carbon copy of most of the recent war pictures. The best part about it is that it's in technicolor."

As they expected, ten days later Harvey and Lt. Spring were sent from Middletown ("by government vehicle") to Maxton Army Air base in Maxton, North Carolina, and from there on to Langley Field in Virginia. After providing camouflage instruction to troops at Langley, they traveled to Fort Dix, New Jersey, to give classes there. When he returned to Olmsted Field, he was issued a .45 automatic pistol, a holster, and a magazine of cartridges.

"I finally managed to see 'Orchestra Wives' last night and the music was really super. Just as you said it would be. I've been just missing that picture for months and now I'm more than satisfied with it. Gosh, when Ray Eberle started off with 'At Last' I just went into a stupor and stayed there. The acting in the picture was just a little on the 'Grade B' side, but I don't think that anyone paid much attention to that. The music was too good.

"You ought to see the gliders at this base. There must be at least 200 of them and more coming all the time. They have one of the biggest airfields here that I've ever seen, and it's parked about 1/3 full of gliders. The only planes we see here are cargo ships and transports with a few light observation planes now and then. I'm angling for a flight to Pittsburgh this coming weekend, but I doubt very much if I'm lucky enough to get it. It sure would be swell if I could go with you to the Hollywood Bowl to hear those concerts. I really like classical and semi-classical music although I don't pretend to understand it too well. I got a big kick out of the Ballet Russe de Monte Carlo when I saw it in Dayton last winter."

Camouflage class at Fort Dix, New Jersey, Jun. 1943

At the end of June, Harvey went back to Langley Field to give another camouflage class. He and Lt. Spring left Middletown at noon on Wednesday, but that morning they took a last look at some of the work their men had done at Olmstead. "We are going up in a C-47 (transport plane) to see how effective our job of camouflage is from the air. We are taking a big plane like that so that all the students can get some idea of how good they are at this business. The only way you can inspect a camouflage job is from the air so up we go. The job this class took on was to cover up a P-39 (pursuit) and even for so small a plane it was a hard job here because the field is flat with very little vegetation. I think our work is going to be satisfactory though."

Harvey was hoping to eventually get overseas, either to Europe or to the Pacific Theater. "I certainly hope that if I do go overseas, I can at least get to see you before I go. That would sure give me a lot to go on while I'm away. If and when I do go overseas, if I can just go into the Pacific Theater of operations, my point of embarkation will probably be San Francisco and if I can get there, I know that we can see each other at least for a short while. But for the present I'm stuck here on the Eastern Coast."

On Thursday, July 8th, Harvey was headed to Fort Dix to provide a camouflage class for the 28th Service Group, which was preparing to go to Bombay. On Wednesday night, he and Ralph had gone to the movies in Hershey. "We saw a picture at the little theater up in Hershey and were rather disappointed in it. 'Hit Parade of 1943' was the name and although Susan Hayward and

John Carroll were rather good, the tunes were sort of sour. Nothing at all worth remembering. Count Basie was his usual rhythmic self in putting over a tune called the 'The Harlem Sandman', but Freddie Martin wasn't up to par. Maybe I'm just getting too critical. I see where 'our friend!' Harry James and Betty Grable have tied the knot. Now to see how long they can keep it going. They should make a pretty fair team because their careers are on a pretty parallel plane. But you never can tell. If James can only make his new marriage work the way he can work a trumpet, they are due for a long, long happy life.

"My C.O., Lt. Col Hinton just came in and told me that Col. Lundberg, the C.O. of this base, will be at Fort Dix on an inspection trip tomorrow and that they will no doubt look me up to find out what we are doing as far as camouflage is concerned. That means that I'll have to be on my toes and on the beam. They probably will ask plenty of questions about past work and future plans and all that kind of stuff. I'll probably spend the weekend in the guard house? How about sending me some hot soup? Well, it's about time I got my wheels rolling toward Fort Dix, so I'll be seeing you (tonight by phone, I hope.)"

Harvey was able to get a phone call through to Betty when he got to Fort Dix that night. "I can't tell you how wonderful it was to talk to you. After I hung up I thought of a thousand things I wanted to say to you but while I was actually on the phone, I must have been just flabbergasted to realize that we were actually talking to each other in person again. There's something about your voice that just picks me up. That's just one more thing to add to all the others that make me think of you as someone very special and very close to me. I hope you feel the same way.

"I was in New York last night and ran into one of the Conover models by the name of Choo Choo Johnson, and between you and I, she is one of the most conceited persons I ever met. I believe that next weekend, if I'm still here at Fort Dix, I'll go into New York on Saturday afternoon and stay over until Sunday night and really give the old place the 'once over lightly' treatment. It's been quite a few years since I was there before." He was at Fort Dix for a couple more weeks and was able to make another visit to New York City. He sent a postcard from the Commodore Hotel on Lexington Avenue and 42nd Street where he was staying. "Just a short note to let you know that I managed to get up to New York again this weekend and I'm really having a wonderful time. I guess by this time you have gotten the little pin and the bar that I sent you. I hope you'll like them." Harvey and Betty had been growing closer and closer, and he had recently asked her to wear his "bar" insignia, and she had agreed. "About the bar, you're wearing it for me has a super special significance as far as I'm concerned, and I'm in hopes that you look at it the same way. New York was loads and loads of fun. On Saturday night I went up and down Broadway and visited every little joint I could find. On Sunday afternoon, I went to see 'Ziegfeld Follies' with Milton Berle and haven't laughed so much in ages. After that I had dinner at Jack Dempsey's place and then went to see 'Coney Island' at the Roxy Theater. It was pretty good but frankly I'm not too crazy about Betty Grable."

Even though none of Betty's letters from this period have survived, it's evident that she wrote often, maybe even more often than Harvey did. "As you've had plenty of chance to find out in the past 14 or 15 months, I'm not great as a letter writer, but believe me I do make a big effort to repay you in a small way for your very wonderful letters by scratching out a few of these unintelligible epistles of mine. I never will forget climbing over those car tracks to wait for a lift back to Santa Monica after leaving your place. And I never had to wait very long either. The people out there sure treated the soldiers royally. I expect to be at Dix for another week after this one and then back to Middletown for a breather of a day or two to get ready for another trip. Where, I don't know yet. One of the quartermaster officers here wants me to go up to Asbury Park with him this week to go swimming in the Atlantic and I think I'll go. Maybe you'll be in the Pacific at the same time...there ought to be a song title there somewhere!"

They did get back to Asbury Park over the weekend and enjoyed themselves. "We were in the ocean or on the beach from 9:00 A.M. until 5:30 P.M. Our schedule now calls for me to be here all this week and then to be back in Middletown the first of next week. I'm trying to arrange it so that I can be here at Fort Dix over next weekend. There's an ulterior motive, of course...another weekend at Asbury Park! When we get back to Middletown, Col. Hinton will probably have another schedule all mapped out but as yet we don't know what it is. The suspense is a little exciting for I don't know whether we will be in Pennsylvania, New Jersey, North Carolina, Virginia or someplace else at this time next week."

The original Broadway production of *Oklahoma* had opened on March 31, 1943, at the St. James Theater on West 44th Street in New York City. "Everyone here is talking about 'Oklahoma' but I don't think I'm going to be able to see it. If I'm here next weekend I think I'll go back to Asbury Park, and also the tickets for Oklahoma are sold out for about a month ahead. It must really be good."

Camouflage class at Fort Dix, New Jersey, Jun. 1943

Harvey had been at Fort Dix for most of July, but it appeared that his extended stay there might soon end. Their last camouflage class was scheduled for the first week in August. "We will be back at Middletown on Monday and then out to some new place. A new service group has just moved in here at Dix and it's possible that we will come right back here, but at least we will be at Middletown for a while. The radio across the hall is playing 'Oh, How I Miss You Tonight'...couldn't be a more appropriate tune. And just now it started into 'For Me and My Gal'. I don't know who's band it is but sounds pretty good. I don't believe we are going to leave here until next Monday morning which means I'm going to try to have another weekend at Asbury Park (Pause here to hear F.D.R.'s speech). It wasn't such a bad speech except that he didn't say a whole lot of anything. Nothing startling I mean." In his Fireside Chat that evening, Roosevelt gave a progress report on American efforts in the war, particularly recent victories in North Africa and Sicily that led to Mussolini's fall. He assured the public that the Allies were already planning for a postwar world and a comprehensive GI Bill of Rights. On Saturday, Harvey went back to Asbury Park and spent the weekend at the Metropolitan Hotel.

As it turned out, Harvey continued to travel back and forth between Middletown and Fort Dix for quite a while, often taking advantage of the opportunity to visit Manhattan and the beach at Asbury Park. He was often accompanied by one of his new friends, Lt. Hammonds (from Georgia) or Lt.

Mass. "I'll probably be here at Fort Dix for quite some time. New outfits are moving in, and they have got to have a certain amount of camouflage training before they move out. That also means that for such a long stay, I'll be put on detached service instead of temporary duty which eliminated my per diem for as long as I stay here. Lt. Mass and I went to New York over last weekend, and we really had a super time just wandering around seeing things. On Sunday afternoon, we went to see Disney's 'Victory Through Air Power.' It's really an education as far as Aviation is concerned. Sunday evening, we went to the Latin Quarter where they have a 1½ hour floor show. Not bad at all." *Victory through Air Power*, an animated documentary, was nominated that year for an Academy Award for Best Music and Scoring of a Dramatic or Comedy Picture.

On August 31st, Harvey submitted a report to his superiors in Middletown concerning the Camouflage courses he and Lt. Mass had conducted at Fort Dix:

FROM: J. H. BROWN, JR., 2nd Lt., C.E., Asst. Cam. Officer
SUBJECT: Camouflage Classes

1. Lts. J.H. Brown and F.A. Mass conducted camouflage classes at this base; the first-class beginning Thursday, 5 August 1943. To date, four classes of six days each have been presented to the officers and men of the 10th Service Group and one class of three days has been conducted with the men of the 383rd Aviation Squadron, separate.

2. In conjunction with the aforementioned classes, Lts. Brown and Mass have supervised the camouflage, dispersion and general tone-down of the 10th Service Group area. At the suggestion of Col. Braswell, Air Base Executive Officer, the camouflage classes erected dummy installations etc. in the 10th Service Group area to help carry out the group defense plan. Paths in the entire area were wired in along with the placement of various trenches ad foxholes to simulate a well-prepared security plan.

3. Rosters of the classes follow

Class beginning 5 August 1943
10th Service Group (inc. names of 31 officers and men)
Class beginning 12 August 1943
10th Service Group (25 officers and men)
Class beginning 12 August 1943
383rd Aviation Squadron (27 officers and men)
Class beginning 19 August 1943
10th Service Group (25 officers and men)

Class beginning 26 August 1943
10th Service Group (20 officers and men)
4. The Camouflage instructors have been given excellent cooperation in the arrangement of classes by Captain Leo K. Steiner, Jr., Group S-2 and Camouflage Officer, and by the Camouflage officers of the subordinate units of the 10th Service Group.

5. To the present time, approximately 150 officers and enlisted men of the 10th Service Group have attended M.A.S.C. sponsored Camouflage classes either at Fort Dix, NJ or at Syracuse, NY, and another class of 30 or 35 men is planned to start on 2 September 1943

The Commander of the 10th sent a note to Col. Hinton at Olmsted: "The above-named officers (Brown and Mass) have been instructors at a Camouflage School conducted for officers and enlisted men of the 10th Service Group. This instruction will be of great value in the saving of men and material in the theater of operations. These officers are to be commended for the efficient, well organized and interesting manner in which these classes have been conducted, both in classroom and field work."

By the end of August, Harvey was still based at Olmsted Field, and his responsibilities as Camouflage Officer included assisting with:

Recommending troop officers for unit camouflage duty
Developing methods for camouflage instruction
Preparing literature for camouflage instruction
Inspecting camouflage fitness of units

These duties kept him at Fort Dix for long periods. "I had some discouraging news today and that is that I'm probably going to stay here at Fort Dix for at least another month or so. We have presented five straight classes here and that's almost too much without a break. Especially with the prospect in sight of presenting four or five more without any relaxation. Last weekend, as you know, Lt. Mass, my cohort, and myself stole a short time in New York, and it was a welcome bit of time off. Saturday night we went to the 'Copacabana' which is supposed to be one of their best night spots, and then on Sunday afternoon we saw 'For Whom the Bell Tolls.' That is a wonderful picture. Don't miss it if you haven't already seen it. Both Gary Cooper and Ingrid Bergman are swell. The song 'Sunday, Monday, or Always' is just starting to really catch on here in the East. Everyone is whistling or humming it."

As his time at Fort Dix dragged on, Harvey was beginning to wonder just when he'd see Betty again. He visited a fortune teller in New York who predicted that he had a trip out west coming soon. "I told her that I certainly did. She also said that there was a dark-haired girl that I was very interested in, and I told her that she had hit the nail on the head. No kidding that's exactly what she told me! I don't know, but maybe this fortune teller saw similar futures for lots of soldiers?"

The classes that Harvey and Lt. Mass gave at Fort Dix consisted of both classroom study and field work. In the field they had the men build large "flat-tops," large enough to hide an entire runway, and smaller coverings for individual planes and trucks. During the week of September 2, they conducted another course for thirty men from the 10th, and the group was able to build a 36-foot by 44-inch flat-top in fifty-five minutes—sixty minutes faster than any previous class. They also erected a drape covering for a P-40 airplane. Another group the following week also did well, but the class had to be cut short because the unit was required to prepare for immediate shipment overseas. Col. Lundberg back at Olmsted was impressed. The 10th Service Group shipped out and a succession of other units (the 501st Service Squadron, the 1113th Service Squadron, the 859th Signal Company, and the 2076th Q. H. Truck Company) lined up to take one-week classes from Harvey and Lt. Mass. In the middle of the month, Harvey and Lt. Mass were able to take a break.

"We came in from Fort Dix yesterday and tomorrow we are going to take off for Tobyhanna, Pa, and then on Sunday we go back to Fort Dix for another stay of three weeks or a month. Fort Dix has been the focal point of all of our activity for some time now, and there are no signs of a let up. We were glad of a chance to come to Middletown because we badly needed a break in the routine at Dix. It'll be nice to go back up to Tobyhanna because I've got a lot of friends up there that I haven't seen for over two months.

"I got a letter this morning from Lt. Haver at Patterson Field, remember him? He was my roommate when I was there and one of the swellest guys I've run into. He's going to be married on the 18th, and he wants me to come to the wedding. Unfortunately, I don't think I'll make it. On Saturday, I'll be at Tobyhanna, which is almost inaccessible, even by railroad. Things just never seem to work out right, but I haven't given up yet."

Both Harvey and Betty were realizing that they had become very close, even though they hadn't seen each other in over a year. Betty had evidently mentioned this in one of her letters, and Harvey tried to put his thoughts in a letter. "We've had only a short time together, about five or six weeks to be exact, and that's hardly long enough for either of us to begin making up his mind about the other. But after talking to you via air mail for well over a year, I've come to feel that everything that is you is a tremendously big part of me. I think lots about you, too. I wonder just when we'll get our chance to really find out for sure." Harvey was able to get into New York again in early October and stayed at the Hotel Dixie on 43rd Street.

Although *Oklahoma* was still sold it out (it would be for years!), he did see a 1936 picture called *Early to Bed*. Two days later, he wrote that he "had a lead on a couple of tickets" for *Oklahoma* for the following weekend.

Harvey and Lt. Mass were to conduct a camouflage course at Fort Dix and then return to Middletown. "This brings up a rather peculiar situation...in this Service Command which extends from Pennsylvania to North Carolina, there is only one base at which there are troops with which we are concerned, and that is Fort Dix. And now, Fort Dix is being taken out of our control so that when we get back to Middletown, we will have no further camouflage assignments in this Service Command. I don't know what plans our C.O. has for us, but it looks like we will be getting a new assignment. I'm hoping for one of three things. One, is for us to be taken off the camouflage assignment; two, is for us to go with a troop outfit somewhere, and three, is that I am sent to the West Coast. There is a remote possibility that I may get an overseas assignment, and if so, I'm hoping to get to the West Coast before going over.

"Lt. Mass and I spent a quiet weekend. We stayed right here in camp and saw some movies. Saturday night we saw Betty Grable in 'Sweet Rosie O'Grady' and Sunday night we saw 'Bataan' with Robert Taylor and 'Saludas Amigos.' On Sunday afternoon we sat in on the 'This is Fort Dix' broadcast which was sent from the Air Base theater over Mutual coast-to-coast. It was a swell program, and the Air Base band was never better. They've got a man who used to arrange for Blue Barron, and he really turned out some sweet arrangements. After the broadcast, they presented 'Sad Sacks', which is a Fort Dix Air Base production with exclusively Air Base personnel. It was wonderful and hilarious. Francis Langford is on the radio now singing 'When Did You Leave Heaven.' She must know who I'm writing to.

"I went over to base theater last night and saw Donald O'Connor in 'Top Man.' I laughed so hard I cried. He's really good, and that Peggy Ryan that plays his sister in the picture is a riot. Suzanne Foster does some operatic yodeling which to me was something more than mediocre. Her voice seems to me to be almost as good as Deanna Durbin's. The stove in our classroom is on the blink, consequently the room is just like a barn. The other instructor

Lt. Mass is talking to the class now, so I'm in the back of the classroom where it is the coldest. We haven't heard any more about what will happen when we get back to Middletown. I've already taken an overseas physical, so I don't have that to worry about. My promotion is still on the fire and as yet I've had no word about it. Since it has gone this long, I'm getting a little confident because I feel that if it had been turned down for any reason I would have heard about it before this."

By Tuesday, Oct. 26th, Harvey still hadn't left Fort Dix. He had thought they would be in Middletown by then, but the move had been delayed a lot longer than expected. However, he did hear some good news. Lt. Haver had written from Patterson Field, saying he had seen Harvey's promotion being processed there and suggesting that it might be waiting for Harvey when he returned to Middletown.

"We had a wonderful show at the Air Base Theater last night. A lot of song-writers from New York came down and sang and played a lot of their own compositions. I can't remember all the tunes they played, but most of them were past and present Hit Paraders. The writer of 'There Are Such Things' was there. Also, the writers of 'Wait for Me Mary', 'Throw Another Log on the Fire' and lots more. It was marvelous! They also had the Metropolitan Opera singer, John Dudley, who has one of the best baritone voices I've heard for a long, long time. He sang a lot of Sigmund Romberg and Victor Herbert songs. Then after the show, they all came over to the soldiers and played while we all sang. You should have been there; you would have been in your glory. It was astronomical to try to realize how much money all those songs repre-sented." "There Are Such Things" was written by Stanley Adams, Able Baer, and George W. Meyer—and was released by Tommy Dorsey's orchestra in 1942, with vocals by Frank Sinatra; it was number one on that year's list of best-selling records.

Harvey sent Betty a cryptic telegram from Middletown on Thursday, the 28th: "DARLING I AM GROWING OLD SILVER BARS REPLACE THE GOLD HARVEY." Second Lieutenants wore gold bars, while First Lieutenants wore silver—he had received his promotion!

"We got in here Wednesday evening, and I've been busy writing reports on our work at Fort Dix. Thursday morning the colonel handed me the letter from Washington which made me a 1st Lt., and I took off right away for the Western Union office to send you the good word. I sent Mother a wire, too, to let her know about it. It came through on October 28th, which was exactly a year from Oct. 28, 1942, when I got my commission as a 2nd Lt. That's an extraordinarily long time for a soldier to be a shavetail, but it couldn't be helped, I guess. It was the 3rd time the recommendation had gone in, but I was transferred just as the first one went in. And when the second one went in, there was a general freeze up on promotions in the whole Air Service Command. There's another bit of news too. I found out that Patterson Field had requested my transfer back there, and it looks very much as if it's going to go through. That means I'll be back on my old stomping grounds again. I don't know what kind of job I'll get but no matter what it is, it's bound to be an improvement over what I'm doing now. It will probably be camouflage work of one sort or another, but I don't believe it will be instructing. It's a possibility that as soon as I get to Patterson, they may send me out to another area. I'm hoping that if I am transferred to Patterson Field, I can get a short delay enroute so that I can stop over at home for a while. I'll send a silver bar with my next letter...be sure to wear it always." The next day, Harvey received orders reassigning him as Assistant Engineer and Engineering Inspector in the Personnel and Training Division, Hd & Hq Squadron,—but he was not transferred back to Patterson Field.

Betty and her parents sent Harvey letters and cards congratulating him on his promotion. Betty also sent some sheet music and a copy of *Capitol*, the Capitol Records newsletter, which included a photo of Mickey Serima, Harvey's Pittsburgh friend who was a drummer with Harry James. Harvey noted that, "looks like he's on the big time to stay. Funny, though, I never hear him giving out with any drum solos. Maybe James just doesn't go in for that. My orders haven't come in as yet but I'm expecting them any day, or any minute. Colonel Hinton wrote an endorsement on a letter to Patterson Field, saying that it was OK to transfer me, and now are waiting either for orders to come back from Patterson or for a letter saying to get orders through headquarters. Are you thoroughly confused? If things go right, I'll be at Patterson by the end of next week."

Captain Spring, who worked in the same office as Harvey, received his promotion at the same time Harvey got his "1st", and the two of them decided to throw a party at the Hotel Hershey for all of the officers in the section. "There will probably be plenty of wine and song, but the women will not be in evidence because it's to be a stag affair. The tariff will be $7.50 a plate, so it had better be good or Captain Spring and I will scream our heads off. We went to Lebanon, Pa. yesterday to see a show because there are none open here on Sundays. Whew."

Harvey had to travel to Harrisburg on Wednesday to see about changes that were needed on a building there and, while waiting for a staff car to pick him up, he wrote to Betty about Tuesday's celebration. "Last night we had that dinner at the Hershey Hotel given by Captain Spring, Captain Reiser, and me in honor of our promotions. The colonel was there with all the rest of the men from our office, and we really had a good time. I don't believe I've laughed so much in a long time. Capt. Spring is a southerner, and of course we rib him unmercifully about it. We had Martinis to begin with, then shrimp cocktail, roast turkey and trimmings, burgundy, demitasse, and dessert all served in the most auspicious style. It's really a swanky hotel with all the airs of the most exclusive places.

"I'm back from Harrisburg, and it was pretty much a wild goose chase. The colonel whom I was supposed to see had just moved his office out here to M.A.S.C., so I just had a good long ride for nothing. I'm still waiting for orders."

On November 8th, Harvey was "...still here at Middletown and as yet have no idea whatsoever about if or when my transfer orders are going to come. It seemed to me that Patterson Field was rather anxious to have the transaction hurried through, but apparently it has hit some kind of snag. If I stay here, I'm almost certain to get an office job, and that would put the finishing touches on me. As for music, it's the same here as it is in your territory. That d___ed 'Pistol Packin' Mama' is driving everyone insane. Not only that one, but 'Roselita' too. If I hear it just once more, I'll be talking to myself. There's a juke box in a joint in Hershey, and 'Roselita' plays on an average of 3,757,621 times an evening. That's too many. Of course, it doesn't bother me, doesn't bother me, doesn't bother me, doesn't bother me. I'm going to a picture tonight that I've been trying to see for a long time. Something has always happened every other time when I planned on seeing it, but I think I'm going to make it tonight. It's 'Hers to Hold' with Deanna Durbin. Everyone says it's really good and that she sings some swell songs."

Harvey was very competitive and loved sports and games. He played football, softball, baseball, volleyball, horseshoes—almost anything. He loved to bowl, and on Wednesday, November 10th, he and three of his friends went to a bowling alley in downtown Hershey. "The thing that hurts all the servicemen here is the 11 o'clock curfew on liquor for soldiers in Pennsylvania. I don't care that much about drinking, but some of the men really moaned last night when we went down to Hershey's only 'joint', and they only had time for one drink."

The next day, Harvey was out on Olmsted's rifle range and qualified as "marksman" with an M-1 carbine. "Well, things have changed again here at Middletown. I'm working in Harrisburg every day now, and I think I'm going to like it a lot better than at the Air Depot in Middletown. We are taking over the Farm Show Building in Harrisburg which is going to be used for engine maintenance work. It's a huge building and we'll have a heck of a lot of changes and alterations to make before the place is ready for us to use. All these new changes are to be made through our office, so it looks as if I'll be down here until it's all finished." While stationed at Olmstead Field in Middletown, Harvey had been assigned to various quarters in nearby Hershey. During this assignment in Harrisburg, he lived in the Hershey Hotel, on a hill near Hershey Park. His office was in the Hershey Community Club, the recreation center that housed a community theater, the public library, a hospital, a dining room, a gymnasium, and a swimming pool. "The biggest trouble is that I have so far to go back and forth to work every day. Harrisburg is just about twice as far from Hershey as is Middletown. I get up at 6:30 to catch a 7:00 trolley to Hummelstown then a bus to Harrisburg, and then another bus to the Farm Show Bldg, and I just barely get here at 8:30. I'm just about ready to go to bed again by the time I get to work.

"The days are stretching into weeks and the weeks into months and still no hope in sight of our getting to see each other soon. It seems funny to me that I should live for such a long time in one spot with no idea that there was anyone like you on the face of the globe, and then one day I join the Army, travel 3000 miles to a dance on a little side street in California and there you are.

"I'm back at Middletown again, but only for a few hours. I'm waiting for a phone call from Col. Hinton in Baltimore about some decisions that are being made in conjunction with our Farm Show Bldg., and then I'm going to take off to Harrisburg again. We've really been working this past week or so and this Sunday I'm to be duty officer again for our section. Captain Reiser is supposed to be on, but his wife is pretty sick in New York, and he wanted to take off, so I'm it. I don't mind, though, because he's a swell guy and would do the same thing for me. There are only a few record stores around here, and I've only been able to get to one of them. He didn't have the records you wanted but I'll keep looking. I haven't heard a radio much lately, but I've been hoping to hear a piece of Harry James in which Mike Serima gets a chance to solo, but so far I haven't heard one. (pause) Okay, just got the information I've been waiting for, so now I'm on my way to Harrisburg."

Lt. Mass and Harvey continued to go to the movies, and on Tuesday they went to see *The Iron Major* with Pat O'Brien. "It's a pretty good show, but I really didn't go into raptures over it. I can't quite put my fingers on what it is I don't like about it. There was just something lacking. It's the story of Frank Cavanaugh's life. He was a really good football coach, and I don't think the picture did him justice....I read Guadalcanal Diary, but I haven't been able to see the picture yet. Most everyone here thought it was pretty good. It's already been shown at one of the theaters here, so I guess I'll have to wait until it comes back to one of the smaller houses."

At Christmas, Harvey was given a two-day leave to go home to Pittsburgh. "It was wonderful to talk to you on Christmas day. Mother was glad to have a chance to talk with you because I've been telling her so much about you. She knows what the situation is and how I feel about you! I drove back to Hershey last night, and it was really touch and go the whole way. It was raining when I left Pittsburgh and I no sooner got into the mountains than the rain turned to ice on the road. It stayed that way for the rest of the trip. I've never seen so many accidents in all my life. I'm enclosing a clipping from the Philadelphia Record which tells how it hit that city."

SCORES HURT AS ICE SNARLS CITY TRAFFIC

Philadelphia traffic was brought to a virtual standstill and scores of pedestrians, motorists and trolley passengers were injured yesterday on icy streets and sidewalks in one of the year's worst accident waves. The Philadelphia Transportation Company, whose trolleys figured in two collisions, injuring 26 passengers, reported its lines through the north and west sections of the cities were paralyzed in many places. Bridge accidents were numerous and dozens of pedestrians, many returning from church, wound up on the casualty list.

The ice storm covered the East Coast from Northern New England to Virginia. Conditions were so hazardous last night that highway authorities in Pennsylvania, New York and New Jersey appealed to motorists not to travel "except in extreme emergency."

"Of course, the Pennsylvania Turnpike is west of Philadelphia, so they don't have much to say about it, but the bad weather covered all of Pennsylvania all the way west to Pittsburgh. I traveled half of the trip going sideways or backward. The car stood up pretty well on the trip and, except for a flat tire, everything was okay."

On the 27th, Col. Hinton informed Harvey that he was being transferred to his old job at Olmstead Field. "I'm back at my old desk at Middletown. The Farm Show Building is getting along pretty well now, so I'll be getting a new job out here. There aren't any signs of a transfer, so I guess I'll be at Middletown for some time. Right now, I'm working on the water supply systems for the test blocks that we've got here, and some new ones they want to install *[Note: test blocks are crushable material used to slow aircraft that go off of a runway.]* These darn things use a whole lot of water just for cooling. I'm glad I'm not paying the water bill. I just took a trip over the test blocks, and by actual test they use 550 gallons of water an hour. That's a pile of water for one test block, and we are going to have 30 of them."

After the busy pace in Harrisburg, Harvey found his new assignment at Olmstead Field to be pretty quiet. "I'm just wasting away for something to do now. Our office must be the most unbusy place in the whole Army. I feel that something's going to break before long, but what it is I don't know. Just so it's something to keep me really busy. Your record just came, and now I can't wait until I get home and find someone to play it for me. I've heard 'G.I. Jive', but I don't think I ever heard the words. I wish you could be here for New Year's Eve. The base is having a big affair at the Officers Club and all officers are requested to be there. It's formal so everyone will really be rigged out in his Sunday best. I'll have to go, at least to put in an appearance, but there won't be much point in staying. A couple of other lieutenants and myself will probably sneak out to some dive in Harrisburg and have a much better time. Col. Hinton has asked me to go to dinner with him tonight which is very unusual. I can't imagine what he has on his mind because he undoubtedly has something special to talk about." There isn't a mention of the dinner after that, and it appears there wasn't anything "special" to talk about. Soon after that, however, he was granted a seven-day leave to visit his family in Pittsburgh, and he suspected this was an indication that he might soon be transferred out of the East. When he could, Harvey listened to his favorite radio programs. "I just heard Fred Allen on the radio, and one of his guest stars was 'Archie', the manager of 'Duffy's Tavern'. Boy, what a screwball he is. I almost fell off the chair laughing. I try to hear his program all the time ('Duffy's Tavern,' I mean), but I can't always manage it."

He spent a week in Pittsburgh, arriving there on Saturday. "We spent the evening talking and feeling good about being together for a while. Sunday evening, we went to my grandmother's for supper after seeing 'Destination Tokyo' in the afternoon. It was really a swell picture and if you haven't seen it, be sure to go. On Monday I went down to the office (Duquesne Light Company) to see all the boys, just talking to them about the Army and what has happened in the two years I've been away. My old boss took me out to lunch. His son-in-law is lost in the South Pacific, so we've got lots to talk about." He spent the rest of the week visiting with his parents, his grand-mother, and various friends and family members.

By January 25th, the staff had changed but Harvey was still at Middletown. "Col. Hinton is no longer here, having been transferred to Patterson Field, and we are expecting his replacement, Col. Maxwell, to come any day soon. Capt. Spring is now on his way to a P.O.E. and will soon be 'over the waves.' That leaves Col. Maxwell (not here as yet), Maj. Aldous, Maj. Nixon (both of whom may also go), Capt. Reiser, and myself. If it turns out the way we expect that it may, only Col. Maxwell, Capt. Reiser and I will be the entirety of the office. It begins to look like I'll be here permanently.

"Col. Maxwell is now in official charge of our section having reported in yesterday (Jan. 27) and started working this morning. We are all pretty sure that he'll be much easier to work for than was Col. Hinton. He seems to be a lot more pleasant and certainly a lot fairer and more considerate. He's the kind of fellow that you know will back you up when you go out representing him. I was talking to a fellow the other day down at the Farm Show Bldg. and it seems he is connected in some way with the Harrisburg Community Theater. He says they are tremendously in need of young men and asked three of us to come down tonight to look around and see if we would not like to try our hand at a play or two. Probably nothing will come of it because I know I could never drag any acting ability out of me, but we may have some fun just the same. They seem to have a pretty good setup for such a small town. Tell you more about it later."

In the beginning of February, Betty and her family had begun to build a new house, still on Caswell Avenue, but three blocks away. "I hate to hear that you are going to move out of the old homestead. When you do that I won't have anything to remember. The house that you're in now is swell. I always felt at home there and I don't like to think of you living somewhere that I can't picture in my mind. Right now, I can just see the piano and the big chair by the door with the records loaded on the table sitting beside it. The couch across the room beyond the piano, the fireplace (I think) at the end of the room. And then it seems to me that your father had his favorite chair with its back to the windows. Remember me sitting on the couch beside you and showing you the shoulder patch I had just sown on all by myself? There are no more changes in our office as yet but there is a rumor going around that Major Nixon is up for reclassification which probably means that he will be given a discharge.

"Tonight, the officers' bowling league will be in session at the Red Crown Alley in Harrisburg. I hope I have a good night tonight because I missed the last two Mondays while I was on leave. My average is not so good that I can afford to roll any bad games. We have about 12 or 14 teams in the league, and they really do raise quite a rumpus when they get started. All the teams are named for planes such as Liberators, Wasps, Fortresses, etc. My team is the Helldivers and tonight we roll the Marauders. We're only about 3 games out of 1st place so if we're on tonight we may bounce right up to the top. 'Besame Mucho' is a swell song and it's a darn good idea, too."

In early February, Harvey and Major William Aldous were ordered to Tobyhanna to survey a proposed site for a salvage storage depot. "The evenings are just a little bit lonely way up here in the mountains and if it wasn't for us doing a lot of drawing and sketching after supper I imagine that the time would hang heavily on our hands. Today we didn't get too much surveying done because of the snow, so at 8:00 I was just about finished and could write you a few lines. We didn't expect to stay here very long when we started out, but there was a real blizzard here all day Friday and Saturday and, when I talked to you on Sunday the snow was at least 2 or 3 feet deep, and in some places it had drifted into piles 10 or 12 feet high. This afternoon the snow started again and right now it's snowing harder than I've ever seen. The wind is awfully strong and the prospects for us to finish our job anyway soon are not very good. If this present snowstorm keeps up we will no doubt be snowed in for the next couple of days at least. The snow is really beautiful when you're not trying to battle it, and as I'm getting seven dollars a day per diem, I don't mind the weather at all. Of course, Gen. Clark, our C.O. at Middletown, is tearing out what little hair he has left because he is particularly interested in this job. But even a general can't pull his rank on a snowstorm.

"I don't imagine you've ever been in a real blizzard before. You can't look up to see where you are going because the wind is driving the snow so hard that it seems to be cutting little pieces out of your face. You have to lean way over to keep from toppling backwards and it's almost impossible to drag one leg after the other against the wind and snow. You can't keep a transit level on the ground, so we are losing lots of valuable time by just waiting for the snow to stop. Even after the snow stops, the wind blows it up off the ground in what just as well might be another snowstorm. I got one of my ears frost bitten on Saturday night after walking only 1300 feet, which is less than 1/4 of a mile. My ear was dead white when I came in and as it started to get some color back, it swelled up and hurt like h____. The funny part is that you don't realize it is happening until too late. Col. Cressey, the C.O. here at Tobyhanna, wants us to locate a few property lines for him with our surveying equipment while we're here. Because of his rank, we are more or less obligated to help him out, but I know we'll have a devil of a time finding any benchmarks in three or four feet of snow.

"I sure hope that our Chicago plans don't fall through. A G.I. plane is next to impossible, and reservations on civilian planes are almost out of the question without official business being the reason to travel. It's almost a dream to think of walking up good old Caswell Avenue again...that is, if you're still living there by then.

"I'm enclosing a ticket to a talk I heard last Wednesday night. I don't think I ever in my life heard such an inspiring and moving talk. In all, it took over two hours and I hung on the edge of my seat the whole time." He was referring a talk at the Scranton Rotary Club by Col. Carlos Romulo, the Chief Aide to Gen. Douglas McArthur. Romulo's talk was entitled "I Saw the Fall of the Philippines." Harvey finally returned to Middletown on the 18th, his train pulling into Hershey at supper time. "I don't know what kind of a job is in store for me, but I hope it is more of the same." What was "in store" was another trip to Tobyhanna to continue work on the site for the proposed salvage storage depot.

A few days later, he heard another rumor about the Army's plans for him: "I may get a chance to go with a Combat Engineer Battalion. It's just a chance and not a certainty by any means but the possibility is there and if it comes along, I'll grab it. It would no doubt mean a chance to go overseas."

Harvey sent several picture postcards to Betty during this period. He called them his "propaganda campaign," sending her pictures of Pittsburgh and sites in western Pennsylvania to entice her to come visit him. He phoned her as often as he could and sent a letter when he could. "I haven't heard anything more about that job with combat engineers, but I know for sure that it's still on the fire. In another month and a half, I'll be eligible for a promotion, so I'd like to stay here that long anyway. It would be really super if I could get a promotion and then go out with engineers to some spot overseas. Did I tell you about the book 'The Valley of Decision'? I read it a couple of weeks ago, and it's awfully good. It takes place around the Pittsburgh district, so maybe I'm a little prejudiced."

By Friday, the situation at Middletown appeared to be shifting. "It certainly looks as if I'm going to be moved from Middletown. The quota of engineer officers at each Air Service Command base has been cut down to two, including the colonel which means that at least three of us will be moved to another assignment. I don't know what the new job will be or how long it will be until I move, but I'm hoping that it comes soon and that I'll be heading west. I'd like very much to be assigned to Combat Engineers but don't know how much chance I have. Col. Maxwell said that he would write to Gen. Miller at Fort Belvoir to try and get me the assignment I want. What are your ideas about me getting an overseas assignment in a combat area? We are still working on the Tobyhanna job, but the end is now in sight.

"Tonight, the bowling league in Hershey is having its playoff games and our team, being in second place, is playing the first-place team for final honors. Should we win, best of five games, each member of the team will get a gold medal. Some stuff, eh? We'll be playing for blood tonight with no holds barred. Tomorrow night I'm going to Philadelphia for the weekend just for a change in the routine. There are a couple of good shows there including 'the Purple Heart' which I think I'll try to see.

"We finished up on the Tobyhanna job yesterday, and the office is very 'unbusy'. I'm waiting now for word from Patterson field about my transfer. I got your letter about Rod this morning, and I sent him a few lines about the Army. . . . The Hershey hockey team won first place in the Eastern Division of the league, and Cleveland won the Western Division, so last night a bunch of us went over to see one of the playoff games, and I was never so disgusted in my life. It looked like Cleveland actually threw the game. Up until last night, Cleveland had won 3 out of 5 and only needed one more to clinch the title. They scored two goals right off the bat and then laid down and let Hershey score 5 straight goals to win 5 to 2. That means another game in Cleveland on Saturday, and of course more money for all.

"I wish that sometimes you would sit down and write me a history of yourself. I don't know anything about you before April 19, 1942, so how about bringing me up to date?"

Harvey sent Rod some advice: "...a letter came from Betty asking me about the Army or Navy as regards your thinking of getting into one of the services. I can see that it really must be a tough problem for a man in your position, certainly a whole lot different than when I enlisted in December 1941. Then, all of us had blood in our eyes and the urge in mind to kill. And I'm not being a bit unpatriotic when I say that it probably would have been a lot better if most of us had waited and tried to fit ourselves into our own particular slots in this business. I've been fortunate enough, and I do mean lucky, to be associated with work that is more or less familiar to me but breaks like that are few and far between mainly because the Army doesn't have the need for the same ratio of need for men with a particular talent as are needed in civilian life. You seem to have talents for and leanings toward the Engineering slant on things, so by all means try to get yourself placed in a spot where the work is not only to your liking but also one which suits your ability. You can't start too soon to start to line things up for yourself because although this is supposed to be a fighting Army, there also a lot of politics concerned. The big thing to remember is that a man going into the Army should try to get a job that suits him, and not attempt to twist his personality to suit his job. It's a cold-blooded way of looking at things, but it's reasonable that if a man likes to do a job and can do it well, he's a whole lot more valuable both to himself and to his employer (the Army in your case and mine.) When the war is over, and the civilians again take control of things, the fellow who's going to be ahead is the one who has continued his education right through the Army. After the last war, many a winner of the D.F.C, Purple Heart etc. was selling apples on a street corner. Any soldier will tell you the same thing. I know you would like the Corps. of Engineers because just wearing a castle on your uniform makes you feel about 3 times better than any soldier you meet. I'm just a little prejudiced about the Engineers, I know. You wouldn't have any trouble fitting yourself into almost any branch of the service, but I think probably you would have more success in the Seabees, Coast Artillery, or Anti-Aircraft (lots of math), Corps of Engineers and the Army or Navy Air Corps as a Pilot, Bombardier, Navigator, or Engineering officer. The title Air Corp Engineering officer is a rather erroneous one, because he is supposed to know all about aircraft and their functions. It doesn't at all coincide with what your idea of an engineer's duties would be. This probably hasn't helped much, but if you have something you'd like to ask, fire away.

"Last night a Lt. Vogt, a quartermaster officer from the base, came out to the club here to play billiards with me. His wife came along and went to the show while we played. Afterwards we went over to the Oyster Bar across the street and met his wife; we had a long talk over a drink and a plate of French-fried potatoes. They've invited me out to dinner at their apartment sometime next week. It ought to be fun, and I'll write you more about when I go there for dinner."

On April 5th, Harvey traveled to Patterson Field to meet with the Construction and Utilities Section there. They discussed the proposed

Reclamation Building and Salvage Warehouse in Tobyhanna, and then Harvey returned to Olmsted. As his trip was designated "necessary for the accomplishment of an emergency War mission," air transport was provided for him.

6

TRAIN COMMANDER

Betty went to Catalina Island with friends for Easter, and when she returned there was a letter waiting. "I had a busy week last week. On Wednesday morning, I hopped a plane (under orders, of course) to Patterson Field to take the Tobyhanna drawings to our headquarters. I had a lot of miscellaneous jobs to take up with them out there, and it was Friday evening before I could start back. Planes were too crowded, so I came on a Pullman, arriving back here about noon on Saturday. Then a few hours later I got another train to Pittsburgh and arrived about midnight. I caught the 9:09 out of Pittsburgh last night and was just climbing between the sheets in Hershey at 3:00 A.M. this morning. I found out quite a bit more as regards to my leaving Middletown. It seems that the job they've got me slated for is Construction and Utilities Officer with a B-29 Service Group. It calls for a Captain and there will be a unit of 37 enlisted men in his charge. The only disappointing thing is that the work won't actually be combat, although our unit would be stationed fairly close to a combat area, and we would more than likely be under fire at times. But the best part of it is this – there will be a ten-week training period, tentatively dated to start around June 1st, and training is slated to be at Geiger Field, in Washington just outside of Spokane. Of course, it will be 1500 miles from Los Angeles, but that's a lot closer than 3000. Surely we can make some arrangements then. Not only that but in going to Geiger Field and when I'm coming back, maybe I can go through L.A.!

"After our ten weeks of schooling at Spokane, we expect to be stationed somewhere in Kansas for training before we go overseas. Before Christmas, I should be on my way across the ocean. It's the thing I've been waiting two years for, and if it comes within my grasp I'm not going to let it slip through. While I was at Patterson Field, I stayed with Lt. Haver and his wife of 5 months. They really made me feel at home. Ralph and I were the best of friends from the time we met, and it makes me feel good to see how really happy he is."

After all the waiting, things sped up for Harvey in the middle of April. He sent Betty a telegram on the 17th: "Orders arrived. Southbound next week. Will call tomorrow night." Harvey was relieved of duty at Olmsted Field the next day and was assigned to Robins Field in Warner Robins, Georgia. Another telegram to Betty, this time from Pittsburgh, on Wednesday the 19th: "I'm home on a six-day delay and taking a train for Georgia on Monday morning. Things point to an early departure for Spokane." (Also on the 19th, Betty sent Harvey an anniversary card; it had been two years since they met in Beverly Hills!) In addition, it appeared that he would be leading a group of troops to Geiger Field in Spokane, which made it unlikely that he would be able to take a side trip to LA to see Betty. His train arrived in Macon, Georgia on Monday night, and he spent the night at the Hotel Dempsey on Cherry Street.

On the 28th, while still at Robins Field, Harvey was reassigned again, this time to the 4050th Army Air Base Unit at Daniel Field. On May 1st he wrote, "This living 'in transit' is rather expensive, and these southerners seem bent on taking the soldiers for every cent they have. Tomorrow makes a week that I've been here, and I know no more about what I'm to do than I did before I came. This post is supposed to issue orders for me to go to Geiger Field with my 37 men but, as yet I haven't seen anyone who knows anything about my orders, much less the 37 enlisted men. I guess that one of these days they will discover that I'm here and then they'll get all excited about the thing and begin issuing orders all over the place. When I left Middletown I felt a little guilty about taking a six-day delay enroute, but I know now that I could have taken a month off and on one have known the difference.

"Surprise!! While I was out to lunch some orders came through on me and now I find I'm being sent to Daniel Field which is outside of Augusta, Georgia. This will only be a temporary stop, here at Robins Field, and it shouldn't be very long until I'm on my way to the West Coast. I'm hoping that they'll let all the officers travel together and, in that case, I'll take off on my own and head for you. If I do get there, I won't be able to stay more than a few hours probably." On May 7th, Harvey sent a telegram to Betty letting her know that his unit was in Augusta but would be leaving soon and he wouldn't be able to visit California as they had hoped. In a second telegram two days later, he indicated that his train would be leaving that afternoon for Geiger Field in Spokane, Washington.

On May 9th, General O'Connor at Daniel Field issued orders for the 4050th Army Base Unit (Section G). Designated squadrons of the 4050th were to proceed by troop train to Geiger Field in Spokane, Washington, arriving on May 15th. Once there, they were to report to the Commanding Officer of the 463rd Aviation Training Center to pursue a 70-day course of instruction as Provisional Utilities Sections. Harvey was designated as the Train Commander for the trip. The Quartermaster at Daniel Field was designated shipping Quartermaster and ordered to provide necessary tickets, make inspections, and render reports, arrange for the installation field ranges on the train, and provide the necessary fuel, ice, and cleaning supplies. Prior to departure, the sales officer provided Harvey with train rations for thirteen meals for all officers and enlisted men, plus three additional meals to provide for delays. The War Department requested that the Pullman Company furnish Harvey and 118 others "at lowest rate the following. From Augusta, Ga to Spokane, Washington. Via Georgia Railway to Atlanta; the Nashville, Chattanooga, and St. Louis Railway to Nashville; the Louisville and Nashville Railroad to St. Louis; the Wabash Railroad to Albia, Iowa; the Minneapolis and St. Louis Railway to Minneapolis; and the Union Pacific to Spokane."

The 2.800-mile train ride to Spokane, with three officers and 115 enlisted men on board, took five days, arriving on May 15th. Harvey was able to get off another telegram during a quick stop in Minot, North Dakota, but spent most of his time "keeping an eye on 115 men and making sure they all got back on the train." He wasn't able to reach Betty when he reached Spokane, but he did send another telegram on the 19th confirming that he was at Geiger Field.

The War Department had purchased the airfield, formerly known as Sunset Field, in 1941, and had renamed it in honor of Major Harold Geiger, an early army aviator who had died in a plane crash in 1927. During the war, Geiger Field served as a major training base for B-17 Flying Fortresses, with new planes coming in from Boeing in Seattle, and was also used as an aircraft maintenance and supply depot by the Air Service Technical Command.

Two letters from Betty were waiting for him when he got to the base. In one of them she suggested they reschedule his California visit to August 11th (these two letters have not surfaced). He immediately wrote back to say he had just learned his unit would be leaving Spokane at the end of July. He hadn't been told where they were going, but he gathered they would be at their next posting for only a short time before being transferred again either to the East Coast—or possibly overseas. He emphasized that he really wanted to see her and asked if she could come to Spokane as soon as possible.

Harvey's unit had arrived at Geiger Field on May 15th, and the plan was that they would be there until about July 23rd. He settled into the Bachelor Officer Quarters at the base, and his roommate was Lt. Yates, the West Virginian he had known at Patterson Field. His first impressions of the base were positive. The field was small, but the Engineers had taken it over almost completely with schools and training programs. It was the biggest group of Engineers he had seen since leaving Fort Belvoir. The food was good at the officers' mess, and the Officers' Club "not much to look at from the outside, but...furnished rather well and they've gone to a lot of trouble to make it as homey as possible." The club included a bar, a lounge, two pool tables, and a large dance floor, along with a barber shop and laundry. There were weekly "tea" dances in the evening, and many of the men brought their wives or girlfriends. As soon as they arrived in Spokane, Harvey and Lt. Yates went into Spokane so they could look around and Harvey could phone Betty. They had a beer and went bowling; the base was six miles from town, and Harvey hoped they could go bowling there often.

By the first week of June, Harvey had been in Spokane for three weeks and hadn't seen Betty for twenty-five months. He received a letter that week that signaled a major change in their relationship: "...you wrote yesterday in your letter that you are actually coming to Spokane!!! When I got the letter, all I got to read was 'Oh, and by the way, I'm definitely coming up to see you'—I didn't even see the part about 'wait, don't collapse' until after they brought me to. I was reading the letter as I was crossing the main street in front of headquarters and was almost run down by all sorts of Army vehicles. About the accommodations here, they aren't too tough to make, although some of the hotels refuse to reserve anything over weekends. I'm glad to hear that your mother is coming with you, because I know she wouldn't want you to make the trip by yourself, and too, it'll be great to see her again.

"The fellow in the next room to me, Lt. Rogers, is a swell guy and as screwy as they come. He just came in and suggested that we go into town. It's almost nine o'clock and only two guys without any brains would think of getting ready at this late hour to go into town. So, I'll go. We'll probably fool around town and get home late, lose a lot of sleep, and then tomorrow wonder why in the world we started in the first place. But I haven't been in town for a long time, and it does a fellow a lot of good to get off the base once in a while." While he was in town, he picked up post cards of Spokane to send to Betty, one of the Davenport Hotel, where he was making reservations for her visit, and one of Coulee Dam, which he suggested they visit.

On June 8th, Harvey and his enlisted men learned they were being reassigned to the Headquarters and Base Service Squadron of the newly formed 75th Air Service Group. The 75th had originated at Tinker Field in Oklahoma and was beginning to get organized at the Warner Robins base in Macon, Georgia. Lt. Col. Muchmore was the Commanding Officer.

The B-29 Service Group with which Harvey was training would eventually go to the Pacific, and the men were becoming a close group in Spokane. "With the rapid movements on every front, I hope that this war will soon draw to a close, and at that time, there is a chance that we will be broken up as an outfit. We naturally don't like the idea, for we have been through a lot together, and seem like a family. But there is one consolation that makes the idea a bit more plausible, and that is that we will probably be demobilized in California and then again I will be able to see you."

By late June, Harvey was becoming excited about Betty's visit, and he was busily making plans. However, he was also worried. "I hope you got my wire about the train schedule yesterday. A sergeant in my outfit asked me down for supper last night so I stopped at the railroad station on the way. It seems funny to me that they haven't any more than one train a day between two large cities like Portland and Spokane. I don't know whether I'll be able to get to Portland to meet you, but I doubt it. If I can get Monday off, it shouldn't be too tough. I'm down in the dumps today and it's because we may not be allowed to stay here to finish our course. It's only a possibility, but you know how the Army operates. I've been thinking of how bad I'd feel if we were shipped from here before you came. There wouldn't be anything I could do about it, legally at least, and when we leave here, I feel sure that we probably won't see the West Coast again before we go across. And there are so many things I've just got to talk to you about before I leave. Things that I'd hate to tackle over the phone. Even the short week you're to have here in Spokane will hardly be more than just enough to mention only a few of the more important things I want to talk to you about. Golly, this really is turning out to be an awfully morbid letter, and there is no reason for it...except that I've just talked myself into this mood.

"We haven't heard an answer to the wire that was sent to Daniel Field about those orders I told you about on the phone. But I'm sure that when the answer does come, it will tell us to stay for the full length of the course. If we should have to leave now, the men will have had only a small part of the intended training and wouldn't be of any use to anyone, the way I see it. By the way, I took another flying lesson Sunday and Mallery, the instructor, says I'm getting along fine. I have an advantage and that is that I've done quite a bit of flying before and all I'm learning now is the actual mechanics of the thing."

On June 8th Betty sent a telegram to Harvey, saying she was coming to Spokane, and ten days later, she sent another saying she had reservations on the Southern Pacific for July 1st. Harvey made reservations for her at the Davenport Hotel. It had appeared that Harvey's unit might leave Spokane before that, but he had just received orders to stay on at Geiger Field until he had finished his training course. Only then was he to report to the newly formed 75th Air Service Group, at Robins Field in Warner Robins, Georgia. The 75th consisted of the Headquarters and Base Service Group (Harvey's unit), the 587th Air Engineer Squadron, the 581st Air Material Squadron and a communication section which included cryptography, radio operators, a messenger center, clerks, messengers, jeep drivers and repairmen. The 587th was sent to Flora, Mississippi on June 8th and was attached unassigned to the 4053rd AAFBU at that base. Their officers at that point were Lt. George Terlinden, Lt. Frank Springer, and Lt. Robert Sprague. They were assigned to the armament and automotive section.

With plans firming up for Betty's visit, Harvey settled into his training regimen at Geiger Field. He wrote to Betty that he thought he would take the opportunity to learn how to fly and took six lessons in a Piper J-3 Cub. The J-3 Cub is an American light aircraft that was built by Piper Aircraft between 1938 and 1947, and "was what pretty much everyone in that era learned to fly in. Reliable, cheap, fun." In a June 8th letter, Harvey reflected on how wartime service in the Army was changing him from "the only child of doting parents, and pretty well spoiled," to "getting to know that the way you've always thought about things isn't the only way to think about them." He found he was developing a broader outlook on various religions and political views, and knew that after his military experience, he would be forever "changed."

7

ENGAGED ON THE
FOURTH OF JULY

On July 1st, Betty sent a telegram saying she was heading to the train station and that her train would leave at 5:30 that evening. She was on her way. Two days later another telegram indicated she had arrived in Portland that morning and her train would leave at 8:00 p.m. She arrived in Spokane early the morning of the Fourth of July, and Harvey met her at the station. He almost missed her train, as he initially went to the wrong station, but he made it. As he waited for her train to pull in, he was nervous. "I didn't know what to expect, didn't know whether life was just about to start or whether it was just to be a burst bubble...believe me it was no burst bubble! When you gave me that one little kiss in the station, something started in me that will be there from now on." They became engaged almost immediately. Betty checked into the Hotel Spokane (for some reason, Harvey had switched the reservations from the Davenport Hotel), and Harvey went back to the field so Betty could get some rest before they went out that night. That evening the two walked all over town and sat in the park watching the fireworks over the ravine. A little boy played in a tree near the bench where they were sitting, and they worried he would fall. They went bowling that night, and "shot arrows" at a nearby amusement park. Two days later, they called Betty's family in Venice with the good news. They both sent letters to Harvey's parents, he being careful to emphasize that he and Betty WEREN'T getting married immediately! After the phone call, Betty wrote to her brother Rod and asked what her parents' reaction to the news had been. She also asked him about the progress being made on the family's new house down the street from the old one.

Betty and Harvey were enjoying their engagement, and Betty came to really like Harvey's friends. On the 6th, they had dinner at the apartment of Harvey's friend, Lt. Henry, and his wife, and then they all went dancing to the music of the Henry King Orchestra at Riverfront Park, which jutted out into the Spokane River. Betty was surprised to learn that this was the only dance spot in Spokane, a fairly large city. In 1936, Henry King had been the bandleader for the Burns and Allen Campbell's Tomato Juice radio program on CBS, and in the forties he recorded on the Decca label. In 1944, he and his orchestra performed regularly throughout Northern California, Oregon, and western Washington; his radio programs were heard all over the country.

Betty, with Harvey sitting next to her, wrote to her family on Monday, the 10th. "We had such a lovely time yesterday. Every day we go someplace or do something fun. We didn't go to church because Harvey was due for a flying lesson at 11:15 and he couldn't miss it. Then, he got out to the field and there was some mix-up about the planes, and he would have had to wait too long, so he caught a bus and came back into town. Just couldn't stand to be away from me!

"We packed our swimsuits and took a bus to Idaho! Can you imagine? We went to Coeur d'Alene, a famous lakeside resort just across the Washington border. Harvey went in swimming. We had dinner there in the evening at a little café near the lake and laughed until I thought I'd burst. Everything we asked for...they were just out of it. We ordered one salad and got two. He ordered iced coffee, and she brought hot. That went on the whole meal...I was so weak from laughing I could hardly walk back to the bus. It's about an hour's ride, and we were both really sleepy when we got back to Spokane. So, we went walking around town to find an ice cream parlor that was open and that we didn't have to stand in line for an hour to get in. Finally, went over to the Davenport Hotel and got some ice cream and coffee there before walking back to my hotel. The stores are open tonight, so Harvey is going to get my ring."

Harvey and Betty only had ten days together before she left to go back to California. On Friday Harvey took her to the station to catch her train back to California. As for countless young couples in similar situations, the parting was not an easy one. Betty wrote to him from the train, mailing the letter when she stopped in Sacramento. On Tuesday, Harvey wrote telling her how much he missed her—a common theme in their correspondence for the next several months.

Harvey and Betty, Jul. 1944

Harvey's mother sent a clipping from one of the Pittsburgh newspapers which reported that three airmen from the local area had been awarded the Distinguished Flying Cross; one of them had been severely wounded in an air attack over Italy, and another, Lt. Robert Benson had completed thirty missions as a navigator out of England. Lt. Benson lived very near the Browns and before enlisting had worked at the Duquesne Light Company, where Harvey had also worked before the War. Clearly, Harvey's parents were worried and were closely following news accounts of the war.

On Sunday, Harvey went to a picnic at Liberty Lake, not far from the base. Although the picnic was for enlisted personnel, the men invited Harvey and another officer, Bob Yates, to join them for the day. Harvey was pleased that his men liked him and wanted him to join them at their event. There was swimming, boating, fishing, and lots of food, and fifty girls from the Spokane USO also attended. Harvey, Bob, and Bob's wife were made to feel welcome by the men, and Harvey was glad that he'd be going overseas with this group.

In a letter he sent to Betty that evening, he described the final project he would be working on at the base before his unit left the following Sunday, the construction of a large unloading dock at the airfield. When they left Geiger Field on the 23rd, there were to be two units on the train, but as he was the senior officer, he would have to be the "train commander," as he had been on the previous trip.

The telephone company had set up a "telephone center" for the army across the street from the Davenport Hotel. Servicemen/women could call their families for free, and Harvey placed a call to Betty on Thursday, the 19th. While he waited for the call to go through, he wrote a quick letter. His orders had arrived, and his unit would leave Spokane Sunday morning at 7:30. They were due to arrive in Georgia some time on Wednesday. The weather was hot and muggy, and he wasn't looking forward to the four-day train trip. He had received another letter from his mother, who had again advised against getting married before he went overseas. Harvey disagreed. Evidently, he and Betty had already discussed the issue, and they hoped to have the wedding as soon as possible. Harvey told Betty, though, that he had no way of knowing when he could get to Los Angeles. It was even possible that his new unit would leave the country as soon as he reached Robins Field. He asked her, only partially in jest, how she would feel about getting married in Georgia. He wrote again the next day and again stressed that he felt they should get married before he went to war because "it will give us something solid to hold onto while we're apart." He added, however, that he would agree to whatever Betty wanted to do.

At 6:30 a.m., Sunday, July 23rd, Harvey and his unit left the base and boarded rail cars in Spokane: the train pulled out at about 7:45. They passed through Coeur d'Alene, Idaho, and as they headed east through Montana, Harvey started a letter to Betty. It was a short one, as Harvey was having difficulty holding his pen steady enough to write. By 10:30, they were in Minot, North Dakota. After supper, the train slowed a bit, and he tried writing again. During a brief stop, it was 103 degrees in the Montana plains. They had several long layovers scheduled and were due to reach Georgia sometime after noon on Thursday. On Sunday and Monday, the train crossed through Montana and South Dakota before stopping for the night at about 10:00 p.m. Monday in Minneapolis. Harvey allowed his men "see the town" in Minneapolis until 1:30 in the morning, which would allow them to get a little sleep and give him enough time to look for anyone that was missing. He knew he was taking a risk that someone would get drunk or cause trouble or even go AWOL, but he felt it was unreasonable to have his men spend four days sitting on a hot train. "At least if any of them get into difficulty, I'll have four or five hours to get them out of it." That night, he allowed himself to imagine his and Betty's Golden Wedding Anniversary—they'd return to Spokane and once again stay at the Spokane Hotel, have dinner at the dining room of the Davenport Hotel, and go dancing at Natatorium Park—"maybe minuets will be our speed by that time?" The next morning, before leaving Minneapolis,

Harvey sent another telegram—the men hadn't gotten into trouble and "had a wonderful time here. We're heading south now."

During a brief stop near Albert Lea, Minnesota, on Tuesday, the men relaxed on the shore of Fountain Lake, and Harvey suggested to Betty that perhaps they should live there after the war. "This town is really one of the nicest I've seen. The people here are so darn friendly that a fellow can't help but feel at home. We had a layover from 12:30 until 4:45 and we turned the outfit loose for about two hours and a half. We had dinner at the Canton Café here in town and the food was really delicious. Of course, we have meal tickets for the enlisted men, but Lt. Jay and I have to pay cash for ours, so today we blew ourselves to a steak dinner. Without any exaggeration, I think it was the best steak I ever tasted. Then, when we were all finished, the man who runs the place told us it was on the house. That was really a treat!! Albert Lea really beats a lot of other towns where we have stopped."

Eventually, they went back to the train station and waited for the trip to start again. Harvey brought the men back to the train a little early so there would be time to look for anyone who might be missing. "It's always a good idea give yourself plenty of time because there's no telling what may turn up."

That evening on the train, Harvey chatted with Sgt. Bill Zierenberg before supper. "We had rather a late lunch at Albert Lea so instead of wiring ahead for a full meal, we wired for a box lunch at Hampton, Iowa. Each man had two sandwiches, one cheese and one ham, two cupcakes, two cookies, an orange, a peach, and a quart of milk. The milk was ice cold, and all in all it really hit the spot. It's really raining now, not hard but steady. The windows of the car are all dotted with streaks and drops of rain. One of the men is playing a sad tune on a harmonica he has brought with him. Everyone has a full stomach and would rather sit and let his thoughts wander rather than waste effort on talking. About halfway down the car, four of the more ambitious boys are playing a half-hearted game of blackjack. I guess it's just one of those sentimental moments, and I'm gelling pretty much that way myself....my thoughts are with you even more strongly than usual."

From Minnesota, they headed south through Iowa and Missouri, stopping for a few hours on Tuesday in St. Louis, and then moving on through Evansville (Indiana), Nashville, and Atlanta before finally reaching Robins Field in Warner Robins, Georgia, on Thursday afternoon. At Warner Robins, they learned that the 75th would be attached to the 315th Bomb Wing, whose flight crews were training at various Air Corps bases in Nebraska.

8

BIVOUAC

Harvey's training schedule at Robins Field was pretty hectic, with work duties from 8:00 a.m. to 4:00 p.m. each day, followed by classes from 4:00 p.m. to 6:00 p.m. and 7:00 p.m. to 9:00 p.m. However, he did manage to send off a letter on August 2nd.

His unit was scheduled to leave Georgia for the "Mid-West" on about September 1st, and he hoped he and Betty could get married soon after that. He planned to apply for a leave as soon as he arrived at his new post, but he was worried that one wouldn't be granted, and he wouldn't be able to see Betty before being shipped overseas. If a leave wasn't granted, he asked if she could come to his new post—Kansas or Oklahoma, or possibly Texas. "We've just got to see each other before the Army makes any definite plans for me."

The next day, Harvey had some interesting news to share, and that evening he tried to put a call through to LA. When the phone office closed at midnight, his call still had not gone through. He was serving as "Officer of the Day" for his group, and although his duties kept him up most of the night, he was up at 6:25 in the morning and wrote Betty a letter. His "news" was that a friend, Lt. Cain, was buying a car, and that he and Harvey had come up with a plan! Lt. Cain would try to get a twenty-day leave and then drive the car to his home in Portland, Oregon. When the unit moved to their next base (probably Walker Army Airfield, near Hays, Kansas), he would drive from Portland to rejoin the group. The "plan" called for Harvey and Betty to get married immediately in the Robins Field Chapel and drive with Lt. Cain and his wife as far as Los Angeles to spend their honeymoon in California. The Cains would pick them up on the way back to Kansas. It was likely that Harvey's change in marital status would mean he would be permanently stationed in Hays. Harvey wrote that he was sure Betty would love the idea and hoped that she would soon be on a train to Georgia. On the 9th, he sent a postcard: "Tonight the officers from our group are going to play a softball game with some other officers on the base. It should really be a hot game. I've set up my own office now and am getting everything pretty well organized."

A couple of days later: "Just finished eating lunch and I've got about 45 minutes before I've got to go to the base hospital and get some shots. I need about 8 of them before I can go overseas, so I thought I'd better get started on them. This afternoon I've got to take a physical fitness test and then this evening I've got to hear a lecture on malaria control. I talked to Lt. Cain today, and now it looks as if he's not going to take his leave until we get to our new station. At least we should have a ride back from L.A. to the base. That's an important item because trains are hard to schedule. No word yet as to exactly when we'll leave here, but the 1st of September still looks fairly certain. If we leave here on the 1st, it will no doubt be the 6th before we hit a new station and then about a week after that before I can arrange a leave, so about the middle of September may be the time for us. You know you are going to have an awful lot of arrangements to make when I'm finally able to let you know that I'm ready to come. You'll have a license to get and a blood test to take and a million and one other things to do. I don't know if the State of California will accept an Army blood test or not for me, but I'll try it to save a little time. I believe I told you in Spokane that I'd like to have Rod as my best man, but if not, here it is now. Do you think I should write him a letter and ask him? As to the church etc., that's all up to you. It's heaven to be talking about such things for our very own wedding. I really do feel engaged now, but I know it will take me a long time to get used to the idea of being married. And to think that in 1918, they thought an Armistice was reason enough for a celebration...if they only knew how lucky I am, they would <u>really throw a celebration</u>."

With no updates by Sunday the 13th, Harvey was pretty sure he was still scheduled to leave on September 1st. There was a bivouac planned for Monday, the 14th, and he assumed it would be the last stage of the unit's training at Warner Robins. When the bivouac ended, he should be just about ready to leave. He was glad that he was now attached to a sizable unit. He could ship all his manuals and books as "organizational equipment" rather than packing them with his clothes. He had a carpenter make a wooden crate for him and "if some of my heavier clothes should slip in by accident, it'll be that much better."

Harvey at Warner Robins, Georgia, Aug. 1944

There was an inspection on Wednesday morning, and then the unit went out on the range to qualify with carbines. The Squadron commander, Major Turner, handled the inspection and since Harvey had already qualified on the range, he was able to take a few minutes to update Betty. He would be going on a four-day bivouac on Monday and when he returned, he would start getting ready to leave. Lt. Cain had decided not to buy a car in Georgia, and instead would bring his old car back to Kansas from Portland after his leave. If he and Harvey could get their leaves at the same time, he could pick Harvey up in LA on his way back to Kansas. In addition to this being convenient, Harvey felt it would be cheaper and eliminate the need to find train reservations. If the plan worked out, he felt he could be back in Kansas before September 10th.

Occasionally, the men provided their own entertainment in the evenings. "One of the boys who sleeps in my hut is Hawaiian and last night before we went to sleep he got out a ukulele and knocked out a few tunes for us. And, brother, can he make that thing talk! I never heard anyone get so much music out of one little uke. He played 'In the Mood' and made it sound like about fifteen instruments were playing. I know you would have liked that."

Harvey was the Group camouflage officer, and on Friday he went out to get the bivouac area ready. "It's really a big job because it's my responsibility to see that everything in the bivouac is accomplished with the least amount of trouble and disturbance to our normal routine. We did a lot of tramping through the woods today and I'm pretty tired, but I want to get a few lines off to you so that you'll know I was thinking about you all day. We've had quite a bit of rain, a thunderstorm today, but it doesn't help the heat any. Just makes everything wet and even more uncomfortable. There are quite a few mosquitoes here but our biggest pain in the neck have been those little gnats that swarm around by the hundreds as soon as you stop moving around. As soon as I got in from the bivouac area tonight, I jumped into the shower and let the streaming water try to wash some of the dust and dirt off. Most of the ground around here is either sand or red Georgia clay and when that stuff raises up as dust, it turns everything red. I was covered in it tonight."

Lt. Jay and Harvey were the only officers to come in from Geiger Field, Jay with the 76th Service Group and Harvey with the 75th. On Friday, the 76th moved out to Great Bend, Kansas, leaving Harvey as "the last one of the boys from Geiger Field. When we leave here on Sept. 1 or thereabouts, it will polish off the last of us".

On Sunday, the men spent the day loading supplies and equipment for the bivouac. A jeep picked up Harvey at 5:30 the next morning, and he then picked up the supply trucks which made up the advance party. "Our job is to get out to the bivouac area and be ready for the rest of the men when they come about an hour and a half later. It'll be a lot of fun for four or five days and good actual field experience for all of us. We'll all be living in tents, so writing during the day will be out of the question and at night we aren't allowed to have lights. I'll get at least a card off to you every day. The other day when I was out fixing up our bivouac, I collected a mess of chigger bites and at that I was only there for a few hours. Their bite is much worse than a mosquito and seems to last a lot longer. We are all going to douse ourselves with sulphur in an effort to keep them off." It was Harvey's responsibility to draw weapons for the bivouac and distribute them to his men: "what a headache that was! I had all kinds of weapons from .45 automatics to bazookas. We expect to be 'camping' until Thursday or Friday, and the following Monday will be the 28th, only 3 days before our tentative moving date!"

Harvey and his men found the bivouac to be "loads of fun" but also very hard work. They were constantly on the alert for possible "enemy attacks" and didn't have a chance to get their ordinary work done. They were attacked on the first day with tear gas and bombs but managed to "stand them off" and took seven prisoners, three officers and four enlisted men. There were several air-raid alarms, when planes from the base here would come out and dive bomb the area—"however they weren't very successful because we were so well camouflaged that they had a hard time finding where we were camped. I don't think I had more than 6 or 7 hours sleep the whole time. We were up almost all night, every night, because we never knew when the enemy would try to break through our outpost system. They tried it a couple of times but never made it."

Orders still hadn't come through, but everyone was confident that they'd be out by the end of the next week. "The squadron commander, Major Turner, said that he'd like to have all of us on hand for about a week following the move so that we could help get things set up and organized before we take off on leaves. That's only fair to him, so we are figuring on staying at our new station for a week after the move."

Harvey was pretty sure that he wouldn't have his captain's bars before he got to LA. "Things just don't work that fast in the Army, except for the things we don't like. It shouldn't take too long, at least I hope not. I don't want to be a permanent First Lieutenant."

At the end of August, Harvey's unit was still in Georgia, with no firm information about when they would move, and he was increasingly concerned about the delay. "I've been worrying a lot about us lately, because the situation here is still pretty much SNAFU. No one seems to know what the score is about our moving out of here and so far we have had no definite word as to where we're going. It's hard on the nerves when I've got someone to go to and can't find out when I'm going to be able to get there. Here it is, the 30th of August already, and originally we were supposed to leave here on the 1st. Now, it doesn't look as if we'll get away from here for at least another week or so. I wish they'd make up their minds. Last night, about 70 more enlisted men came in and that puts us almost up to strength with the exception of our Ordnance Section. The men that came in last night are our Guard Section, and they really are a rough bunch. They've had a ten-week course at Barksdale Field in Louisiana, and after spending that long a time in that place, they'll be ready for anything."

That night, Harvey went to the theater on base and saw *Dragon Seed* with Katherine Hepburn. It was hot and humid, but he enjoyed the picture. "Should be a 'must' on your list of movies if you haven't already seen it."

9

LANDING STRIP IN MISSISSIPPI

The 1st of September had come and gone, and the 75th was still in Georgia. "Everybody's just a little on edge actually waiting on orders, and most of us are pretty anxious to move. From the way things look now, it probably won't be until late September before I can get out there to you. In one way, that's best because it will give you a little more time to get ready, but I don't know whether or not I can make it." There was an inspection parade scheduled for Saturday morning. The major was going to be in the reviewing party and had asked Harvey to take his place as squadron commander for the parade. "Not only that but today I was given charge of the Fire Fighting section which makes four duties I've got now...Utilities Officer, Camouflage Officer, Acting Group Ordnance Officer, and now Fire Marshall. One thing about all this, I guess—it shows that that the Major has confidence in my ability to handle the extra work. He and I get along fine, and I know that when he gets the opportunity to put in my captaincy, he'll do it.

"Tomorrow night the Officers Club is having another one of its weekly Saturday night dances, and I guess I'll go again with Lt. Cain and his wife, Paula. The three of us get along really well. They're the couple that we may ride back to Kansas with."

On Tuesday, September 5th, Harvey got word that the wedding would have to be delayed even longer. "We aren't going to Kansas before October 1st. That choice bit of news was told to us this morning at officers' call. The base in Kansas where we're going isn't ready for us yet and won't be until about Oct. 1st so it will be at least that long until we leave Georgia." In the meantime, Robins Field was expecting many more troops to come in, and the 75th had to move out to make room for them. The orders were to move to Herbert Smart Airport, about thirty miles from Warner Robins, until the base in Kansas was ready. "We're due to leave here Thursday morning, day after tomorrow, and what a job of packing we've got on our hands. None of us want to go there because it isn't as nice a field as this, but there's nothing we can do. None of us know just how long we'll be at Herbert Smart, but I do know that higher headquarters is making every effort to get us out there by Oct. 1st. I'm pretty low right now because up until the last minute, I've been hoping against hope that we'd get to Kansas on schedule. It looks fairly certain now that I won't be able to get to California before the middle of October. You'll find out a lot about the Army after we're married, but for now, just have a little patience with the Army and trust in me to get to you as soon as I can."

Little of Betty's correspondence to Harvey from this period has survived, as he didn't begin to save letters until after their wedding in November. But in one letter, she included a clipping from a local paper, the Herald-Express, that caught her attention and, obviously, caught his as well. A father and son had both served in Europe during wartime, one in World War I in 1918, and the other in World War II, and their experiences were captured in the letters they wrote to each other:

Son and Father Exchange Notes on Two Wars
Dear Dad: Dear Son:

History is repeating itself in many ways as events of World War II unravel in Europe. A picture of this repetition is found in the story of Harold Whitman and his son, Sgt. Don Whitman. The father fought in France in World War I. Now his son is fighting there in this war. Here are excerpts of letters reflecting the spirit of the typical Yank overseas and World War I dad at home.

"...I am writing this letter from somewhere on the French countryside, where you fought in World War I. Everywhere there are people standing by the road with glasses and bottles of cider, waiting for a convoy to stop..."

"...that first bombing is something that I will never forget even if I live forever. They dropped flares over us and light up everything like daylight. I was so scared I couldn't talk or hardly think. I have never been so scared and mad in my life. You just lay there like a clay pigeon and let them drop..."

"...and then they started to lay their eggs. The awful swishing sound those 1000-pound bombs made was almost worse than the actual explosion and concussion. Each one sounded as if it was going to land right on you. Some of them dropped within 100 yards of us..."

"...we had just begun to dig in our position when the crew on watch saw four ME 109's hedgehopping straight for us. They had already strafed some other guns. The crew fired on them, and I think we might have damaged one...Tell mom not to worry because her lil' boy can duck 'em faster than the Boche can throw 'em, and all this isn't as bad as it sounds, ... Don"

"...when the time comes for you to go into battle and you begin to get scared, you shouldn't be ashamed. Anyone who says they are not afraid in their first battle is just a fibber. I don't want you to do anything heroic, just for the sake of being a hero...but do what is expected of you...Dad"

Harvey saved the letter.

By September 9th, Harvey was well situated at Herbert Smart Airport and was feeling that it wouldn't be as bad as he had thought. It was a small place and didn't have all the facilities that Robins Field had, but he thought they'd get along fine. "We really have been terribly busy getting set up here, and I've had to do quite a large share of it myself because the other officers, with the exception of the Major are young and rather inexperienced at this business of moving an outfit from one place to another. You can hardly imagine how hard it is to arrange facilities for 650 men, especially at a base that is only supposed to handle a total of 1000 men. Setting up supply rooms, mess halls, orderly rooms, and troop housing, and laying out areas where there aren't any is a large order. But everything is starting to calm down a little, so I ought to be able to get a little more of my own personal stuff done. This airbase is about 35 miles from Robins Field, and we are now 10 miles from Macon, instead of 22 as we were before. Of course, the Officers Club here isn't nearly so expansive as the one at Robins Field but it's not bad and really seems to be a lot chummier. Everybody here knows everybody else which helps. Of all the officers on the base, the officers from the 75th make up about 50% so we are evenly matched when it comes to any kind of dispute."

Rumors now had it that the 75th would be leaving on about October 1st. It had been over two months since Harvey had seen Betty. He typed his Saturday morning letter while sitting at the Major's desk in the orderly room. "He just came in and is sitting beside me on a footlocker waiting for me to finish. He's a swell guy and I know that you'll like him a lot. He's only 29 years old, but his early rank hasn't gone to his head. We all really like working hard for him."

Two days later: "These men of mine are really working now. We have all kinds of work to do all over the area such as wiring, carpentry, plumbing, and excavation. Not only that but they're really cheerful doing anything they have to do. They are all pretty anxious to meet you because they feel they have to pass on what kind of girl is going to marry their lieutenant. That should tell how we feel about each other here. They would no sooner let someone take advantage of me than they would themselves. I frankly can't understand why some officers have so much trouble with their enlisted men because all you have to do is remember they are human too."

At about this time, Betty's family moved into a new house, and she sent a picture of it to Harvey in Georgia. The new house was about three blocks from the old one, both of them on Caswell Avenue. "The letter came today with the picture of your new house, and it looks really swell. Now I can understand why you and your family have wanted to spend so much time getting it ready. Went up to the dispensary at noon today and got two more shots...a typhus and a cholera. After that I can go anywhere in the world and not be afraid of catching anything....but malaria. So far they haven't found any kind of a shot to give a man to keep him from getting malaria. We're supposed to have a dance at our Officers Club this next Saturday night, but I guess you can't make it....can you?"

On Sunday, Harvey went to church and his roommate, Sol Mayer, went with him. "He's Jewish and told me that if I went to synagogue with him this evening, he'd go to church with me this morning. So, this morning, I tried to convert him, and this evening he's going to try to convert me. He's a good guy, and we have lots of fun together." He filled Betty in the next day. "I went to the Synagogue last night and really enjoyed myself. It was the first time I had ever been inside one, and so Sol kept me straight on proceedings. After the service (Jewish New Year service) one of the men of the church asked us out to his house for a bite to eat to celebrate. They had a typical Jewish meal with everything from gefilte fish right on down. And it was really good. I didn't care much for the fish, but the rest of it was delicious. I was the only one out of 10 at the table that wasn't Jewish, so they all had a big time trying to convert me. It really was fun. Incidentally, Sol decided I'd have to have a Jewish name to go into the synagogue, so he nick-named me Izzy Finkelstein. What a crazy bunch of officers we have.

"Yesterday we had our first parade here at Herbert Smart, and again I was

Squadron Commander of Headquarters Squadron. The base band played for us and, all in all, everything went off smoothly. This time we had the whole ceremony from start to finish which took about an hour. That includes Adjutants Call, Presentation of Officers, Retreat, and all the rest of it. The 75th only has about 650 men which is only around a third of the men that you saw at Geiger Field, but it makes a good-looking parade just the same. Our own colonel reviews us and of course all the men try to look especially good for him. He said that Hq. Sq. was by far the best in yesterday's parade. Most of the rest of the officers in Hq. Sq. aren't too familiar with the procedures of a parade, so it looks like I've got a permanent job every Saturday."

Thursday had been an exciting day at the field. Herbert Smart was a small base ("if they're landing two planes the same day, it's a big deal"), but on Thursday a hurricane warning came from the East Coast. An hour later, forty Navy fighters landed at the airfield to park until the danger passed. They only stayed the night, but "in that one night Herbert Smart Airport saw more planes at one time than it had ever seen before. It was a pretty sight to see all those formations of Hellcats and Corsairs come swooping in. The Navy boys certainly can fly."

On Sunday afternoon, Harvey and a couple of friends found time to see a couple of movies at the base theater: "One was 'Casanova Brown', and if you get the opportunity to see it, don't miss it. Gary Cooper and Teresa Wright are really super. Another good picture is 'Arsenic and Old Lace'. I laughed at that one till I thought I'd split my Sunday shirt. It's every bit as funny as the stage version if not funnier. The scene where Cary Grant is tied up in a chair is a scream."

By September 20th, the 75th was still in Georgia and there was no indication that they would be moving out soon. The men had only expected to be at Herbert Smart for about twenty-five days or until the 1st of October, but now they weren't even sure they would leave then. There wasn't even anyone Harvey could ask about it since all orders came from a higher headquarters. One consolation, at least as far as Harvey was concerned, was that the base at Herbert Smart had six bowling alleys, surprising for such a small place. Major Turner asked Harvey to take a look at the electrical fixtures and the general condition of the alleys to see if they could be put into shape. The alleys hadn't been used since 1943, so it turned out to be quite a job. Harvey and his men worked on them all day Tuesday and some on Wednesday evening "and now I believe that they are almost in first class shape for use. The switch boxes were all screwed up, and we had to take them all apart to see what made them tick.

After putting in a system all our own, the lights didn't work bad at all." They sanded and refinished the alleys. "It's probably not as good as the Brunswick people could do, but it'll serve the purpose for us."

There had been a rumor circulating about Harvey going to Flora, Mississippi, on detached service for a week or so. He didn't want to get excited about it before actually seeing the orders telling him to go. "I'd like to get the job but I'm afraid that I wouldn't have very much of a free hand in doing the job." The project involved a runway at the Mississippi Ordnance Plant that someone else started but hadn't finished. It appeared that the orders would come from Patterson Field, the same place that would be issuing the orders for the 75th to move to Kansas.

The Mississippi Ordnance Plant was located in Flora, Mississippi, about twenty-three miles outside of Jackson. It was initially established in 1942 as a bag-loading facility, but those services were already being provided by more efficient plants. It was placed on standby until August 12, 1942, when it was activated as the first Army Special Forces Ordnance Unit Training Center (OUTC). The MOP produced propellant and igniter charges for large-caliber guns; the site also had firing ranges for submachine guns, rifles, antiaircraft guns, live grenades, and demolition explosives. The Ordnance Unit Training Center would become the third largest training center in the United States. This center trained Ordnance troops as technicians for heavy machinery in order to work on the front lines to repair and maintain critical ammunition and tools. These troops then became specialized units, with each unit able to cover a certain area of equipment/ammunition, and they were eventually sent to duty assignments throughout the world. The OUTC put heavy machinery and maintenance operations on display at the Mississippi State Fair in order to show the public what they were doing to help the war effort.

The next day, Harvey received his orders to go to Mississippi. "I'll probably take off for there on Sunday. I'll stay only a couple of days looking the situation over and then I'll come back to get some more men to work on the job, whatever it is they want me to do. I'm still in the dark about that part of it. I've told them that I want to take Bill (T/Sgt. Zierenberg) with me because, after all, that will be his job when we get overseas. I think they are going to let me take him. The bowling alleys opened up tonight!"

The Group photographer took some pictures of Herbert Smart, and Harvey sent some of them to Betty. The photos no longer exist, but Harvey's description of them gives a good idea of the scene. "One of them show the kind of huts that we are using for both living quarters and for offices. Another of the pictures shows one of the company streets, of which we have six. When we have Squadron formations, that whole street is filled with troops. It's a nice orderly looking place but I'm ready to leave for Kansas any time. The other pictures show a couple of my boys operating a skill saw, our first Sgt., Major Turner, and Lt. Cain. Cain is the one I've told you quite a bit about. He has bought a car now and if we can get our leaves together, we'll come to California in it.

"Went to the theater again last night and saw Arsenic and Old Lace for the second time. Then after the show we went bowling again and although I didn't burn up the alleys, I did do a little better."

On Monday, Harvey and Sgt. Zierenberg arrived in Jackson, Mississippi, checked into the Hotel Heidelberg, and then went out to look at the Mississippi Ordnance Plant in Flora, about twenty-five miles from Jackson. "We got here this morning and have had a short look at the situation. They've got a very small landing strip that they want lengthened and improved. As soon as we get the details worked out, we are going back to Herbert Smart and get a crew of my men to work on the job. It looks like about a week's work or maybe a little more. Not a tough job at all. Calls for a little work with bulldozers and graders but that's about all. We think we'll probably be able to leave here tomorrow or the next day to pick up our men at Herbert Smart. Then after a few more days, we'll be back down to start work. I've got to run now because one of the officers from this post is waiting to take us to supper. That's southern hospitality for you!" On Saturday: "I'm supposed to leave tomorrow again for Mississippi to go to work on the runway down there. It will probably take about two weeks to complete it. It is the 30th of September and still no word as to when we are going to leave here." Harvey's trip to Mississippi was delayed because they were unable to get Pullman reservations for his men. He decided to wait and travel with them. "These boys would be pretty darn tired after sitting up all night on a train, so I don't feel as if I'd be justified in asking them to work after we got there. So, I'm just going to sit tight till they break down and get reservations for us. Should get them tomorrow. The colonel has told me that in case our unit gets orders while I'm away, he'll wire me to come back right away so that I can move with the outfit rather than have me come along later. That's probably the best idea, even though it may interfere with the job we'll be doing down there." The time changed on Sunday, and the men had an extra hour of sleep. After a combined breakfast and lunch, they all went to a 2:00 movie. "It was 'San Diego – I Love You', a pretty sad movie but it helped pass the time."

Pullman reservations for the men never materialized, so they all, including Harvey, took a regular train. When they arrived, they were assigned housing at the post in Flora. "We started our runway today and should finish it by the middle of next week. The equipment they've furnished isn't the best, but I think we can make it do. We were pretty tired after sitting up all night on the way down, but we're rested now and really feel like working." On Sunday, Harvey sent an update on their progress. "We put in a full day of hacking away at our runway. The dust is really thick out there, and when we come in at night it's hard to tell one of us from the other. It just lays on in a solid coat. The heavy equipment that we're using raises up such a dust that the air is cloudy with it all day long and, of course, we're standing right in the middle of it, so we get the full benefit. I figured that by the time we finish here we'll have moved just about 4000 cubic yards of dirt, and that's quite a bit considering that we have been able to beg, borrow, or steal only three pieces of equipment – a grader, a 5-yard scraper, and a very small bulldozer. That's not nearly as much equipment as we could have used, but we can't be too choosy here. Everyone has been more than nice to us, but the equipment just isn't available. The strip is about 3 1/2 miles from the main part of camp so we have a truck to carry the men back and forth and a jeep for me to run back and forth. The jeep comes in handy because there are lots of little things that I have to take care of back here while the men are working out on the strip. It looks as if we have the job just about half finished now so about Thursday or Friday of this week we should see the last of it and be ready to start back to Georgia. This has been more or less of a test for my boys and really, they are all A-1. They like to work for me, and I like to work with them and with a situation like that we can't help but be a good outfit. We're trying to get some pictures taken from the air so that we'll have some kind of a record to take back to Herbert Smart with us. Haven't had any chance to go into Jackson yet, and even when we do have time, we're so tired that our thoughts run to going to bed rather than to town. So, I guess the city of Jackson will just have to do without me. If they can stand it, I can."

They were working hard, trying to get the runway completed by the end of the week. Harvey had requested transportation back to Herbert Smart on Saturday night, and if they got it, they needed to have the runway finished by then. It was going to be close. "The finished job will be 1700' by 60' and although that isn't near big enough for large planes, it will easily serve for the small ships they intend to use here.

"I saw another of Donald O'Connor's pictures the other night, 'The Merry

Monahans', and it's just as good as the rest of them. He's fast becoming my favorite comedy star. He and Peggy Ryan are a good team. Jack Oakie was in it, too, but his stuff is getting a little bit on the stale side."

The weather turned cold in Flora, getting down into the low forties. "We were out working on our air strip all morning and my hands are pretty stiff. The job looks pretty good, and I'm beginning to think that we may get it done by Saturday. They haven't found out whether or not they're going to be able to get us pullman reservations for that night, but they should know by this afternoon. I hope that we get them because an all-night ride on those trains is no fun if you have to sit up in a coach seat. I called Lt. Mayer and had him get a couple sets of my winter clothes pressed for me so that I can start wearing them when I get back...he says that Georgia is plenty cold, too. I saw 'Ever Since Venus,' last night and didn't think too much of it. Ann Savage plays in it, and as she comes from Pittsburgh, I thought I'd better check up on the hometown talent. Frankly, I thought Pgh. could do a whole lot better. Maybe it's just that she lacks experience, but she certainly lacks something...It's the 13th....We got quite a bit done out there on the runway yesterday afternoon and this morning, but I don't think we are going to finish by Sat. evening. We haven't found out yet whether or not we have Pullman reservations, so maybe we'll have a little longer than we thought to finish the strip. Berths on the R.R. are really tough to get, even when you travel on military orders...It's the 14th...this letter is going to weigh over a pound if I don't hurry and mail it. We worked hard all day and managed to get within 3 or 4 hours of finishing the job. We also found that we can't possibly get reservations before Monday night so that means another weekend in Mississippi. All we have to do now is finish making ditches along the sides of the runway and smooth down the surface a little with a roller. We can do that easily on Monday and then we'll be ready to go. Our orders call for us to be here 15 days which means that we can wait until Tuesday evening at the latest in order to try for Pullman space.

"The American Legion has put out a folder on the G.I. Bill of Rights and it's got quite a bit of good information in it. After we get married, we may want to take advantage of some of the benefits of the Bill?"

They finished the Flora project on October 16th. The next morning a plane came in from Red River, Texas, and the pilot took Harvey up to inspect the air strip from the air. He was very pleased with the efforts of his men and wrote to Betty later that day that it "made me feel pretty proud of my little outfit." Major Bean, the Post Engineer at Flora came out to see the completed runway and promised that he would send a very favorable report on the job to the headquarters at Patterson Field. As good as his word, Major Bean submitted the following report:

WAR DEPARTMENT
Office of the Commanding Officer
Mississippi Ordnance Plant
Jackson, Miss
20 October 1944

SUBJECT: Report on Air Strip Construction

To: Headquarters, ATSC, Wright Field, Dayton, Ohio
  Attention: Major Jack Gall

1. Reference is made to telephone conversation with Major Gall, your station, with Capt. Berry, this station, on 3 August 1944, requesting report rating performance of the officer and enlisted men furnished to accomplish this work, which is herewith submitted:

a. Description of work accomplished:

Length of strip	1750 ft.
Width of strip	6 ft.
Surface, compacted earth	
Drainage, runway crowned	
Approximately 12″ "V" type ditches on both sides to natural drain lines.	
Amount of earth moved	4500 cu. Yds.
Time required	12 days

Unit accomplishing work:
  Detachment of Utility Section
  Hq. Squadron, 75th Service Group
  1st Lt. John H. Brown, Jr.
  C.E., Commanding

b. This work was accomplished in an excellent manner and with good engineering practices. The results are very satisfactory. All equipment furnished was handled by this Unit in a workman-like manner and turned back in good condition.

2. The Post Engineer rates the performance of the officer and enlisted men of this Unit as excellent.

Ralph W. Bean
Major, C.E.
Post Engineer

Cc: Commanding Officer
AAB Herbert Smart Airport
Macon, GA
Lt. Col. E.C. Muchmore

That evening Harvey and his men boarded a train in Jackson and departed at 11:30 p.m. for the overnight trip back to Robins Field in Georgia. They had to change trains a number of times, including in Meridian, Mississippi, and they reached Macon, Georgia, sometime after 5:00 the following afternoon.

At about the same time Betty got Harvey's letter from Jackson, she also received one from his parents in Pennsylvania, a response to a letter Betty had sent them earlier. In her letter, Betty had described her recent wedding shower in Venice, and Harvey's mom described the gift (silverware) that they were sending. Obviously, plans were firming up regarding the wedding!

"It seems almost certain that orders are due to come in any day now, by the 1st of Nov. at the latest. There have been several wires come through from Patterson Field saying that orders have started and then been stopped for one small reason or another, but it shouldn't be long now. It's getting a little cool now, and last night for the first time this year, I put on my winter clothes, and I began to feel like a soldier again. Those darn summer uniforms make you feel like a gas station attendant. Sol Mayer and I went down to Macon to have dinner and see a show. I've missed 'Going My Way' for one reason or another until last night. It was really super. I think Barry Fitzgerald almost stole the picture from Bing Crosby. And Rise Stevens was especially good. She's a much better actress than I thought she would be and of course her singing doesn't leave a whole lot to be desired either. Naturally, I'm a hard-bitten old soldier but I don't mind admitting, to you anyway, that I was as close to having damp eyes during that show as I have been for many years. I thought about you all through the picture.

"Remember when I left Spokane, I had to leave one of my boys there in the hospital with a broken ankle? Well, yesterday he came back to us, apparently as fit as a fiddle. The doctors out there told him that he was completely okay and now he's back for duty. He'll have to take an overseas physical exam here, of course, and we're all hoping that he doesn't have any trouble with that. If he passes, we'll be all set to roll. His name is Sgt. Doyle and a boy with that much Irish in him just couldn't help but be a good man. There was a whopper of a football game in Atlanta yesterday – Navy and Georgia Tech. I wish I could have gone to see it because from the papers, it will probably be one of high notes of the season. It would be swell if we could get to see Rod play a game while I'm out in L.A. I've asked Mother to send me my little radio from home. Our little hut is awfully quiet with music of one kind or another, and I can't be singing all the time. The big debate now is whether or not my singing is allied to music or not. It's doubtful."

The evenings were cold, and Harvey and his bunkmates kept a fire going in the little stove in the middle of their hut. "We don't try to keep it going during the day because it so darned hot that just being in the sun causes perspiration. My radio came, and now we can listen to music while we lie in bed. I didn't realize how much I miss the darn thing. We just found that the station we have on the radio is KDKA from Pittsburgh (730 miles from Macon!), and it's as clear as a bell. Tomorrow evening a crowd of the officers are going to a smorgasbord (sp) in Macon, and we really should get a feed there."

Harvey's mother wrote to Betty on the 28th and enclosed a handout she and Harvey Sr. had received about "Navy Day."

Navy Day 1944 in Pittsburgh

On behalf of the United States Navy, the Navy Day Committee of the Pittsburgh Chamber of Commerce welcomes you aboard LST 831. It is hoped that by giving the people of Pittsburgh an opportunity to see one of the warships built in "Victory Valley," the great industrial area surrounding Pittsburgh, there will be better understanding of the importance of this district's contribution to our Navy.

This great ship, one of some 200 tank landing craft build in the Pittsburgh district, was launched at the Ambridge shipyard of United States Steel's American Bridge Company on October 6. Its outfitting has since been completed, and it is now manned with ferry command and combat personnel, who will take the ship from here down the inland waterways to join other invasion ships in combat duty.

The people of Pittsburgh wish LST 831 Godspeed and happy hunting.

Navy Day Committee
Pittsburgh Chamber of Commerce

The LST 831 was assigned to the Asia-Pacific Theater and participated in the assault and occupation of Okinawa Gunto from April through June 1945.

On Friday, October 31st, Harvey and his unit were on the firing range at Herbert Smart, where they qualified with an M-3 submachine gun; Harvey score was considered "expert." That night, he was able to get a call through to Betty. Although it was good to speak to her, there was some news that he wasn't able to share over the phone. "Last night talking to you was like a dream come true. I did want to tell you all about our moving to Oklahoma City but, after all, that's military information and over the phone it could get to quite a few ears without our knowing it. The truth of the matter is that we are leaving here on the 5th of November and expect to arrive in Oklahoma on Tuesday, November 7th. As of now, the orders call for us to stay there only until the 15th of November, but heaven knows we may be there for months just as we were here. Then, after leaving there, we are supposed to go to Walker Army Base, which isn't far from Hays, Kansas. The Group has a technical training period to go through yet and that should be a matter of several months before we go overseas...and you and I should be able to have all that time together.

"I'm going to ask for a leave as soon as we arrive in Oklahoma and as soon as I find out how soon I can get away, I'll let you know when to expect me. The Major has told me that he sees no reason why I shouldn't get a leave when I ask for it. Then, if Lt. Cain can get his leave at the same time, I'll have a ride to L.A. and we'll both have a ride back to wherever my station will be by that time.

"We are really busy here now getting the outfit ready to move to Oklahoma. The address you see on the envelope (75th Service Group, Hq. Sq. Tinker Field, Oklahoma) is the one we'll have when we get there. Time to hit the hay, and tonight I really need it. I'm ass't train commander for the trip and that is really keeping me on the go all the time." The next day, he was issued his M-1 rifle.

They spent the next day packing and crating equipment. His section didn't have much to pack, but since they had the only carpenter tools, they had the job of building boxes and crates for the supplies and records of all the other sections. They needed to be ready to load everything on baggage cars at 7:30 a.m. on Saturday. They also needed to make arrangements regarding the troop train itself. "Equipment and supplies for a mess car is a large problem, and we also have to make arrangements for all of the baggage of the enlisted men. Clearances have to be made out and signed for all the officers so that none of them will leave the base with supplies or equipment that is supposed to stay here. Getting the desired number and type of sleeping cars is a job, too, so you can see we have our hands full."

Note: In Harvey's letter of November 2nd, he added some thoughts that resonate with the current situation as I write this, two weeks after the 2020 presidential election. "The political situation is getting pretty hot now. It's hard to tune in the radio without finding someone slinging mud in one direction or another. The territory here is predominantly Democratic and everyone is boosting Roosevelt to the sky. The latest issue of Newsweek says that the election will be plenty close with Pennsylvania's vote swinging the decision either way. Good ol' Pennsylvania, 'the Keystone State'!!"

On November 5th, the 75th boarded a troop train at Herbert Smart Airport in Macon, Georgia for the 1,000-mile trip to Tinker Field. They arrived on the 7th, and "upon their arrival they marched, in formation, from the train to their barracks hoping to impress the brass."

10

MALIBU HONEYMOON

"We're finally getting settled here at Tinker Field. It's a deluxe base with all the facilities possible at an Army Air Base. I've covered just about half the distance to California and now if I can work out this leave business, I'll take off on the other half. Since Major Turner comes in tomorrow morning, we should know then just how long it will be before we can leave. As far as I know, I should be able to take off in a week or ten days. I'll know tomorrow for sure. We had a swell trip out here, and the whole outfit was pleased when we found out what a nice place we were coming to. It's too bad we're not going to stay here until we go overseas." The unit expected to stay about a month and then move on to Walker Army Air Base at Walker, Kansas. Harvey was surprised to find a number of old friends at Tinker Field. "Not only Ralph Haver and Frank Hammond that were with me at Patterson Field, but Bob Yates too!! I almost fell over when he walked in on me. So, Yates, Hammond and I went over to Haver's house last night after work for supper. I didn't want to go because Millie, Haver's wife, is expecting a baby in about two weeks but they insisted and really we had a wonderful time. After a swell supper, we all sat around and talked over old times over three or four highballs. We almost laughed ourselves silly." Bob Yates had the same job as Harvey, but with the 24th Service Group. They had been training in Fresno, California, and were just about as far along as the 75th. "Betty's not with him now but when he goes to his next station he's going to send for her so they can be together as long as possible. That's what we'll do too. If you and I get back here before the 75th moves to Kansas, you'll get to meet these Engineers that I like so well. It seems that all the Service Groups are converging on Oklahoma, so maybe we'll get to see more of them...Jack Dangers, Fleming, Jay and a few more that you met in Spokane.

"I'm sitting here writing on my footlocker and the radio is playing 'Tico, Tico'. That piece really knocks me out. Rhumbas are my favorite when it comes to listening to music. Sure wish I could dance to them...wish I could dance to anything for that matter. You're going to have to teach me!"

By the middle of November, Harvey had been promoted to the rank of Captain. He and Betty were making final wedding plans, but the exact date for the ceremony was still dependent on when he could get a furlough from his unit. On the 14th, Harvey wrote that the dates of his furlough were firming up, and he was pretty sure he would leave Oklahoma City on Monday, the 20th. He had been granted an eleven-day furlough, with three travel days tacked onto either end, a total of 2 1/2 weeks. The 75th was ordered to transfer to a "permanent" assignment at Walker Air Base in Hays, Kansas, and this move was likely to happen while Harvey was on furlough.

How he would get to California from Oklahoma, though, was still very much up in the air. Travel during leaves from the Army involved hitchhiking on military aircraft that had a free seat. Harvey was trying to arrange for a spot on a plane headed to California, hopefully somewhere near enough to Los Angeles so he could catch a train the rest of the way. He reassured Betty that if all else failed, he could still take a train ("the plane's substitute"), though that would take a bigger chunk out of his allotted furlough. He also alerted her that he hadn't had time to get his uniform cleaned and pressed—they might have to squeeze that in before the wedding ceremony. Harvey's friend, Lt. Cain, was hoping to come down to LA on his way back to Tinker Field, and in that case, Harvey and Betty could drive back to Kansas with the Cains.

Plans changed again. Harvey sent a telegram on Saturday the 18th that flights had been delayed due to bad weather, and he had hitched a ride. He was driving to Los Angeles on Route 66, and would arrive some time on Tuesday, the 21st. The telegram was sent from Oklahoma City, and the drive from there to Southern California was a straight shot on Route 66, one of the original highways of the US Highway System. The highway had been established in 1926 and would become one of the most famous roads in America, known as the "Will Rogers Highway," or sometimes the "Main Street of America." However, on November 18, 1944, Harvey was less interested in the history of the highway than in the fact that it led directly to Santa Monica, California.

A year later in Guam, Harvey would think back to this day. "Next Sunday will mark a year exactly from the day (the 18th) when I stood in front of the Biltmore Hotel and waited for my ride to come along, the ride that was to carry me halfway across the country to the one I loved." Two of them stood waiting there, Corporal Harris and Harvey, and they tried to guess what kind of a guy they would be riding with, and what kind of car he would be driving. There had been a note on the bulletin board at the field and both of them had seen it. The note said there would be room for two riders, and as both had been unable to catch a plane ride, they both snatched at the chance to get a ride straight through to Los Angeles. "I can remember how excited I was all the way. Neither of the other two were married but Harris was going to see a girl that he said he was going to marry when he got out of the Army, and Loren Tindall, the guy we were riding with, was starting to get more or less serious with some new movie starlet, so the whole way out all we did was to talk about you and the two girls that they were interested in."

Betty and Harvey were married in Santa Monica on Friday, November 24, 1944. The scheduling had been tight, and they had to take care of the rings, the blood tests, and the marriage license on the day of the wedding. They were married by an Army Chaplain, and Betty's family attended the ceremony, including her seventeen-year-old brother Rod, who served as Best Man. The couple honeymooned for two nights at the Las Tunas Isle Motel on Las Tunas Beach in Malibu. The motel, located on Pacific Coast Highway had been built in 1931 and was known as a 1930s hideaway spot for wealthy and famous members of Hollywood's movie colony. The motel was famous not only for its privacy, but for its quirky "Tiki" décor. The rooms were decorated with either bamboo or leopard skin, and each had its own name—the larger bamboo room was "Big Bam"; the smaller one was "Baby Bam." There was a pool, but the weather was cool, and Harvey and Betty spent most of their time in their room.

Harvey's parents weren't able to come out from Pennsylvania for the wedding. The uncertainty about the timing had been a problem, and train tickets were reserved for servicemen. Harvey and Betty called the Browns from the Malibu motel.

Soon after the wedding, Harvey received a letter from Rev. H. Boyd Edwards, the minister of the family's Episcopal church in Pittsburgh. Rev. Edwards wrote, "I do wish you both God's blessing and every happiness in your married life. We will be very glad to see you both when you return to Pittsburgh. The old parish goes on about the same as ever. Did you hear that Thomas James has been missing in action over Germany? Apparently, he was flying from Italy to Germany and his plane was brought down and the entire crew was lost. So far they have had no report from him. I hope and pray that everything comes out all right and they will discover, as they did in the case of Clifford Breakiron, that he is a prisoner in Germany. He is too fine a boy to lose."

The 75th had moved from Oklahoma City to Walker Field in Victoria, Kansas on December 4th. They had traveled the 340 miles in a truck convoy, and the weather was so cold that straw had been put in the trucks to keep the men's feet from freezing. By the next day, the weather had warmed up, and the area became a "sea of mud." The men's quarters at Tinker Field consisted of uninsulated plywood shelters with shutters that could be raised in summer and lowered in winter. There were coal-burning heaters in the shelters, a source of heat and soot during that very cold winter of 1944–45.

Harvey had to return to his unit, which was now at Walker Field, soon after the honeymoon, and he and Betty took the train. Lt. Cain had received new orders that didn't allow a side trip to LA to pick up the newlyweds, so they took the train to Denver, and then on to their new "home" in Hays, Kansas. As a married officer, Harvey was allowed to live in town, and they found a room in an apartment on West 12th Street in Hays. A Mrs. Staab rented rooms to several officers and their wives, and the Browns became good friends with the other couples they met while living there for the next couple of months.

The 75th Air Service Group was preparing to head overseas, and on December 27th, Harvey, along with Major Justice of the 581st Material Squadron, was ordered to spend a week in Omaha securing "morale equipment" the men would need in the Pacific. The two traveled by rail and came back with several crates of recreational supplies including an ice maker, a juke box and a supply of records, and assorted sporting equipment.

he 1st of September had come and gone, and the 75th was still in Georgia. "Everybody's just a little on edge actually waiting on orders, and most of us are pretty anxious to move. From the way things look now, it probably won't be until late September before I can get out there to you. In one way, that's best because it will give you a little more time to get ready, but I don't know whether or not I can make it." There was an inspection parade scheduled for Saturday morning. The major was going to be in the reviewing party and had asked Harvey to take his place as squadron commander for the parade. "Not only that but today I was given charge of the Fire Fighting section which makes four duties I've got now...Utilities Officer, Camouflage Officer, Acting

Group Ordnance Officer, and now Fire Marshall. One thing about all this, I guess—it shows that that the Major has confidence in my ability to handle the extra work. He and I get along fine, and I know that when he gets the opportunity to put in my captaincy, he'll do it.

"Tomorrow night the Officers Club is having another one of its weekly Saturday night dances, and I guess I'll go again with Lt. Cain and his wife, Paula. The three of us get along really well. They're the couple that we may ride back to Kansas with."

Betty and Harvey's wedding in Santa Monica, California, Nov. 1944

11

SECRET LETTERS

Harvey knew that he would soon be going overseas, and he and Betty tried to make good use of the time they had together in Kansas. Later in Guam, he would remember one particular outing when they took a bus to Salina, about one hundred miles away. He remembered "walking all over town in the rain looking for a knife and shoes for me, playing the pin ball machine for hours 'cause you knew I wanted to...We went in to see the picture right as we got off the bus on the way back from Salina and our arms were pretty full of packages." They saw *The Woman in the Window*, with Edward G. Robinson, and Harvey laughingly helped the boy take tickets at the door of the theater.

In preparation for the trip overseas, Harvey, along with Roy Justice and James Ray, was sent to Colorado for a conference on "supply matters." The meetings were at Peterson Air Force Base in Colorado Springs, and the three traveled by rail. When Harvey returned, he was granted a four-day leave plus three travel days.

At the beginning of February in 1945 Harvey filed a change of address form directing that future mail be forwarded to the Squadron Headquarters of 75th Air Service Group in San Francisco. He had received word that the 75th would be leaving Walker AFB in a few weeks, probably headed for the Pacific Theater. For security reasons, he wouldn't know their exact location until his unit was under way, but he could share with his family that he would soon be heading overseas to support combat crews of the B-29 aircraft.

The new commanding officer of the 75th, Lt. Colonel Joe Neyer, had reported to Walker AFB shortly after Christmas. He knew that the unit would soon be heading overseas, and he secretly contacted wives, parents, and sweethearts of his men, asking them to "write letters addressed to their sons, husbands and sweethearts, but not to tell them and to place the letters in an envelope addressed to the Chaplain at Walker Air Base." These letters would be distributed later when a boost from home was most needed. Betty alerted family members, both in Pittsburgh and in Venice about the "secret letter project," and a number of letters were sent to the Chaplain's office. These letters were full of love and prayers, of course, but they also contained family updates. Many of them were written on the same day, March 24th. In her letter, Betty tried to imagine life on the ship; was the food good? Was Harvey playing his favorite card game (hearts)? She asked him to remember everything he saw and did so he could tell her about it in letters.

Harvey's mother also added a letter, asking what he thought of the ocean voyage and hoping that he wasn't seasick. She suggested keeping a diary, and wondered what life was like aboard ship, "when you cross the equator they say they dunk you and shave your head." She clearly was worried about him but channeled her anxiety into small details: "I hope the mosquitoes aren't bad," and "I hope the meals are good." She voiced feelings shared by most families of servicemen overseas: "We don't mind doing without at all at home here if you fellows are getting all you need." She ended her letter with "... please don't take any unnecessary chances. All our thoughts and prayers and love are with you. Mother." Harvey's Aunt Peggy was a clerk at the Veteran's Hospital in Pittsburgh, and she reported that the office was busy giving loans to veterans and helping them get established in local universities. "I believe we have them in every school and university in Western Pennsylvania as students of law, medicine, engineering, dentists, teachers, etc."

Two letters came from his mother's sisters. One, from Aunt Agnes, was filled with news about his cousins in Butler. She suggested that Harvey keep a scrapbook to share one day with his children and grandchildren. In another letter his Aunt Alice wrote, in pencil, that she liked Betty and, calling Harvey her "favorite nephew," was glad he was so happily married. She went on to talk about her experiences with the food rationing system, saying, "It's really fun trying to figure out what to eat with the number of points you get....the oddest Sunday dinners sometimes!" She went on to say "I was just thinking what a kick yours and Betty's children will get some day when we tell them some of the unbelievable experiences we all have had during these times. Too bad we didn't all keep a diary!" (Yes, Alice, but many of you did write letters! —DB.)

There were also letters from the California family. Betty's mother referenced the 'letter project', saying, "This letter is addressed to you in Hays, but you will probably be somewhere on the Pacific or Atlantic when you open it. This is a mighty fine idea and a very sweet gesture on the part of your Chaplain to have letters for you men while on the way."

12

PRESIDENT STRICKEN

On Monday, April 2, 1945, Harvey put Betty on a Union Pacific train for the trip back to California. They wouldn't see each other again for several months, and the parting was emotional. Betty cried until the train reached its first stop in Ellis, Kansas, but by the time they stopped briefly at Oakley, Kansas, she had calmed down and began the first of many letters, at least six, that she wrote to Harvey from the train. The stop in Oakley was a brief one. She had been riding in a coach car, but during the Oakley stop she moved to a lower berth in the sleeping car. (The fare for her berth from Oakley to Denver was $1.55 plus 22 cents tax!) At first, Betty had trouble writing and just stared out the window. It was raining in Oakley, but it began to snow as they moved through Colorado. The heavy snow reminded her of times she and Harvey had spent together that winter in Hays—walking home from a movie in the snow and traveling through bad weather during their trips to Colorado Springs and Pittsburgh. She thought about how good it was to meet Harvey's family in Pennsylvania, and she tried to imagine where he would be when he received these notes. She told Harvey about the other people on the train: a polite little boy who noticed the captain's bars and engineer's earrings she was wearing, and a group of soldiers just back from overseas. She chatted with one of the soldiers, who had just returned from twenty-seven months in Europe and was heading for a "redistribution center" in Santa Ana, California. *(Note: When I read this letter to her some fifty years later, she could still remember the conversation with this young serviceman.)*

It was snowing heavily by the time she reached Denver (about 4:00 in the afternoon). Betty mailed her first letter and a post card to Harvey and sent him a telegram saying she was feeling a bit better and already awaiting his return from overseas. She also sent a packet of letters to the Chaplain at Walker for the "secret letter project." The next day, her train continued through Wyoming and Utah, and she described the snowcapped Rockies and the Great Salt Lake. She finally reached Los Angeles on Thursday morning, and her parents met her at the train station. She sent off another telegram to let Harvey know she had arrived safely.

At about the same time on Thursday that Betty's train was pulling into Los Angeles, a troop train with part of Harvey's unit, the 75th Air Support Group, was pulling out of the Hays station. They were headed for Fort Lawton, near Seattle, Washington, and as the train left Hays, wives and girlfriends that were still around waved from the platform. Harvey, along with the rest of the unit, would leave the next day. Like Betty, he had been pretty upset when they had parted on Monday. He wrote to her late that night, talking about how hard it had been to watch her train pull away. He had received her telegram from Denver and was relieved to hear from her. On Wednesday, he tried to call her, but all lines were down because of the snow. He sent a telegram instead.

The engineering squadron had requisitioned the tools needed to service the B-29 bombers, and specialists were busy training to use the equipment. A number of people had donated items that would help the morale of the men while overseas. The comedian Joe E. Brown donated baseball and basketball equipment, and Beau Brummel (a men's wear company) gave the unit playing cards, pencils, and score pads. The men themselves contributed money and other items: someone donated an ice cream maker, much to the delight of the rest of the men. The "morale equipment for overseas" was packed for the trip and included the ice cream maker, an ice maker, a juke box with records, sports equipment, coffee, sugar, milk, etc. The government had also given the 75th an allotment of beer and soft drinks, and these were also packed for the trip.

At eight thirty on Harvey's last night at Walker, he wrote Betty one more letter. The weather had warmed up a bit, and they had been able to get most of the loading done, ready for their departure the next day. He reported that his men were "really on edge" as they prepared for finally heading overseas. On Friday, the 6th, Harvey mailed the letter just before his troop train pulled out at 1:00 p.m. During the trip, Harvey stuck with his friend "Mac"; both were feeling "blue" and spent most of their time playing contract bridge. All the officers in the unit were beginning to hang out together. In a letter written from the train, Harvey described some of the scenery (rocky snow-capped peaks, little vegetation, the occasional coyote or antelope). Because of the Army censors, he couldn't be specific about his location. Two post cards he "sent," one from Paradise, Montana, were not forwarded until after he left the country. All he could say was that they were due to reach their "destination" on Tuesday, the 10th. He did manage to place quick calls to Betty and his mother during a stop on Monday night.

Betty continued writing to Harvey after he left Hays. She addressed her letters to his new APO address in San Francisco, knowing they likely wouldn't be delivered until he was overseas. On the 5th, she wrote that she had received a couple of the foot lockers they had shipped from Hays.

On the Saturday after she returned from Kansas, Betty's father and brother spent the day building a trellis and planting fruit trees and a Victory Garden in the backyard. That evening, Betty went to the movies with Rod. Betty, Harvey, and Rod all loved the movies, both going to them and talking about them. Culver City, the area where Betty lived, advertised itself in the late 1930s and early 1940s as "Where 'Hollywood' Movies Are Made," and both Betty's home and the music store where she worked were within a few blocks of several motion picture studios. The letters beginning to fly back and forth between the newlyweds were filled with details about movies they saw, and these letters give a glimpse into the motion picture industry of the era. On that Saturday evening, Betty and Rod went to see a double feature at the Majestic Theater near the beach on Santa Monica Boulevard. The Majestic had originally opened as the Santa Monica Opera House in 1911, had booked vaudeville acts and silent films in the 1920s, "talkies" in the 1930s, and by 1945 was featuring big budget movies being produced in the local studios. The theater itself later appeared in several films, including *Young Frankenstein* in 1974 where it was the scene for the "Putting on the Ritz" sequence. It was finally torn down after the 1989 Northridge earthquake. On that April night in 1945, Rod and Betty saw *Tonight and Every Night*, starring Rita Hayworth, and *Let's Go Steady*, both newly released by Columbia Pictures. In addition to the feature films, the show at the Majestic also included a cartoon (which Betty described to Harvey at great length), a newsreel with clips from the war in the Philippines, and a community sing-along, which closed with a very somber "I'll Be Seeing You."

Harvey's unit arrived at Fort Lawton (their "destination") near Seattle, on the 10th. Harvey had a pass from the Adjutant, Captain Carter, to go into Seattle that evening, but was too tired to leave his room. He later found the pass still tucked in his pocket and sent it to California so Betty could see it. On Wednesday, the unit worked outside in a pouring rain, getting ready to head out.

On Thursday, April 12th, the world learned that FDR had died in Warm Springs, Georgia, and that Harry Truman had been sworn in as President. Harvey, at Fort Lawton, would have heard the news through military channels but also in radio reports and in the newspapers. Headlines read: "ROOSEVELT PASSES: Nation Shocked by War Chief's Sudden Death," and "PRESIDENT STRICKEN: Nation's War Leader Dies." Harvey wrote: "This afternoon we got the sad news about President Roosevelt, and almost everyone I met had kind words to say about him. Regardless of political performance, I think that everyone will have to admit that we have been fortunate to have lived in the life span of one of the greatest statesmen of all time. It may prove to be quite a blow to the Allied war effort, but I have no doubt that the much publicized 'American Way of Life' will come out on top. Too bad he couldn't have lived to see one of his most trying problems come to a successful conclusion as it most certainly will do." On a lighter note, Harvey joked about writing a book called "The Life and Loves of J. Harvey Brown, Jr.," with the contents simply being Betty's name repeated a billion times. Several times in their correspondence, they both kidded about writing a book about their experiences. He also mentioned that he had received a letter from Betty's folks, but "gave it to the Chaplain to save until the proper time." Evidently, he had helped plan, or at least was aware of, the "secret letter program"!

In California, Betty also heard the news: "This afternoon the President passed on, and this evening all programs on the air are cancelled. The stations all have on programs dedicated to his memory, and patriotic in theme. They keep playing hymns, and I just have to sit here and talk to you, or I will start bawling, I know." The Lundins were registered Republicans, but they had supported Roosevelt and were saddened by his passing; after the war they became Democrats.

On the 13th, Betty's parents and Rod sent three "Personna Blade Mail" packets to Harvey's APO address in San Francisco. Razor blades were expensive and hard to come by, and the Personna company packaged them so they could be sent to servicemen with enclosed messages. Betty's family knew he would need razor blades while he was overseas, and they each enclosed a note. Her dad reported that "Rod has a good chance of making West Point. So far he has met all requirements and all letters of recommendation have been OK and received with favor in Washington. Entrance examinations will be held in July."

On Friday night, Harvey called Betty from Seattle and then wrote to her, "Just a little while ago I was talking to you for the last time in probably a very long time, because I'm not going have the opportunity to call again....I'll be darned if I could think of anything appropriate to say...all I really wanted to hear you say was 'I love you' just once more before we are completely shut off from each other, except by mail." Evidently, several of the other officers were leaving for the war zone not knowing whether their wives were pregnant. One of them, Lt. Arthur "Mac" McKinney, had become one of Harvey's two best friends in the unit. The other was Major Harvey Turner, and the three friends had spent a lot of time together and come to "like each other a lot and understand each other's weaknesses and strong points."

As Harvey was writing his letter, Betty was also putting down her thoughts. When he had called, she had been sitting down to a dinner of eggs with her family—her father hadn't been able to find a store that had any meat. After talking with Harvey, Betty came back to the table but couldn't control her tears. She finally went for a walk while the rest of the family finished dinner. All the radio programs were about FDR's death and "sad as they could be." Rod talked Betty into going out to see a movie. They went to the Carthay Circle Theatre on San Vicente Boulevard in Culver City, and saw *Sudan* and *I'll Remember April* (which Betty described as the "usual Universal talent parade"). The theater was one of the iconic "movie palaces" of Hollywood's "Golden Age" and had hosted many glamorous Premieres, including those for *Snow White and the Seven Dwarfs* in 1937, *Gone with the Wind* in 1939 and *Fantasia* in 1940. At the red-carpet premieres, stars of the films would arrive in limousines to be greeted by hundreds of fans in bleachers as searchlights scanned the sky. The mood this April evening in 1945 was much more somber, but the night at the movies seemed to help both Betty and Rod feel better.

13

THE KOTA BAROE

At 9:30 Sunday morning, April 15th, after their final processing at Fort Lawton, Harvey and the rest of the 75th boarded their troop ship docked at Pier #42 in Seattle, a Dutch liner called the *Kota Baroe*. On the dock as they boarded, the troops were served coffee and doughnuts by the Red Cross, and a band played "Don't Fence Me In." Harvey noted "it wasn't a bad send off at all. I'd always read about the Army having bands at the port of embarkation, but I had no ideas that they actually did have them. It was plenty nice of the Red Cross to supply the coffee and doughnuts and stuff...." Before boarding, Harvey shipped his suitcase to Betty via Railway Express. Evidently, the censors missed that the enclosed receipt noted "Seattle, Washington" as the point of origin.

Information about the *Kota Baroe* was evidently given to staff before the ship left the dock. It's unclear how widely this information was shared with the men, but Al Seelof, in the Communications Section, later referred to it in his "History of the 75th Air Service Group." A few months later, Harvey and fellow officers in the Utilities Section came across the document, and Harvey sent a copy to Betty:

THE GOOD SHIP KOTA BAROE

YOU MIGHT BE INTERESTED IN A FEW FACTS ABOUT THE SHIP THAT IS TAKING YOU OVER.

IT WAS BUILT IN 1929, IS LESS THAN 500 FEET LONG, HAS A GROSS TONNAGE OF CLOSE TO 8000 TONS AND A SPEED OF 12 TO 14 KNOTS.

THE NAME OF THE SHIP IS "KOTA BAROE". IT IS A MALAYAN NAME MEANING NEW OR BEAUTIFUL TOWN.

THE MASTER OF THE VESSEL IS CAPTAIN A. VOORDUYN. THE FIRST OFFICER IS MR. NUBOER, WHO WAS SAILING IN THE PACIFIC AT THE OUTBREAK OF THE JAPANESE WAR. HE, TOO, HAS BEEN SAILING FOR US DURING THE ENTIRE TIME.

THE CREW ARE ALL MEMBERS OF THE DUTCH MERCHANT MARINE AND ARE TRAINED SEAMEN. MANY OF THEM HAVE LOST MEMBERS OF THEIR FAMILY AND FRIENDS AND NONE OF THEM HAVE SEEN THEIR NATIVE HOME FOR OVER FIVE YEARS.

THE WAITERS, CABIN BOYS, ETC., ARE FROM GOA, A PORTUGUESE PROVINCE ON THE WEST COAST OF INDIA. THEY ARE CHRISTIANS AND BELONG TO THE ROMAN CATHOLIC CHURCH.

THE TRANSPORT AT PRESENT IS CHARTERED TO THE ARMY. IT IS A MATTER OF INTEREST THAT IT IS A DUTCH VESSEL, CHARTERED BY THE ENGLISH, RE-CHARTERED TO THE WAR SHIPPING ADMINISTRATION AND ALLOTTED TO THE ARMY.

THAT THIS SHIP, AND ALL OTHERS OF THIS TYPE, ARE USED AS ARMY TRANSPORTS IS DUE TO A PARTICULAR REASON. THIS SHIP NAMELY WAS DESIGNED TO CARRY MOHAMEDAN PILGRIMS. THEREFORE, THE LOWER DECKS, D AND E, WERE CONSTRUCTED SO AS TO ASSURE LIVING SPACE, AND, ABOVE ALL, SUFFICIENT HEIGHT WHICH FAVORS VENTILATION IN THE TROPICS. THE NUMBER OF PILGRIMS WAS FROM 1000 TO 1200. THE PILGRIMS, NATIVES OF THE NETHERLANDS EAST INDIA, WERE FAITHFUL MOHAMMEANS. THE WISH OF EVERY MOSLEM, RICH AND POOR, IS TO BE ABLE TO VISIT THE HOLY CITY OF MECCA IN ARABIA ONCE IN HIS LIFE. THE POORER ONES HAE TO WORK HARD AND FOR LONG YEARS TO BE ABLE TO SAVE THE MONEY TO TRAVEL OVER SEAS AND TO REMAIN AT MECCA FROM THREE TO SIX MONTHS. WHEN THEY WERE ABLE TO GO THEY BOUGHT A TICKET AND BOARDED ONE OF THE KOTAS AND EMBARKED WITH THEIR FAMILIES WHEN WEALTHY, OR ALONE WHEN POOR. THEY HAD TO CARRY FOOD --- NOT FOR THE SEA VOYAGE, AS THEY WERE FED ON BOARD–BUT FOR THE TRIP OVERLAND. WHEN THE SHIP LEFT PORT, THOUSANDS OF MOHAMMEDAN NATIVES WERE ON THE DOCK TO SEE THEIR RELATIVES OFF. AFTER ABOUT THREE WEEKS THE PILGRIMS WERE LANDED AT THE PORT OF JIDDAH, ON THE COAST OF ARABIA, HALFWAY UP THE RED SEA. THEY WERE BROUGHT ON LAND BY ARABIAN CRAFT, AND ONCE

ASHORE, THEY HAD TO TRAVEL ON CAMEL BACK IN LONG CARAVANS THROUGH 100 MILES OF DESERT TO MECCA. THE TRIP WAS FULL OF WEARINESS AND PRIVATIONS, AND MANY PILGRIMS, ESPECIALLY THE ELDERLY, CAME BACK ON THE SHIP THAT WAS TO TAKE THEM HOME, IN BAD CONDITION. HOWEVER, THEY DID NOT CARE; THEY HAD BEEN TO MECCA. NOWADAYS THE AUTOMOBILES AND BUSSES HAVE DONE AWAY WITH MANY OF THE DIFFICULTIES OF THE PILGRIMAGE.

IF YOU ARE A LAND LUBBER, PERHAPS SOME OF THE TERMS USED ARE CONFUSING. MOST EVERYONE KNOWS THAT "FORE" REFERS TO THE FRONT OF THE SHIP, "AFT" TO THE REAR OF THE SHIP; THAT "STARBOARD" IS THE RIGHT OF THE SHIP WHILE FACING "FORWARD" AND "PORT" IS THE LEFT. HOWEVER, THERE ARE SOME TERMS THAT ARE NOT QUITE SO FAMILIAR. YOU NEVER GO "UPSTAIRS" ON A SHIP; YOU GO "TOP-SIDE" OR TO THE NEXT DECK. YOU HAVE "HATCHWAYS" INSTEAD OF DOORS LEADING IN AND OUT. YOU DON'T HAVE "FLOORS" ON THE SHIP; YOU HAVE "DECKS." INCIDENTALLY, THERE ARE SIX DECKS ON THIS SHIP --- A,B,C,D,E AND THE BRIDGE DECK. IN ADDITION, THERE IS THE STORAGE HOLD BELOW "E" DECK AND A FLYING BRIDGE ABOVE THE BRIDGE DECK. THE FLYING BRIDGE IS OFF LIMITS, EXCEPT TO THOSE WHO HAVE TO DO WITH THE RUNNING OF THE SHIP. THIS IS SOMETIMES CALLED THE "MONKEY BRIDGE" FOR OBVIOUS REASONS---A MONKEY LIKES TO CLIMB AS HIGH AS POSSIBLE.

THIS SHIP WAS A MIXED CARGO AND PASSENGER SHIP PRIOR TO THE WAR. IT CARRIED A MAXIMUM OF 60 PASSENGERS AND APPROXIMATELY 70 CREW. NOW, OF COURSE, IT HAS A REGULAR CREW PLUS THE ARMY CREW. THE TRANSPORT COMMANDER, MAJOR RAMIRES OF SAN JUAN, CALIFORNIA, IS HOLDING HIS POSITION FOR THE FIRST TIME. HE HAD ANOTHER SHIP FOR A WHILE BUT WAS TRANSFERRED TO THIS SHIP JULY 7, 1944.

MAJOR PRAG, THE SURGEON, HAILS FROM PORTLAND, OREGON. HE, TOO, IS AN OLD HAND AT HIS JOB, HAVING HAD THE SAME POSITION ON ANOTHER TRANSPORT. HE HAS HIS HANDS FULL THIS TIME BUT IS ABLY ASSISTED BY OTHER MEMBERS OF THE MEDICAL PROFESSION.

THE POST EXCHANGE OFFICER, 1ST LT. TODD, IS ALSO ASSISTANT TRANSPORT COMMANDER.

THE TRANSPORT CHAPLAIN, CHAPLAIN TOOGOOD, IS IN CHARGE

OF RECREATION EDUCATION-INFORMATION, AND RELIGIOUS SERVICES.

IN ADDITION TO THESE FOUR ARMY OFFICERS, THERE ARE 26 ENLISTED MEN WHO TAKE CARE OF THE OFFICE WORK, ASSIST THE SURGEON AND THE POST EXCHANGE OFFICER, AND OPERATE THE RADIO SHACK.

OUR SAFETY FROM ENEMY ACTION DEPENDS ON THE NAVY ARMED GUARD AND COMMUNICATIONS. THERE ARE THREE NAVAL OFFICERS; LT. CORPRON IS THE SENIOR OFFICER, AND LT. PALMER THE JUNIOR OFFICER IN THE ARMED GUARD. LT. DUCHENE IS THE COMMUNICATIONS OFFICER. THERE ARE ALSO A NUMBER OF MEN WHO STAND WATCH ON THE BRIDGE AND IN THE GUN TUBS—FOUR HOURS ON AND EIGHT HOURS OFF OUT OF EVERY TWELVE HOURS.

THERE ARE MANY THINGS WHICH YOU MIGHT DESIRE FOR A PLEASURE CRUISE, BUT ALL IN ALL WE ARE PROUD OF THE "KOTA BAROE." IT HAS ABOUT THE BEST FOOD OF ANY SHIP WE HAVE BEEN ON; PLENTY OF DECK SPACE, AND, SO FAR, SHE HAS BEEN KEPT SAFE FROM ANY ACCIDENTS OR ENEMY ACTION. WE ARE ALL LOOKING FOR THE DAY WHEN WE SAIL BACK WITH ALL THE PORT HOLES OPEN AND THE LIGHTS ON.

The ship pulled away from the Pier at 4:00 p.m., and the sea was calm that first day. Harvey spent some time on deck after playing a few hands of poker with his friends. Gulls and albatrosses flew around the ship, and Harvey could see the Navy blimp that escorted the departing ship for most of the day. He found the blimp a welcome reminder that they "weren't all by themselves in this huge stretch of water. When you look on all sides of the ship and see nothing but water it kind of gives you the idea that everyone else has forgotten about you." Still getting used to the censorship rules, Harvey noted "I think I'm allowed to say I'm on a (this word was censored) vessel, and it looks like a pretty good ship."

Harvey's job was to act as the Police and Sanitation Officer, with two officers to help him. He found the food aboard the *Kota Baroe* to be very good. On Wednesday afternoon, there was a movie in the officers' wardroom, *South of the Border* with Gene Autry, and the PX opened so the men could buy cigarettes. Each soldier was allowed one carton, but Sol Mayer, a nonsmoker, gave Harvey his so he could have two. A total investment of one dollar and five cents a pack! In the evening Harvey played poker again with his friends.

He won five dollars. One of the men had spotted a whale earlier in the day; Harvey was disappointed that he had missed it.

On Friday the 20th, the ship had naval gunnery practice, and on Saturday, there was a rifle inspection. Many of the men wrote letters to be mailed from Hawaii. While at sea, the men occasionally had "singing periods" up on deck. They sang lots of old songs, songs that everyone knew, and the act of singing together seemed to strengthen the sense of family that was building. Harvey noted that the northerners sang "Dixie" and the southerners sang "Yankee Doodle"..."without so much as one wisecrack....things like that get way down inside of a person." One day, the men saw their first whales, or at least the spouting of whales, some six hundred yards from the ship. Harvey noted that he hoped to see one up close "so he could identify it if he ever bumped into one on the street somewhere.

"The Kota Baroe docked on the 23rd of April, a Sunday, at pier #28 in Honolulu's Hawaii Harbor at 19:00. From the 75th, only Colonel Neyer left the ship, but the men could buy ice cream and pineapple juice for a quarter at the dock." Harvey sent Betty a packet of picture postcards, saying "we didn't see much of this stuff, but I thought you'd like to see the pictures."

Harvey wrote to Betty from Honolulu. His letters were opened and screened by the "U.S. Army Examiner" (censor), and occasionally, words were clipped out. However, there were clues to his whereabouts between the lines. He talked about being aboard the ship while they were stopped, about the warm weather and blue water, and about still not knowing his final destination. He had dated his letter, and although the date had been clipped out, the postmark showed when it had been sent. So, his ship was in port, and Hawaii was the obvious location. In his letter of the 24th, he also mentioned that he knew of the Colonel's "secret letter project" and was eager to get some mail. The ship needed some minor repairs, and they remained in port until the 25th. When they did leave, no escort boats were with them.

Harvey did most of his shipboard writing at a little table he had set up on the bridge. On the 28th, the sea was calm, except for the occasional "rolls," and the sun was bright. As he wrote, the public address system was playing "I'm Beginning to See the Light" by Stan Kenton, and it reminded Harvey of the time he and Betty had seen Kenton at the Hollywood Palladium. Spike Jones tunes were also mixed in. Poker and Bridge were pastimes for the men, and Harvey reported that he was constantly playing bridge with his friends: Colonel Turner, Peck, and Mac. He hoped that Betty would learn the game so they could play when he came home. He had seen two more films on board:

San Francisco, a 1936 film starring Clark Gable and Jeanette McDonald, and *Hi Diddle Diddle*, with Adolphe Menjou and Martha Scott. They were supposed to see *The Lives of a Bengal Lancer*, but the showing was called off because of a rifle inspection. Most of the films on board were "pretty old and decrepit," but the men appreciated the entertainment and the break from the monotony of the trip.

On the 29th, the *Kota Baroe* broke down near the International Date Line, about halfway between Honolulu and Micronesia. Without support vessels, the ship was quite vulnerable while the sailors repaired the engines. On the 2nd, the ship broke down again and drifted for a while, "The group were left alone in the middle of the ocean, just drifting, not knowing when the ship would be repaired, just open targets for the enemy....the men of the 75th, while sitting in the middle of the Pacific, were blue, dejected, etc. when they heard over the ship's speaker 'the 75th Air Service Group please report for mail call!' The men could hardly believe their ears." Lt. Col. Neyer had decided that the time had come to activate the "secret letter project," and he had the letters from home delivered to the men. The Chaplain had forgotten to include Harvey's letters with the others but sent word to Neyer that he would bring them with him when he rejoined the unit. Following the mail call, every man in the 75th was given a cold bottle of beer or a soft drink; this had also been planned before the group left Kansas. "Needless to say, the 75th was the envy of the other men on the ship." While still at sea, Lt. Col. Neyer received his promotion to Eagles— Full Colonel. The timing of the promotion wasn't lost on Neyer's men, and as there were no Eagle insignia available on the ship, the men in the machine shop made one for him out of tin. In the evening, Harvey and about twenty others were in the mood to sing. They gathered around a piano in the mess hall and sang while Chaplain Cooper played the piano.

14

BACK AT THE
RECORD STORE

Betty, not knowing where Harvey was headed, or even that he was already on his way, continued writing to his APO address in San Francisco. On Monday the 16th, she had dinner with the family of her good friend Peggy Irving. Peggy's boyfriend was being discharged from the Army in Europe because of "battle fatigue." Rod picked up Betty on the way home from his band practice. On Tuesday, she went shopping in Santa Monica with another friend and had coffee and a piece of pie in Manning's Coffee Shop on 3rd Street. That evening after dinner she and her parents listened to Bob Hope and Fibber McGee on the radio: "they are doing wonders for morale." That same evening, Harvey's mother, Elsie, wrote a letter to her son, urging him to stay safe. She had heard that all American ships at sea would hold services for Roosevelt, and she wondered if Harvey had attended one.

On Wednesday, Betty called Mr. Stella, who offered her old job back at the music store. The 19th was the third anniversary of that first dance at the American Legion Post, and Betty sent a Valentine's Day card, saying "Somebody made a big mistake! Valentine's day should be April 19, not in February!"

While the 75th was having gunnery practice in the Pacific, Betty was writing to Harvey from California. She had received a card he had written on board ship and had mailed from Honolulu. The postmark gave her a clue to his location, and she joked about him being in "paradise" without her. Her brother Rod was captain of the Venice High School track team, and on

Friday (the 20th) she watched the afternoon meet with Fairfax High. Rod was entered in the low hurdles, broad jump, and high jump events and had to fill in for an injured runner in the relay race (which Venice won to win the meet). She stayed to watch his baseball practice, and then walked home with him. After dinner, his band played for a school dance—as Betty said, "he sure makes every minute count." On Saturday, John Owen came to the house to visit Rod. He and Betty's father were charter members of the City Hall post of the American Legion, and Betty described him as "high up in Democratic circles in California." He was interested in Rod's application for appointment to West Point, and he offered to have his influential friends write recommendations.

A letter from Harvey's mother was tinged with worry for his welfare. They had an illuminated globe and would often try to figure out where his ship might be located.

On Sunday night, Betty noted that it had been a week since Harvey's ship left Washington: "someday you can tell me all about it." That afternoon, she and her brother had gone to the movies at the Pantages Theater in Hollywood. They saw *It's a Pleasure* with Sonja Henie and Michael O'Shea, and then drove to North Hollywood to see friends. Later, she listened to news about the United Nations Founding Conference to be held in San Francisco that week. The purpose of the meeting was the establishment of a Charter for the new organization. The US delegation was headed by Secretary of State Stettinius and included representatives from both Houses of Congress. Betty was hopeful and wrote "That is certainly turning into an important gathering. It will be wonderful knowing that our children will grow up in a peaceful world." In her letters, Betty often enclosed war-related cartoons or news clippings from the local newspapers, and sometimes the two had very different tones. On the back of a pair of silly cartoons enclosed with her Sunday letter, were a story and photographs about memorial services for FDR. In Monday's letter, she enclosed more cartoons, one showing a soldier in a foxhole reading a travel brochure about Florida: "He likes to read about far away distant places!" She and Rod went to the library (he was writing a term paper on West Point), and she picked up reading material for herself: *In My Father's House* (J. Street), *The Gals They Left Behind* (M. Shea), *We Are the Living* (E. Caldwell), *This Above All* (E. Knight), and *Quietly My Captain Waits* (E. Eaton). She and Harvey were avid readers, and they often talked about books in their correspondence. The titles of Betty's Monday collection clearly reflect what was on her mind. On Wednesday, Betty read *The Gals They Left Behind* while sunning in the back yard. She wrote that she would try to send a copy to Harvey as soon as possible. While reading, she listened to the "Lucky Lager Dance Time" on the radio. She also enclosed a George Clark cartoon showing a girl saying goodbye to her sailor on the dock saying "And promise you'll write every single day! I'm going to rush home and start waiting for a letter!"

On that same Wednesday (the 25th), Elsie sent another letter. She guessed that Harvey was headed for Okinawa because of reports that the Americans had occupied two-thirds of the island and were planning to construct several airfields there. She was wrong, but her letter reflected the guessing game obsessing families and friends of the men on the *Kota Baroe*; no one knew where they were or where they were going. She noted that some friends had received a letter from their son who was also in the Pacific, and he had asked about the welfare of his Aunt Marian. The reference to his non-existent aunt was a thinly veiled clue to his presence in the Marianna Islands; Elsie remarked that the whole world would soon know where they were since the censors were missing such obvious hints.

On Friday night, Betty and her friend, Peggy, went to the movies at the Dome Theater on the Boardwalk of Lick's Ocean Park Pier in Santa Monica. They saw *Roughly Speaking*, starring Rosalind Russell and Jack Carson, and a murder mystery, *Fashion Model* with Robert Lowery and Marjorie Weaver. *Fashion Model*, a low budget film, had just been released by Monogram Pictures and had been filmed at their "movie ranch" in Placerita Canyon near Newhall. Tom Mix had filmed many of his silent westerns at the Placerita ranch. *Roughly Speaking* had just been released by Warner Brothers and had been filmed at their Burbank Studios, with some scenes shot on Terminal Island in Wilmington. Betty enjoyed both films, but she found herself crying during a scene in *Roughly Speaking* where soldiers left for war at a railway station. "It seemed so real, and so like us." She had recently spoken to two friends whose new husbands were both missing in action, one at Iwo Jima and the other in Germany, and the film had touched her constant worry about Harvey's welfare.

On Saturday, she and Peggy visited the USO center in Santa Monica, and Betty was asked to come back and help out. She preferred not to return to hostessing—"just can't see dancing with all the men on the West Coast!"—but did agree to help. The center needed someone to head the Poster Committee and help with the Traveler's Aid desk, so Betty agreed to help out. She also thought she could help with the center's "servicemen's wives club" which planned teas, beach parties, card-playing evenings, and guest speakers. That evening she and Rod went to see the opening of Abbott and Costello's *Here Come the Coeds* at the Pantages Theater in Hollywood. The LA Times reported "Bud and Lou's latest screen adventures are as a pair of zanies who turn an exclusive girls' college upside down when they set out to save the institution from bankruptcy." Betty hoped that Harvey would be able to see the movie and was sure it would make him burst out laughing.

Elsie's letters were filled with chatty news of life at home, but her growing worry about Harvey was mentioned over and over. Betty was also worried, but she allowed herself to focus on her future with Harvey, on their children and grandchildren. She imagined "...quiet evenings and family discussions at dinner whether our son should have the car or not, or if our daughter is old enough to go that dance...you'll be such a good grandfather, so secure and understanding."

On Monday, Betty's family gathered around their radio and listened to the Peace Conference in San Francisco. Delegates argued for two hours, in several languages, about Argentina coming into the conference; the session lasted over three hours. Betty wondered if Harvey could listen to these live broadcasts, or whether tapes would be forwarded to them later. It was "boys' week" in Venice, and boys and young men were able to serve as honorary city officials: Rod was Lieutenant Commander of the Venice Police Department. He went to the rifle range, watched "the men show off trick shooting" and, in the afternoon, rode around Venice in a patrol car. Betty turned in early, as she had to return to work in the music store in the morning.

15

TWENTY-SIX DAYS, 5,700 MILES

Harvey wrote to Betty on Wednesday, May 2nd. Censors cut the date from the letter, but Harvey left Betty a clue, "does it seem like a month since we last saw each other?"—Betty had boarded her train in Kansas on April 2nd! Harvey wrote that the sea was rough, but the sun was shining brightly, and it was the hottest day of the trip. The meals aboard the *Kota Baroe* were "sumptuous" (Harvey's description), but the weather was too hot and muggy to want to eat.

The men had just gotten the news that Hitler had committed suicide, and some of the men felt he deserved a more violent end. Harvey disagreed but did feel that the world was well rid of men like Hitler and Emperor Hirohito. In the afternoon, another movie was shown on the ship, a Bette Davis film called *Jezebel*, but Harvey decided to skip it. Because of blackout regulations, films were screened indoors, and he felt it would be suffocating on such a hot day. After dark, Harvey and Mac went up on deck and stood for a while in the moonlight. It was a quiet opportunity to share their feelings about being so far from Betty and Dottie (Mac's wife).

The nights were stifling inside the ship, and Harvey decided to do his letter-writing in the afternoons, at least while still on the ship. The next day, he wrote while sitting under a lifeboat... "it's the coolest place on the boat at any time." That morning they had received an unconfirmed report by shortwave, that it was finally VE Day and all armies in Europe had ceased fighting. Harvey predicted that the Americans could now concentrate completely on

Japan, thus shortening the Pacific war. Unfortunately, the news was premature, and the war in Europe wouldn't end for another week. The *Kota Baroe* had already stopped twice and would probably make one more stop before finally reaching its destination. Harvey wasn't allowed to be more specific but told Betty that he would fill her in when he could.

The ship finally docked on Friday, May 4th, at Eniwetok in the Marshall Islands. The harbor was full of American vessels—cargo ships, small carriers, and submarines. The mail was taken off the ship, and some of the men fished in the harbor: "a few deep-sea fish were caught but died as soon as they reached the surface."

Two days later, the *Kota Baroe* left Eniwetok as part of a convoy, and the men still didn't know where they were ultimately headed. The ship was soon separated from the rest of the convoy. On Wednesday the 9th, Harvey wrote again. They were still at sea, and he admitted that he hadn't thought they would be on the water this long. "It hasn't been that bad at all, but it is getting really monotonous now." The men, Harvey included, were eager to find out exactly where they were going and what kind of job lay ahead. They reached Guam the next day and learned that this was where they would be stationed. It had been twenty-six days and 5,700 miles since they had left Seattle. The squadron would be building runways and serving as ground support for B-29s flying to Japan.

The next day, the unit disembarked from the *Kota Baroe* and went to Northwest Field, the headquarters of the 315th Bombardment Wing. "Barracks were waiting for Headquarters & 581st Materiel Squadrons on the south side of the runways in Service Center 'G'. The 587th Air Engineer SQ along with the Engineering teams from the three other Service Groups, were quartered on the north side of the runways in Service Center 'H'". Harvey's group was on the north side.

His letter next letter was dated May 12th and included the cryptic note "on an island in the South Pacific." He was apologetic about not writing sooner, saying "I hope you'll understand when I tell you that I'm now on dry land for the first time since we left the U.S., and that the past couple of days have been a madhouse of unloading and getting settled. We are now occupying the place that will be our home for quite some time, and we've got quite a bit of work to do to make it into some semblance of home." He was apologetic about his lack of correspondence, especially since seventeen letters from Betty were waiting for him when the ship docked. Her letters were accompanied by photos, a carnation ("still in fine shape") and cake crumbs. Censorship regulations were still very strict, and although he was now able to date his letters, he couldn't tell Betty where he was—Guam.

The Engineers lived in two-man tents for a while. This was to be their home, and since no one knew how long they would be there, they went about the business of making the area livable. They made paths and roads from pieces of coral, and coconut trees were planted for landscape. They also worked with the Seabees building air strips, parking ramps, etc. Runways were built in readiness for the 315th Bomb Wing to use. There was talk about trucks, bulldozers, and even jeeps disappearing, so armed soldiers accompanied the trucks as they moved supplies and equipment from the ship to the camp. The Service Group soon began to settle in, building a day room and an enlisted men's club to house the "morale" equipment, which included the Wurlitzer juke box and the soft drink fountain.

Not long after the unit settled in, they had a picnic at Talaforo Bay to celebrate their return to dry land. Unfortunately, the picnic lunch had been left in the sun, and almost everyone became ill.

At that point the unit only had tents with a few barracks for the enlisted men, but the rest of the camp was being readied as soon as possible. He wasn't able to share his exact location, but Harvey was able say that the camp was on a "typical tropical isle," with coconut, banyan, palm, and banana trees. He and Mac shared a tent, and they lay awake at night talking about how fortunate they were to be surrounded about such beauty, especially after over a month aboard ship. He and Mac had started their letters outside that day, but when it had begun to rain, they retreated to their tent. Generators had not yet been set up, and it was very dark inside, so letter-writing was finished for the night.

The generators were still not set up the following day (Sunday), and as it got dark early in Guam, Harvey began his letter in the afternoon. He was dressed only in his shorts, and as he wrote "a lot of small jungle insects are taking advantage of my bare back....the little brown ones are the most persistent." While he wrote, one of his men brought him a pot of hot tea, "the first hot thing I've had in two days!" He described the camp for her. The officers' barracks would be finished in a couple of days, and they would leave the two-man tents they were in. The mess halls weren't finished, and they had been eating K-rations and C-rations. Harvey had knocked coconuts off of trees and found he enjoyed both the milk and meat. There were also bananas and papayas growing wild near his tent, but they weren't yet ripe. He was surprised at how moderate the weather was, not as hot as he had expected. The sun would come out between the frequent, intermittent, rain showers. They quickly learned not to bother to get out of the rain since it cooled them off, and the sun quickly dried their uniforms. The unit had unpacked the short-wave radios, and Harvey listened to Jimmy Durante as he wrote. He had been named "Roads and Grounds Officer" for the entire unit, and he expected to be kept extremely busy over the coming weeks.

That Sunday (Mother's Day back in the States), he spent the day handling bulldozers and other heavy equipment. The mess hall had opened for the noon meal, and the shift away from constant K-rations and C-rations was welcomed. The first meals "weren't much to talk about" but at least they were hot and served with hot coffee. After lunch, Harvey's section worked late into the night and, since the showers were only turned on for a short period at supper time, most of his men missed "much needed" showers.

Harvey shared that there were still Japanese soldiers on the island. He thought that comment might be clipped by the censors, but they let it go. The Japanese were bottled up by Marine patrols and were waiting to be captured. Harvey didn't expect to see any of the Japanese while he was there. On Sunday, he was working in a back area of the camp and saw one of the biggest lizards he had ever seen, "fully five feet long and looked like a miniature dinosaur." He and his men threw chunks of coral at it, making it run away "at the speed of a horse." His letters were taking such a long time to reach Betty that he had decided to abandon the V-mail system and stick to regular air mail.

Harvey appreciated the hard work and positive attitude of his men, who often worked well into the night. They were beginning to make progress setting up their base in an area that had been only jungle and coral when they arrived. He was also bonding with his fellow officers. On Friday (May 18th), three of them borrowed a jeep and drove to another outfit that was showing a movie, *Gentle Annie*, starring James Craig, Donna Reed and Marjorie Main. Harvey was delighted to find that there was also a Pluto cartoon. Harvey was beginning to find the censorship rules tedious. He wanted to share the details of his surroundings and his life in Guam with Betty, but there was little that he could share.

In his Saturday letter, he noted that it had been exactly thirty-seven months since he and Betty had met at the Legion Hall in Beverly Hills. The army was supposed to be on a seven-day work week, but many of the soldiers in Guam took Sunday afternoons off. Harvey's unit was the exception. He felt it was good for he and his men to keep busy rather than just "have time hanging heavy on (our) hands." In addition, they were moving parts of their camp to a new area, and Sunday was the only time they were able to obtain the needed heavy equipment. The new area was heavily wooded, and they spent the whole day with bulldozers and cranes. Harvey bragged about the skill and work ethic of his men: "real professionals. That makes my job a whole lot easier because I don't even pretend to be an expert on any of this equipment. I can operate most of it, but it takes a skilled technician to get the maximum amount of work out of it. Take a look at the next road construction job you see, and you'll have an idea of what sort of equipment I'm fooling around with." They moved into their new barracks that day, and Harvey built himself a desk (to make letter-writing easier). He also built some shelves and planned to work on a small chest of drawers. He wished Rod (who was a better carpenter than he) was there to help with the furniture. The Chaplain brought over the letters that were supposed to have been delivered aboard ship, and Harvey also finally received the newspapers from Pittsburgh and the comics that Betty had sent.

On Monday, Harvey went to the movies at the camp's open-air theater and saw *After the Thin Man*. He and Betty had seen it together in Hays. He had been eager to see the second half of the double feature, a film about Chopin called *A Song to Remember*, but rain cut short the evening. Tropical storms in the area "came hard and often, but not for very long at a time." The camp would get soaked, but during the day the hot sun quickly dried it up.

On Wednesday, the censorship regulations were finally relaxed a bit. Harvey was able to let Betty know that he was on an island in the Marianas "but which one will still be a secret." He could tell her that there were natives on the island, as well as a few Japanese hiding in the jungles. He was also able to give some information about their trip across the Pacific—that they were in Hawaii for three days, but not allowed to leave the ship. They had not been in Pearl Harbor, but in Honolulu Harbor adjacent to the city. He told her they had made one more stop (he couldn't be more specific about that one) where mail was put off. He noted that mail delivery should become more regular now, and that cablegrams could be sent using the standard EFV forms (Expeditionary Force) using the address AMUGDO, which was a code for his location.

On Friday, Harvey noted that he had been saving all of Betty's mail. Unfortunately, the letters were starting to pile up in his footlocker, and he wasn't sure what to do with them. The men were allotted a ration of one can of beer a day, and although Harvey rarely drank beer, he had one that night after supper. It wasn't particularly cold, but he liked it because it was Duquesne beer, which was produced in Pittsburgh. The humidity on the island was tough on leather, and his watch band was beginning to fall apart. He clipped off a piece and sent it to Betty so she could look for a couple of spares. The dirt around the camp was a red clay, and when the weather dried up, the entire camp was covered in red dust. Harvey was looking for some relief from the heat and was hoping to use his free time on Sunday to go swimming at a beach on the other side of the island.

Saturday was a busy day for Harvey's unit. The base wasn't completed yet, and plans were underway for a coordinated "blitz" air attack on Japan. The B-29 had been developed as an intercontinental bomber, originally intended to fly from the continental US to Europe if Britain fell to the Nazis. Three hundred thousand of them were produced during the war, and many of them were now based in the Marianas. Many of the B-29s involved in the bombing runs took off from Guam, and there was pressure to enlarge and improve the base, especially the runways. Harvey's heavy equipment team was using dynamite to blast through the thick coral, and they were working three shifts, twenty-four hours a day. Occasionally, the men would watch the bombers take off for their missions. B-29s from their airfield had been involved in the recent strike against Nagoya and would be central on the proposed attack on Tokyo. Harvey was proud that his men had an important role in the process. "My job is to help maintain a base from which these boys can operate. It is only a small part of the operation, and not very close to any action, but at least it's something. I sure wish I could see a little bit of what's happening.... but I'm glad for your sake that I can't." That evening, the lights in the barracks had gone out, and Harvey was forced to write his letter in the Squadron Orderly Room. He was "as tired as I have been in a long time" and, during the afternoon's blasting, he had gotten moisture on his hands from the dynamite and "that always gives me a splitting headache."

On Sunday, the unit worked well into the night. Typically, Sunday mornings were spent doing maintenance on the equipment, and during the afternoons they could relax a bit. On this day, however the amount of "rush" work kept them pushing all day. Harvey noted that they didn't complain and knew that keeping busy was how all of them, he included, kept their minds off those who were waiting for them at home. He noted that "we've really got some fine equipment to work with. It's a real pleasure to see this stuff operating, especially when the men operating it know 'their' stuff." It hadn't rained for several days, and the roads were so dusty that one car or truck couldn't follow another because the driver couldn't see.

The Utility Section had been reorganized, and now four officers were in charge of four different units. Harvey was in charge of the Heavy Equipment section (the other units being Shops, Airport Maintenance, and Control), and he felt the new structure would work well. The officers were beginning work on an "Officers' Club," a place where they could gather and relax when they had free time. On Wednesday, Harvey and his unit unpacked specialized tools and equipment he had picked up back in the States, and they felt well prepared for the work ahead. They also set up the refrigerators, ice machine, and ice cream machine they had brought with them.

Harvey and Betty started getting congratulatory letters from friends who were just now hearing about their marriage. Some of the servicemen Harvey had known were still in Kansas or Oklahoma City, while others had moved on to other assignments. One, now the Post Engineer at Bruning Army Airfield in Nebraska, had just heard he was being sent to the Pacific to serve as a replacement Utilities Officer, and wondered if he would see Harvey. Other friends were now stationed at different bases in the States or had been shipped overseas to Germany or China.

On Tuesday, the officers continued their discussions for the proposed Officers' Club. They weren't sure whether they wanted separate clubs for each unit, or a consolidated club for the whole base. It was complicated because some units had brought along a lot more equipment for a club than others had. The officers in Harvey's unit, for example, had each donated forty dollars back at Walker field and had purchased a coca cola dispenser, ice making machines, ice cream machines and a lot of other equipment, including the supplies needed for the machines. The number of mixes purchased for the machines had been based on the size of the unit and wouldn't meet the needs of the entire base. Other units had not made plans before shipping out, and Harvey's unit felt that a consolidated unit would be a bit unfair. Nevertheless, Harvey was confident that some sort of compromise could be worked out.

He was amazed at how the boxes and crates of equipment had survived the trip overseas. "Everything is in perfect shape which is truly amazing considering the beating they have taken in shipment. We had just two light bulbs broken out of the hundreds and hundreds we packed." While the unit unpacked, music was playing over the loudspeakers, and tunes like "A Little on the Lonely Side" and "I Walk Alone" hit close to home for Harvey and the others. "Boy, how true to life are those titles...Not only do I walk alone but it will be that way till I get back to you and then—Never again!" The pouring rain wasn't helping his mood, and the men were hearing that they could expect three months of heavy rain.

16

SALESMEN FROM

CAPITOL AND DECCA

Betty went back to work at the music store on May 1st. A number of her friends stopped by to welcome her back, and Betty worried that she bored them with her constant talk about Harvey. She had to answer the same questions over and over again: "Oh, you're back home again. Has it really been that long? Is Harvey overseas? Which way did he go? Pacific or Atlantic? Where is he going?" She thought her friends would know better than to ask these questions—big LOOSE LIPS SINK SHIPS signs were all over town. Most of the day's chat concerned the War; one friend showed Betty a letter she had received from her sister who had just been liberated from a concentration camp in the Philippines. On Tuesday, Betty went over to the Irvings' for dinner, and then she and Peggy went to see Peggy's mother at Culver City Hospital. The hospital was only two blocks from Main Street, and the two young women went to Bray's Grill for a coke. Two boys who used to buy records at Stella's offered to drive them home so they wouldn't have to take the bus. "They used to really tease and torment me but now they treated me with all the respect due to a married woman!" When they got back to the Irvings', they realized they didn't have a key and had to crawl into the house through a window. The next-door neighbor was a police detective, and he was able to get the window open for them. She and Peggy wrote Harvey and Eddie while listening to Dinah Shore and eating Hershey bars and drinking cokes at the dining room table. At some point, the radio program was interrupted with the news of Hitler's death and Italy's surrender. Betty noted "Supposed to be true. I hope so." She spent the night with Peggy and went to work from there. Betty swept the store while Mr. Stella cleaned the inside of the piano with a wire brush. The salesmen from Capitol Records and Decca Records stopped by with some new releases that would be on sale in a couple of weeks. Capitol had just signed Peggy Lee, and Betty particularly liked her first big hit, "Waitin' for the Train to Come in." Betty also liked the music from the recent movie *Here Come the Waves*; she enclosed the lyrics of Bing Crosby's "I Promise You" from that film.

Later in the afternoon, Betty took a call from a woman who asked to speak with "Betty, who used to be called Betty Lundin." When Betty identified herself, the woman went on to ask if her name was now Brown and was she married to a Captain J. Harvey Brown Jr. By now Betty was terrified because she had heard that morning that two American transport ships had just been sunk near the Philippines by the Japanese. The woman went on to explain she had received a "V-mail" from her "favorite" nephew, a Captain Yoder, who said that he was sitting right across the table from Harvey. Betty now remembered the woman. She'd volunteered at the USO and had a small shop in Culver City; the two agreed to meet soon.

Elsie also wrote to Harvey on the 2nd. She was worried because her friend, Mrs. Glaes, had received a letter from her son, Gordon, who was serving in the Marianas. Gordon reported that his unit had come ashore on an island that had been retaken and supposedly cleared of enemy forces. They were instructed to stay on the road, but five men had strayed slightly out of bounds, and all five had been killed by snipers. Elsie reminded Harvey to follow closely any "boundary line instructions."

During the war, the Army had established a secure method for communicating with servicemen stationed abroad. To reduce the cost of sending original letters through the mail, the V-mail (short for Victory Mail) process consisted of censoring letters, copying them to film, and then printing smaller paper copies upon arrival at the message's destination. Elsie had received a V-mail letter from Harvey and decided to try the system on May 5th. Surviving V-mail letters from the period are legible, but the print is quite small.

Elsie told Harvey about a special communion church service for families of servicemen the previous Wednesday. Harvey's name was among those posted on the altar, and the pastor read each one of them aloud. On Friday evening, Harvey's parents went to the Stanley Theater in Pittsburgh to see a performance by the Ink Spots. Harvey's Aunt Peggy wrote to him on the

5th. She told him about her work at the Veteran's Hospital in Pittsburgh and passed on news about the rationing of meat in the city; during the past week, she and Harvey's mother had only been able to obtain three-quarter pound portions of ground meat, and butcher shops had only pigs' ears to sell.

On Saturday evening Betty and Rod went to the movies at the Westwood Village Theater on Broxton Avenue. The foyer of the theater featured murals depicting the California Gold Rush, and the connection with nearby UCLA was emphasized in the depiction of sports teams and "college coeds doing classical dance formations." The neoclassical tower of the theater dominated the neighborhood, and the theater (now called the Regency Village Theater) still exists. That Saturday, Betty and Rod saw *Brewster's Millions*, a new Universal comedy starring Dennis O'Keefe, and *Three Caballeros*, an animated Disney film featuring Donald Duck along with live actors. Betty and Harvey both loved cartoons, and she hoped that he would see this one soon.

Betty worked that Saturday afternoon at the music store. Before getting married she had been making sixty-five cents an hour (up from fifty cents when she was first hired!). However, that afternoon, her pay slip showed she was now making sixty cents/hour. Mr. Stella's explanation that this was all he could now afford didn't sit well with Betty, and she said she would quit at the end of the month if she didn't make more.

As Betty was writing to Harvey on Sunday night, she listened to a radio program about a 1929 raid on Tokyo. The Americans, the 20th Air Force, were stationed on Saipan, and Betty wondered if that was where Harvey was headed. The Associated Press reported that V-E Day would be announced on Monday morning, and all radio programs starting at six o'clock were delayed making room for comments by Truman and Churchill. Although the AP had evidently jumped the gun a bit (V-E Day was actually Tuesday), wild celebrations erupted on the East Coast. Betty noted that celebrations on the West Coast were more subdued: "people seem to realize that we are only 1/2 through – that the Pacific War is in full swing. They rejoiced over the European victory, there were no demonstrations in the streets at all. Everyone I saw was rather on the quiet, sober side today." It was reported that the official announcement would coincide with all bars being closed for twenty-four hours. Betty spent the day filing records at Stella's.

On Tuesday, Betty's letter was had the heading "VE Day – May 8, 1945." She noted that things were pretty quiet on the West Coast, with the only difference being the constant news from around the world. She had the day off and got up early so she could hear radio programs from Guam, Manila, and London. Later that day, she went shopping for Mother's Day gifts in downtown Los Angeles. On Wednesday, she went back to work and spent the day filing records; she wrote her daily letter to Harvey on "special paper" (an empty Capitol Records record folder).

Back in Wilkinsburg, Elsie was happy that V-E Day had come but, like Betty, didn't feel much like celebrating until, "Japan is beaten, and you are back safe and sound." She put in a few hours that day at the USO canteen in South Park. Most of the four hundred men they served were Purple Heart recipients being trained for MP duty in Europe. She saw a newsreel about conditions in Okinawa and wondered if Harvey was there.

In her May 10th letter, Betty noted that several articles in the LA newspapers that morning dealt with the final stages of the European war. One described a point system for releasing servicemen from overseas, and another reported that Adolph Hitler's body had been tentatively identified as one of those found in the rubble of his Berlin headquarters. She had a busy day at the music store, sorting and displaying stock that had just come in. A butcher from across the street was so excited to find that the new batch contained a record he had been searching for ("Goodnight Soldier" by Judy Canova) that he saved some bacon and pork chops for her—a big deal in those days of rationing. In the evening, the family went to the high school to see the annual band concert. Rod was first chair trumpet. Afterwards they went home for dessert, and Betty and Rod danced to the records that she was packing up to send to Harvey. She then sent the records in a tin given to her by a friend at Selznick Studios.

On the 11th, Betty received the V-mail letter Harvey had written aboard ship two weeks earlier, on April 28th. It had been mailed on the 7th from Honolulu, and Betty noted it was a bit hard to read because the print was so small.

Harvey's father didn't write often, but the imminent end of the war in Europe prompted him to write on the 11th. He and Elsie wondered where Harvey was. He had been gone about a month, and they expected he should have reached his final post; they guessed it might be Okinawa. Elsie was out at a meeting, and Harvey Sr. went to the movies at the Enright Theatre in East Liberty. He saw *Key to the Kingdom*, starring Gregory Peck, and enjoyed it. In the afternoon, he had visited the Pittsburgh Blood Bank and had given his ninth pint since the beginning of the war. The blood banks in the East would soon close, since those on the West Coast could supply the needs in the Pacific. Harvey's father felt that the Eastern closures were a mistake because of the possible effect on Eastern morale, and the tendency to think that the war was over.

On Saturday, Betty sent Harvey two V-mails. Both she and Harvey were becoming frustrated by the V-mail process, both with the limits on length of messages and the difficulties in reading the small print. Both hinted that they would send only regular letters, even though the delivery time was longer. In one of her V-mails, she noted that her mother had appreciated his Mother's Day card. Betty had sent Elsie a few of Bing Crosby records: "Mother's Waltz," "Just a Prayer Away," "Too-Ra-Loo-Ra-Loo-Ra," and "I'll Remember April"). She added "That'll be a great day when I become the mother of our baby... please finish the war quick, and hurry home!" A friend of Harvey's from home, Dick Whitfield, also sent him a V-Mail on the 12th. Like Harvey, Dick was frustrated with the repeated announcements of VE Day, only to have them later dismissed as rumor. However, the most recent announcement had proven to be accurate, and the celebrations in Pittsburgh, including a snow-storm of paper thrown out of tall buildings, had been going on all day.

Sunday was Mother's Day, and it rained most of the day in Southern California. Betty missed Harvey, and she wondered where Rod would be headed in the coming months. She played Bing Crosby records all day: "they are all such beautiful songs, and I think his voice is in a class by itself," and at dinner, the family listened to sentimental programs on the radio. Finally, Betty needed to go outside to cry and gather her thoughts. She started to feel better as she wrote to Harvey about their future together. In Wilkinsburg, Harvey's mother was also feeling blue. "Do you suppose that (the end of the war) will ever be in my lifetime?"

On the 18th, Betty spent the night at the Irvings', and, after dinner, she and Peggy took the streetcar to the high school to see the setup for the Senior prom. Rod's band would be playing, and he and a friend had been decorating the bandstand. Betty visited briefly with Rod and his date, and then she and Peg went home. They stayed up until 2:00 a.m. writing letters.

On Sunday, Jean Green and her family spent the day with the Lundins. Jean and Rod had dated for quite a while, and the two families were close. Jean's current boyfriend had just left for the service and had given her a ring before he left. Later, after everyone had gone home, Betty looked through some things she had saved from the time in Kansas. She found a list she and Harvey had made of possible names for their first baby [usually referred to in these letters as "Junior"], and she wondered if they would actually settle on one from this list.

Harvey's parents wrote to him that Sunday, the 20th. They had been anxious and unable to sleep because they hadn't received a letter from him. They were still guessing that he might be in Okinawa and had no way of knowing that he had left Seattle two days earlier on the *Kota Baroe*.

After work on Monday, Betty and two friends went to the movies at the newly reopened Meralta Theatre on Culver Boulevard in Culver City. They saw *Bring on the Girls* and *Rough, Tough and Ready*. She recommended both pictures to Harvey, particularly the second one, which was about Army Engineers. The Meralta had been built by the traveling vaudeville duo Pearl Merrill and Laura Peralta (they performed as "Ella Fant and Miss Kito"), and Will Rogers had appeared at its opening in 1924. At that event, an Our Gang comedy had been shown "which had all the kids leaping through their on-screen likeness when the projectionist stopped the film!" In the 1920s, local studios used the theater to preview their films, and in 1928 general releases also began to appear. During that period, Christian Science lectures were occasionally held on "dark days," and it is possible that Betty's mother (a Christian Scientist) was in attendance at some of them. In the 1940s, mainly war-themed pictures were shown at the Meralta. The original theater burned down on August 9th, 1943, and it reopened in 1945.

Betty had the day off on Tuesday, and while she worked around the house, she listened to the Lucky Lager radio program. She enjoyed new songs by Betty Hutton, Peggy Lee, and Harry James. She noted, though, that the popularity of the James band was slipping. A letter from Harvey reached his parents, letting them know he had arrived at an island in the Marianas. His mother had heard that the Japanese had spotted American ships steaming out of the Marianas, and she wondered if Harvey was on one of them. She was worried about the reported casualty numbers in the Pacific Theater.

Harvey and Betty both played the clarinet. On Wednesday, Betty took hers to the music store and played all day in between helping customers. Her coworker, Elsie, accompanied her on the piano. Stella's had a wide variety of sheet music, and the two women sampled everything. After work, Betty's family celebrated her mother's fifty-first birthday by having dinner, giving presents, and going to the movies. They saw, and enjoyed, *Royal Scandal* and *Bring on the Girls* at the Village Theater in Westwood. Betty had just seen the second picture only two days earlier, but her mother really wanted to see it. Accompanying the feature movies was a short film about Colorado, and it brought back memories of a trip she and Harvey had made to Colorado Springs shortly after they were married. They had visited the Will Rogers

Memorial and the Garden of the Gods and had danced at the hotel where they were staying. Harvey had asked that the band play "their" songs, "You Made Me Love You" and "My Dreams Are Getting Better All the Time."

On Friday, Betty went to lunch with a friend from MGM studios. When she wrote to Harvey that evening, she enclosed an "In Memoriam" poppy made by the local American Legion. The next day, Rod took his physical exam for the Naval Air Corps (he passed). His West Point exam wouldn't be until July, but he had decided to take the NAC exam in case the offer for it closed; he still planned to take the West Point exam. Rod understood that Harvey had been disappointed that his own West Point appointment hadn't come through, but if it had, he never would have met Betty.

Harvey's parents had gone to the Penn Theatre to see a newsreel about the first bombing raid on Tokyo from Saipan. There were also reports that nineteen B-29s had been lost on a Friday raid over Tokyo, and that Japanese "suicide planes" were targeting American bases in the Marianas. They were anxious and sleeping poorly. On a more hopeful note, Elsie had read that Bing Crosby would soon be doing a show in the Marianas, and she hoped Harvey would see him.

On Sunday, Betty helped her father in the garden and then went to the movies with Rod. They drove to Grauman's Chinese Theatre on Hollywood Boulevard and saw *Diamond Horseshoe* with Betty Grable and Dick Haymes and also *Faces in the Fog*. Although Grauman's was very close to Culver City, Betty hadn't been there in a long time. It was one of the great "movie palaces" of the era and had opened in 1927 with the premiere of Cecil B. DeMille's *King of Kings*. When he opened the theater, Sid Grauman shared ownership with Mary Pickford, Douglas Fairbanks Sr., and Howard Schenck. Several high-profile premieres have been held there over the years, including *Star Wars* in 1977. Among the distinctive features of the theater are the concrete blocks in the courtyard with the handprints and footprints of Hollywood stars, the earliest being that of Pickford in 1927. On March 15th, two months before Betty and Rod's visit, Grauman's had hosted its second Academy Awards ceremony, with Bing Crosby winning Best Actor for *Going My Way* and Ingrid Bergman winning Best Actress for *Gaslight*.

During her lunch break on Monday, Betty took the P.E. (Pacific Electric) Short Line train, known as the "Red Car", into town to deposit a check Harvey had sent from Guam. That evening Rod received word to report on Wednesday for his V-5 medical exam, and he and Betty tried to cheer up their mother who was upset at the prospect of him leaving for military service.

After supper, Rod and Betty went to the movies again. "It's getting as bad as back in Hayes! – we go practically every night." This time, they went to the Bruin Theatre in Westwood and saw *Dark Waters*, a movie Betty had already seen in Kansas with Harvey, and a Jack Benny film, *The Horn Blows at Midnight*. The Bruin was a relatively small theater that had opened in 1937 on Broxton Avenue, across the street from the much larger Village Theatre. After the film, they had malts across the street at a place called Crumper's.

By Tuesday the 29th, Harvey's mother hadn't heard from him for several days and was becoming increasingly worried. She wondered where he was (Betty had written that she thought he might be on Guam), and she worried about everything—about his health, about suicide attacks, even about snakes. That Tuesday, Betty spent the whole day waiting on girls "who are waiting for husbands who are overseas. Sort of a lonesome look in their eyes."

Wednesday was Memorial Day, and Stella's was closed. Betty helped Mr. Stella and the rest of the staff paint the store's floor for a couple of hours, and then they all headed for a party at the beach. They went up the coast highway to Malibu, not far from where Betty and Harvey had spent their honeymoon. After a big lunch and an afternoon on the beach, she headed home. Rod came home soon after that from taking his V-5 test for the Navy. He hadn't passed it. The family had just learned that the group he was being considered for would be sent overseas to replace men killed in combat, and they were relieved that he hadn't passed the test. He planned to continue to study for the West Point exam. Betty was relieved that Harvey had finally received his packet of letters from his Chaplain. On Thursday evening, she went with her parents to an Eastern Star show and dinner. Music was provided by a "professional cowboy band," and they all danced, even Betty's mother and dad.

Ten cartons of new records arrived at the store on Friday, including new songs by Dinah Shore ("Counting the Days" and "Along the Navajo Trail") and the Chopin music from *An Affair to Remember*.

17

"GECKO" THEATER

On Friday night, June 1st, Harvey and his friend Mac went to a little out-door theater that had been set up in one of the other camps (there were evidently several of them). "The theater is an open-air job, as all of them are on the island, so we drove right up and sat in our jeep to watch the movies. Regular Drive-In style!" The theater didn't have a feature picture, but rather was showing short films, all of them fairly new and many of them published by the Army-Navy Screen Magazine. When they returned to their officer quarters after the movies, all the lights had gone out, so they headed out with flashlights to take their showers. That afternoon, Harvey had unpacked more of his stuff, including a gooseneck lamp for his homemade desk and a small electric fan. With his letter to Betty that night, he included a sketch of his living quarters and an explanation: "The building is twice as wide as it is from the wall to the center of the double doors and four times as long as it is wide. The building is supposed to be partitioned off into four rooms with four officers per room but as yet they haven't put in any of the partitions. I guess they'll get around to it one of these days." The men were trying to adjust to their new environment and to being so far from their loved ones. Harvey was no exception. "I hope you're not worrying about me, 'cause there isn't a single thing to worry about. Physically I'm in better shape than I've been in for years. I've lost a little weight and feel like a million dollars. I'm working pretty hard and liking it better every day. Mentally, I'm missing you so much that it tears me apart at times when I think about it. That's something I tried to prepare myself for when I left. I knew it was coming but I never suspected the feeling would mount up like this. The day we meet again will be one we'll remember for the rest of our lives."

Harvey also worried about his men. "Sgt. Patton took sick today, probably a recurrence of his trouble back at Walker. Not serious, I hope. Bill Zierenberg borrowed my jeep tonight to go and see Pat in the hospital, so I'll know in the morning just what the score is. Pat isn't working directly under me now, so I won't be short a man, but I hate to see a swell guy like that getting sick." Unfortunately, five days later, Sgt. Patton was still in the hospital and would need to be sent home: "...it looks as if his ulcerated stomach is going to keep him there for quite a while. A man with an ailment like that should be discharged because he can't possibly maintain any kind of a diet on army chow. Plenty of eggs and fresh milk are the usual prescribed items and although we have eggs almost every morning, we haven't seen fresh milk since we landed. That's not so good for a man in his condition. I'd sure hate to see Pat leave us, but deep down inside I know he should be discharged. He doesn't want it himself, but you can't go by that at all." Five weeks later, Sgt. Patton was released from the field hospital. "Pat is going to leave us before very long and right now is sweating out transportation back to the States. He's getting a discharge and isn't too happy about it because he hates to leave the outfit. He's a good guy, and I hate to lose him."

On Sunday, the heavy equipment unit worked hard all morning, and Harvey told everyone to take the afternoon off. "Before you could say 'Please pass the butter', there wasn't a man in sight." It was the first time off they had had since arriving in Guam, and he thought they needed a rest. Accompanied by his buddies, Mac and Peck, he drove his jeep to the beach where they swam for an hour. Many of his men were also at the beach, as were some of the women attached to the unit, mainly nurses and Red Cross workers. For some reason, the women were getting a lot of attention. After leaving the beach, the three of them drove around a bit, taking back roads they hadn't been on before. Although they didn't see anything noteworthy, the motion of the jeep stirred up a welcome breeze. They returned to camp just before the mess hall closed and enjoyed a Sunday supper of roast pork, mashed potatoes, corn, tomatoes, and cherry pudding. Harvey reported to Betty that the food in camp was surprisingly good.

After supper, the three drove to their favorite outdoor theater to see a movie, but unfortunately the projector broke down before the picture started. They drove around, finally finding another theater that was showing *Tonight and Every Night* with Rita Hayworth...the same movie Betty and

Rod had seen in April. (Harvey didn't make the connection.) In order to keep the men entertained, there were movies almost every night. On Monday, the three buddies saw *The Story of Louis Pasteur* with Paul Muni and Josephine Hutchinson. The film was an old one (1936), but Harvey hadn't seen it. Before the movie started, there was a talk by a native Baptist minister, who described his experiences during the Japanese regime before US troops had arrived.

A major accomplishment of the Service Groups in Harvey's camp was the construction of their own outdoor amphitheater. The Navy Seabees and Army Engineers joined the Service Groups, and the site was bulldozed, terraced and compacted. Seats were constructed from discarded wooden crates. The stage was built from various materials and was large enough (40' by 90') to attract live entertainment. The theater opened for the first time on Wednesday, June 6th, "and even though they've got a lot of work to do on it yet, it really isn't bad….Our stage is large enough to accommodate any of the travelling shows that may come our way so we're hoping for the best and most glamourous ones to hit our island. Naturally, there are quite a few other theaters here, but as ours is the only one in this particular area we may be lucky enough to have the show. With a jeep, though, we can still travel to see a show if we have to." The movie on opening night was *Dark Waters* with Merle Oberon and Franchot Tone. Harvey had stocked up on cigarettes, six cartons of them. "The normal allotment is one pack a day, but I ran into a PX that was closing out, so I managed to lay in a supply. Running down every day to pick up one pack at a time is pretty much of a nuisance, but now I'm pretty well set."

From time to time, Harvey tried to give Betty a feel for the environment where he was living. For example, he described the large toads that were all over the island. "We've noticed, while driving back from the show at night that they seem to like sitting in the middle of the road. We must have seen at least twenty of the on the road tonight. I didn't hit any of them tonight, but I don't see how we did it. The stupid things just sit and blink at the headlights as you go by. When they are sitting down, their heads are five or six inches off the ground so you can get an idea of how big they are."

For several days, Harvey's men had been preparing an area for the storage and maintenance of their heavy equipment, and they were about ready to move into it. "We've done a lot of clearing with our bulldozers and then covered the whole area with the coral of which this island is composed. We built a small building for use as an office, another for the mechanics shop, and a large one for use as a garage for machinery that is being repaired. It sounds a lot more elaborate than it really is, but I'm sure it's going to make our job here a lot easier than it has been so far. The hardest part has been to keep operating at the same time we are attempting to set up an organization. Now that the organizing is just about completed, we can throw everything we have into operation." By Thursday, the unit was pretty much operating at full strength. "We've got our heavy equipment set up pretty well organized by now and are in operation with every available piece of equipment. The Army certainly has invested a lot of money in this kind of stuff, and we've really got our share of it. Now it's up to us to put it to good use. I guess we can do it if anyone else can! For our new location we chose a spot that was back in the jungle and thick as could be with trees and underbrush of all kinds, but the ground itself was gently sloping which gives good drainage which will mean a lot a little later if it rains as much as they say it does in the rainy season. The job of clearing wasn't too tough for us because we've got all the equipment to do it, and if we ran cross anything that our equipment couldn't handle we used dynamite or TNT. We had lots of fun doing it, too!?"

All letters were monitored by Army censors, and anything related to military activity, or where troops were based, was clipped out before the mail was allowed to go out. Harvey was pretty careful, and very few of his letters ended up with "clipped out" sections. Clearly though, he and Betty had talked about where he might be sent, and occasionally he would send a vague clue in a letter, like "you know that island we always wanted to see?" Interestingly, incoming mail was not censored. "In Mother's letter yesterday, she said she had heard from you, and you had made a statement that you thought you knew where I'm now located. Funny, you never told me anything about it. Let me know what you think because, as I said before, your letters to me are not censored and I'm interested to know your ideas about of my location and how you arrived at your estimate." On the 8th, a note appeared on the headquarters Bulletin Board to the effect that "censorship regulations have been lifted enough to permit us to say that we are on Guam. I hope it's not an error and the censors cut that word out...even so, I'm sure that you know where I am. I can't see any reason for not saying so because it certainly can't help (the enemy) any now to get hold of that information!" A week later, Harvey noted that the censorship rules continued to relax. "They've opened up the censorship quite a bit, but they still don't allow us to take any pictures. Too bad, because there are lots of non-military pictures that could be taken and sent to you. Items of interest to you who haven't seen the place."

Even in Guam Harvey and his fellow officers found outlets for their love of sports. They had formed a softball team while training in Kansas, and that Thursday they had their first overseas game. "Our game tonight was with the enlisted men of the Engineering Squadron (aircraft engineers, not Corps of Engineers) and even though they have a pretty hot team we managed to beat them 12 to 8 by scoring 6 runs in the last inning. Had two hits and a walk out of four times at bat so I felt as if I had helped out a little. I'm doing all the catching for our team, probably because no one else wants the job, but I like it because there is always lots of action no matter how slow the game is." The game started at 5:30, and the men missed supper, which was at 6:00. However, they were able to talk the cooks into giving them coffee and sandwiches, and afterward they went to their new PX to have a cold can of beer (one each!).

On Saturday, Harvey and Mac went to the movies again, seeing *The Woman in the Window* with Edward G. Robinson and Joan Bennett. Harvey remembered seeing the movie with Betty back in Hayes, Kansas. The film had been produced by the Christie Film Company, an independent film company with offices on Santa Monica Boulevard in West Hollywood. In 1944, when this movie was filmed, Christie rented studio space from larger studios (Goldwyn, Paramount, RKO, Selznick, and PRC). Christie went out of business in the early 1950s.

The unit worked hard the next morning, and the men were looking forward to another free Sunday afternoon. On a hunch, though, Harvey checked back at his "little" office and found an officer there with truckloads of heavy generators that needed to be unloaded. Harvey spent the next four hours doing the job himself, "...until almost four o'clock I operated a crane because I didn't have another operator available.... I didn't mind too much, though, because it's a lot of fun to operate a piece of machinery that can lift up to eight or nine tons. Gives you a sense of power and control to know that with just the touch of a lever you can swing all that weight. I'm glad I know a little about this equipment, because I'd hate to ask an operator to do anything I couldn't do." Later in the afternoon, Harvey and Mac drove around the island looking for a soldier, Gordon Glaes, who had lived next door to Harvey in Wilkinsburg and was now also stationed in Guam. "Didn't have much luck except to find out that he had been here and may be back a little later." The ride did give the two a chance to explore a bit. "A little about the island here, it's the biggest island in the Marianas as you can see from your map. It's well wooded with all kinds of tropical trees, and the climate is quite a bit hotter than that in Los Angeles. There are quite a few natives here, and they are called 'Chamarros'...they don't seem at all handy with their hands, which accounts for the terrific lack of any kind of souvenirs. The capital of the island is Agano, pronounced "A-gan-yo", a pretty beat up place. There are a couple of smaller towns scattered around over the island...in this climate the natives naturally go in for thatched roofs and very light buildings. But every now and then they've attempted something that resembles concrete. Not too bad." That night, the two of them took in another movie, *Mrs. Miniver*, starring Greer Garson and Walter Pidgeon. The film had won Academy Awards in 1942 for Best Picture, Best Director, Best Actress, Best Supporting Actress, and Best Screenplay. Harvey especially liked it, however, because he thought that Garson looked a lot like Betty. Ironically, the movie had been filmed at the MGM Studios on Washington Boulevard in Culver City the very same week that Harvey and Betty had met at the USO dance three miles away in Beverly Hills!

The next night, they went to the movies again, this time seeing *Between Two Women* with Van Johnson, Lionel Barrymore, and Gloria DeHaven. "You should have heard the whistles and stuff when Marilyn Maxwell came on the screen!" On Tuesday, they were back at the movies. "Tonight, for the first time since our new theater opened, they had a picture that I hadn't seen before. I had almost forgotten what that was like. They had 'Gambler's Choice' with Chester Morris and Nancy Kelly. Strictly a class D picture, but pretty good entertainment at that. I can't imagine what people did for entertainment before movies were invented. Lucky thing for me."

The rainy season had come to the Marianas in June. The wet weather, though uncomfortable, did little to interrupt the hard work being done in the daytime or the movie-going in the evenings. "Honey, you've probably seen newsreels of a lot of soldiers sitting in pouring rain, watching a movie in an outdoor theater. Well, tonight it happened to us. About halfway through the picture it started to sprinkle and before you could say 'scat' it was pouring down. Funny but hardly a man got up and left. The picture wasn't too spectacular, 'Enter Arsene Lupin,' with Ella Raines, but here in the island it just doesn't make any difference if you get wet or not. We just turned up our collars, pulled down our hats, and took it. And didn't mind a bit! When you first arrive at an island like this, it's a little disturbing to see men working outside right through a rainstorm but you get used to it and do the very same thing yourself without a second thought. You'll really have to look out for me when I get back. Things like pulling me in out of the rain etc. should be a daily occurrence for you for a while. Hope you won't mind!"

"Gecko" theater, Northwest Field, Guam, 1945

The string of movie nights continued on Thursday, and Harvey and Mac saw a Judy Garland and Mickey Rooney film, *Girl Crazy*. Both had seen it before, but so long ago they had forgotten most of it. "Funny thing, right in the middle of the picture, someone had spliced the film and had put in about five seconds of a bomber dropping bombs on some city or another. It had everyone baffled for a minute or two, and then the place just roared!!" The camp was scheduled to get its first traveling road show the following Monday, but the men suspected that it wouldn't be a "name" show.

The first container of records from Betty arrived on Friday the 15th. The records were packed in a film can and had arrived completely undamaged—quite a feat since the 78 rpm records of the day were very fragile. Harvey was anxious to listen to them. "We have a player that provides music for everybody at the theater up until showtime...I'm going to have them play all of your records for me." He took them to the movies that night but arrived too late and "sat through the whole picture with the film can in my lap." He planned to bring them earlier on Saturday. The movie on Friday was *Boys Town*, with Spencer Tracy and Mickey Rooney, and Harvey had been wanting to see it for a long time. Before the main feature, the men were shown a couple of Navy films about the retaking of Guam the previous July. "They were actual battle scenes and actually showed the rescue of that fellow named Tweeds who was the lone survivor of the Guam garrison at the time the Japanese captured it. The most realistic movie I have ever seen. In some scenes they actually showed how the enemy, when they knew that the island was going to be retaken...vented their full fury on the natives. These people are Nationalists of the United States and if given half a chance could be donators of wealth in many ways. Politically, socially, physically, scientifically and lots of others. They are really fine people as we've found after living among them for a while. It's a pity that they had to suffer so miserably." After the film, there was one more treat waiting for Harvey—at the PX, they had Fort Pitt beer for the first time, "and I had to have a bottle of that because it's another Pittsburgh product."

The unit did more blasting on Saturday. "I've got a pretty good-sized headache tonight because all I've done all day is handle gobs and gobs of dynamite and by golly it'll do it to me every time! We are clearing a large area and ran into quite a few large trees that our bulldozers couldn't knock down. So, we had to blast. It's loads of fun placing charges and knowing beforehand just how much damage your stuff will do and knowing just where the tree will fall. Some of these guys know nothing at all about explosives so they think we're plenty smart to be able to blow up a few trees. If they only knew how easy it all is. Tomorrow is Sunday and I hate to disturb the peace with a lot of explosions, but we've still got a few trees to blow out. It's for a good cause so I guess no one will mind."

Later that day, he found that a soldier in his unit had been in Middletown, Pennsylvania, at the same time Harvey was stationed there and living in Hershey—April 1944. The private "had just received two copies of the Post paper from a friend of his there and what do you know if my old C.O. didn't have his picture on the front page sporting a new promotion! One of the best Commanding Officers I ever had. I guess I'll have to drop him a line to congratulate him on his 'eagles' but he'll have to wait his turn because I've got quite a few other letters to get off first." He was hoping that he wouldn't have to work all day Sunday because he wanted to take a little time off to relax. He thought he might take a long ride or maybe have a swim at the beach. He also wanted to stop by the hospital "because there are a couple of our boys there and I know they like to have someone think about them."

Luck was with Harvey on Sunday, and he was able to take the long ride he was hoping for. "We managed to get cleaned up with our work about noon, so right after lunch Mac and I took off in the jeep for a long tour of the island. Naturally, we didn't expect to cover it all in one afternoon, but we really did see quite a bit that we hadn't seen before. We saw all the places where the main battles had taken place, and around one end of the island we found lots of caves in the cliffs above the beaches where (the enemy) had probably died attempting to hold off the U.S. troops. These places are all pretty well blackened and scarred and for the most part, practically blown to bits. The trees in these areas are short, shot off, stubs and the ground is pretty well pitted with the remains of a tank or two lying abandoned here and there. After that picture last night, we could practically refight the battle in our mind's eye as it must have actually happened. Looked like pretty rough going to me. We saw lots of beautiful sights too, what with all the palm groves and thick, green jungle almost everywhere. Before the island was occupied, it must have been a solid mass of jungle, so thick that a man can't see more than 10 feet away and can't walk more than a step in any direction without cutting bushes, vines, weeds and all kind of growth. Any installations the Army has erected have been hewn out of this wall of jungle! I've often read of the thickness of tropical jungles, but I never imagined it could be true! Part of our trip took us on a road that wound up to the top of a tall cliff overlooking the ocean. We stopped there for a few minutes because the view was too good to pass up. The rocky, coral cliff fell away almost straight down from our feet to a ribbon of sandy beach which held back the white breakers of the ocean. The water was as blue as your eyes and stretched all the way to the horizon with hardly a ripple. There were pillows of clouds all over the sky which looked like a light blue ocean over our heads. It was really a beautiful sight, and I wish I could describe it to you as it really looked....We saw quite a few native villages, at least four or five. The names of some of them are Agat, Asan, Dedado, Sumay, Sinajana, and of course the one I've mentioned before is Agana, the capital. They are small places with the most predominant type of buildings being the thatched roof variety. The huts are not laid out in any pattern, but just build in any spot that the owner likes. No cooking is done in the living quarters but in an open sided building which houses a large oven which appears to be made of baked earth and stone (coral). The people are very quiet and unpretentious and don't attempt conversations with anyone. However, I'm told that about 80% speak English and the rest speak their native Chamarro language which is a mixture of Japanese, Filipino and Spanish....this letter has turned into quite a travelogue. I suppose I should end it with something like 'And now as the golden sun sinks into the West, we take our leave of the beautiful, tropical isle of Guam...etc.'. Just like the movies. Maybe Zanuck will give me a job when I get back! Me and Barrymore!!?" Later that night, the records that Betty had sent were played over the theater's loudspeakers before the movie. "Everyone noticed that they were new records and, especially when they put on Dinah Shore, the G.I.'s really screamed for more... I felt very close to you then...Thanks for that little bit of home and you."

The dedication ceremonies for the 75th's new theater took place on Monday evening, June 18th. It had a capacity of five thousand and, over the next several months would usually be filled to capacity. Soldiers had submitted their suggestions for the name of the place, and a case of beer was presented to the man with the winning entry, "The Gecko," the name of the small lizards that were everywhere on Guam. Harvey explained to Betty that they were "absolutely harmless and interesting to watch as they flash back and forth catching flies. Good at it too!" Following the dedication there was a stage show presented by a group of GIs calling themselves "the Guamatics," and the response was wild: "...it's been a long time since I've laughed so hard. Lots of music and jokes, all of them good. We expect to have one stage show a week and some of them should be first class jobs from the States!"

The rain kept up, but there were dry periods from time to time. After a couple of rainless days, the dust would settle in the roads making driving hazardous. The weather on Wednesday was a mix. "I guess the weatherman couldn't make up his mind whether to have rain or sunshine, so he had both—at the same time. We had rainbows all over the place all day long. Sometimes the rain was pretty heavy, but the old sun stuck it out and had his face showing continually. Looks as if our rainy season was doing its best to get started." Because of the weather that day, it was difficult to get a lot of work done, so the unit had a chance to work on paperwork in the office. "The Army requires quite a lengthy procedure in the keeping of maintenance records on all kinds of vehicles and heavy equipment, along with a lot of inspections and reports that have to be made. We have to have a complete and accurate record on the mileage, hours of operation, gasoline consumption, diesel fuel consumption, engine repairs and overhauls, and a thousand and one other things. Really keeps my men on the ball to keep track of it all. It was pretty tough at first because I didn't have a single experienced administrative man to set up the office, but we're managing to work our way out of the woods. It looks now as if it could possibly turn into a smoothly functioning unit."

The heavy June rain became a constant theme of Harvey's letters. On Thursday, he wrote, "Spent practically my whole day just trying to stay out of the rain. I don't think we have had more than half an hour all day without at least a little bit of rain coming down and most of the time it has been really pouring. Most of the low areas here are well covered with large quantities of water, which will drain fairly quick if the rain will only stop for a while. But it doesn't look as if it's going to let up for some time. Our barracks are on fairly high ground, so I don't think there is much danger of our barracks ever getting water on the floor except from cracks in the roof. And we've found quite a few of those since the heavy rain started. One thing we can be thankful for is we've gotten rid of that d_____ dust problem, for a while at least. The dust, like the rain, is the worst I have ever seen. We'll make out all right because each of us is griping about the same things and after a little while of that, the situation gets to be funny. Mac and I stood out in the pouring rain today and almost died laughing at each other. I guess if things keep going that way, we can stand most anything."

Like most of his men, Harvey and Betty spent a lot of time thinking about their life after the war. Betty saved the money he was able to send her, and they shared their ideas about buying a home. Harvey thought they could maybe find a four- or five-room house for under $5,000 (Note: that would be about $72,000 as I write this in 2021.) Betty had thoughts about opening a music store of her own or going into partnership with someone else. Harvey noted, "...the money won't earn anything if it's kept in the bank, and it's just possible that we can use it to an advantage in another way." Harvey had been wanting to send home some souvenirs, and he sent Betty a couple of small pieces of the local coral. He also hoped to send Rod a metal watch band like one he had seen a fellow officer wearing. The bands were made by a local from metal collected from a Japanese "Zero" that had been shot down over the island.

On Friday night Harvey was up late, writing his letter to Betty as he waited for a message. "I expect to be called out at any minute for a night job. They're expecting a plane part to come in about midnight, about half an hour from now, and I'm going to take the job myself rather than wake a couple of my crane operators out of a sound sleep. It's a heavy part, and rather delicate, so I'd rather tackle it myself. Besides, I like to operate these big cranes." The unit had worked late that afternoon, and they barely had time to grab a bite to eat before heading for the theater to see the evening's film. The movie was *Ladies of Washington*, with Trudy Marshall, Ronald Graham, and Anthony Quinn. Harvey had already seen it but felt it was still a good way to spend an evening.

Saturday night's film was a bigger hit. *Saratoga Trunk*, starring Ingrid Bergman and Gary Cooper. "It was one of those pictures that leaves you feeling as if you've seen something special.... It's supposed to be a new picture, and it was as far as we are concerned, but probably you've already seen it. If not, please don't miss it, I know you'll like it. Ingrid Bergman makes a performance that will be remembered for a long while." *(Note: Ingrid Bergman did receive an Academy Awards nomination that year, not for this film, but for The Bells of St. Mary's.)* Before the movie began, a GI band from another part of the island played a half-hour program: "they were really good and would rank with quite a few of the top bands I've heard! ...But our real treat will come on July 1st when we are to have Dick Jurgens and his band. Boy, that will be the day! Looks as if our little theater is beginning to break into the big time. Sure hope they keep bringing on big shows like that! I'll bet there won't be one vacant seat that night."

Another officer, a Lt. Milleville, had been assigned to help Harvey. He would be responsible for the maintenance of all equipment, and Harvey was happy to have the help. The two seemed to quickly hit it off, and Harvey felt, "that between the two of us we can turn out a crack job. I hope so because there is a big job to do."

Another Sunday rolled around, and this one marked seven months since Harvey and Betty were married. As usual, the unit worked all morning, but Harvey was in a melancholy mood and spent the afternoon hanging out in his quarters. Actually, he now had a bit more space to hang out in. "The four officers occupying our end of the building have been reduced to two...Lt. Leonard and myself. Lt. Teach has an indefinite stay in the hospital with some kind of blood disturbance, and Capt. Loader is on detached service for a couple of months. So, Leonard and I have spread out in a big way. Mac and Peck are in the next room but as partitions haven't been put up, it's all like one big room. Leonard is a good guy from Texas that I didn't know until we got here." In his section of the quarters, Harvey had packed everything he had brought with him (including his chess set) in a "wardrobe" he had built out of packing crates. After the build-up about Guam's "rainy season," the lack of rain the past few days was almost disappointing: "we haven't had any rain for almost three whole days. This is supposed to be the local rainy season and all we've had is one day and a night of hard rain. None of us are kicking about it at all, but after being all built up for three or four months of steady down pour, we feel a little let down. If it would rain hard for three or four hours in the middle of each night, the dust would stay settled, the days would be sunny, and everyone would be happy about the whole thing." Harvey's letter to Betty was a long one that day, and he filled her in on some details of daily camp life: "We're getting a limited amount of fruit juice at our PX now and it is given out according to ration cards that everyone has. The beer, cokes, and now fruit juice is punched on a card so that every man, officers and enlisted men alike, gets a certain amount of the stuff each week. Tuesday is our 'drinkless' day every week so most everyone tries to stock up on everything to hold him over. We get six bottles of beer, four cokes, and two-pint cans of fruit juice each week, and you can buy it every day in the week or buy your whole week's supply at once. That's a good deal because lots of times some of the men want to go on a small sized binge, and in that case they get up to six bottles of beer at one time. I couldn't drink more than one bottle at a time, but some of these guys pour it down as if they had a hollow leg." In a later letter, Harvey said what he really missed in Guam was "a glass of ice-cold milk!" A marine had come around the camp that day, wanting to trade a Japanese flag for four quarts of liquor, he didn't find any takers, mainly because no one had four quarts of anything. The marines and a few of the other outfits had been in Guam for some time and had picked up most of the "souvenirs" that were to be found. Since no one had money, there was a thriving souvenir-for-liquor barter operation. Harvey thought that the flag seemed authentic but had to pass on it.

The movie that night (*True to the Army*, with Ann Miller and Alan Jones) was, as Harvey put it, "pretty much of a stinkeroo."

The roads around the camp and airfield were a problem, and on Wednesday Harvey's men began to address the problem: "we made preparations and procured the equipment to begin oiling the roads around the area. We have quite a few roads and... what a difference it'll make, both with the condition of the roads and the dust problem. After we finally get our roads in shape, their maintenance will be a very minor problem. As it is now, I've got to have two or more pieces of equipment permanently assigned to road maintenance just so they are barely smooth enough to ride on. From now on, though, things will be different." The movie that night was *Keys to the Kingdom*, with Gregory Peck. Harvey liked it. "Kind of solemn, but once in a while a picture like that does a guy a lot of good. It keeps a man from losing himself in his own self-centered ideas.... With acting and a story like that in front of you, it forces you away from thinking about yourself. I don't mean that it is a cure all, but it does put your thinking along other lines for a change."

The weather changed again on Thursday. "Just as I was griping about how dry the weather was, it cut loose with a big fat rainstorm tonight. And right in the middle of the movie!! It came up so fast that we were all soaked before we knew what was happening, so none of us bothered trying to keep dry. We just sat there and watched with the rain coming down in sheets. When I got back to the barracks I was soaked to the skin, not a dry stitch of clothes. My shoes were full of water as were all of my pockets. It was sure a mess but lots of fun at the same time because every man in the barracks was in the same fix!" It had dried off by Friday evening, and the men were back at the theater to see *She Gets Her Man*, a comedy with Joan Davis..."talk about screwy shows. This one took the cake!"

Harvey tried to keep in touch with his friends from Pittsburgh, especially those who were in the Service. It was difficult, as he often didn't know where they were stationed, and communication with them was challenging. Occasionally, though, a letter did get through. He had sent a V-mail note to Howard Sperber, a good friend he had worked with at the Duquesne Light Company in Pittsburgh before the war. Both were engineers. The V-mail message reached Howard, and he wrote a reply. Unfortunately, the letter was misaddressed, and it took the US Army Postal Service over three weeks to finally find Harvey and deliver his mail! Howard was a Pfc. with the 129th Airborne Engineering Battalion, stationed in Auxerre, France. The 129th had been sent to France in the closing phase of the European war. After VE Day, they were part of the Occupation forces and were awaiting redeployment to the Pacific. Howard's letter has survived and gives an interesting glimpse of the situation at the time. "Dear Harvey, I had heard you had left, headed for the Pacific somewhere. Keep up your good work, keep the B-29's flying, fields to land on, etc. They are certainly pounding the heck out of Japan. Boy, anything like that I'm all for because we'll be headed that way some day and the more damage they do, the easier it will be for the soldiers...You have been in a long time now, haven't you, Harvey? 3 1/2 years? Art [another of their friends] was, shall we call it lucky, to get out. I hope he has fully recovered and is O.K. now. You are still in the Engineers, aren't you? You must be attached to the Air Force as the Engineer Officer? Do you remember George Wilson who played football for Wilkinsburg about the same time you did? He's a paratrooper now, a lieutenant in the Medics attached to our division. I don't care much for the country of France. Paris is OK, though. It's altogether different from the rest of the country. I didn't get to see much of Germany, but the parts that aren't laid waste and ruined by bombs are very beautiful. Sadly, all those stories of atrocities there are true.... I'll try to drop you a line from the States...it is rumored we may go through the States on our way to Japan. Howard." Another old friend, Ralph Haver, who had graduated with Harvey from Fort Belvoir and had been his roommate at Patterson Field, wrote from Smoky Hill Army Airfield in Salina, Kansas. Harvey and Ralph had also been stationed together in Spokane. "In your letter, I was particularly interested in the Utilities setup you described. It sounds like an efficient way of doing business. Rumors...seem to indicate that we're bound for an area a little closer in than you are. I'm going to practice up for my running, so I can dive into a foxhole!"

Another Pittsburgh friend was Jean Robinson, a girl he had once dated and whose family went to the same church as the Browns. She and her family remained close friends with him, and Harvey's parents kept in touch with them as well. Jean had married Regis "Rege" Dietz, an airman and another of their Pittsburgh friends. Seven months after the wedding, his plane went down in the South Pacific, and he was listed as Missing in Action:

The Department of Defense POW/Missing Personnel Office (DPMO) announced today that the remains of a U.S. Serviceman, missing in action from World War II, have been identified and are being returned to his family for burial with full military honors. Army Air Forces 2nd Lt. Regis E. Dietz, 28, of Pittsburgh, will be buried on April 8 in Bridgeville, Penn. Dietz, along with 11 other crew members, took off on Oct. 27, 1943, in their B-24D Liberator from an airfield near Port Moresby, New Guinea. Allied plans were being formulated to mount an attack on the Japanese redoubt at Rabaul, New Britain. American strategists considered it critical to take Rabaul in order to support the eventual invasion of the Philippines. The crew's assigned area of reconnaissance was the nearby shipping lanes in the Bismarck Sea. But during their mission, they were radioed to land at a friendly air strip nearby due to poor weather conditions. The last radio transmission from the crew did not indicate their location. Multiple search missions in the following weeks did not locate the aircraft.

Following World War II, the Army Graves Registration Service conducted searches for 43 missing airmen, including Dietz, in the area but concluded in June 1949 that all were unrecoverable. In August 2003 a team from the Joint POW/MIA Accounting Command (JPAC) received information on a crash site from a citizen in Papua New Guinea while they were investigating another case. He also turned over an identification card from one of the crew members and reported that there were possible human remains at the site of the crash. Twice in 2004 other JPAC teams attempted to visit the site but were unable to do so due to poor weather and hazardous conditions at the helicopter landing site. Another team was able to successfully excavate the site from January to March 2007 where they found several identification tags from the B-24D crew as well as human remains. Among other forensic identification tools and circumstantial evidence, scientists from JPAX and the Armed Forces DNA

Identification Laboratory used mitochondrial DNA - which matched that of Dietz's nephew - in the identification of his remains.

Lt. Dietz was awarded a Purple Heart, and his remains were later moved to the National Cemetery of the Alleghenies in Cecil, Pennsylvania. When Jean wrote to Harvey on July 5, 1945, she knew that her husband's plane had gone down, and that he was listed as MIA. Jean didn't talk about her own loss in her letter, but shared news about other friends. She noted that "There was a picture in Life Magazine last week of a portion of Guam. It has been made into quite a place, hasn't it? There was also quite an article in today's Post-Gazette about the airfields you fellows are building there."

The predicted heavy rains had finally arrived in Guam. The weather slowed progress for Harvey's unit, but they continued to work on setting up the camp and on runway construction. By the end of the month, the pace was hectic: "We really had a busy day at our heavy equipment unit today. There were more jobs to do than we could even begin. By stretching things quite a bit we managed to get a little done on each job and keep everyone happy so that we don't have anyone on our necks. If we get much busier though, I don't know what we'll do for bulldozers and graders. It seems everything has to be done at once, and each officer thinks his job should be done first. Gets pretty hectic sometimes, but that keeps us well occupied."

Harvey received a letter from Rod with his graduation announcement and a school newspaper. He was sorry he'd miss the ceremony because "It's the only chance I could have had to see someone close to me graduate from high school. That is, until you and I sit in the front row and watch our children as they get their diplomas."

Harvey finished a letter to Betty on Friday, June 30th and then turned in early. He had another busy day scheduled for Saturday, and he wanted to have enough energy left for the Dick Jurgens show coming to the camp that night.

Meanwhile, Harvey's parents were listening to a weekly radio program, *Meet Your Navy*, broadcast from Guam. "Of course, I know you wouldn't be on a navy program, but I wish I could hear your voice...your work is helping in a big way...the commentators and the different ones that come back from the war areas certainly give the engineers all the credit in the world. They say (you) are doing a magnificent job.... you are getting experience and education that no one can ever take from you and will be of value to you the rest of your life. Now we are listening to crewmen talking from a submerged submarine in Pacific waters..."

18

SNEAK PREVIEW OF

ANCHORS AWEIGH

Friday was June 1st, and Betty continued to be busy at Stella's. Stacks of records came in, and she spent the afternoon on the phone with customers who had placed orders. That evening on the ten o'clock news, she heard that the war effort in the Pacific was far ahead of schedule "due to the hard work of the Army Engineers and Seabees in Guam," and that "officials in Washington send congratulations." She was happy to hear war news that struck so close to home. She and Harvey had been discussing the pros and cons of his staying in the regular Army for a ten-year tour of duty. He would be young enough when he was released to go into some other line of work, and she said she would support whatever decision he thought was best. Saturday was always a busy "record buying day" at Stella's, and Betty worked all day. She had told Mr. Stella she would quit at the end of May if her salary wasn't increased, and she worried all day about how she would handle the situation if there was no resolution by the end of the day. However, when he wrote out her paycheck at the end the day "he casually said that starting this week he was going to pay me the 65 cents an hour we had discussed. And he said if things worked out any better at the store he would see about more." That day she also received her first uncensored letter from Harvey. June was off to a good start.

On Saturday, Betty and Rod went to the movies. They went to the Wilshire Theatre on Wilshire Boulevard in Santa Monica and saw *Earl Carroll Vanities* and *Flame of Barbary Coast*. Both films had recently been released by Republic Pictures, which primarily made low budget B-level movies. The Wilshire had opened in 1930, an example of the Art Deco style theatres built during the Depression era. Although Rod and Betty enjoyed the earthquake scenes in the second film, the movies were quite long, and they left feeling "almost numb."

Mr. Stella was away on Monday attending a funeral, and Betty and the other girls at the store kept busy sorting another load of new records. As usual, business picked up in the afternoon when the high school students got out, and a thirteen-year-old boy came into the store, talking loudly and looking for records. The store was crowded, but the boy yelled out to ask Betty if she liked Tommy Dorsey and if she was going to see him that weekend at Casino Gardens in Ocean Park. When she said she hadn't planned on attending, the boy asked if she wanted to go with him. She politely declined, "but would give a dime to have a picture of everyone's faces standing around listening to us. I'll most likely be teased about that for some time."

When writing to Harvey, usually late at night, Betty would feel especially "connected" to him. But sometimes her loneliness would take over. Wednesday was one of those nights, and as she listened to music by Gilbert and Sullivan (*Pirates of Penzance* and *Yeoman of the Guard*), she missed him terribly. She had been active in the Job's Daughters organization for many years, and she still helped out with meetings and Installations of new officers. At the Installation on Saturday night, she ran into a couple of friends whose husbands were also serving in the Marianas. Mary Alyce Cole's husband was on Tinian Island in the Northern Marianas, about 120 miles from Guam—(a bomber called the Enola Gay would later take off from Tinian's North Field for a bombing run over Hiroshima). Betty wrote that another friend (Betty Lou Graner Jones) "has a husband near where you are, in fact he's in the 75th and was at Walker when you were. Betty Lou wasn't with him for they had a small son and couldn't find a place to stay with the baby." Talking with Betty Lou made Betty think of the family that she and Harvey were planning, and she sent Harvey a Father's Day card.

YANK, the Army Weekly was a magazine published by the military during World War II. Betty had a subscription, and she enjoyed reading each issue and looking for news about the war. She had just received the June 1st issue, and there was a spread on Guam and a story about the Pacific Theater.

Harvey's Aunt Peggy wrote with news from Pittsburgh. She had been appointed Assistant Finance Officer of the Veteran's Administration Hospital and was hoping to transfer again to the hospital's planned new site near the University of Pittsburgh. The new hospital would be the second largest in the

East. She wondered if Harvey had heard the news that Omar Bradley was the new Administrator of the Veteran's Administration.

Like most cities around the country, Los Angeles was still wildly celebrating the end of the European War. On Friday, June 9th, Gen. Patton and Lt. Gen. Doolittle flew into Municipal Airport (later known as Los Angeles International Airport), about six miles from Betty's home.

> George Patton and Jimmy Doolittle came home to Los Angeles yesterday - and Los Angeles took them to her arms.
>
> From the split second that their C-54 Skymaster planes - three of them - roared over the Municipal Airport, they were given thunderous welcomes in the style to which only conquerors are accustomed. As Gen. George S. Patton's plane rolled to a stop at the airport, scores of civic officials led by Mayor [Fletcher] Bowron, Army generals and the enlisted men right on down to the buck privates went to the side of the ship and welcomed him home. Attired in shiny steel helmet and bearing the four stars of his high rank, polished boots and a studded pistol, the leader of America's victorious 3rd Army stepped from the plane and snapped his salute to the "old hometown."
>
> After only a brief stop at the airport-until all the heroes could climb into command cars and jeeps provided for each one-there began the journey to Pico Blvd. and Broadway.... Strung all along the line, over the highways to City Hall, it was estimated that 1,000,000 persons - the occupants of the homes for which the generals and their men fought - waved their shouts of greetings to the soldiers.
>
> On June 10, the generals toured several cities around Southern California. During the visit Patton gave several speeches, believed to be the only time he addressed large numbers of American civilians. The Times reported that Patton's speeches were "peppered with profanity -- but mild to those who soldiered with him.

The parade ended at the City Hall in Los Angeles, where Betty's father worked as a clerk in the City Treasurer's Office. That evening 105,000 people filled the Los Angeles Colosseum to hear speeches by the Generals and presentations by city luminaries. Betty was unable to attend either the parade or the gathering in the Colosseum, but she and her family listened to radio coverage of the speeches. (She noted that the station finally had to shut off General Patten's microphone because of his profanity!) The weekend was emotionally charged, and for Betty, the presence of Doolittle made it even more so. She remembered that his famous raid on Tokyo in 1942 had happened only one day before she and Harvey had met at the USO dance. She sent Harvey a copy of that day's *Los Angeles Times*.

On Sunday, Betty and Rod went to the movies at the El Portal Theatre on Lankershim Boulevard in North Hollywood. They saw *Without Love* with Spencer Tracy and Katherine Hepburn, which Betty described as "one of the craziest pictures I've seen in a long time." She hoped Harvey would get a chance to see the film in Guam. She also mentioned a new Donald O'Connor and Peggy Ryan film (*Patrick the Great*); it hadn't been released yet, but she was eager to see it. With her Tuesday letter, she enclosed an article clipped from the *LA Times*. It had been sent from Guam and noted that 150 B-29 "Superfortresses from India have arrived at Tinian to join the Marianas based aerial offensive against Japan."

Early that next week, Rod, along with four other boys from Venice High, was interviewed on the General Electric Radio Program. Rod's father was unable to hear the show, but his mother called the station for recordings of the program to be used as a Father's Day gift.

On Thursday, another shipment of records came into Stella's. There were several RCA recordings by Glenn Miller, including "Moonlight Serenade," "Little Brown Jug," "Pavanne," and "Pennsylvania." Miller had died in December when his plane went down over the English Channel, and his recordings were wildly popular, especially with big band fans like Betty and Harvey. In her letter that night, she included a newspaper clipping about the recent wedding of Deanna Durbin and her producer, Felix Jackson, and the upcoming wedding of Judy Garland and Vincente Minelli. The Garland marriage would take place at Judy's home in Southern California, and Louis B. Mayer, head of MGM would give away the bride.

Stella's had opened in 1935, and on Friday there was a celebration of the store's Tenth Anniversary. Mrs. Stella sent a basket of flowers, and Betty brought flowers from home. Occasionally people from the nearby entertainment industry would come by the store. For about a month, a pretty teenaged girl had been buying records from Betty, who was hoping to introduce her to Rod. When she got home from work that Friday, Betty was surprised to see the girl's picture on the cover of the July issue of *Woman's Home Companion*! In a letter that day, Betty told Harvey about the girl and about an MGM actor who regularly came in to buy records. His name was Arthur Walsh, and Betty and Harvey had seen him in *Two Girls and a Sailor*, playing a shy sailor who danced the jitterbug with Gloria DeHaven. Walsh was working on a new war movie with John Wayne and Robert Montgomery (*They were Expendable*). Betty found him to be shy and friendly, and she hoped that she and Harvey could see another of his films.

Betty and Harvey often shared their thoughts about having a family and buying a home after the war. "It will be wonderful to have our own home... just think of it—an American home, full of peace and love to bring up our children in." *(Note: as I went through these letters in 2020, it was interesting to hear how certain Harvey and Betty were in 1945 that the world after "their war" would be safe, peaceful, and conflict-free for their children.)*

Betty was considering buying a season ticket for the summer *Symphonies Under the Stars* series at the Hollywood Bowl. Box seats cost $24 for the series, which would begin in the middle of July. "Someday I hope we can go to these concerts together—they are held at the Hollywood Bowl. It is really beautiful and inspiring to sit in that big amphi-theater under the stars and hear such moving music."

Sunday was Father's Day. Betty's family went to Venice High School for the Baccalaureate service, and then after her dad had opened his gifts, they all went to the movies. They saw *Strange Illusions* and *Patrick the Great*, the movie she had told Harvey about earlier. It was a busy week for them all, with Rod graduating from high school on Thursday the 21st. Given the ongoing war, it was an especially emotional ceremony. Betty noted "everything was so serious—the trend of the times makes the high school age so much older. They seem to have to accept so many responsibilities—but I guess they can do it."

Betty and Rod tried to get to as many concerts as possible. In June, they attempted to get tickets to *Carmen Jones*, the climax of the Los Angeles Civic Light Opera Association's season at the Philharmonic Auditorium. Billy Rose's jazz adaptation of Bizet's opera *Carmen*, with the original Broadway cast, was completely sold out, but they were determined to get seats for *Rose Marie* during its LA run at the Philharmonic.

Betty and Harvey saved all of their letters (little did they know that they would serve as the source material of this current project—seventy-five years later!). In her letter to Harvey on Friday, Betty wrote "I have all your letters tied together now with red, white and blue ribbon, and I keep them in my little stand by the bed. There is quite a stack by now." In Guam, Harvey was concerned that his footlocker would soon overflow.

On Sunday, it had been exactly seven months since Harvey and Betty's wedding. Betty sent a letter written on an anniversary card. He also received a letter from his aunt: "We are having quite a parade in Pittsburgh tomorrow (Monday, June 25th) ...64 Army heroes will land here after a 19-hour flight from Paris. Three generals and 35 other officers, Gen Devers, Lt. Gen. Simpson and Gen McNarney!" Devers commanded the 6th Army Division in the European Theater, Simpson commanded the 9th Army Division, and McNarney served as the Supreme Allied Commander of the Mediterranean Theater. The parade, twenty-three-miles-long, began at the County Airport and ended downtown at the City-County building:

> Three huge, four-engined Army transports will roar into County Airport tomorrow afternoon from the battlefields of Europe, bringing 64 be-rib-boned heroes to the most thunderous welcome in Pittsburgh history. They will be men who helped to plan the campaign that licked the Axis. They will be men who won undying fame in foxholes, tanks and planes. They will be men who knew the hedgerows of Normandy, the Anzio beach-head, the Remagen bridge, the Battle of the Bulge, the Battle of Germany. Many were wounded, nearly all were decorated, all have done their part, and more.... Ten of these heroes are from Pittsburgh...The official welcome will be given at the City-County Building by Gov. Edward Martin, Mayor Cornelius D. Scully and John J. Kane, Chairman of the County Commission. The top three rankers, Gen. Joseph T. McNarney, Gen. Jacob L. Devers, and Lt. Gen. William H. Simpson, will give brief responses to speeches of welcome. Following the official welcome, the group will go to the William Penn Hotel, where rooms have been reserved for each man, so that they may have private reunions with their families and friends.

Similar celebrations, featuring Gen. Eisenhower and Gen. Bradley, were held in Washington and New York. Peggy worked for the Veteran's Administration and had heard that Bradley would take his leadership position with the VA on August 1, 1945.

That week Betty expressed worry about Harvey's headaches related to dynamite blasting. She also discussed the "problem" of saving the mounting stack of letters that she was sending him. She had been sending him tin containers filled with records, and she suggested filling the tins with her letters and sending them back to her. She could then use the tins to send more records (a 1945 version of recycling?).

She told Harvey about a visit from an old friend, Jack Cassett, (their two families had been close for years). He had served for three years with the 32nd Infantry Division in the Pacific and had been wounded the previous November during the Battle of Limon in Leyte (the Philippines). There had been 1,498 American casualties in the battle (killed, wounded, and missing in action). As noted in the 32nd's website: "The cost had been great, but X Corps had secured the northern entrance to the Ormoc Valley and could now continue its push south to link up with XXIV Corps to eventually complete the eviction of the Japanese from Leyte."

The proximity of the music store to the motion picture studios paid a dividend for Betty on Friday. A friend from the cartoon department at MGM told her about a sneak preview of the studio's new movie *Anchors Aweigh*. After buying a fifty-dollar War Bond, she went to the movie with her friend, Elsie. "There is one bit of cartooning in it where Gene [Kelly] dances with a mouse that's really wonderful. We got to the Fox-Westwood Village at 7, and it was 8:15 before we got in! The line was over 2 blocks long—sneak preview! I think everyone in California must have heard about it, mostly 'bobby sockers.' – It really had an all-star cast with Kathryn Grayson, José Iturbi, Frank Sinatra, Gene Kelly. I hope Guam gets hold of it right away for it is wonderful, and it's California! Some places in it made me remember the places we'd been, especially the candle shop in Olvera Street. Had some real good shots of M.G.M. Studios. It's hard to believe I work in walking distance from the place."

19

OUT OF THE JUNGLE

TO SURRENDER

That Sunday was a busy day at Northwest Field. The men worked all morning, stopping at noon for a large turkey dinner served in the mess hall. However, the evening's entertainment was the day's highlight. Harvey and the others had been looking forward to this show for days.

Dick Jurgens was an American orchestra leader from California. After a successful, seventeen-week run at San Francisco's St. Francis Hotel in 1933, the band toured up and down the West Coast and in Chicago at the Aragon Ballroom. They spent eight years on Catalina Island, performing at the Casino there. They appeared regularly on national radio broadcasts and recorded for a number of labels, including Decca, Columbia, and Mercury. In 1943, Jurgens broke up his band and joined the Marines as a radio operator. He switched to the Entertainment Section and formed The Dick Jurgens All Marine Show, a music and comedy revue "recognized as one of the first and most successful non-USO 'soldier shows.'" On March 25th, 1945, the troupe began an extensive tour of the Pacific. "For two years, they played 148 shows, often in outdoor theaters...in, or near, active zones, where USO shows rarely penetrated: Tarawa, Kwajalein, Eniwetok, Saipan, Leyte"—and Guam. Harvey and his unit saw them there on July 1, 1945!

"Then at 6 o'clock we had the big stage show that we had been waiting for. Dick Jurgens and his All-Marine band. It was a super duper show, fit for any Hollywood production. A first-rate performance if ever I saw one. It lasted for an hour and a half and could have gone on for hours more. We loved it!

I took a few notes on the program so you can get some idea of what it was all about. The band consisted of 6 saxophones, 4 trumpets, 3 trombones, a piano, an electric guitar, a bass fiddle, an accordion and a drum man plus a spare singer, three comedians and two extra men, a violinist and a guitarist who played hillbilly songs along with the bass fiddle player. The program ran something like this:

1. 'Somebody Stole My Gal,' with Woody Johnson, the guitarist doing the vocals
2. a little skit by a ventriloquist with two dummies
3. 'My Dreams are Getting Better All the Time' with Dick Smith, a saxophonist, singing
4. a skit by two comedians
5. 'Saturday Night is the Loneliest Night in the Week' with Wood Johnson
6. 'I'm Making Believe,' with Emmett Haugen doing vocals (he was really good!)
7. 'Accentuate the Positive' with Emmett Haugen again
8. 'Easter Parade'...Emmett Haugen
9. 'I Can't Give You Anything but Love', a band specialty number
10. 'Trolley Song' with a comedy skit
11. A medley, 'Tea for Two', 'I'll Get By', 'Just a Baby's Prayer at Twilight', 'Don't Get Around Much Anymore,' 'Porters Love Song to a Chambermaid', and 'Mama's Going - Goodbye'.
12. 'One O'clock Jump', a band specialty number
13. then a really silly skit about a Marine first sergeant
14. a special arrangement of Ravel's 'Bolero'
15. a trio playing cowboy and hillbilly songs (Billy Falcher, guitar; Jack Looney (violin), Zeke Zimmer (bass)
16. the finale - 'Rum and Coca Cola' with Dick Smith doing vocals

You can imagine what a wonderful show it was. All those G.I.'s just screamed and whistled all the way through." In October, Jurgens and his troupe performed for President Harry Truman at a White House press banquet.

After the Jurgens show, the unit unpacked their ice cream machine and made the first batch of ice cream. "...every man in the 75th had at least one pint of ice cream! Not the fine stuff that you buy in the States, but plenty good for G.I. ice cream. We don't have fresh milk to put in it, and we have to use a ready-made mix that we brought from the States, but it was the first we have had since we landed here, and I didn't hear a single man griping about it.... that's not bad at all for being out in the middle of the Pacific!"

On Monday, it had been exactly three months since Harvey and Betty had said goodbye at the train station in Hays, Kansas: "exactly 3 months since I saw you last, and strangely enough, it's again a Monday. I'll never forget that morning! The saddest day I've ever known! You were so beautiful and sweet, and yet so sad. The idea that hit me hardest was the fact that you were sad, and yet there was nothing I could say or do that would help." He was trying to find something special to send to Betty, perhaps a bracelet made by the local man who had fashioned a watch band for him. "I'd like to find something really nice to get you, but the natives don't make very many things, and what they do make is rationed for sale at various Post Exchanges. Our particular PX may not have any items for sale for several months yet. Possibly not at all. We saw a picture tonight, 'Music in Manhattan,' that made me really lonesome for you. I missed you so during the show that, if it hadn't been so funny in spots, I think I'd have walked out in the middle of it."

Wednesday was the Fourth of July, but on Guam it was quiet. Few of the men stationed there even mentioned the holiday. The government was selling savings bonds to servicemen that were offering various enticements, some more successful than others. "They made a big to-do about buying bonds last Saturday and used as a selling point, the fact that every bond would have printed on it 'Purchased on the island of Guam.' Well, I thought I'd buy one to put in Junior's fund. So, today they came back to us with those exact words on them, but <u>typewritten</u>. Can you imagine that? Shucks, that doesn't mean a thing. Who's to say that you didn't type it on yourself? It's a pretty good way to sell bonds, but it made a lot of guys pretty mad, too! And I'm one of them."

Harvey drove to Agaña today to try and find some items of heavy equipment that he needed. On the way back, he picked up a Marine officer that had seen action on most of the fronts in the Pacific and South Pacific. "When we came to his station, he asked me in for a drink. It was a revelation! He took me into a bar they had built, and a boy behind the bar served us one of the most delicious drinks I have ever tasted. It was a Lord Calvert whisky with plain water and ice. Actually, it was no different than any such drink I've had in the States, but coming at a time like that, and in a hot, dusty place like this, it tasted delicious. It's the first drink of liquor I've had since leaving the States, and I really did enjoy it. I ordered your bracelet today, too. I don't have any idea how long it will take him to finish it, but when he gets it completed, I'll send it to you. Incidentally, I saw the Japanese Zero that he's using for his aluminum supply, so that makes it authentic."

On Thursday, Harvey and his team focused on routine maintenance. "We had to dynamite one big tree in the middle of the motor pool but that's about all. This tree was really a big one, and it took 15 1/2 pounds of explosive to cut it down. That's quite a bit to use on one tree, but it had to be used because of the tree's size. It really made quite a blast and then laid the tree right on the ground beside the stump. A pretty good job, if I do say so myself. The movie tonight was 'Having Wonderful Crime', which has been ballyhooed long and loud. Even though it was a pretty good picture, I was a little disappointed. Guess I expected too much. The picture did have Carole Landis, who drew 'oohs' and 'ahhs' from everyone."

On Friday, the men were treated to an offshore spectacle. "We saw a waterspout off the coast of the island today, and talk about thrilling sights. It looked like a long, wavy, black snake extending from the ocean to a huge black cloud that hung rather low in the sky. It didn't get close enough for us to see what was happening on the surface of the water near it, but it came plenty close enough for me. Those things are wicked, especially if you happen to be out in a small boat when it hits you." The men had heard they were due for a typhoon. There hadn't been one for four or five years, which was the usual interval between these storms. "I hope I'm well tied down to something when that comes along. The natives say that there isn't much danger so long as you stay flat on the ground while it's going on. I suppose that's to avoid being hit by flying objects and if that's the case, you can bet that little Harvey will have himself a great big hole handy to dive into. None of this 'flying object' stuff for me!"

Harvey went on duty as O.D. (Officer of the Day) at 4:30 Saturday afternoon. After lunch on Sunday, he went back to his barracks, hoping to relax before going back on duty. "Who should walk in but Bob Anthony and two of his buddies! He's Peggy Anthony's brother...she's the girl that lives up the street from us in Wilkinsburg...you met her at our house when we were home in February. He was so grown up that I didn't even know him at first. He's an Aircraft Mechanic's Mate, second class, which makes him the equivalent to an Army Staff Sgt. He lives down on the other end of the island, about 30 miles from here, so I threw them all in my jeep and we took a long ride to have some time to ourselves, O.D. or no O.D. He's only 19, and isn't married yet of course, but he's got a special girl back home. He gets in some flying time because he's a qualified gunner and said if I'd come down sometime, he'd fix me up with a flight in a Navy fighter. He showed me a Japanese Zero that had been wrecked alongside a Japanese Mitsubishi. I got a piece of the Mitsubishi right out of the 'rising sun' painted on its wing. I'll send it as soon as I can. Also, we found a Japanese whisky bottle that I'm keeping (empty, of course). On the way back to his station, we stopped at two different cemeteries to look for a Lt. Richard Bull, U.S.N. He's a boy from Wilkinsburg that we both knew. He was killed here, and I'd like to find his grave. At one cemetery, we found a little plot set aside where seventeen Marine War Dogs were buried. Those guys really thought a lot of their dogs."

Harvey went to the movies again on Sunday and saw a double feature. As far as he was concerned, both were "stinkeroos." "One picture was 'Carolina Blues' with Kay Kyser, and I don't even remember the name of the second one. They were both pretty bad and except for the singing of a girl in the second picture, the whole evening would have been wasted. I think her name was Betty Rhodes but I'm not sure. Somebody said she used to sing with Bob Chester, but I'm not sure of that either. It started raining about halfway through the first picture, and it's still coming down...not hard, but steady with lots of lightning." It's likely that Betty Rhodes' film, *You Can't Ration Love*, was the movie that Harvey saw that evening. It was to be Rhodes' last movie, after which she concentrated on her radio and recording career.

Harvey was still having trouble sleeping. "Last night I went to bed pretty early, thinking that I'd be in much better shape today, but actually I think I'm more tired tonight than I was last night. Sleep is something you just can't get enough of in this climate...I can't understand it.

"It looks like we're going to get a break next on a U.S.O. show next Tuesday and are scheduled to see the Eddie Bracken show with Peggy Ryan! That should be a super duper one, especially with that crazy Peggy Ryan in the cast. I haven't seen her in a movie since I left the States, and I've been looking forward to seeing her new picture, the one you mentioned, never expecting to see her in person. I'll write you all about it after the show."

Eddie Bracken and Bob Hope took separate USO "camp shows" to the Pacific during the summer of 1945. Bracken's troupe, the only USO show sponsored by the Navy in the Pacific Theater, visited military bases, hospitals, and aircraft on Guam, Saipan, Tinian, and Ulithi, as well as Peleliu in the Palau chain—while Hope's group went to other locations, including the Solomon Islands. Bracken's tour included Peggy Ryan, singer Maxine Conrad, dancer Roberta Stevenson, the comic duo Gil Gilbert and Virginia Lee, and a young accordionist, Shirley Gallagher. Gallagher, who passed away in April 2020 (at the age of 98!), kept a diary and later wrote a book about her experiences on the tour. She remembered that the show was always the same. She opened with "Wall Street Rag," "Alabama Bound," and "St. Louis Blues." "I never got tired of playing the same songs. The men were so appreciative and always clapped for an encore." On one occasion, Rear Admiral Richard Byrd, the noted Arctic and Antarctic explorer, gave her the stars off his collar as a keepsake. She kept in touch with Bracken until his death in 2002.

Bracken later told a story about being awarded a medal by the military for a curious episode on Guam. "An Army base was showing his movie, "The Miracle of Morgan's Creek", when two Japanese fell out of a tree, and they gave me credit for capturing them. They were UCLA men and could speak English fluently, and they literally fell out of the tree laughing and were captured."

However, despite the big build up for the Eddie Bracken show, Harvey and Mac along with many others in their unit, were a bit disappointed. "Parts of it were pretty good, Eddie Bracken himself, for instance, but Peggy Ryan wasn't at all good. Besides those two there were three other girls, a dancer, an accordionist and another dancer, acrobatic this time, and a male comedian making a total of six people in the cast. The dancers didn't do much but toss the 'body beautiful' in the faces of a lot of very eager G.I.'s. Bracken was plenty good and put on two very good pantomimes, one of a baseball player and one of a boxer, that had us all rolling in the aisles. Peggy Ryan danced with four or five G.I.'s on stage and did a tap dance, all of which weren't bad, but not nearly as good as she is in the movies. We had the biggest crowd I've seen since the last time I was in Grand Central Station."

A rumor circulated that Bing Crosby would be coming for a show on Guam. "That will really be a show that I'd break my neck to see. There will never be another Crosby, and I aim to see this one as often as possible. He's my boy!!" Unfortunately, despite the rumors, Crosby's tour didn't include a Guam appearance.

"We just stopped writing for a few minutes to listen to a couple of news broadcasts, and they sound pretty darn good. We've just heard about the huge raids that are being made by planes from Admiral Halsey's fleet along with the B-29's from our islands. I wish those [Japanese] would give up and let us come home! If we can keep up the pace of bombing that we are setting now, it shouldn't take too long. I hope there doesn't have to be an invasion of Japan proper because it would mean a tremendous loss of life and I can't see the need for it. With the number of planes from here plus those from Okinawa, Iwo Jima, the Chinese coast, and on carriers, we should be able to crush the whole of Japan to a pulp. Sorry if that sounds a little blood thirsty, but that's the only way we'll beat them."

A rumor started circulating on the island that photography regulations would soon be relaxed. "So, if you can get hold of any #120 film, please grab it up and send it to me." He wanted to show Betty pictures of his Guam "home," and in that same vein, he asked her to send a copy of a recent magazine article. "Someone was telling me that Life Magazine ran a series of pictures on Guam not very long ago and we haven't been able to get a copy of it here. If you can get hold of that issue, send me the pictures so I can point out to you a few places that I've seen and know about."

The officers had reorganized their softball team and were scheduling games with other units. "We had a game tonight except that it was called off on account of a wet field. We have four more games scheduled for this week and I know darned well that all of them won't be rained out. The only trouble is that it gets dark awfully early and that forces us to start games around five o'clock. One team that we play has fixed lights on their field, so we usually play them a night game starting around 8:30 or 9:00 p.m. I would bet that we have one of the best officers' teams on the island, and that takes in a lot of territory. After we have a little practice and get into shape, we'll be hard to beat." This particular letter had been opened by a censor—perhaps a short-stop on an opposing team?

Betty had asked Harvey about the officer who had been assigned to help him. "You asked about Lt. Milleville. He's from the 76th Service Group which is one of the ones in our unit here (24th, 73rd, 75th, 76th). He's a Quartermaster Corps officer and was handling his group's transportation before they came to Guam. We have a good time working together, and I think we are doing a fairly good job of handling the heavy equipment. You also asked about Northwest Field. That's exactly where I am. That's our baby, and we aim to make the [Japanese] fear that field more than any other."

Mac and Harvey went back to the theater on Saturday. They weren't particularly impressed by the movie, but they enjoyed the show that preceded it: "...before the movie started, we had an all-native show that lasted over an hour. It wasn't professional at all, but it was so homey that it was good. They had seven or eight kids ranging from four to twelve and some of them were pretty good. They sang and danced and one little girl about seven years old played boogie-woogie on the piano. There was a girl about sixteen that did a grass skirt hula dance, and all their music was furnished by a piano and two guitars, all played by natives. The piano player and one guitar player were especially good.... actually, they got more cheers and whistles than the Eddie Bracken and Peggy Ryan show. These natives are touching in their efforts to remind us that they are proud of being Americans, and they strictly resent any references that they are anything other than U.S. citizens. They are citizens the same as Hawaiians or the inhabitants of any other United States possession."

Harvey had been working at the Duquesne Light Company in Pittsburgh when he enlisted in 1941. Many of his fellow engineers from Duquesne were now in the service, and they still tried to keep in touch. One of them, Ralph Horner, was the head of the Engineering and Construction Department and sent Harvey a list (typed, no less) of updates on everyone's whereabouts, including Harvey's:

Capt. Harvey Brown - at B-29 base in Guam.

Col. Bill Conwell - currently Chief of Staff of the A.A.F. Engineers in Naples, Italy.

Lt. Earl Dubas - on leave after being a prisoner in Germany for 10 months.... wants to get back to flying. His leave is up August 5th.

Lt. Art Dubel - discharged after foot injury which kept him in the hospital for several months.

Sgt. Eichner - now in the Philippines, engaged in emergency rescue work. Says he has seen Manila both from the ground and from a "flying bathtub."

Corp. Fred Fraer - back in India after a 30-day furlough during which he was married.

Lt. Ed Gue - last word was March 28th. The Marines had moved again into wetter and deeper mud. He is somewhere practicing electronics.

Ensign Bob Jarvis - married in February. Last word was from Norfolk.

Capt. Logan - no word since January, but at that time he was in France.

Capt. George Harper - no recent news. Last word was from Italy.

Cp. John McKree (sp?) - last letter on June 9th from Finschhafen, British New Guinea.

Sgt. Jim Fletcher - returned to U.S. after being interred in Switzerland for 9 months.

Pvt. Howard Sperber - he was in France when he last wrote (note: Harvey had received a letter from him).

Lt. Charles Stott (Navy) - at the Brooklyn Navy Yard. Has been transferred from ship repair to new construction. The Franklin put in there for repairs, and he said it is really messed up. *(Note: the USS Franklin, an aircraft carrier, had been bombed March 19th, in the Pacific, with 807 killed and 487 wounded, second most in the war, behind only the battleship Arizona.)*

Lt. Mac Vetter - long time no news. Last word was from Chante Field, Illinois, where he was in Air Technical Service Command training.

Lt. Craig Williams - recently received letter of commendation for devising a mirror system for orientation of 40 mm. guns.

Capt. Don Young - distinguished Flying Cross for "extraordinary achievement while serving as lead navigator."

Sgt. Jean Francis - returned to U.S. after long stretch of duty in Africa and vicinity.

Cpl. John A. Cohan - confined to a hospital in Arizona.

T/Sgt. James Morrison - Air Control Tower Chief on air strip in Saipan. Written up in an Army magazine for ability of his crew to bring in B-29's in the shortest time ever established.

C.M. 2/c Ed. J. Saltece - somewhere in Pacific.

S/Sgt. George R. Kerr - released after being prisoner in Germany for 14 months. Lost 25 pounds in prison on a 60-day furlough before going to a Miami rest camp.

C.M. Ralph H. Jamieson - with the U.S. Navy Seabees in the Survey Corps working on an air strip on Samar.

Cpt. John McKinley - in the Philippines.

Pvt. Frank Flanders - last heard as he was about to leave San Francisco for overseas duty.

Pvt. Ed L. Auth - in basic training at Camp Wheeler, Georgia.

Seaman 1/c E.V. Rymer- just finished boot training at Great Lakes, expect to go to Radio School in Chicago.

Lt. John W. Lambert (Navy) - flying out of the Aleutians.

Seaman 1/c J.D. Hutchinson - not heard from Jan. was somewhere in France doing work for the Navy on shore.

GM 3/c Jack Wallace - somewhere in the Philippines doing office work for the Navy.

Yeo 2/c Jimmie Craig - yeoman on USS Chauvenet in the Pacific.

Seaman 2/c William Koecher (sp?) - stationed at U.S. Naval Repair Base, San Diego. Waiting for assignment to a ship.

Pfc. Eddie Miller - stationed at Compiegne, France. Expects to be moved to Munich, Germany with the Army of Occupation.

Bernard McCullough - discharged from Seabees after 2 years in South Pacific.

Two things jump out when reading this letter: the number of men from Pittsburgh and, by extension from the whole country, that were away from home serving in the military was unbelievable; and those with engineering backgrounds were needed everywhere.

Betty wrote to Harvey with some remembrances of their time in Spokane, and her letter brought back his own memories. "It was really a beautiful two weeks, wasn't it?" As expected, picture-taking regulations were relaxed, and Harvey again asked her to send him film. "We are allowed to take pictures of very limited subjects but even as limited as it is, we can get a few good pictures. I managed to get a few on the boat, but I haven't had them developed yet so I don't know how they will turn out...we did see quite a few things that I want you to see.

"We had a brand-new movie tonight at the theater, 'Rhapsody in Blue' and it is really one of the classics. Please don't miss it whatever you do! Joan Leslie and a new male star play the leads along with Oscar Levant, Paul Whiteman, Hazel Scott and Walter Damrosch. And the music will have you sitting on the edge of your seat with your mouth open. It's the story of the life of George Gershwin and it's done to a turn. The best picture with the best music in a long, long time." The film was nominated for two Oscars, one for Best Sound Recording and the other for Best Music, Scoring of a Musical Picture. The "new male star" that Harvey mentions was Robert Alda, the father of Alan Alda.

That day Harvey discovered his unused day pass from Fort Lawton in Seattle and enclosed it with his letter. The pass had been issued for an overnight leave on April 10, 1945, two days before his ship, the *Kota Baroe*, had left for the Pacific. Harvey had been exhausted by the train trip from Kansas and didn't used the pass.

On Friday the 13th, the officers had a softball game..."and in the fifth inning, I came sliding home, ripping up the turf as well as my left hip and shin. I scored the run, but I don't it was worth it. I came back, took a shower, and then went down to the dispensary and had myself 'painted up.' I'm sitting here on an angle, trying to keep one 'cheek' from touching the chair. Incidentally, we lost the blame game, 4 to 1. Phooey on the whole works."

The heavy rain on Guam was becoming a problem. "We've been getting plenty of rain lately, in fact almost every low area around here is full of water. Drainage problems come to my department so I'm plenty busy trying to get rid of the water. The medics are after me too, because standing water in this climate always collects a lot of little 'wigglers' ...that means mosquitos. We don't have the facilities nor the material to initiate a large drainage project, so we are resorting to digging large sumps in the low areas. We use small bulldozers and dynamite to get a hole about 15 or 20 feet deep and at that depth we usually find fissures in the coral that will carry water away fairly rapidly. It's a slow process but it seems to be the only thing we can do. We are having trouble with the roads, too, because this hard rain washes away anything we try to use as a road surface. We've been able to get a little waste oil to coat the roads, but we'll have to get them in shape before we use it. And then pray for dry weather for a day or so after we apply the oil, to give it a chance to soak in before it's washed away. Sorry, here I go again, giving you a free lecture on road building when you don't give two hoots about it. I wonder how long it's going to be before we're back together again. It seems like years already, and yet I feel as if I'd never left you."

Saturday was "Hank" Milleville's day off, so Harvey worked during the morning. There was a softball game scheduled, but the field was still too soft. The team practiced for a bit, but finally gave up. "It's only now and then that we manage to sneak in a game or two. We play all we can, though, because that kind of exercise comes in handy." Betty had asked about of Harvey's friends, and he gave her a few updates in his Sunday letter. "The last we heard about Capt. Wood was about two months ago and that was very little. He had been released from the hospital and given another assignment. He has been given his majority and seemed plenty happy about it. 'Pat' Patton is going to leave us before very long and right now is sweating out transportation back to the States. He's getting a discharge and isn't too happy about it because he hates to leave the outfit. He's a swell guy, and I hate to lose him."

Ever since the Americans had retaken Guam, there were continuing incidents of Japanese coming out of the jungles to surrender. Harvey's mother had forwarded him an article from *Time* magazine, and he forwarded it to Betty.

THE ENEMY: Come with Us

For two hours the sound truck howled Japanese into the silent bamboo and sword grass of southern Guam's jungle. Suddenly from the green wall emerged a chubby, medium-sized young man, blinking in the sun. While U.S. officers watched, the Japanese man trudged up the hill and saluted. Then months after the U.S. recapture of Guam, the last Japanese officer was willing to talk surrender.

Asked the Americans with a face-saving phrase: did the officer "wish to come with us?" Said the officer, after considerable discussion, he would consider it. "Come-with-us" day was set, and the man returned to the jungle. Nine days later, while a Marine battalion gaped, the Japanese officer marched out with 33 infantrymen, plump from eating stolen U.S. C-rations, wearing stolen U.S. fatigue uniforms.

In more places than Guam, U.S. soldiers were beginning to detect some response to the blandishments of "come with us." On Okinawa 6,932 Japanese were prisoners (2,433 were Koreans and Okinawans). In the last few days, they had appeared in groups sometimes 50 strong, waving red, white and blue U.S. surrender leaflets. In the Philippines 609 surrendered to the 37th Division in 36 hours.

Some fissures were at last appearing in the armor of "Bushido" - the stern warrior code. By Western standards, the rate of surrender was still low indeed, but Japanese prisoners, once a rarity in the Pacific, were coming in as never before. Psychological warfare units worked hard to encourage more.

Another show at El Gecko on Tuesday! "We had another stage show tonight and it was one of the best so far. An all-G.I. cast with loads of talent. All of these boys belong on the professional stage. The show was followed by a lot of movie shorts and like a damned fool, I stayed to watch all of them. I should have come back and gone to bed...I've been up past midnight for three nights in a row, and I just can't take it in this climate. Tomorrow night I'm sure I'll get to bed early because there is no show or movie so all I'm going to do is write your letter." Along with the letter, Harvey also sent a package.... a bracelet... "made out of a metal strip from the red 'sun' on a Japanese Zero."

Harvey and an enlisted man in the unit took care of a blasting job the next day. "Sgt. Zierenberg and I did the job and its funny, but the fumes from that stuff (dynamite) affected both of us exactly alike. We both got mild headaches, which went away after a short while. The job was to make a soakage pit for one of the dispensaries. After our jack hammer and rock drill went down about four feet they were stopped, so we had to use dynamite. The hole was only 2 feet away from a Quonset hut, but we were lucky and did no damage to the building. Everyone was afraid we would probably level the place. Tomorrow we'll have a little more blasting to do on the same job, but there won't be the same chance of damage."

That evening after supper, the officers played a volleyball game with the men of the Utilities Section, and the officers team won two straight games. "Our team had Capt. Spellman, Lt. Leonard, Lt. Yarnas, Lt. Mayer ("Sol"),

Mac, and me. I was supposed to play softball, but I didn't get out of a meeting until after five, so I didn't have time to get to that game. Volleyball is loads of fun too, though, especially with these guys playing. We sure have a swell bunch. I don't think I've ever seen a better group of men and officers, both, all in one organization." They didn't go to the movies that night since Mac and Harvey had both seen it. "I don't remember the name of it, but Vera Hruba does the main honors – something about ice skating or some such stuff. It wasn't very good, if I remember." *(Note: the picture was Lake Placid Serenade.)* Harvey didn't go the next night, either.... "I had already seen 'Meet Me in St. Louis' twice, so I stayed home and wrote a letter to your folks and one to mine. I suppose they both fell over with the shock, but when I sit down to write a letter, I don't feel like writing to anyone but you."

The unit's workload on Friday wasn't especially heavy, but two pieces of equipment broke down and, combined with the heavy rain, it was a difficult day. The censorship regulations again eased up a bit, and Harvey was able to share a few more specifics. "The stop we made between here and Honolulu was at Eniwetok in the Marshall Islands, and it is a barren place if I've ever seen one. I'm sure glad we kept on going instead of parking there for the duration. Guam is bad enough. We can also now say that we are part of the 315th Bombardment Wing, which is in the 20th Air Force. When I get back, I'll be wearing one of those patches I bought in Los Angeles. The 315th B.W. is composed of 4 Service Groups and 4 Bomb Groups. The Service Groups are the 24th (Yates), the 73rd (Dangers), the 75th (me), and the 76th (Jay), while the Bomb Groups are the 16th, the 501st, the 502nd, and the 331st. Our flying field is almost completed, and most of our work is now concerned with improving our living conditions and getting our administrative setup in order. We are sending out pretty large numbers of B-29's on frequent raids against Japan and points West, not our full strength as yet, of course, but enough to give a darned good account of ourselves. It won't be long now before Japan will be feeling the full strength of the 315th." The B-29s of the 315th Bomb Wing concentrated their attacks on Japanese oil refineries and, in one fifty-day period, flew fifteen combat missions. Between August 30th and September 2nd, they also flew two major, and three smaller, POW missions, dropping food and supplies to American soldiers being held prisoner.

Harvey was an avid reader and would be for the rest of his life. Although access to books was difficult in the Pacific, the officers had established a small library and passed around their reading material, both books and periodicals. Harvey almost always found something that interested him. "Did I tell you about the book I read about a week or so ago? It's called 'The Scarlet King,' and is the story of Mary Magdeline. Pretty good, too. I've just started 'One Foot in Heaven' and it also looks like a good one. The author, Hartzell Spruce, has written another one, 'Get Thee Behind Me,' so if you see it anywhere, send it to me, will you? We have a number of books in our group library, and as soon as we get a more substantial building set up, we can draw about 2000 more books for the library. That should keep us all occupied for a while."

Saturday was another full day, although the morning began rather calmly. The barracks had been leaking under the heavy rains, so they managed to find nine rolls of roofing paper for the roof. After lunch, Harvey and four or five others stripped down to shorts and started putting on the roofing paper. None of them were experts, and it took a long while to get started, but after they got a system worked out, it moved along pretty well. They began work around two o'clock and finished a little after five, just in time to take a shower before dinner.

After supper, Harvey and Mac went down to the Chaplain's office where there was an electric record player. "Your four records came today, and I had to hear them right away.... they are really swell! 'You Made Me Love You,' is the most wonderful song ever written, and when Harry James plays it, my heart melts. While it was playing, I really felt how badly I miss you.

"An 'oldie', 'Destination Tokyo' was our movie tonight and I saw it for the second time. Just as good this time as before. In the picture, Cary Grant played lots of the feelings that I feel for you every minute of the day. If you have a chance, see it again and you'll know what I mean. It rained a little during the picture, but I hardly noticed."

Harvey had a chance to relax on Sunday and, after seeing Charles Laughton's picture, *Suspect*, with Mac, he wrote his daily letter to Betty. The two of them occasionally used code words when they wrote, but the relax-ation of the censorship rules allowed Harvey to open up a little. "You are cute when you ask me to talk about 'sunsets' [their code for his return to the States: ie., the end of the 'Rising Sun'], but I don't think I need to be nearly so secretive. We have no word here about any invasion yet and probably the first we hear about it will be by shortwave broadcast, possibly an hour or so before you hear it. From all indications, I feel fairly certain that our job here will be a 'duration job' which means there will be no "sunsets" on Guam for me until the war is over. I can say, though, that the planes from our field have been really plastering the Japanese homelands. I've watched several missions take off this week. It's getting to be more or less a 'milk run' with practically no resistance at the other end. The 315th Bomb Wing is making a pretty good name for itself.

"I took a ride in an ambulance tonight – on a stretcher in the back, too. Lt. Leonard took Bob Yates to the hospital for kidney observation, so I went along for the ride. Only room for two in the front, so I rode the stretcher rack in the back.

"We saw Ann Dvorak in a picture tonight with John Wayne. I haven't seen her since way back when I was in high school. She's still plenty good looking!"

Arthur "Mac" McKinney was Harvey's best friend on Guam. The two shared living space in the BOQ, worked closely with one another, and spent much of their down time going to movies, playing on various officers' sports teams, and teaming up for card games. "We sure have been sticking pretty close together since we left the States. We walk to work together and then I pick him up at noon in my jeep for lunch. At night, I pick him up for supper and after that we go to the show, and then write a letter or two. Sometimes, if the show doesn't sound good, or if we have seen it before, we just write letters and then lay on our bunks for a while talking. Since the four of us were together so much in Kansas, it gives us a lot to talk about and a lot of things in common." They talked about home, their wives, and their hopes to have children after the war. "We are really looking forward to the time when we can come down a gang plank and find you two at the end of it. I hope Dottie can see her way clear to getting out to California when we do come home."

The 24th was Betty and Harvey's "eight-month" anniversary. "It was only fitting that on our day, they have a really super deluxe show at the theater. It was the 128 Seabees Swing Band, and it couldn't have been a better show. Every doggone one of them was an accomplished musician and the band as a whole was better than most. The program lasted almost two hours, but I could have listened for two more, easily. They provided a background for my dreaming of you. Just eight months ago today...

"Hank (Lt. Milleville) and I had a tough day today. Nothing seemed to go right. No matter what we tried, it just wouldn't work out the way we had intended. We have slack days and busy days and tomorrow promises to be a busy one, so that should keep us out of trouble. Also, Pat is leaving here by plane in the next day or so, and it's very likely he'll stop, at least for a while, at Santa Monica Redistribution Center. I've given him your address and phone number so he can get in touch with you. I went to the hospital today to see him, probably for the last time before he goes. It's tough for him because he doesn't want to go, as long as the rest of us are staying here. I know that if I were in his place, I'd be knocking myself out because I was going home, but at the same time I'd feel a little funny at leaving the rest of the gang here...of course, once the war is over, it'll be every man for himself."

Harvey was Officer of the Day again on Thursday, and he missed the movie at El Gecko. "I think I missed a good show at the theater tonight, and all because of being on duty. It was 'Christmas in Connecticut' with Barbara Stanwyck and Dennis Morgan. From all that I've heard it must have been pretty good. But I'm glad that it's tonight that I'm on duty and not tomorrow night because then we've got a good stage show on schedule... 'Al Pearce and his Gang.' I sure don't want to miss that one. Then on the 31st we've got a show coming called 'Shapes Ahoy' which has been advertised pretty widely in Stars and Stripes. All the performers, both men and women, are from Hawaii which means we should see some genuine hula dancers. Al Pearce's show advertises five girls 'direct from the States' but I'm trying not to get excited because of the big disappointment we had with Eddie Bracken's show."

On Friday evening, Harvey sat down to write a letter before even taking his shower because "the entertainment was something that I want to talk about before I forget anything. Hope you don't mind me sitting here smelling like an old goat while I'm writing! To begin with, we had Al Pearce's stage show, and it was exceptionally good. I never made much of an effort to hear him on the radio, but in person he can really put on a show. With him he had four girls, actually three girls and a woman, because one of them was Arlene Francis who always talks so fast and so much. The others were a dancer and two singers. Then he had a man who was absolutely marvelous at manipulating puppets. The biggest laugh of the evening was caused innocently enough by one of the singers. I didn't catch her name, but she has recently graduated from Hollywood High School and has a very nice classical voice. Her figure, though, is what caused all the commotion!! She wore a tight-fitting silk dress, and although the men didn't enjoy her singing tremendously, they clapped and clapped after each song so that she had to walk back and forth from the wings to the microphone to do encores. She sang about seven or eight encores before Al Pearce, acting as M.C. had to break it up. Then after the stage show we had a movie called 'The Women.' Seemed to be an old picture so maybe you've already seen it, but if you haven't, try to see it. There are quite a few stars in it, all women and not one single man, although the men come in for a lot of discussion. Norma Shearer, Rosalind Russell, Paulette Goddard, Joan Fontaine, Marjorie Main, Joan Crawford and quite a few others. It's really good."

With his letter that night, Harvey enclosed a couple of items, one of them a copy of the *Stars and Stripes* issue advertising the Al Pearce show (with a photo of the Hollywood High graduate, Audrey Dodd), and the other a pair of clippings his mother had sent from Wilkinsburg. Two of Harvey's childhood friends from Wilkinsburg, Jeanne Counsel and Bill Price, had married in 1942, just before Bill entered the service. At the beginning of July, Bill had been killed in an accident in Oregon, and Harvey's mother had sent him an article from the local newspaper.

Lieutenant Killed in Jeep Accident

Lt. William Zeigler Price, 23, of Mt. Lebanon, was killed Tuesday in a jeep accident while going to the scene of a Navy plane crash, his family has been notified. The accident occurred near Klamath Falls, Oregon. A graduate of Wilkinsburg High School and Mercersburg Academy, he was attending Pitt when he enlisted in July 1942. He was soon to have been sent overseas. Lt. Price is survived by his widow, the former Jeanne Counsel of Wilkinsburg; his mother Mrs. Gertrude M. Price, and a sister, Marion Price.

Harvey's parents had attended Lt. Price's funeral in Wilkinsburg. Another of Harvey's Wilkinsburg friends had been killed just the day before:

Captain Dougall

Services for Capt. William M. Dougall, 28, of Glenn Avenue, Wilkinsburg, who was killed Monday near Pueblo, Colorado, when lightning struck a B-29 bomber, will be held tomorrow.... Capt. Dougall, a graduate of Wilkinsburg High School and the University of Pittsburgh, was one of 13 men killed when the Superfortress exploded after being hit by the bolt approximately 20 miles from Pueblo. Capt. Dougall had been in the Army Air Forces for four years, serving 22 months in anti-submarine patrols in the Caribbean theater.

Harvey skipped the Deanna Durbin movie (*Can't Help Singing*) on Saturday. He had seen it already and was too tired to leave the barracks. Betty was learning to play the ukulele in California and had asked him to find her one in Guam. He had tried, but with no luck. "There doesn't seem to be any ukes on this island. We've still got that Hawaiian lieutenant with our outfit so I'll ask him if his folks wouldn't like to buy one or two ukes and send them to you. If I can't make that deal, I'll do my best to try to get one if we stop in Honolulu on the way home. You are two chords better than I am [Betty had learned five!] ...I know three! Pay lots of attention to Stella, and by the time I get home you'll be an expert and able to teach me. I wish I could learn to play like this Hawaiian officer—he is really good. Funny thing, he learned to play <u>after</u> he started college in the States. That's like Babe Ruth going to Japan to learn to play baseball!"

He stopped writing for a minute so he could chase a rat in the BOQ! "I've had to interrupt this letter every five or ten minutes to help chase rats. There are quite a few of them on the island and naturally, as soon as buildings are put up, they come inside. We almost always have one or two around for us to chase. As soon as someone spots one, four or five of us take after him with knives, brooms, and anything else handy. We don't very often catch one, but we sure have a picnic going after them. Tonight, we had two rats cornered in the barracks, and we chased them from one end to the other. Then we'd lose them for a while, and everyone would settle down again to reading or writing. Pretty soon, someone would catch sight of a rat again, and the chase was on. Jimmy Ray almost hit one with a broom tonight, but it ducked between his legs and got away." On Monday, there was another hunt. "We just finished our nightly rat hunt but still haven't had any luck. Maybe by the time I finish your letter, we'll have caught one. We've got about half a dozen traps set all over the place, but only one has caught anything. Ray spotted this one tonight, and before you could swallow your gum we were all after him, whooping and hollering and waving any weapon we could find. I got a couple of swipes at him with my knife, but he got away."

Harvey sent a bit of each paycheck to Betty so she could put it into their account. "The more we can salt away, the better off we'll be when all this foolishness is over and done. Too bad we can't think of some way to put all that money to work for us, but at least we won't lose anything this way. This is one benefit that we're getting out of this war, because if I were back in the States and away from you (which I can't imagine), we wouldn't be able to save nearly so much of my salary. Another thing that we can count on, too, is my mustering out pay which will be $300.00, and then of course there will be all my accrued leave. I've got about 60 or 65 days of that piled up now. This morning we had the biggest and longest rain so far. These tropical rains are not at all what they're cracked up to be...they're worse!"

Servicemen in the Pacific theater had access to *Time* magazine, which ran a column called "U.S. at War," and occasionally Harvey would send articles on to Betty. He sent two clippings with his Monday letter, one about the men in charge of the units in Guam: ("These are the big wheels in our machinery!"), and one describing conditions aboard troop trains like the ones he had been on in the States: ("Boy, I've ridden a lot of trains like this!")

Bandit Chief

In a week when Under Secretary of War Patterson declared that battered Tokyo was no long a primary bombers' target, the War Department announced the name of the man who will run the heavy bombers' assault on Japan to war's end. To no one's surprise, he was 54-year-old General Carl Andrew Spaatz (TIME, July 2). "Tooey" Spaatz will be chief of a new U.S. Army Strategic Air Force of the Pacific.

On the record, no one was better qualified to direct the aerial destruction of Japan than the onetime fighter pilot who was chief of the U.S. Strategic Air Forces in Europe. German propagandists hated West Pointer Spaatz, called him the "aerial bandit." Japanese propagandists would soon have their own ideograph for the precise, mild-mannered Pennsylvania Dutchman who is impatient to get the war over so he can go sail boating.

The man who directed the operations of Flying Forts and Liberators over Europe will have mostly Superforts in his new command. His assistant destroyers will be rough, tough, morose major General Curtis LeMay, who last week became boss of the Twentieth Air Force, now based on Guam, Tinian and Saipan; and rough, tough, merry Lieut. General James H. Doolittle, boss of the famed Eighth Air Force, which is being transferred to the Pacific from Europe. Jimmy Doolittle's base will probably be Okinawa, from which MacArthur's Far Eastern Air Force began operating last week. Tooey Spaatz will direct his giants from headquarters on Guam.

And

WARTIME LIVING: Home Sweet Home

In the daytime, as they rolled through the sweltering prairie heat, they ran out of water. The toilets wouldn't flush. At night, they curled up against green-plush, straight-backed seats, fitfully brushing at insects and soot that kept pouring in the windows.

Soon they learned to take the backs off the seats, improvise hot and prickly beds from two seats with the chairbacks in between. Another man would sleep on the other chairbacks---in the aisle. Some dozed on their luggage.

For six days and five nights they traveled in this fashion from Boston to California—500 veterans of the European war, now on their way to fight another war. When they got off the train at Camp Beale, Calif., they let out a G.I. gripe that could be heard all the way back in Washington. Other trainloads of soldiers went through the same sort of experience—and they all griped. It did not cool them off to see civilians whizzing by in air-cooled Pullmans, or to hear a rumor that German prisoners of war were also riding in Pullmans.

As July ended, Harvey's unit was working on multiple projects, and he was getting tired. "We had a pretty tough day today with almost everybody in the Wing on our necks for something or other. Our biggest heckler was a major who wanted two Quonset huts moved. That's a delicate job because those huts, although strong on the ground, are flimsy when you hoist them in the air. That job gave us a few headaches, but I think we'll polish it off tomorrow."

Harvey went to the theater with Mac on Tuesday to see *Shapes Ahoy*, and they both enjoyed it. It was the first show at El Gecko that had brought a backdrop with them, and it seemed more like a "stateside" show. "The girls were pretty fair, but the backbone of the whole deal was their comedians. Mac and I made d____ fools of ourselves laughing. None of their stuff was smutty or crummy at all, and it went over a lot better than some of the ones that struggle for laughs by getting dirtier and dirtier. They had one little Hawaiian girl who couldn't have been over 5'0" tall, and talk about blues singers – she was as good as they come. She came out in a sleek silk dress, and how she could put those songs across. 'Cow Cow Boogie' was a masterpiece! It seemed like we had only been watching for about fifteen minutes when the show was over...actually it lasted over an hour and a half."

Mark Peck's wife Marie sent him a book called *Robinson Crusoe, U.S.N.* "It's the story of a Navy man's stay on Guam during the Japanese occupation. That guy really had some tough experiences while the [Japanese] were chasing him all over the place."

20

BORIS KARLOFF ON SELZNICK LOT

As Betty wrote her July 2nd letter, she realized that exactly one year earlier she had boarded a train to meet Harvey in Spokane. "I remember after I got on the train I couldn't yet believe I was really on my way. It seemed as if any minute I'd wake up and find myself at home. I don't know where this year has gone, but it has been beautiful. You ask if I'll go to the port to meet you? I'd go over to Guam to meet you if I could!" The next day, she wrote, "A year ago tonight [Pacific Coast time] I was on my last leg of the trip up to see you. I wasn't really excited about the whole trip until just about an hour before we pulled in. Oh brother, I thought that hour would never get finished."

Monday was a slow day at Stella's, possibly because of the holiday. Betty had lunch with her friend, Helen, and another friend, Gloria Lee, came over from the studio where she worked to join them. At about 2:00 p.m., Gloria's brother visited Betty at the store and stayed all afternoon. "It was first good talk we've had for over a year. He's been all over the U.S. training, and said he used to fly over Tinker Field a lot when he was stationed in Oklahoma. Then he spent six months flying in South America. This is his last leave home before going over ...he flies a Navy bomber (forget its name.) I spent most all my end of the conversation talking about you. He's another good old friend that I want you to meet and get to know. Another fellow, Jerry Siggins, came in this afternoon and it's been 2 years since I've seen him. Jerry plays the bass fiddle simply out of this world! He's always some place or other every night in a jam session. Wish you could hear him. He used to buy records from me when I first worked at Stella's. Right now, I'm listening to Ray Noble's Orchestra on the radio, and he sounds really danceable. 'The Charm of You' is really a cute tune - have you heard it yet? The mailman brought two letters from you today, and the pictures of Hawaii are special. We would really have fun at the Royal Hawaiian Hotel, wouldn't we? Another place we'll have to go when you come back is the Hotel Del Monte down near San Diego. The pictures reminded me of it.

"We pulled a trick on E.A. [Mr. Stella] today. Beverly, a friend of Elsie's, bought some 'smoke bombs' when she was in San Francisco in Chinatown – so since there are no firecrackers here of 'course (thank heaven!), the kids put the bomb in Stella's old Ford. The car always has something wrong with it anyway, and you should have seen his face when the smoke started pouring out from under the hood! George and I were in his car, Mr. Greengard was standing talking to us, and Beverly and Elsie were in Bev's car...all of us just waiting. After Mr. Stella stepped on the gas and just about fell out of the car, we all went over to his car and enjoyed a good laugh. We wished everybody a glorious 4th and went on home. Such is life in Culver City!"

That month's copy of *Life* magazine had an eight-page spread on Guam, with many photos of the island. Betty wondered if Harvey had seen it and if he had been to the places pictured. Specifically, she asked if he was located anywhere near Northwest Field; actually, that's exactly where he was stationed.

On the Fourth of July, Betty and Harvey had been engaged for exactly a year. "A year ago today was certainly a happy one, wasn't it? From the moment I saw you dash into the station in Spokane, I knew for sure that 'this was it!' I was so excited and so tired, I remember I couldn't eat anything for breakfast, and I slept practically all day. But that night!... I'll never forget 'The Fourth – 1944.' I remember watching the fireworks in the park. We had two years of conversation to get caught up on, and there was so much to know about each other. I remember we talked a mile a minute and then just saying nothing. I held your hat...it's funny what little things you think of, isn't it? I was thinking of how we'd get 'our' key at the desk and go up on the elevator and walk around the corner to turn right and then left, down the long corridor to the last room on the right – across from the staircase.

"Remember when we first went up to the room and the maid didn't have it made up, so she kept working while we put my things down. You decided to get back to the field and let me get some rest before you came back in the evening. After you left, the maid said it was a shame that my 'husband' had to go out to the field and was he stationed in Washington long, etc.? That's the first one who said that to me (outside of being kidded here around home.) Lots of beautiful memories have been crowded into this year. Thanks for all of them. We had such a beautiful two weeks together in Washington when we hadn't seen each other for such a long period of time. Just think how it will be next time we meet after a similar interval!

"Well, out of the past to the present. Today, I've heard exactly 5 firecrackers and seen 2 skyrockets. This afternoon I packed another box to send you and the whole time I listened to a 4th of July program on the radio. They played all of Cohan's numbers – 'You're a Grand Old Flag,' 'Yankee Doodle Dandy,' 'Over There.' It's the first time I've heard 'Over There' or even thought of it since you left, and you'll never know the pride I felt when I realized again that you are a big part of the U.S.A. Patriotism isn't for talking about, it's a feeling way inside, and it sure hit me then. As I put your address on the box, I thought of the millions of other wives and sweethearts who were doing the same thing, and how proud I am of you. Tell everyone there 'hello' for me." She and Harvey had been thinking about where they would live, and with her letter that night she included an article from *Collier's* magazine on home-buying. "Houses built ten years ago are now selling for as much as twice the original price. There's a reason: It's inflation. It hits the home-yearning G.I. harder than most of us, but here is advice for every potential homeowner."

After work on Friday, Betty and Elsie had dinner at Tips, a pancake restaurant on La Brea (with her letter that day, she enclosed a calendar of theater listings she had picked up the restaurant), and then went to the movies at the Ritz Theater at Wilshire and La Brea, "across from the little jewelry store where we waited for the bus the night we got home so late about three years ago! We saw 'The Thrill of a Romance,' with Van Johnson, Lauritz Melchior, and Esther Williams!! The picture itself was sort of stupid, I thought, but the photography was beautiful. The mountain scenes were all taken up in Yosemite – it is really beautiful up there. I remember over a year ago, Eddie Wright (the fellow you met at George's) was telling about the picture. He was supposed to go on location up there but wasn't well at the time. The cartoon with it was wonderful too! An M.G.M. one of 'Swing Time Cinderella.' It has that sexy gal in it that the wolf really howls over...I can just hear you and Mac and George laughing over it. Virjeanne was ushering at the theater, so we waited until she was through and went out to her house. It's the first time I've seen her mother and dad since I've been back home. Afterwards, Virjeanne and her mother walked Elsie and I to the car stop, and we took the Short Line on home." There was a lot of mail waiting for Betty when she finally got home, including a letter from Harvey's mother, one from Rae Terlinden, and three from Harvey, one of which included a copy of the *Stars and Stripes*. "That program you had with Dick Jurgens band really sounded like something. It was wonderful hearing so much about it...he has always had a swell outfit and I like him even better for playing over there for you fellows!"

While Betty wrote to Harvey on Saturday, she listened to Bing Crosby singing "I'd Rather Be Me" on the radio. "It's from the picture 'Out of this World'—I'm looking forward to seeing it, but you'll likely see it first over there." Eddie Bracken played the lead in the film, with Bing supplying his voice.... "Imagine a shy young singer with Eddie Bracken's looks and the soothing voice of Bing Crosby and you have a picture of the hero of this film... That trick of movie prestidigitation is the novel twist of the show and is good for a laugh whenever Eddie opens his mouth and Bing's warbling comes out."

Harvey's mother also wrote to him on Saturday, telling him she had just read about a new airplane that the government was building: "...a CX99 or something like that. Supposed to be about twice as big as the B29. That is beginning to sound almost unbelievable. Also, I heard yesterday on the radio where 600 B29s left on a raid and returned without a single loss. They were from the 21st bomber division. Are you the 20th Air Force or the 21st? I think it's the 21st, but your dad thinks the 20th." Harvey's father was correct; it was the 20th. His mother may have been referring to the 21st Air Force Fighter Group, which was based on Iwo Jima and had accompanied B-29s attacking the Japanese mainland.

Betty was late getting up on Monday morning, too late to catch her usual Short Line car. She ran to catch the next car but missed that one too. A passing motorist saw her running to catch the streetcar and asked if he could give her a lift. Normally, she wouldn't accept rides from strangers, but she was late for work and her instincts said that this would be safe. The driver was a neighbor and had recently been discharged from the service. Like Harvey, he was a Captain and said he was still trying to get used to civilian dress. "He collects jazz records, and I imagine he'll be buying a few records from us. Nothing like drumming up business!! I ate over at the Sweet Shop at lunch and ran into a fellow I graduated from high school with in '37. His name is Marsh Henry, and he works at Selznick Studio—worked at M.G.M. for six years and just changed during the last big strike. I also saw another friend, Jack Holland, who is leaving in the morning for Pensacola, and then overseas. His uncle works for Douglas in Long Beach, and he says the C-74 (maybe it's the C-47?) is being flown on the 28th. I hope I get to see her flying around!"

The C-47 was essentially a modification of the civilian DC-3 and included a cargo door, hoist attachment, strengthened floor, a shortened tail cone for glider-towing shackles, and an astrodome. During the war, it was mainly used for the transport of troops, cargo, and wounded. More than ten thousand of the aircraft were produced at the plants in Long Beach, Santa Monica, and Oklahoma City.

After work on Tuesday, Betty met Mary Alyce at the RKO Studio. "She had some more work to do so I went into the Publicity office to wait for her. I thought Stella's was a madhouse! I take it all back. She finally got finished and we drove over to the Hollywood Bowl. Had a heck of a time trying to find a parking place, because it was just packed for blocks around. Mary Alyce didn't stop for anything to eat, thinking 'The Pepper Tree Inn' would be open. It's on the grounds. But it isn't open this season because of food shortages, so we filled up on hot dogs.

"Our box - #831 - is just off-centered and about three tiers up. The night was perfect. It started at 8:30, and it was still light. Little by little the sky turned to black, and the stars pop out as you listen to the magic of music. I could go every night just to relax. I don't especially like Stokowski, but it wasn't bad tonight. There was a huge crowd, and they were quiet as can be all evening. I really appreciated that because some audiences at outdoor affairs are so noisy. They played Bach- 'Passacaglia' and 'Fugue in C minor' (which I didn't like), Wagner 'Love Music' from 2nd and 3rd acts of 'Tristan and Isolde' – that was really very beautiful even though I wasn't very familiar with it. After the intermission, they played Tchaikovsky – 'Symphony No. 6 in B minor'...that has the theme from which 'Story of a Starry Night' was taken. I really like that and know a little more about it. We just about died laughing during the third part (the allegro) ...the fellow who played cymbals had about 4 times he was supposed to hit them, and each time he would just about knock himself over! Afterwards, Mary Alyce and her mother took me over to Hollywood Blvd. where I caught the La Brea bus and transferred to the Venice Short Line. I'm so sleepy and it took such a long time getting home, waiting for buses and street cars. After this, I'm going to plan to stay with Mary Alyce out in the Valley or have her come home with me. She is good company, and we enjoyed our 'first night' at the Hollywood Bowl so much. Between listening to the music, we talked about her Sgt. Will in Tinian and my Capt. Harvey on Guam."

Harvey's mother also wrote to him on the 10th while she listened to a radio report from Guam. "That raid on Tokyo last night must have been a lu-lu. The reporter said 70 airfields in the Tokyo area were hit and that 3500 tons of bombs were dropped. It is, he said, the greatest combined air and sea battle of the Pacific War so far. Before he came on I heard a Gene Rider, with Halsey's fleet aboard a battleship, talking about a sea battle that was raging. I'll bet you saw plenty of activity last night with those B-29's taking off, and the ships are based at Guam too, aren't they? I saw in Life magazine that picture of the new base for B-29s on Guam which is the longest paved runway in the world. Buddy [their nickname for Harvey], we appreciate your hunting around for souvenirs for us, but really the only thing important anymore is that nothing happens to you and that you get back safe and sound before too long. So many aren't, you know."

After work on Wednesday, Betty and Peggy took the Venice Short Line to the USO in Santa Monica. "It is the first night I've been down there since I got home. The reason we went was that Peg wanted to show off her ring - can't say I blame her. I remember doing the very same thing only too well. I only saw 2 people I recognized. Peg introduced me to the lady at the desk as a former President of the Junior Council, and I felt about 60 years old. We walked upstairs and down to the playroom in the cellar and then left. That was enough for me. Then we took the Pico bus to Ocean Park to see 'Murder, He Says' at the Rosemary Theater– it is really a riot. Reminds me of 'Arsenic & Old Lace'. We also saw 'Escape to the Desert.' All I've heard on the radio for months is the ad for this picture, and it is pretty good at that. It's about the best double feature I've seen in a long time. We missed the comic, though.... darn." That night, Betty put together another tin of 78s from Stella's, and she started a card to slip in with the records. "Here are a few more records for all of you to enjoy. They're especially from me to you, but maybe it'll mean something to the other boys too. It is the melody of Tchaikovsky's 6th that we heard last night at the Hollywood Bowl. The words of 'Brazen Little Raisin' are cute as they mention California...just don't want you to forget this spot on earth as you travel around the world! Thought I'd put one classical record in this can. It is pretty, and I think you'll like it. Bing has a new record too... just listen to the words of 'Your Socks Don't Match'! If the weather is too hot, just put these records in the ice box – and I'm not trying to be funny. They'll warp all out of shape if you don't. I hope these all arrive in good shape.

Betty's father went with her to the Hollywood Bowl on Thursday. "On the way home, he told me it was the first time he's ever been in the Hollywood Bowl. I didn't know that. Living here all these years too. Why, I've even played in a Girl's Band on the stage...don't know why he wasn't there then. Helen

Frankel was supposed to be a guest vocal star tonight, but a throat infection made her cancel. A young 23-year-old girl from San Francisco, Miss Alba, stepped in at the last minute and has really stepped up a rung in the ladder of success. She is very lovely and sings like a bird. Otto Klemperer was guest conductor tonight and followed the scheduled program. All the songs Miss Alba sang were in foreign languages except her last encore. She sang Frimal's (sp?) 'Someday,' and it really made me lonesome for you. I'm back home now, it is midnight, and somebody just started playing Chopin on the piano next door so loud you'd think it was noon instead!"

Harvey had been telling Betty about a storm heading for Guam, and she sent him an article from the *Los Angeles Times* describing the heavy damage caused by a typhoon near Japan in June:

TYPHOON RIPS U.S. FLEET
21 WARSHIPS DAMAGED IN GALE OFF JAPAN
By. Leif Erickson

A raging typhoon lashed Admiral William F. (Bull) Halsey's Third Fleet with 138-mile-an-hour winds last June 5, tore the bow off the cruiser Pittsburgh and damaged at least 20 other warships, Adm. Chester W. Nimitz announced today after virtually every damaged ship was back in action.

At least four of the damaged ships - the Battleships Massachusetts and Indiana, the Carrier San Jacinto, and the Destroyer John Rodgers - participated in last Tuesday's 1000 plane carrier strike at Tokyo.

Many of the ships were badly hurt by towering 100-foot seas. None was more heavily hit than the fast, new heavy cruiser, Pittsburgh, which was caught near the center of the storm off the Ryukyu Islands. "A thunderous sea ripped off 104 feet of her prow and tossed it aside as though it were a match box to wallow in the storm off the ship's port side" reported Associated Press Correspondent Robbin Coons.

Capt. John E. Gingrich ordered the engines reversed and swung the 665-foot ship precariously around in a circle to escape a collision with her own bow.

Sealed bulkheads kept the Pittsburgh afloat and the cruiser, normally capable of 44 knots, lumbered back to Guam at 9 knots for temporary repairs. The bow was taken in tow by a tug and brought back to port.

Betty had written a couple of times to Mac's wife in St. Louis, and Dottie wrote back to her on July 12th. "That plan to meet the boys at the port when they get back sounds wonderful to me. I'd like very much to meet you and then go on together to meet our boys. I guess it's pretty far off to plan, but I'll be glad when we can really plan further."

On Saturday, Betty was back at the Hollywood Bowl. "Such a crowd at the Bowl tonight. Mother and Dad took me there, and we got wound up in a beautiful traffic jam. They then went over to the Hollywood Paramount to see 'Out of This World' with Eddie Bracken, etc. After the Bowl performance, I walked down Highland and met them at the show. It must be a couple of miles, or maybe I'm exaggerating. You'd have enjoyed the program tonight. It was the Gershwin memorial, and they played all the tunes I love. 'Someone to Watch Over Me,' 'Embraceable You,' 'I Got Rhythm,' excerpts from Porgy and Bess, and Carmen Cavallaro playing 'Rhapsody in Blue.' It was all simply beautiful."

The music store received a monthly newsletter from Capitol Records detailing the Hollywood music scene. In addition to promoting Capitol artists, the sixteen-page publication contained schedules for local music venues and articles about prominent personalities. Betty sent the July 1945 issue to Harvey because it contained a description of the Hollywood Bowl season and highlighted the Gershwin concert she had just attended.

"Every Type Music" for Hollywood Bowl
Leopold Stokowski Promises Many Innovations for Season of 1945

Leopold Stokowski is sweating it out these warm summer days and nights, preparing for the opening of the Hollywood Bowl season this month. His honeymoon concluded, the white-maned maestro has high hopes for the coming series. He recently signed a contract to serve as the Bowl's conductor for three years.

Stokowski's overall dictum concerning works to be performed in the famous amphitheater is in accord with his own catholic views on music. "There'll be every kind of music played this season - something for everybody's taste," he declared.

The equipment will be placed so it will not be visible to the audience, and Stokowski is presently working with sound engineers to get it in operation before the opening concert. For the orchestra, which will be known as the Hollywood Bowl Symphony, Stokowski has chosen his own ensemble, man by man. Many, of course, are from the Philharmonic orchestra, and several are musicians formerly with that body. For the few remaining chairs not yet filled he is holding auditions at which applicants are passed upon by a committee of 17 resident musicians.

Tuesday nights will feature symphonic programs, also conducted by Stokowski, and Thursday nights, soloists and guest conductors. So far, Otto Klemperer and Constantin Bakaleinikoff - the latter teamed with pianist Oscar Levant - are the only guest conductors definitely set. Soloists, to date, include Artur Rubenstein, Lawrence Tibbett, Claudio Arrau and Levant. The Ballet theater will give nine performances, on Thursday, Friday and Saturday evenings of the final three weeks. Another "Night in Vienna" program, featuring vocal artists, will be presented July 21, and a Pan-American Night, featuring Claudio Arrau, will be given July 26. The season will conclude with a performance of Beethoven's Ninth Symphony, conducted by Stokowski.

There is also talk of holding a Gershwin memorial concert on July 12, the anniversary of the composer's death in Hollywood in 1937.

Sunday, July 15th, marked the one-year anniversary of the day when Betty had left Harvey in Spokane. "As a background to this 'Sunday love letter' I'm listening to the 'Standard Symphony Hour' on KFP from the Hollywood Bowl. This is the first Sunday evening broadcast, and I wonder if you are hearing it over there. They played Grieg's Piano Concerto in A, one that Freddy Martin has recorded in dance time. The announcer just said that the program was short waved to South America and Alaska, so I guess you won't be hearing it unless it is transcribed. Right now, 'The Haunting Hour' program is on the air! How gruesome! I used to love to turn all the lights out and listen to these programs."

The news from the Pacific was non-stop, and Betty was increasingly worried about Harvey. "The news on the radio all seems to come from Guam these days. Plenty important spot in the Pacific war, the center of everything. All day we've been hearing talk of a near invasion of Japan, and it sounds like it should come soon. If you can, let me know if anything happens. If you aren't supposed to, of course don't, but anything you can send would really be of interest to those who love you. If you are going to be moved to one of the new air bases nearer Japan, mention "the sunset on Guam" ...then I'll know. I sort of have a feeling you'll get there one of these days. I hope you stay in Guam, though."

On Tuesday, Betty and Rod met Mary Alyce at the RKO Studio, and they went to the Hollywood Bowl. "It was very good again tonight, as they played more familiar music. Clair du Lune of course headed my favorites. Rod liked it a lot. The other girl in our box is Anne (Dillinger) Jeffries' sister and is very pleasant. Did I tell you that Dana Andrews is just three boxes away, as if it makes any difference to me. We all get a big kick out of watching the bobby sockers getting his autograph. That show you had sounded pretty bad. I'm sorry it wasn't as good as you thought it would be. Those shows should be tested here before they are sent over." With her letter, Betty included some clips and photos about a new airplane being built at the Hughes Culver City plant:

> Facts and figures concerning the world's largest airplane - Hughes Aircraft's "Hercules" - were released today in an announcement by Charles W. Perelle, vice-president and general manager of the company's Culver City plant. Wingspread of the huge plane, formerly known as the HK-1 and housed in two mammoth buildings in Culver City, is 320 feet or large enough so that a B-29 Superfortress could be placed under each wing, Perelle said. Gross weight of the cargo plane is 425,000 pounds and it's cost of production, including research, fabrication and purchase of a grading dock at Long Beach for its launching, will exceed $20,000,000, the company official said. Eight engines to be manufactured by Pratt and Whitney and to be completed sometime in January 1946, for the first flight of the sky giant, will have 3000 horsepower each to propel the ship. It's capacity for cargo is enormous. It can carry on 60-ton tank, complete with armor and crew, or three light tanks. Used as a hospital ship, it could accommodate 350 patients on stretchers with doctors and nurses enough to care for the wounded and surgical equipment as well. As a transport plane, it will be able to carry 750 fully armed infantrymen from Honolulu to Tokio on a non-stop flight.

Over at Selznick Studios on Washington Boulevard, Boris Karloff was filming a picture called *Bedlam*. After work on Thursday, Betty met Mary Alyce there, and they watched for a while, "...while on the lot I saw Boris Karloff and some of the characters out of a horror picture they are shooting now! They look awful.

"Mary Alyce, Marion Smith (a friend of M.A.) and I then went over to Sunset Blvd to a Drive-in, and our car was right next to Merle Oberon and her new husband. She really is a beautiful gal!" Merle Oberon was filming *This Love of Ours* at Universal Studios and had just married the cinematographer,

Lucien Ballard. Oberon and Ballard had met on the set of Oberon's film *The Lodger*. She had sustained facial injuries in a near fatal automobile accident in London in 1937, and "Ballard invented a key light to be mounted by the side of the camera. The light, nicknamed the 'Obie' after his wife, directed light onto the subject's face to wash out blemishes and wrinkles so they would not be caught on film." He is probably best known for his later collaborations with Sam Peckinpah on films like *The Wild Bunch* in 1969.

"Then we went to the Bowl, and it was the best ever! Patrice Munsel, the 19-year-old soprano soloist of the Met was the star of the evening. She had at least 10 curtain calls. The program is usually over at 10 or so, but tonight she was still singing encores at 11 o'clock. She has so much poise and such a beautiful voice. Well trained but not too 'formal.'"

During spare moments at the music store, Mr. Stella was teaching the girls to play the ukulele..."you should hear us play 'My Bonny!" Betty asked Harvey to bring a couple of ukes back from the Pacific if he could.

Betty kept track of her "anniversaries" with Harvey, and on Tuesday they had been married for exactly eight months. She took a trip into Los Angeles to do some shopping (wallpaper with a bamboo design, badminton racquets (!), and some magazines to send to Guam). She and Rod tried out the new racquets and ended up playing for two hours. That evening Betty headed back to the Bowl, and she really enjoyed the program. "The Bowl was wonderful tonight. Very familiar music – in fact it was the best night that Stokowski has conducted. During the intermission, Mary Alyce, Kathryn Lytle (Ann Jeffries' sister) and I went over to Pepper Tree for some coffee. When we came back and got settled down for the rest of the concert, I thought I'd have hysterics. A fellow was standing behind us (we have the last box by the aisle) and ate popcorn. Through most of the program it is so still in the Bowl you can hear the crickets on the hillside. Well, this character was munching popcorn and rattling the paper. M.A. and I looked at each other and got to laughing...very quietly, of course. Then he just about fell through the hedge when he lit his cigarette! Then, he sneezed and hiccupped.... anyway, he snapped me out of my melancholy, anniversary-without-you mood!"

Rod stayed home from work on Friday to study for his West Point entrance exam, which was scheduled for the next day. Friday morning, he went in to Los Angeles City Hall to have lunch with his father and then stopped by Stella's to see Betty on the way home.

Harvey's parents went to the movies in Pittsburgh on Friday and saw Van Johnson in *Thrill of Romance*. His mother wasn't particularly impressed: "...

just fair. They are sure spending a lot of money to try to put Van Johnson across, but not for my money. Esther Williams is in the picture with him...a peach of a swimmer. We saw 'Valley of Decisions' last week, and it was pretty good. I always like Greer Garson. The scenes were supposed to be laid in Pittsburgh, but it was before my time, and I didn't recognize them. We did see some pictures taken on Guam last night at the movies. They didn't show much of the place but piecing together all these different pictures, we are getting a rough idea what the place is like."

Business was brisk at Stella's on Saturday, and Betty didn't get off until six. "I had to go to Hollywood on the bus and streetcar because Mary Alyce left early. I got off the bus on Hollywood Blvd. and ate dinner at Pig n Whistle. Then I walked up Highland to the Bowl. Took me 30 minutes...all uphill! I got there in plenty of time, though, because the show didn't start until almost 9. It was beautiful, and I heard a new musical instrument called a 'theremin.' There are only 3 people in the U.S. who play it. It's a new idea in sound waves; vibration of the motion of hands in front of the instrument produces sounds, very weird – sounds like a human voice. The used it in the 'Halloween' number that was narrated by Lionel Barrymore. When he was wheeled out on stage, the Bowl almost all rose as one person, applauding him. It was wonderful. The dance routine of Sally and Tony DeMarco, with colored lights changing as they danced, was almost unbelievable. They are so very graceful. It reminded me of the night the you and I went with your folks to the Wm. Penn Hotel for dinner and saw that good floor show. I had to come home on the streetcar because Rod had the car for a date with Georgia Ott. She's real cute and they had a good time. They saw 'Out of this World' at the Paramount. A girl we knew at Venice High, Laverne Higham (I don't know her stage name) had a good-sized part in it. She sings a song and is in quite a bit of the picture. I haven't seen it yet." Laverne Higham's stage name was Nancy Porter. She was born in Salt Lake City and appeared on Broadway in the early 1940s. While she was Ethel Merman's understudy on Broadway, Paramount scouts noticed her and brought her to Hollywood. She was a popular pinup during the war, but her acting career never took off. The movie that Rod and his date saw was her last film.

Betty sent Harvey a copy of the Saturday issue of the *Los Angeles Herald-Express*, not because it contained a review of the Hollywood Bowl program, but because of the front-page headlines:

EMPIRE STATE BLDG. AFIRE: Army Plane Hits 79th Floor; 15 Die in Flames, Elevators Drop 80 Stories. A B-25 bomber crashed with a thunderous explosion into the seventy-eighth floor of the Empire State Building today showering flame and debris throughout the upper part of the world's tallest building and trapping hundreds of office workers a thousand feet above the street..... The plane, lost in a fog, zoomed down fashionable Fifth Avenue and crashed headlong into the north side of the building at the seventy-eighth floor. Office workers in the building itself and pedestrians in the street below watched in horror.

Ironically, in the same issue was a brief description of an earlier sea battle in the Philippines. A Japanese suicide plane had crashed upside down into the USS *California*, a battleship badly damaged during the Pearl Harbor attack in 1942.

Rod knew his sister was sending news to Harvey, but he sent his own letter on Sunday with a couple of additional items. "Friday I went to S.C. to find out about the Scholarship. I went up to Gus Shavers office, and he was there with Dean Cromwell and Jeff Cravath. More fun. I had to see if my grades were OK, and they were. Gus told me that Kile and I would start practicing on September 1st but wouldn't start classes until the first of November. I'm really excited about it." Gus Shaver had been an All-American quarterback and fullback at USC and had led them to a national championship in 1931. In 1932, the Olympics were held in Los Angeles, and American football had been an exhibition sport during the Games. Shaver had been the captain of the winning West team during the game between All-Star players from American universities. When Rod met him in 1945, Gus Shaver was an Assistant Coach at USC, serving under Jeff Cravath (whom Rod also met that day). Dean Cromwell served as the SC track coach from 1909 to 1948, had been the Assistant Track Coach at the 1936 Olympics in Berlin, and would be the Head Track Coach at the 1948 London Olympics.

"Then yesterday (Saturday) I took the West Point test. Wow, what a test. It lasted 8 1/2 hours. First I had an hour's test for Officer Qualification, and there were three sections: English, Mechanical Aptitude and Math Comprehension. Then I had a straight 3 1/2 hour math test. It was hard but I knew most of it. I fell down in the Literature section, I think. The U.S. History wasn't bad. I won't hear anything for about a month." He also told Harvey about his new girlfriend, Georgia, and about seeing Laverne Higham in the Eddie Bracken movie.

CELEBRATION

On Wednesday, August 1st, Harvey was busy with the Quonset huts and several other jobs. After dinner the entire 75th attended a special briefing, the same briefing being given to combat bomber crews. The Wing's commanding general, Gen. Armstrong, wanted all his men to know the details of the mission. "It's interesting as the dickens to see how the bombing mission is all laid out. Every detail is worked out with precision that would do credit to a flock of watch factories. When the pilots and their crews get information like that, I don't see how they can help dropping the bombs right down the [Japanese] chimneys. And they'll be hitting more and more chimneys, too!!"

With his letter, Harvey included articles clipped from the latest issue of *Stars and Stripes*, one which detailed American psychological warfare tactics, and two others which described entertainment troupes headed to the Pacific:

Psychological Warfare Does the Job Guns Can't
by T/4 Joe Fisher

We are fighting the Japanese with more than B-29s, flame throwers and harbor mines. We are attacking with propaganda - based not on lies, Nazi-fashion, but on facts which, once driven home to the enemy soldier and civilian, may shorten the war and save lives.... At present one-half to one million OWI leaflets are being sprinkled daily over Japanese cities by high-flying B-29's and navy carrier planes. Others are being dropped on hopelessly resisting Japanese pockets from Bougainville to Burma. It has been found advisable to minimize U.S. victories and treat Japanese defeats as due to overwhelming superiority of U.S. manpower, equipment and supplies, rather than to any deficiency of Japanese fighting spirit.

Show Troupes Heading West

Islands to be visited in the near future by Hollywood film stars touring MidPac have been announced by Army Special Service and Navy's Fleet Entertainment Section.

The Jack Carson show, currently on Oahu, goes to the outer Hawaiian Islands of Kauai, Maui and Hawaii in early August and then will head for the Marshall and Gilbert Islands.

Gene Autry, now playing Tinian, will proceed to Iwo Jima, Angaur, Peleliu, Ulithi and Guam before returning to the states the end of August.

The troupes headed by Eddie Bracken, Al Pearce and Charlie Ruggles, all Navy sponsored, will play the Marianas area only.

"This is the Army," Irving Berlin's all-soldier musical production, is on Tinian, and will give performances on Saipan, Guam and Ulithi during August. The CPBC Entertainment Section also gives news of its four-star revue, "Shapes Ahoy." The cast is on Guam and will play Angaur, Ulithi, Peleliu and Iwo Jima before heading back to Oahu.

Live Shows (Pacific)
Guam

Foxhole Medleys (USO Camp Shows), July 30 – Aug. 5
Free and Easy (USO Camp Shows), July 30 – Aug. 5
Gene Autry (USO Camp Shows), Aug.5
This is the Army (SSO), Aug. 2

Harvey wrote back to Betty's brother on Thursday, and he described his life on Guam in terms he thought Rod would understand. "I hope this feeble attempt will be enough to let you know that I'm alive and kicking and sweating out our end of the war on this damned little island. Really, it's not such a bad little place but after so long a time, a guy sure would like a look at some different scenery. Something besides jungle, jeeps, and airplanes would sure look good.

"You've never seen such weather as we are having here. Sometimes it's unusually hot and then sometimes it's unusually wet, but no matter how it is, it's never normal. When it's wet, we get barrels of water, and when it's hot, the old sun just boils down. Drainage here is a bigger problem than I've ever seen before. Most of our equipment is busy all the time either filling in low spots or constructing ditches and culverts. The whole island sits on solid coral which is just a few inches below the topsoil, and that coral won't allow one drop of water to soak itself in. However, in very low areas we find that by digging down about fifteen feet, we begin to find fissures in the coral which readily carry off excess water. By making French drains in those areas, we can ease the situation a little. It's a big problem, though, and means quite a bit of work.

"I managed to get myself an air mattress today, but it was quite a struggle to make the grade. The only way the guy would trade was for a quart of liquor, so now I have to mooch the liquor so to give him for his mattress. It's worth any trouble I go to, though, because these mattresses really make sleeping a pleasure. Just like the Biltmore or the Waldorf-Astoria, but without room service.

"I wish you could be here to see some of these missions taking off for Japan!! Boy oh boy, to see all these B-29's taxiing up to the runway...kind of gives a man a feeling of pride and satisfaction in being on this end of the bomb run...on the other end, somebody's liable to get hurt."

Harvey didn't receive a letter from Betty on Thursday, but Mac had picked up two packages from her and brought them back to the barracks. One package was a tin of records from Stella's, and Harvey planned to take them to the Chaplain's office to play on the record player. "The titles sound plenty sharp!!" After dinner, he went to the movies with Mac and saw *A Tree Grows in Brooklyn*. "It was so depressing and made me so lonesome for you that if I hadn't been sitting down front, I'd have left in the middle of the picture. I never did care too much for Dorothy Maguire, or whatever her name is, and this picture put the finishing touches on her for me. They're installing 35 mm projectors at the theater now so our selection of pictures should be much better from now on."

It was hot and muggy on Friday afternoon as Harvey sat in his office. As he looked out the window, he could see some of the rigs pulling into the yard. "We've got equipment working on all kinds of jobs all over the entire area and it's really a sight in the morning or evening to see all this stuff pulling in and out of the Heavy Equipment Yard. The piece of equipment I like the best is a

P-1 Michigan Crane. It's a truck mounted crane that has a lifting capacity of 10 tons. Since I've been here, I've learned to operate the thing fairly well so if I ever have to fool around with that equipment in civilian life, I'll know a little bit about it. It's really a lot of fun to operate on of those big devils, and every now and then, when a job shows up for one of them and I can't find an operator, I take the rig out myself. I probably shouldn't do that, but I do anyway. One of our biggest problems is having enough coral to satisfy everyone's needs and demands. Coral is the only thing we have to use for roads, fills, walks, runways, taxiways, or anything else. It's even used for concrete when mixed with cement. So, you can see that it's a big problem supplying coral for a base with growing pains like ours. It's a good thing that coral is so plentiful because otherwise we wouldn't have a thing to use.

"George Terlinden just came in and passed out cigars. He's now the proud father of a baby boy, and he's stalking around here beaming. Riley Hayes and Jimmy Rae are both expecting their babies in December, and that's supposed to be the month for the Skinners too. And who should walk in today but Lt. Rice! Remember him? He's the young kid we called 'Junior' in Kansas. He's on his way to Tinian where he's been assigned as Special Services Officer. Sure was good to see him again and hear all the latest dope from the States."

Mac and Harvey went to El Gecko again on Saturday night. "I don't know why I stayed to see the darn picture all the way through because it really was pretty sad. I guess if we get pretty hard up for entertainment, we'll stay to watch most any picture. This one was a British film about Nazi spies in North Africa. You know the kind." They went to another film the next night, but Harvey was more interested in telling Betty about a new Italian dish he had heard about. "Our mess sergeant here is an Italian boy by the name of Renato Porfaro, and I was talking to him about Italian dishes the other day. he says his mother has a good recipe for that 'tomato pie' I was telling you about back in Hays. The Italians call it 'Piza' or something like that, and if he gets the recipe, I'll send it to you.

"There's a man staying with us in the B.O.Q., a civilian by the name of Jim Bristow. He's about 40 years old and we all call him 'Pop.' He's the technical representative for the U. S. Rubber Company and is sent by the government to furnish technical advice and assistance on things like self-sealing gas tanks, tires, de-icer boots, etc. He lives in East Los Angeles, and his wife sends him clippings from the L.A. papers all the time, so he always gives them to me to read. One is a note about the So. Calif. Edison Co. switching from 50 to 60 cycle electric service, which means you'll have better electrical light service in your house when it goes into effect. Steadier light. The other item is a column by Bill Henry that gives a pretty fair idea what life is like on an island in the Pacific that is more or less removed from the war. Maybe you've already seen both of them? 'Pop' is a pretty swell guy and is really working his head off over here. Pop has seen quite a bit of the war so far, having been in Italy, the Aleutians, and now here. I hope you will get a chance to meet him some day."

Harvey was on rotation as Officer of the Day, and his turn came around again on Monday. "I'm sitting here at a desk in Group Headquarters sweating out another tour of duty as O.D. Boy oh boy, it sure seems to me to come around fast, too fast to suit me. It's an awful waste of time and energy because nothing ever happens to warrant an officer staying here all the time, but I guess if I left for any reason, all hell would break loose, and I'd be in the soup up to my neck. Today was really a dull, listless day with hardly a thing doing. I spent my time all day just checking up on jobs that I've got under way in different parts of the area. Didn't start any new jobs at all and couldn't even manage to finish any that we've got in progress. The sun was hot as blazes all day with not a hint of rain until about eight this evening. Then it really poured. It begins to look as if we've gotten through the worst part of the rainy season now, so we'll probably get days that are hotter and hotter from now on. Wouldn't you know that I'd get O.D. tonight when the movie is going to be 'Mr. Big' with Donald O'Connor. A fine deal!! I guess one of the other officers would have taken the job for me, but I hate to ask a guy to take this job. Maybe you had better see the picture seven or eight more times so you can tell me about it when I get home. There is a radio beside me playing all kinds of dreamy, sentimental tunes that carry me right back to you. Just a few minutes ago, they played one of _our_ tunes – 'You Made Me Love You,' and before that 'Who Wouldn't Love You.'"

Mail delivery was becoming spotty, and for servicemen awaiting news from their families, it was tough. "Can you imagine how Hank Milleville feels – his wife was supposed to have had her baby last week, and he hasn't heard from her in three days. He's really tearing his hair out!! The Army can cut down on food and the men won't gripe too much, but you should hear the h___ they raise when the mail system goes haywire. It's terrific!! The show tonight was 'Cobra Woman' with Maria Montez and Jon Hall. I think you and I saw it together, but I went to see it again. Plenty colorful and lots of beautiful women running all over the place. That Maria Montez is a close second to Loretta Young for my money, along with Maureen O'Hara."

The biggest news hitting the camp on Guam that day, though, was about a new weapon—the atomic bomb. "We heard today over the short wave from San Francisco about the new atom bomb that's so powerful and deadly. Morale here on the island has gone up a thousand percent. They say that one plane load of atom bombs is equal to a 2000 plane Superfort raid. If that's so, can you imagine the effect of a 2000 plane raid if all the planes were carrying these new atom bombs? It's almost unbelievable!! Sounds like something that you'd read about in Buck Rogers. I don't see how the Japanese can possibly hold out very long if we begin to use those things. They said that while the bomb was being tested, two men were watching a test explosion with binoculars from a distance of six miles away and were knocked flat by the concussion."

What Harvey didn't tell Betty—either because he didn't know or, more probably, because of censorship regulations—was that the atomic bomb had already been dropped on Hiroshima the previous day!

"I hope you've been able to get that book I told you about – 'Robinson Crusoe, U.S.N.' because it's plenty good and will tell you a whole lot more about this island than I could even begin to write down." The book, published in 1945, was written by Blake Clark about the experiences of George Tweed, a Navy warrant officer who had escaped when the Japanese captured Guam at the same time they attacked Pearl Harbor:

When the enemy landed, Tweed, with the permission of his commanding officer, who said there would only be token resistance, jumped into his 1926 auto and under fire raced out of Agaña. The American navy would bound back in six weeks, he and a fellow fugitive were certain, and planned to make their supplies of canned food last that long. They hid in the spiny underbrush where natives took more food to them. Later they met five other Americans but eventually split up.

The Japanese knew Tweed and others were still alive. They organized Chamorro searching parties and, when those failed, took over the task themselves, combing the countryside systematically. Once, when surrounded, Tweed in desperation tried to surrender but didn't succeed. Afterward, learning that the Japanese intended to execute him and informed further that if he stayed free his example would encourage the local people, he decided to stick it out if he could.

His five companions were captured and beheaded, he heard. He seems to have owed his own phenomenal escape to a combination of luck and wit. The luck in having native friends who refused to give up his secret even under torture. The wit was his ability to forage for himself, to guess when natives were too terrified by unrelenting enemy pressure to continue to be dependable.

The last 21 months were spent in a cave overlooking the sea some 15 miles north of Agaña. This exploit was unique. Robinson Crusoe is tame compared to Robinson Crusoe Tweed, but the facts in this book, which has photos and illustrations, are almost beyond belief.

Reports about the new bomb, and its possible role in shortening the war, continued to pour into camp: "...the magnitude of this new atomic bomb is incredible! The stories we hear, and the radio broadcasts are fantastic! The whole island is really excited about the possibilities if this bomb can be put into everyday use. And I see no reason why it can't be done. There was a rumor circulating today that the war was actually over, but no one has heard an official announcement as yet. If that's true, maybe we can spend Christmas of 1945 together. Wouldn't that be wonderful? One thing that I do want to mention is that even when the war is over, it will probably take every bit of six months or longer to get all of us back to the States again. That seems like an awful long time, but when you remember just how many men there are to ship back, you can realize how long it will take to get them all started home. That is going to be the transportation problem of all time. Some guys will have to stay longer than others, and there will be lots of weeping and wailing, but it can't really be helped. I'm just praying that the Army ceases to have a job for me at the earliest possible minute. I'm ready to leave any time. I'll have had four years in the Army on the 17th of December, and that's long enough for me." On a lighter note, he added: "The movie tonight was a Class A stinkeroo! The name of it was 'Dangerous Passage,' but I can't remember any of the players. They are probably better off being forgotten anyway. Even the cartoon wasn't very good, and it's really a bad cartoon that I don't like! After this week we are supposed to start getting much newer pictures, so I guess that then, it'll really be a pleasure to go...maybe we're just getting extra particular!"

There was a major rainstorm in Guam on Thursday. "It seems like every time I tell you about one of our rainstorms, I call it 'the biggest one we've had yet' but it's true. And this one we're having now is the granddaddy of them all!! I mean it's really coming down. If they get any worse than this, the whole island will be under water. You've never seen anything like this in your whole life. The sky just seems to open up and drop half an ocean on us all at once.

We had to shout to each other right here in this room in order to hear above the noise of the rain on the roof!

"I came in after lunch today, and Hank Milleville rushed up to give me a cigar!! He had gotten a letter saying that his wife had given birth to a baby girl on the 31st of July. His mother-in-law sent him a cable at eleven o'clock that same night and he still hasn't gotten the cable...I guess that air mail is really the fastest way to communicate. I'm smoking his cigar right now and although it's a good one, I could never be a real cigar smoker. Just one every now and then tastes good."

After a break, Harvey resumed his letter. "I've just gotten back to writing after a lapse of about two hours. The rain stopped just as suddenly as it began, and the phone began ringing steadily. Almost every building on the base had water on the floors, and quite a few areas were completely flooded out. Every available piece of equipment was put to work digging ditches and trying to provide drainage in some way or another. By now, everyone has cooled down a little, and any water damage is being repaired. Fortunately, we have been working on drainage as much as possible during the dry spells, or we would have suffered a lot more.

"The radio reported today that more atomic bombs had been dropped on Japan today. This time on Nagasaki. I hope the [Japanese] realize pretty soon just how futile it is for them to hold out any longer." Harvey had still not mentioned the bombing of Hiroshima.

Sunday, August 10th: "We just got in from the movies, and a big fat rumor was going around that the war was over. A little later we found out that it wasn't over yet, but that the [Japanese] had offered to accept the peace offer concocted at Potsdam if they could keep their emperor. There are all kinds of radio reports floating around back and forth, and it's hard for a guy to actually know just what is going on. I can't see why the war should last more than a day or so longer anyway. Everyone around here is d---ed going crazy with happiness about the way things are turning out. It sounds like a good-sized war going on outside with every guy and his brother grabbing his gun and shooting away for all he's worth. So far, all of them are shooting in the air... hope it stays that way! Lots of rockets of all kinds shooting all over the sky. These guys are really raising a rumpus. Darling, do you realize that all this means that we are getting closer, much closer to the time when I'll be home again. Boy, if they end this war in the next day or so, maybe they'd get everything straightened out so we could start home in a few months. I can hardly believe the possibilities that this new peace offer brings.

"Now the officers in the barracks are really getting noisy. They've all had quite a bit to drink and from the sound of things, it's starting out to be an all-night party. I know I'm not going to be able to write much more with all this noise, so I'll stop now and try to tell you all about it tomorrow."

Ralph Haver, Harvey's friend from Fort Belvoir, Patterson Field in Dayton and Geiger Field in Spokane, was headed for the Pacific and wrote to Harvey from his ship. "Finally, they rounded up enough manpower to shove me up the gang plank and I can tell you, that they had a job. This traveling by ship gets a little monotonous after a couple of weeks, which I presume you became well aware of on your trip out. We're crammed on pretty snug like and consequently we 1st lieutenants and lower type officers are quartered in troop space – you know (4 berths high, 2 wide with a 2-foot aisle.) Our compartment (which we call 'torpedo junction') is well forward and well down so we get the benefit of any motion. The air gets a little thick towards morning, in fact I'm trying to get an oxygen tent for use at night. The last 3 nights I've tried sleeping top side which I've found to be much better in spite of the hard steel deck and occasional rain. Don't get me wrong, I'm having a helluva good time. If this atomic bomb deal is all they claim it is, this here war might wind up quicker than we thought. Anything that's as powerful as this bomb is said to be should change the enemy's point of view. How's 'Utilities Inc.' making out? Give my regards to Dangers, Yates and Jay. I ran into some of the old fraternity brothers...Jack knows them all – Ted Fisher, Bob Chambers, T/Sgt. Maines, Lt. Hollingsworth, Hal Bashar and Jules Brady. It was quite a reunion."

Harvey filled Betty in on the big celebration in the Guam camp. "After reading last night's letter, you've probably figured out we didn't get very much sleep. Well, you're certainly right. I got into bed at five this morning, and a lot of the men didn't go to bed at all. Most everyone was as drunk as a lord and making noise in any shape or form that he could. I had a few drinks myself but not enough to make me feel more than a little effect. One officer went to the mess hall and made a flock of sandwiches, and the rest of us popped popcorn and drank beer and stuff. Naturally, most of the conversation centered on whether the Japanese peace request would be accepted by the U.S. and, if so, how long would it take us to get back to the States. Everyone guessed at lengths of time varying from two months to well over a year. Personally, I can't see that it's possible for us to be sent back in two months, but I feel certain that our stay here won't drag on for a year after hostilities cease. More than likely, it will be around six to eight months. We haven't heard any reports today as to whether or not the U.S. is considering an acceptance, but it seems that the civilian population back home is more or less in favor of <u>not</u> accepting. None of us here can quite understand that attitude because even if the [Japanese] do keep their Emperor, he would have little or no bearing on their militaristic feelings. Maybe, we are wrong in looking at it that way – and it's very possible that our opinions are flavored with a strong desire to get home as soon as possible. In the meantime, despite a large blowout last night, everything went along as usual today except that the air is almost electric with everyone listening for any indication of V-J Day. Today, I managed to pick up a couple of the leaflets that the B-29's have dropped on Japan along with the translations that go along with them. I'm sending one to you so you can see the kind of propaganda (if you want to call it that) that the U.S. is using."

On Sunday morning, Harvey had to make a trip to the other side of their field, and as he drove his jeep across the taxi strips where the bombers were parked, he noticed the nicknames that the pilots had painted on many of the planes. "Some of them are pretty good. We've got 'Dark Angel,' 'Rebel Raiders,' 'Hubba Hubba', 'Twentieth Century Fox,' 'Fleet Admiral Nimitz,' 'Fluffy Fuzz III,' 'Captain Chuck,' and a whole lot more. The two best ones are 'Miasis Dragon' and 'Beegaz Burd'.... I almost fell out of my jeep when I saw that last one!!" On shortwave, they were hearing that five million men would be released from active duty in the twelve months following the surrender. The Japanese had just ordered their soldiers to stop fighting while the peace was being considered, which meant that surrender was probably imminent. "We've been sweating out the end of the war, and now I guess we'll have to sweat out the trip home. I was sure that the war would last a lot longer than it has."

The rumors were still flying around that afternoon, but the officers took a break and played a little baseball. "We had a baseball game this afternoon at one o'clock and what a fiasco it was. Our team has been playing softball right along, and this is the first time most of us have played baseball in years. Naturally, we were beaten, but it was a lot of fun. We didn't even have a chance to toss the ball around before the game. After batting that big softball around for so long this d___ed baseball looked like an aspirin tablet when we got up to the plate. I got one of our three hits, but it was only a little chop over the second baseman's head. Riley Hayes had a long two base hit and Bruce Ridgeway had a single to score him for our only run. Outside of that we didn't do much but fumble the ball. We have another game scheduled for Tuesday evening, and we should be a lot better after getting the feel of the ball today. We certainly can't be much worse!"

After dinner that night, Harvey went to the movies and saw a picture that he and Betty had seen together in Hays, Kansas: "'Music for Millions'. Remember it? I liked it just as much and laughed just as hard at Jimmy Durante as I did the first time. There is some wonderful music in it, especially Handel's 'Messiah' which they played with full orchestra and choir. Reminds me of all the times we sang it back at church. Oh, to be a boy soprano again instead of a gravel-voiced baritone. I don't care, though. I love my singing anyway."

The war wasn't officially over, and Harvey still needed to use "code" references regarding his likely next destination. "Remember that map I told you to throw away? Well, don't! I'm sure you'll want it and need it! It might be very handy for us, and our posterity might enjoy looking at it. I'm sure glad we bought those in Hays because they are probably as good as any you'd be able to find now. Especially that one with the sunset on it! *[Note: This was a map of Japan!]* The war situation hasn't changed any as yet. Everyone is holding their breath waiting for the (Japanese) to either accept or turn down our latest peace terms. It seems to me that they have been deliberating an awfully long time on this thing – maybe they've some sort of a sneaky deal up their sleeves.

"Mac and I didn't go to the show tonight because the picture was 'Sahara' with Humphrey Bogart, and we've both already seen it. We can't afford to miss tomorrow night because Gene Autry, sans horse, will be the stage attraction! It promises to be a whopping big show and a good one, too! We're averaging about one stage show per week, and all in all they haven't been at all bad. Most of them are small local shows, but some have pretty big-name stars. I'll tell you about this one tomorrow."

By Tuesday the 14th, it seemed that the rumors of an imminent end to the war might be true. "Late this afternoon, we intercepted a message from Radio Tokyo which said that the Japanese government had accepted the terms of the Potsdam Conference. That isn't official yet, and won't be until Washington actually makes the announcement, but at least it looks like the beginning of the end. By tonight sometime we should get a confirmation from Washington, and that will finish the whole deal once and for all. I can hardly believe that this whole mess is almost finished. I know that I won't get home to you right away, but at least I'm sure it can't take too long. Everyone is hanging around a radio somewhere to be sure to get the news as soon as it comes in. As I sit here writing, you're no doubt in bed, still sleeping and entirely oblivious to all that's taking place as you sleep. When you do wake up, the war should be officially over with all the radios bursting with the news. God bless you for making this war and anything else that comes along, bearable for me!

"Two swell packages came from you today, one of them with some beautiful recordings. I haven't had a chance to play them yet, but I'm going to take them down to the Chaplain's hut tomorrow evening with your note, so I'll know just where you want me to listen most closely! I'll have the Victrola turned down real low and be sitting real close so that no one else will hear. We went to the show tonight, Mac and I, to see the Gene Autry production, and it was plenty good. He was supported by a small string ensemble that he picked up on the island to help put his shows over. The whole thing was swell all the way through. He had six in his cast – a girl who sang and played an accordion, a girl who just sang, the usual sexy dancer and singer, a comedian, Rufe Davis, who stole the show, an M.C. who was plenty good, and Autry himself. The show as long, clean, and funny, which is more the exception than the rule for G.I. shows. Most of them get the idea that G.I.s only want a lot of smutty jokes and stuff which is so wrong. The show tonight was just what the doctor ordered. Mac and I just roared at this Rufe Davis character – he's the big farmer guy who performs all the facial gymnastics with noises to match. Haven't seen him for years. I hope the Special Services officer keeps up the good work."

The long-awaited news came on Wednesday, August 15th—*the war was over!* "Today was the day we've all been waiting for. I don't suppose that today will be officially called V-J Day, but at least President Truman announced that the U.S. had accepted Japan's terms. Or rather, he agreed that Japan should surrender under the Potsdam terms. Now we'll be sweating out the day when we'll arrive back in the States. I can't see why they'll want to keep us over here for any great length of time, but it's hard to say just how they'll work it out. There wasn't any great show of jubilation here, just a real pleased and satisfied look on everyone's face. You see, the war won't actually be over for us until we land back in the good 'ol U.S. again. The jobs we've been doing will keep on until the day they tell us to pack up and leave. The bomber crews will be flooded with leisure time, but most of the rest of us will be just as busy as ever. The news today was just another radio announcement as far as changing our daily routine is concerned. We shouldn't have to work quite as hard, but there will still be plenty to do. My heart is with you today, wondering how you feel today and how you plan to celebrate the end of the war. I'm sure you feel happy today...it's a pretty swell world after all, isn't it?"

The next day, the war was officially over, and the men of the 75th were trying to adjust to a new routine. "Almost everyone seemed to prefer a day of sitting and waiting for something to happen, rather than a day of getting out and making something happen. And, believe me, I was no exception. I barely moved out my chair. The sun didn't help matters either, because it just boiled all day, draining all energy from everybody. I had a couple of power shovels and a few dump trucks working but that's all. We haven't received any orders to stop construction yet, but no one has the urge to finish jobs that existed the day before yesterday. No doubt one of these days an order will be issued to stop all of our new construction projects and merely perform a few of the necessary maintenance jobs needed to keep the base operating. These enlisted men of mine need a rest bad, so I'm not doing a bit of yelling for work. We'll just go along with the crowd until they decide to send us home. This island has become a hot house for rumors of all kinds, shapes and sizes. Ever since Japan first offered to surrender, we've been hearing rumors that have promised everything from an immediate trip home to at least two more years in the service. Some of them are really wild and woolly. I'm hoping that the most optimistic ones are true, but to contradict what I told you the other day, I don't believe you'll need that map after all. And I'm hoping and praying that I see my next sunset with you.

"We saw a fine picture tonight over at the theater, 'A Royal Scandal,' with Tallulah Bankhead, Charles Coburn and Anne Baxter. It was really good! The most nonsensical picture I have ever seen – nothing at all made sense but it was so darn funny, we hardly saw the screen for laughing. Tallulah Bankhead played Katharine, the Second, the Czarina of Russia and really does a bang-up job of acting, as usual. The whole thing is absolutely impossible which is what makes it so darn silly. See it if you can."

Usually, Harvey began his letters to Betty with the date and his location: "Guam." However, on Friday "Guam" became "Still Here," an indication that the long-awaited end of the war hadn't changed things much. "Just sitting here in the office and have managed to take the typewriter away from the clerk long enough to bang out two or three lines to you while I'm waiting for something to happen. As soon as the peace was made official by Truman's announcement, our work fell off to almost nothing. We've still got enough to do to keep us busy, but nobody is pushing us any longer. There isn't any particular point to our work now, but I imagine that the Utilities Section will be busier than anyone else. We've been laughing all day about that picture we saw last night. The d___ silly look on Tallulah Bankhead's face as she tried her best to maintain some sort of regal atmosphere in her Russian court was enough to bowl us all off our seats. The picture was full of bearded Revolutionists and all kinds of subversive plots attempting to get the czarina off her throne. Charles Coburn, as the Exalted Chancellor, played his usual comical, fat, fine role with Anne Baxter as an attentive and fiery Lady in Waiting. The whole darn thing was such a farce that the crowd was in stitches the whole way through.

"The rain has just started and, wonder of wonders, it's a gentle spring rain instead of the thunderous cloudbursts that we are used to having. The air smells so sweet and clean. This kind of a rain makes a guy want to get out in it and let it fall on his face and run down his cheeks. The water is dripping off the coconut trees but is hardly wetting the ground. A day like this puts a lot of vitality back in a guy's system, and that's fortunate because the sun really takes it out. On Sunday, the day after tomorrow, the whole Utilities Section is having a picnic and beer party down at the beach on the other side of the island. We've been gathering beer rations for days in order to have enough to go around. It'll probably turn out to be a pretty wild affair, but I guess these guys deserve a brawl now and then."

"Still Here" had been replaced with "Still on the Rock" at the top of Harvey's Saturday night letter. "I didn't go to the show tonight because it looked so much like rain. I should have had time to write a long letter, but these guys kept talking all night about the war, and then by the time I had finished with my censoring, my eyes were pretty heavy. I want to get some sleep too, because tomorrow is the Utilities picnic, and we'll no doubt knock ourselves out all day. I'm going to take my camera along and try to get a few pictures. I spoke too soon yesterday when I told you about the nice, gentle rain, because we had one of our downpours this afternoon. I'm glad I didn't go to the show, because it came down pretty hard then, too hard to sit outside in it anyway.

"We still haven't had any word one way or the other about just how long we'll have to sweat it out here on Guam. All the rumors are still floating around with new ones popping up all the time. The best policy is to pay no attention to anything until orders come out, and then we'll take off.... for home, I hope. If they're going to make me stay overseas for any length of time, I hope they move us around a lot, so we'll at least see new places and scenery all the time. Old Mac is the one who's really sweating it out. He has the worst case of homesickness I've ever seen. Not that all of us aren't anxious to get home, but we don't go around with our feelings on our sleeves. I feel really sorry for him."

Harvey slept until almost 9:00 on Monday morning, and since everyone else had left for the picnic at 8:30, he drove out by himself in his jeep. "It took me an hour and a half to get there. They had their spot picked out on the beach on the Southwestern side of the island where there was a ball field and lots of ocean to play around in. There were 10 truckloads of men and 15 officers, with 25 cases of beer, 12 cases of Coca Cola, lots of sliced cheese, sliced Spam, and a mixture of peanut butter and jelly along with some cake for dessert. We played five games of softball and did lots of fooling around in the ocean. The beach was rocky and full of sharp coral that can cut your feet to ribbons, so everyone that went into the water wore shoes of some kind. I wore my tennis shoes because they'll dry out faster than leather shoes."

In the afternoon, they set up a PA system, and a couple of the men with guitars and violins played some hillbilly music, while everyone else sat around and relaxed. Colonel Kennedy arrived in his jeep, and they asked him to say a few words over the microphone: "He told the men not to get too excited about going home because we would no doubt be here for three or four months yet. That didn't sound bad at all to me because my hunch has been that we would have to spend seven or eight months on this rock. I got back here a little after five this afternoon in time to get a few bites of supper. Mac wanted to go to the show tonight, and I did too, but it was raining, and the sky was looking dark. So, I stayed here to write a letter, while Mac went with a couple of other guys. The picture was 'My Reputation' with Barbara Stanwick and George Brent, and from what I hear it's supposed to be pretty good.... but I didn't want to stand out in the rain. It's not so bad if the weather is ok when you start out and it starts to rain halfway through the picture, but I'll be darned if I'll go when it's already raining. I'm glad I didn't go because the rain is coming down in buckets now. Old Mac is going to look like a wet turkey when he gets back." There was more rain on Monday, but it held off long enough for Harvey to go to El Gecko for the day's movie. "Considering the picture, it might just as well have rained!! It was 'Keep Your Powder Dry,' Lorraine Day, Susan Peters and that sweater-filler Lana Turner. The picture was a crude representation of the WACs and turned out to be little else than propaganda. Pretty funny in spots but not a top-notcher. Donald Duck knocked himself out in 'Donald's Crime,' where he swipes $1.30 out of a piggy bank to take Daisie out to a hot spot. Plenty good.

"More rumors today, a few that sound pretty good (if they are to be believed.) One of them has us starting for home within a month. I'm getting to the point now where I won't believe I'm leaving until I actually get on the boat, or plane, or sled, or however it is they'll send us. Maybe that's better anyway."

Irving Berlin's *This is the Army* is considered by many to be the most successful and popular patriotic show of World War II. Berlin had insisted that African American performers be included in the cast, and it became the only integrated unit in the military at the time. The production had opened on Broadway on July 4th, 1942 and was so successful that the Broadway engagement was extended to twelve weeks and was followed by a national tour. Eleanor and Franklin Roosevelt both saw the show, she on Broadway and he at a special White House performance. Warner Brothers made *This is the Army* into a Technicolor movie in 1943, filming it on fifteen different stages at their Studios in Burbank—about ten miles from the music store where Betty worked. Two of the stars, George Murphy and Ronald Reagan, would both later go into politics. Murphy served as a US Senator for California, and Reagan was Governor of California and later, US President. With a reduced cast, Berlin later took the production overseas to the European, Far East, and Pacific theaters. The international touring company, went to England, North Africa, Italy, Egypt, and Iran before heading to the Pacific in December of 1944. The company, directed by Irving Berlin himself, landed in Guam early in August 1945, just a few days before the atomic bomb was dropped on Japan.

Harvey and his unit saw the production at their outdoor theater on Tuesday, August 21, 1945. "At the theater tonight we had 'This is the Army,' and without a doubt, it's the best show of its kind that I have ever seen. All the entertainers are potential stars and I'll bet all of them will be playing stage shows of one kind or another long after the Army releases them. I'd sure like to see the movie now to compare the two. It (the stage show, not the movie) is going to run at our theater for four days to allow all personnel in this area to see it. They have quite an elaborate prop set up, so they are centralizing rather than move from theater to theater. I think maybe I'll try to sneak in and see it again!!" The show struck some personal chords with Harvey. The romantic leads were a serviceman with the production troupe and his girlfriend, who worked at a record store back in the States. Also, there was a musical number ("I Left My Heart at the Stage Door Canteen") about a soldier falling in love with a girl he met at a place very much like the Legion Hall in Beverly Hills. With his letter, Harvey included the program for the production:

THE UNITED STATES ARMY
Presents
IRVING BERLIN'S
ALL-SOLDIER-SHOW

THIS IS THE ARMY

Music and Lyrics by Irving Berlin
Entire Production Staged under the Personal Direction of Mr. Berlin
Production in the Pacific Ocean Areas under Supervision of United States
Army POA Special Services Section

OVERTURE

OPENING CHORUS

"THIS IS THE ARMY, Mr. JONES"

SGT. DICK BERNIE

"I'M GETTING TIRED SO I CAN SLEEP"

"DON'T SING - GO INTO YOUR DANCE"

SGT. JULIE OSHINS

"MANDY"

MILITARY VAUDEVILLE (with a juggler)

LADIES OF THE CHORUS

MILITARY VAUDEVILLE (with acrobats)

"WITH MY HEAD IN THE CLOUDS" AND "AMERICAN EAGLES"

"WHAT THE WELL-DRESSED MAN IN HARLEM WILL WEAR"

FINALE

Intermission

STAGE DOOR CANTEEN

"I LEFT MY HEART AT THE STAGE DOOR CANTEEN"

MILITARY VAUDEVILLE (with magician)

A SOLDIER'S DREAM

"OH, HOW WE LONG TO BE HOME"

DADDY'S FURLOUGH

FINALE

"That wonderful letter came today in which you tell all about the peace celebration and hearing the final announcements about Japan's surrender. I wished that I could have been with you that special day. I'm awfully glad you tried to call my folks, honey, and I hope you can get through to them when you try again. I sure wish I knew when they are going to send us home. We talk about little else all day long."

That same day, Harvey's mother wrote to him and was able to give vent to the worry that she and Harvey Sr. had been dealing with. "We are so glad this mess is all over and nothing has happened to you. I used to think our luck just couldn't be that good. I'll sure be glad when everything is signed, sealed and settled and you are on your way back home. I can just imagine how glad you and Betty both are that it is just a question of time now, and believe me, dear, daddy and I are just as happy for you. I hope Uncle Sam doesn't have anything too involved in mind for you that would keep you over there too long. Betty says if you are to be there for an extended period of time she is going over to be with you. After MacArthur goes into Japan on Sunday, I have an idea things are going to wind up pretty fast. I would have liked to have seen you when peace was declared. It was really something here, and I could just imagine what it was at a military base and especially in Guam. Guam seems to be the hub. All the news and reports and information we get comes from there.

"You know the war is over because the Fuller Brush man was here yesterday! Talk about getting back in the groove. They are laying off right and left everywhere now. Whole sections of Westinghouse have closed down entirely, putting thousands out of work. Mine Safety has closed down with the exception of a skeleton force in the office. But I haven't heard too much griping. Everyone just seems to be glad the war is over. I feel really sorry for the ones who haven't any reason to be glad, and there are lots of them."

Harvey enclosed a clipping from the *Baltimore Sun* with his Thursday night letter. It was an article about Mrs. Margaret Johnston Goetz who was born in Agaña and was known as the "First Lady of Guam." Mrs. Goetz had saved the life of an American Naval Officer, George Ray Tweed, who had gone into hiding when the Japanese invaded the island in 1941. Despite being tortured, Mrs. Goetz had refused to tell where Tweed was hiding, and had gone on to become a leader in the Guam resistance movement. "With liberation, she became head of the Island Red Cross. She distributed cloth to the ragged natives, organized committees to see to the American service men. Among the members of her troupe is her daughter, Marian, who dances the hula. On the side she serves again as consultant for everyone, including Americans, with problems to solve, and as a member of the committee for the new Agaña, for the town is to be rebuilt on higher ground." Harvey had seen Mrs. Goetz's troupe when they had performed at El Gecko.

As the war ended, the men paid close attention to news about the ASR. The Advanced Service Rating scoring system (ASR) was being used to determine which soldiers would be sent home, and even more importantly, when. The regulations had been introduced in September of 1944, and revisions were made in February and March to account for changing conditions in Europe and the Pacific. Roughly speaking, points were awarded for time in service (one point per month), overseas time in service (one additional point per month), combat awards (five points each), and dependent children at home (twelve points each). Harvey still hadn't heard much about when they'd be leaving Guam, but "I don't have much of a chance to be sent home very soon because the points required for captains is 70. Right now, I'm credited with 42 which puts me in 'Class E.' The points are figured as of May 12th or 13th of this year at which time I had 42. If they refigure the points in the future, I'll have some more but it'll still be some time before I have 70. The men in Classes A and B are being sent home pretty soon, within a month, but there aren't many of them so in order to release the desired number now, they'll either have to refigure the points or lower the points required for release. All officers over 42 years of age can be released upon request, so maybe I should go to work on my birth certificate?"

The officers of the 75th were preparing a baseball field so they could have a "home field," and Harvey worked on it on Saturday. "I'm pretty tired tonight because I took a bulldozer out again tonight after supper to work on our proposed ball field. These bulldozers we have are awfully small, and consequently you take an awful beating while you're working on it. It gets dark here about seven thirty, so we don't have a whole lot of time to get much work done after supper, but we'll make it if we keep plugging away. Most of the guys will have some spare time on their hands before very long, so we'll be needing a baseball diamond of our own. The games we've played so far have all been played on someone else's field, but as soon as we get this one finished we'll be able to have home games of our own. I'm trying to teach a couple of these other officers to operate the bulldozers so we can use two or three of them at one time and finish up a lot faster. It's kind of a ticklish deal because the equipment is my responsibility, and I can't afford to have one of these officers ruin a bulldozer. Parts are too hard to get. Tomorrow, I don't have one single thing to do, so I'm going to spend most of the day on my back, reading and thinking of you. By the way, if you see any more of those books like you sent before, send them on to me, will you? Those little pocketbooks are really small, and some of them are very good. Any that you would like I'd like, so don't worry too much about the titles." Harvey's mother wrote on Saturday and asked about the typhoon in the Pacific. It had delayed the peace process forty-eight hours, and she was worried about the impact on Guam.

A letter came for Harvey from Jean Dietz, the friend from Pittsburgh whose husband had been shot down in 1943. She passed on news about common friends and asked if celebrations were going on in Guam. "I suppose you and the boys had a big blow out on August 14th when you heard the news. A week before the official announcement, we kept hearing reports that the terms had been accepted...and then the reports would be contradicted. There was quite a lot of celebrating in Pittsburgh too."

On Sunday, Mac and Pop talked Harvey into taking them for a ride in his jeep. "It was a little cloudy which made it ideal for riding, so we traveled over quite a few of the main roads on the island. At about four o'clock we decided to start back in order to be here for supper at five. Well, that's when the jeep started acting up. It would spit and cough and jump along for a few hundred yards and then quit altogether. After we fiddled around with it for a little while, it would start up, but then go through the same performance again. I guess I must have taken the sediment bowl off the fuel pump at least 1000 times. The trouble seemed to be either water or dirt in the gasoline, so after proceeding in fits and starts for over an hour we managed to work a system by adjusting the mixture of the carburetor and running with the choke all the way out, so that we could limp home. We couldn't make more than 10 miles an hour, so we didn't get back until past 6:30. Sgt. Porfaro, the mess sergeant (he's the one who's going to get the tomato pie recipe for you) was still in the mess hall so he fixed up some chow for us. It was lots of fun though, because every time the jeep started to go into one of its coughing spells, the three of us would go into spasms of laughter.

"While we were out this afternoon, we found the Graves Registry Office, so we went in and inquired about the location of Paul Bright's grave. He's a boy from home, a Lt. J.G., who was killed on the 10th of December 1941, and buried in Guam. We went out to his grave and took a couple of pictures of it to send to his folks. He's buried on a sandy track beside a row of bushes with large red flowers on them. Really a pretty little cemetery. We also got a picture of a new monument that has been put up on the beach where the Americans landed on July 21st, 1944, to retake the island.

"The officers had been eating in the enlisted men's mess hall up until Monday of last week, but at that time our own mess hall became ready for operation so we moved in. It's a little more like a cafeteria with the food being served from a home-made steam table and eating at four-man tables rather than at the standard 8-man, picnic type tables that most mess halls use. Sgt. Porfaro is our mess Sgt. and talk about good food! Guests who eat in our mess hall says there is no better food to be found on the island. We get the same rations that are given to every other mess hall, but the difference is in the preparation. Porfaro knocks himself out trying to make it taste good.

"There was heavy rain again on Monday, and the camp was flooded. The automotive shop was completely under water, and the men couldn't get into the large coral pit where they kept shovels and several dump trucks. "That tied things up for a while because we use a lot of coral for building roads and for making fills under buildings etc. Things were pretty hot around here for a while, until we explained to everybody right up to the General that the coral pit was shut down because of an 'Act of God'. I hope that we don't get another rain like that right way because we'd be working out of rowboats!

"We saw 'Heavenly Body' last night, with Hedy Lamarr and William Powell, and I thought we'd die laughing. It was a new picture to me, although I understand it is comparatively old. One of my sergeants, Sgt. Van Eman, just came in and we were talking about the picture and one thing led to another and before we knew it we got to talking about some of the cartoons we had seen. Sure enough, we got to talking about the one, 'Innertube Antics' that I told you about a little while back. Before long we were laughing like a couple of fools. I hope someone starts a theater back in the States that shows nothing but cartoons. I'll be a regular customer at that place. Incidentally, this Sgt. Van Eman is a swell guy. He's about 45 years old and has a son in the Army in Germany. Because of his age, he's getting a discharge in a very short time so that I'll have to find a replacement for him, which won't be easy to do. He handles all the water hauling trucks that operate out of the heavy equipment pool and has been doing a d___ good job. We haul from 150,000 to 200,000 gallons a day and to keep the trucks on the road and on schedule is a pretty stiff deal."

That evening, Harvey went to El Gecko again to see a picture he had already seen. "It was 'For Whom the Bell Tolls' so I really made an effort to go. I'd like to get hold of the book to read, so if you see it around anywhere, get it for me, will you? Have you seen the picture? You'd like it, I know. After we came back from the show, one of my mechanics came up and said there was a Marine that wanted to see me. I didn't think any Marines on the island knew me, so I took a look to see who it was. I had never seen the guy before, but he told me that his girlfriend was a very close friend of my wife. He said her name was Jeannie and that really stopped me because I don't know any of your friends by that name. He said her last name was Whitman, and it still didn't register. I took a stab in the dark and asked if her name couldn't possibly be 'Virjeanne', could it...and that was it! Can you imagine that?" Virjeanne and Betty had regularly gone together to weekly dances at the American Legion Hall in 1942. She had been there when Betty and Harvey had met for the first time. "His name is Earl Sexton, and he seems to be a darn nice guy. We went down to my room and had a long talk over a bottle of beer. His outfit won't be here for very long now, but he's going to come back up here before he goes so we can have another long 'bull session.' He gave me his last 'dog tag' to send on to Virjeanne, because he's apparently not allowed to send anything at all home. His home is in North Carolina, and as I was stationed at Maxton, N.C at one time, we had plenty to talk about." Earl came over again later that evening and brought a bracelet that he hoped Harvey could forward to Virjeanne. He also gave Harvey two Japanese hand grenades that he had picked up somewhere, and Harvey planned to bring them home with him."

Wednesday was a busy day for the Heavy Equipment Unit. "We've been having lots of rain the last few days, but it hasn't been that heavy downpour that is common around here. It's still raining right now and has been for at least the past 48 hours. Lots of the work we do depends on the ground being at least in a semi-dry condition, and this continual rain has managed to keep everything pretty soggy. If it would just stay dry for about two days we'd be able to get a lot of work done that is hanging fire right now. For instance, we've opened up a new coral pit to provide new fill for roads etc., and the entrance road to the pit is as mushy as can be. That entrance road is about two hundred feet long, and with all this water on it, it stays so mushy that the dump trucks have a hard time getting through. It slows us down, and we are only getting about 25% of the coral that we should be getting. We'll get it all straightened out in time, but it sure makes it rough for now.——There was a long interruption here because we had a phone call from an Engineer Supply unit on the lower end of the island in answer to a letter of ours requesting some additional equipment. We need some larger stuff for some of these jobs we're doing, so we put in a requisition for it about two months ago. Just today they called and said that they thought they could help us with a few of the items we had asked for. So, I took off right away to see about it. Sure enough, they do have a small surplus of equipment, and I think we are going to be able to get some of it!! We are especially interested in two bull dozers and a 3/4-yard shovel. The bull dozers are bigger than anything we have now, and we've got quite a few jobs that are too large for our small dozers to handle. The shovel will go right into our coral pit and ought to allow us to increase our output about 100%. We're also getting some other stuff including a half dozen more dump trucks, a ditching machine, an 8-ton roller, a scraper, and a concrete mixer, but they aren't nearly as important to us as the dozers and the shovel. The supper bell is ringing now, so I'd better run for my chow."

Gradually, some of the men from Guam started to head home. "Some of the men here have sufficient points to go home, and they have been leaving in little dribbles every now and then. Naturally, the big problem is transportation so sometimes it takes quite a while before a man can get started even if he has enough points. Captain Dangers of the 73rd (Jacques) has been sweating out a ride, and last night it came through so he's on his way back now. He's planning on surprising Jeanne, so don't say anything to her if you should happen to be talking to her. It seems to me that it'll be a shock when he walks in on her, but I guess he wants it that way and I'd hate to be the one to spoil it. It will be a good long while yet before I can hit that homeward trail, so I'm not doing too much sweating. I sure hope they cut down the number of points required for release. As soon as these high point men get on their way, then some of the rest of us should fall into line. A few more men are leaving tomorrow, but they are all 'high point' men. There are still a lot of them to go yet before there is much chance for the rest of us. If the point system stays just as it is, I won't have enough accumulated to leave until next June. There are lots of rumors and guesses as to how and when the point system will be altered, but as yet the War Dept. has not given us any information about it. Even if they decide not to change it to our benefit, we can't be too disappointed because there are quite a few other men in the Pacific who have been here lots longer than we have and deserve to go home first. But, if we should get a chance to go soon, you can bet we're not going to turn it down. Mac has a pretty fair chance of going home before some of the rest of us because he only needs a couple more points to reach his critical score (58 points for 1st Lts.)!

"We saw Eddie Bracken's movie 'Bring on the Girls' last night, and it wasn't bad at all. Spike Jones' band played a super number at the end of the show that really was the ultra, ultra in foolishness! They played on everything but the kitchen sink and would have played on that too if they had had one. Eddie Bracken is much better on the screen than he is in person. I guess that stage show of his was quite a flop. At least it's getting a lot of negative reviews in all of the newspapers we've seen over here. It has already been pulled off its current tour. Tonight's movie was 'Crimes Inc.' and talk about lousy pictures. This one was the world's worst. Leo Carrillo and Martha Tilton were in it, but they couldn't keep the rest of the characters from ruining the show. We stayed through it all because it was so bad that it began to get funny after a while. We laughed at the most serious scenes, booed the villains, cheered the hero and everything else!"

On the last day of August, for some reason Harvey decided to start to rave about the meals in camp! "The food here lately has been really good. Since we opened our own mess hall (that's the officers mess), we've had food that some restaurants in the states couldn't match. We're getting the same food as all the other mess halls, but our cooks are performing wonders with it. Yesterday, we had liver and onions which, in the army, has a reputation for being rather sad food. Our cooks breaded it and fried it with bacon and fried the onions right with it and talk about good eating... Man, that was the best yet. They make 'C' rations taste like chicken ala king. I'm sure that all the credit should go to Mess Sgt. Porfaro, because he's really worked to make the mess hall a success. Breakfasts are always delicious and consist of either hot cakes, French toast, or fried eggs, along with some kind of hot cereal. We can't get any fresh milk for the cereal, but even with powdered milk it tastes good. The coffee is always fresh and as different from regular GI coffee as day from night. Breakfast has always been my favorite meal anyway so I'm in my glory now as far as chow is concerned.

"Sunday is the day that has been picked for a show of air strength over Japan, so we expect a lot of activity about then. I'm doing my best to get a ride on that mission, but so far I've had no luck. I've got feelers out all over the Wing, so if there are any vacancies on any of the planes, I should have a chance to get on. There won't be any bombing, but it will be a sight to see just the same, and maybe I'll have a chance to take some pictures on the flight.

"One of the officers in one of the other groups is leaving today, so the other officers had a big party for him last night. When I say party I do mean a big one. They drank everything in sight including the native liquors that are made here on the island from the sap of the cocoanut tree. They call it tuba juice and agi juice. I've tasted it, and, believe me, it's like drinking liquid fire. It's white and clear like water, and I guess I must have had about as much as would fill a medicine dropper. I thought it would burn a hole right straight through me! How those guys can drink that stuff and then say they like it is beyond me. The medical officers here say that they can't understand why all the natives on the island aren't blind from drinking the blamed stuff. They say it's much harder on a man than the 'canned heat' that some people in the states insist on drinking." The "canned heat" that Harvey referred to was Sterno, an inexpensive alcohol-based gel used as a cooking fuel for portable stoves. It was made from ethanol, methanol, a gelling agent, and pink dye, and it came in cans. Sterno had been consumed as an alternative source of alcohol since Prohibition, and during the Depression, hobos had made "jungle juice" (also called "sock wine" or "squeeze") by squeezing the gel through cheesecloth or socks and then mixing it with fruit juice. The problem was that the drink was highly poisonous, often causing blindness and death.

"I cut an article out of the Saturday Evening Post by Colonel Stoopnagle, and I know you'll get a kick out of reading. Whenever I see an item by Colonel Stoopnagle or Ogden Nash, I always take time to read them. Ogden Nash spends most of his time writing poetry, and if he can't find a word to rhyme, he just manufactures one. He put out a whole book of that kind of poetry one time, and I read almost all of it."

22

MOVIE STARS SERVED

IN "FUM-POO"

The fiancé of Betty's friend, Peggy Irving, had been discharged with "battle fatigue," and she was leaving town to be with him in Texas. Peggy wanted Betty to see her off at the train station, and the Irvings asked if she and Elsie would stay at the house to take care of the dog. Betty liked the idea, but she needed to talk it over with Elsie. On Thursday, Betty and Mary Alyce went to Selznick Studios to pick up their friend Marion so they could go to dinner and on to the Bowl. While Marion finished up her work for the day, the girls waited in the office of Geraldine Mavor, the Publicity Coordinator at Selznick. "Around the walls are large glamour shots of Joseph Cotton, Robert Walker, Gregory Peck, Rhonda Fleming, Jennifer Jones and others. There are five desks in the office, and I am sitting at Geraldine Mavor's desk – ...<u>the big boss herself</u>! She and several hundred others at the studio are out on strike." Mavor, originally from Calgary and with a Master's from Columbia, had worked for many years as a literary agent. She had been Publicity Coordinator at Selznick since 1944. Later, she would marry A. E. Hotchner, a good friend of Ernest Hemingway and the author of *Papa Hemingway*. At the time of Betty's visit in August of 1945, Mavor and many others from all major Hollywood Studios were on strike. What had originally begun as a minor labor dispute involving a few set designers had exploded:

> In March of 1945, an estimated 10,500 CSU workers went on strike. They
> put pickets at all the studios and later started picketing movie theaters

also. By that time the studios had 130 films on the shelves – a nine month's supply. This was not necessarily the most fortuitous moment for a studio strike. Still, shortly after the strike was launched, Disney, Monogram and some independents bargained with Local 1421. Columbia, RKO, Universal, Fox and Warner Bros. did not and were affected most severely, with MGM and Paramount right behind.

The strike really started to hurt the producers. RKO was forced by the strike to suspend production of the Selznick epic "Duel in the Sun", starring Gregory Peck, Jennifer Jones, Joseph Cotton, Lillian Gish and Walter Huston. The star cast refused to work when mass picketing began. Jennifer Jones, leading lady in the $4,000,000 spectacle, walked out when she saw the pickets. Lillian Gish walked past the studio waving to the picketers. Other players, including Gregory Peck, Lionel Barrymore, Walter Huston and Charles Bickford did not show up at all.

On October 5th, there was a violent confrontation at Warner Bros. Studio, an incident later known as "Hollywood Bloody Friday."

That evening, the three friends went to the Hollywood Bowl, and they agreed that the program was wonderful. "I'm so glad I didn't miss it. Rubenstein played several concertos on the piano and, as an encore, he played Chopin's Polonaise. That man can really make the piano talk. I made good bus connections, so here I am ready for bed and talking to you...it's only a quarter to twelve."

It was Mr. Stella's birthday on Friday, and the girls went with Mr. and Mrs. Stella to dinner at Carter's Restaurant in front of the Cathay Circle Theater on Wilshire Boulevard. "The veal cutlets were delicious...but it was so hot in there I thought we'd all pass out before we finished dinner. We drove all over the place trying to find a good show, or one that didn't have a big line out in front. We finally wound up at the new Drive-In theater on Olympic Blvd. First time I've ever gone to a drive-in. It really was fun. The pictures we saw were 'The Clock' with Judy Garland and Robert Clark, and 'Main St. after Dark.' I'd already seen that but had missed the other...it was cute. It was so warm there in the car that none of us had coats on, and we had all the windows open." Betty got home at about the same time as her brother. "Rod just got home from his date with Nellie – another new one. They saw some picture on Hollywood Blvd."

Betty and Mary Alyce, along with Rod and his date, Georgia, went to the Bowl again on Saturday evening. The event was a joint program of the

Hollywood Bowl Association and the Academy of Motion Picture Arts and Sciences—and a number of Hollywood stars, including Claudette Colbert, Danny Kaye, Frank Sinatra, and Frances Langford were featured. The first part of the program was conducted by Leopold Stokowski and included scores from a number of motion pictures. After the intermission, Ms. Colbert read a narration by Nunnally Johnson with the orchestra playing behind her. Then Kaye presented a scene from one of his films, and the program concluded with songs by Sinatra and Langford. "As far as I'm concerned, Danny Kaye stole the show! I thought we'd all die laughing at his antics. He's a good-looking guy, too. He and his wife sat in a box in front of us during the first part of the show. I think we would have enjoyed the show even more except for the fact that we had a flat tire on the way there. Right off of Hollywood Blvd.! We left the tire to be fixed while we were at the Bowl, and when we walked back to the car at midnight Rod had to change the tire – and to top it off, it happened on a hill, and the darn car kept slipping. I was supposed to be over at Peggy's at midnight but got there at 2 o'clock." Betty still managed to write to Harvey that night, and she included a couple of newspaper clippings. One was an article about a Japanese ship captured in the East Indies while posing as a Red Cross hospital ship. The other was about "Tokio Rose." Betty and her friends at the record store had gotten a kick out of that one!

Tokio Rose Asks New Records for Program so Yanks Supply Them

Tokio Rose, the Japanese radio propagandist, knows the meaning of "American Service." Col. William C. Farnum, chief of staff at the Santa Ana Air Base, who recently returned from the Seventh Air Force in the Pacific, related today that Tokio Rose had complained on her broadcasts to American forces that her records were scratched, and she needed new ones.

A Rotary Club in the south co-operated by purchasing the records, which were flown from the mainland to a B-29 base in the Marianas. Col. Farnum was commander of the Army Garrison Forces on the island of Tinian and the records were placed aboard a Tokio-bound Superfort.

The records were parachuted down on Tokio. Colonel Farnum heard them on his radio the next day.

Meanwhile, Harvey's parents were closely following the news from Guam. "Guam sure is given a lot of publicity in the newspaper. Until you were stationed there, it meant nothing to us. We hear a lot about the 20th Air Force and what they are doing. Boy, that would be a thrill to watch them leaving for their attacks. Do you see them coming back? .... Just listened to Wesley Edwards broadcasting from Guam, and he talked about the planes leaving Guam loaded with 3 million leaflets to be dropped on Japan telling them to quit now. Are you ever anywhere near these daily broadcasts when they are sent? I dreamed about you last night. Are you all right?"

Sunday morning, Betty went to Union Station with the Irvings to see Peggy off. "It's the first time I've been in the station, or gone through to the trains, since we left for Hays and then, of course, when I came home alone. I couldn't hold back the tears, I missed you so much. I didn't feel weepy for Peg, because she seems very happy and was excited at the prospect of the trip and the wedding. Her mother took it pretty hard, and 'Pop' just smoked his cigar harder than ever. I never hear a train whistle that doesn't remind me of listening to the train go by in Hays.

"Yesterday something happened that restored my faith in people! Just as I was leaving for work, Mother called in and asked me if I had my ticket for the bowl. I said 'yes' and just to be sure I looked in my purse – and the whole book of season tickets was gone. I dashed around my room trying to find them and couldn't. Mother called in the afternoon and said I had a letter from Spring Street from someone she's never heard of. I told her to open the letter...and it was from the man who runs Harry's Deli and Restaurant on Spring St. in Los Angeles, telling me he had found the ticket book and was holding it for me until I could pick it up! I'm going down to L.A. Tuesday so will pick it up then!"

Betty and Rod had joined the community orchestra in Los Angeles, Betty playing clarinet and Rod playing trumpet. Her father met her after work on Monday and took her to an orchestra practice at City Hall. "It was a good practice...boy, am I rusty. Especially when the music is in <u>5 sharps</u>!" On Tuesday, Betty went back into LA with her parents and retrieved her Hollywood Bowl tickets from the restaurant on Spring Street. "The man was so nice, and he wouldn't take any money for saving them for me. Tonight, Mary Alyce and I played hooky from the Bowl and went to a show instead! We went to the Bowl first and gave our tickets to some girl marines...I hope they enjoyed the box seats! We went over to Hollywood Blvd. and saw 'Christmas in Connecticut.' It was really a howl! ... if it happens to come back, be sure to see it. There was also a short, 'America the Beautiful', that was really lovely – all in technicolor and showed scenes from all over the country."

News stories that day focused on the atom bomb and the death of the war hero, Richard Bong. "Are they loading the bombs on the B-29's in Guam? If you are anywhere close to them be extra careful! Wasn't that a shame about Major Bong? I didn't know a thing about it until this afternoon. They'd only been married 6 months. Remember when we saw the news of their wedding?" Major Richard Bong, a pilot in the US Army Air Forces, was widely considered America's top flying "ace," a war hero. After shooting down a record thirty-eight Japanese fighters, he had been presented the Medal of Honor by General MacArthur in December 1944, after which he shot down two more Japanese planes before being returned to the States. He married his sweetheart, schoolteacher Marjorie Vattendahl in February 1945 (the wedding that Betty referenced in her letter), and then helped with a testing program for Lockheed's new P-80 fighter. Ironically, on August 6th, during a test flight in California, Bong died (at the age of twenty-five) when his P-80 crashed in a North Hollywood vacant lot, near the intersection of Oxnard Street and Satsuma Alley....some seven miles from the Hollywood Bowl. The August 7th headline in the *Los Angeles Times*, JET PLANE EXPLOSION KILLS MAJOR BONG, shared the front page with an even larger headline: ATOMIC BOMB HITS JAPAN!

At about 1:45 in the afternoon on Thursday, the telephone rang in the music store, and Mr. Stella answered it. "He got all excited, and when he hung up he said that at 2 p.m. the announcement of the end of the war was to come. The call had been from the Newspaper office who had some inkling of a special broadcast. I tried to act calm and serene through all the commotion in the store and did – but I was doing flip-flops inside. I went into the little girls' room, combed my hair, washed my hands and talked myself out of tears. When the news started there were about 30 people standing around the radio – just looking at each other and not saying a word. When the news came through, it wasn't the end of the war, but news about the conference the (Japanese) were having, discussing how they could get out of the mess. What a let-down feeling...these people that start rumors! I guess I should have known better.

"Mom and Dad went to the Bowl tonight, my anniversary present to them. They enjoyed it and said it was packed. Jeannette McDonald was the soloist and did 7 encores."

On Friday, Betty wrote again... "Another big day in history! I've been wondering all day what you were doing and what all of you were saying and thinking as all the big news breaks. It's getting near that day the whole world has been dreaming of, and I find it almost too hard to believe. It always seemed some day in the far future – and bang, here it is. We had a big radio out in front of the store with the news on all day. Most of the stations cancelled all programs and commercials in favor of the news items. On the window I printed:

LATEST

~~WAR~~

PEACE

NEWS

"Of course, it hasn't come yet, but it is coming any day, or hour, now! Excitement has been in the air all day – but people have been calm and there hasn't been any celebration here for the war isn't over yet. We've got the different war "Extras" and put them in the front window too." With her letter, she included an article about celebrations in Guam:

GUAM TARS NEARLY TEAR OFF ROOF

Enlisted men at Guam fleet headquarters nearly "tore the roof off the barracks today as news spread like wildfire over Guam that Tokio was willing to talk peace. In view of the atomic bomb and the Russian declaration of war, the news seemed convincing to the men who had steeled themselves for additional long months of combat against a fanatical enemy.

Staff officers at Fleet Adm. Chester W. Nimitz' quarters said: "We have had no other word than that which has been broadcast to the public. We'll let you know if there are any further newsworthy developments."

Harvey's mother sent Pittsburgh reactions to the week's news. "All the things that have happened this week. Just one good surprise after another – the atomic bomb, Russia's entrance into the war, the offer of surrender from the [Japanese], and the cocoanut from you!... [She stressed the last one!] We were wondering what you were doing when all this excitement was going on about Japan insisting on surrendering on their own terms. Pittsburgh was very calm and not convinced. I believe it will be a reality in a short time though, and it can't come too soon. We went to the Penn [Theatre] last night and saw Bette Davis in 'The Corn is Green.' Pretty good, too. She certainly can act, can't she? And that Van Johnson picture is held over for a third week at the Stanley.

"A news bulletin just now says there will be nothing new on the Japanese reply to our terms until Sunday night or Monday. I hope when I write you next the war will be history."

Rod went to the Bowl with Betty on Saturday. "It was simply beautiful this evening. Yehudi Menuhin was soloist for the night, and Antal Dorati directed. He had that orchestra right at the tips of his fingers! – and I like violins when they are played like Menuhin plays his. They played an oriental piece I'd never heard of before. If you get a chance – listen to it. If I find it has been recorded, I'll buy it. The Colas Breugnon Overture by Kabalevsky – How's that for a mouthful! Mother and Dad went to a show and saw '1,001 Nights' and 'Son of Lassie.' Kathryn Lytle, one of the girls with us in the box, is one of the flower girls in the picture '1,001 Nights.' Everyone is still waiting around here for authentic news to reach us. There surely has been a lot of premature celebrating, hasn't there? Betty Lou Jones came into the store today and brought her little boy in for me to meet. Her husband is the one in the 75th that I told you about. She says he is taking care of wheels and tires now...will that help in your locating him?

"Darling, how does the war ending affect you? Do you have any idea if you'll come home in the next 6 months or become part of the army of occupation or be stationed some place over there in the regular army? If the latter is the case, you realize, of course, that I'm coming over there as soon as I'm allowed to. One day nearer peace.............

"Just heard on the radio that it may be that meat rationing may go away next week. Hope so, but just the same we are going to hang onto our ration books because you never can tell. There is so much going on in the world these days, it almost makes your head swim. Planes bigger and better than the B-29's - millions out of jobs from the war plants – most all metals are off the priority listings...mostly wondering if the war is over or not! On the radio the other night we heard that troops are already on-board ship, completely equipped to leave immediately to occupy Japan, or invade if necessary. They said that Manila has no water at present because for two days they've pumped fresh water into the ships. Does this make sense to you?

"I got a big kick out of the names of the planes. With humor like that in fighting planes, how could the boys help but come out in front. Those leaflets will be something to save for souvenirs, won't they? Souvenirs of our mighty B-29's and the marvel of this age...the atomic bomb."

Sunday's news about the war was typical of the ongoing coverage. "Late this afternoon a flash came over all stations that the Japanese had accepted our terms – war was over! The folks came in from the kitchen, and we cried happy tears with them. Then, after all this was over, the commentator came on again and said that the previous announcement of peace was premature and that there was no official word from the President. Then, I really felt like bawling...just think of the millions of people who heard the declaration of peace and then heard the cancellation of it."

Some local Army and Navy servicemen, just back from the South Pacific, came into Stella's on Tuesday. "They used to buy records from us and just wanted to let us know that they were still kicking!"

Bold lettering at the top of Betty's Tuesday letter read:

"PEACE" AT LAST!!
August 14, 1945

"It's come for sure. The whole wide world is at peace today. It still seems like a dream because there have been so many false rumors the last week. I wish you were here so we could really celebrate this wonderful day together. I'm staying home this evening. Listening to the mobs on the radio from Times Square, and every large city, is enough commotion at the present to suit me! I'm sure I will sleep like a log tonight for I don't think I had more than 3 hours of sleep last night. We were up until the 10 o'clock news, and as there wasn't anything special on, we all went to bed – to sleep, we thought. I had just dozed off a little when I heard the radio blaring next door and Mrs. Jones yelling that the war was over. I turned on our radio just in time to hear the fellow saying that nothing was definite, but all were standing by! About 1:49 a.m., though, people started going up and down in front of our house, banging on pans and yelling. Then we knew it was all over – so we all put on our robes and got up to listen to the radio in the living room. Again, it was just overly anxious announcers. So, we got back into bed, and I left my little radio on all night. This morning I got up about 10. Rod and Daddy had left for work really early, and Mother was sound asleep, since she had gotten up to get their breakfast. I put the news on right away, and nothing new came on. Mother and I had some tea in the backyard. Just after 4 p.m., she went in to hear the news....and there it was! The actual declaration we've all been waiting for. Whistles started blowing, horns tooting, people yelling and happy, relieved tears flowed at last. Rod drove in a few minutes later in the mail truck, and we listened to the news hit the different cities. Heard Guam too! Right now, there is a 'Radar' program on the air. A B-17 flying blind from Santa Barbara to Hollywood is talking to a Navy destroyer off the Southern California coast. They are giving each other their positions by radar. Until peace came today, of course, all of this would have remained a military secret. They are explaining all the intricacies of radar...certainly is amazing."

Betty was glad she was home when the news hit. Elsie called from Stella's and said they had taken all the old records and broken them all over the store! They closed at 4:30 and would also be closed the next day, and possibly Thursday as well. "I have never heard a 'New Years' like this – people with cow bells and horns are going by in front now, and more reports from cities all over the world. This will be going full blast all night and on into tomorrow from the looks of it. I didn't even attempt to call your folks when the news did finally come for the wires were all swamped. I'll call later this week. I bet they are just about as happy as can be.

"Over the radio from Guam just now it said that the whole island was going crazy. That the boys were starting to realize the war was actually over, and they could really start making plans for the future. I wonder what you are doing right now. Honey, do you realize this is the first time in either of our lifetimes that the whole world has been at peace!"

Harvey's mother relayed her own feelings about the ending of the war, and she described the scene in Pittsburgh. "Words could never express how thankful we are that this war is over, and we are all able to finally talk about it. I sometimes thought our luck just couldn't be good enough for us all live to see it over, and for nothing to happen to you. I'll always be grateful for that. As soon as it was official, we heard a broadcast from Guam, and they begin their broadcasts now by saying this is so and so speaking from 'Allied Victory Base on Guam.' I'll bet the celebrating there was really something. We feel awfully proud that you played such an important part in the winning of this war. Attention was called many, many times to the gigantic job the engineers had to do and how well they were doing it. The work on Guam was especially stressed in a broadcast on Sunday."

Harvey's parents went into town on Tuesday night, and they had never seen downtown Pittsburgh so crowded. Fifth Avenue was packed solid from the buildings on one side of the street to the other. They stopped briefly in Trinity Church and then pushed through the crowds for a while. "In all those thousands and thousands of people, we ran into Florence and Herb. If you could have seen the amount of people, you would see how impossible that was. Do you know what plans the Army has for you now? I hope they won't keep you over there too long, because I know how anxious you and Betty are to take up your life. Will you ever forget that Sunday afternoon in 1941 [Pearl Harbor]? That changed our whole lives." In a letter to Betty, she shared memories of the end of World War I. That day they had taken Harvey, then ten months old, to downtown Pittsburgh to see the wild celebrations.

On Wednesday, Betty wrote, "Today was a holiday, as proclaimed by President Truman. We will work tomorrow as usual, and then whenever V-J Day comes, that will be a national holiday. I hope we celebrate that day together next year."

With the end of the war, rationing of various products was relaxed. Gasoline rationing stopped on Wednesday. Soon, canned fruits and vege-tables were taken off the list. Meat, fats, shoes, and tires were still on the ration list. "You should have seen the cars lined up to get gas as soon as the restriction was lifted. Rod goes on vacation next week, and he and Mike are planning to go up into the mountains – probably to Big Bear – now that they won't have to worry about having enough gas to get home. There hasn't been very much in the papers or on the radio as to who is coming home. They did give figures on the number of men to be released from the various services in the next 18 months, though. I wonder if the point system will change? President Truman declared August 19th as a day of prayer for the nation. V-J Day will not be a holiday. I just heard a radio report from Fleet Headquarters on Guam...it comes on every night around 10:30, and it really sounds good to hear voices from Guam, even if it is somebody else talking."

"Rod, Georgia and I went to see 'Anchors Aweigh' tonight and had to wait in line for an hour...after standing at work all day! Rod hadn't seen it yet; both of us girls had, but it was so good I could see it again. Jose Iturbi plays the Hungarian Dance No. 2 in the Hollywood Bowl scene that is worth the whole show. I hope it plays over there for you to enjoy." Betty enclosed a brief Herald-Express article about another post-war change in the States:

Auto Speed Limit Lifted

The nationwide 35 mile an hour speed limit was lifted today by the Office of Defense Transportation. ODT director J. Monroe Johnson has notified all state governors that the ban has been removed effective tomorrow.

Johnson urged motorists to "think twice before attempting to increase regular driving speeds in old cars no longer capable of high-speed operation". With cars in their present worn-out condition, he said, highspeed driving will increase the frequency of accidents and undue wear particularly on tires. The order establishing the federal speed limit was issued September 26, 1942, as a tire conservation measure on recommendation of the Baruch rubber committee. It was later made a law by some state legislatures and by proclamations of governors.

Harvey's father wasn't much of a correspondent, even with his son. However, the end of the war was a special occasion, and he sent off a letter to Guam. "Here comes another of my rare letters. It is 9 p.m. Saturday night…11 a.m. Guam time. Every time we mention the time, we think of Guam time. We just got a special delivery letter from Betty. She wanted to call us but couldn't get the call through. She is very much thrilled, as we are, about peace being here again. We had a two-day holiday, going back to work yesterday, Friday morning. Did they give you any time off, or did you work as usual? Guam seems to be the center of everything. We hear several broadcasts a day from there. Are you near any of the stations? We are listening to the Barn Dance on the radio, and the Dinning Sisters just sang the Victory Polka. Mother said it is one of your favorites. Did you know about the bomb before it was dropped, or see them being sent? They must be terrible. Tell us what you can. We are just now listening to a special broadcast of the happenings on Iwo Jima (sp?). The announcer is describing the types of planes soon expected there, carrying the [Japanese] on their way to see Gen. MacArthur. We heard last night that there still are several hundred [Japanese] on Guam. Do you see or hear about them? Say, Bud, how big is Guam? Tell us what you can about it. You should see the cars on the road here now. They abolished gas rationing the day after peace was declared, and everything that can run is now on the road. They had better lift tire rationing too, or these wrecks will be running around on their rims. I guess all restrictions will come off soon. Do you have a radio so you can hear what's going on? I hope so. We think we will go to Calvary Church to hear the Bishop. Hope to hear from you soon. Love, Dad."

Sunday was the day President Truman had set aside for National prayer, and Betty and her mother went to church. "By just looking at everyone's faces, you could tell that Peace had come. Everyone looked more relaxed than I've seen a crowd of people look in a long time. There is some Oriental music coming from the Bowl Broadcast. Do you like that mysterious music? Rod is playing records in the living room now, so we're each having our own private concert. Tchaikovsky's 'Romeo and Juliet' is on now – the theme 'Moon Love'. Another one I used to love was Debussy's 'My Reverie.' Rod just slipped 'Octaroon' on – the toad! It was a long time ago that you found that one and sent it to me, wasn't it?" Betty sent a page from that day's *Herald-Express*. One side was covered with baseball scores and news ("Feller Leaving Navy to Rejoin Indians"). The other had articles about job losses at Douglas Aircraft, the easing of wartime rationing, and the lifting of the travel ban in the country. There was also an article about the impending wedding of Shirley Temple to John Agar, an Army sergeant stationed in Washington.

On Monday, Betty went through her record collection. "I went through a whole stack of my records tonight. I'm going to sell a lot of them while there is still a demand for the old numbers that aren't being reprinted. It will be hard packing them around the country anyway, so we might as well benefit from them while we can. I didn't realize I had so many. I see now it is going to take more than one evening to sort them out. Also looking through some old magazines before I put them out. I found some good recipes I'm going to put aside. I'll try them first before I try them on you, though, so don't worry. On Tuesday, Rod went to a political meeting in town, and he hoped to meet Ellis Patterson, the man in our district who is going to appoint Rod for West Point...at least so we hope."

Mr. Stella took the day off on Wednesday, and Betty and Elsie were alone at the store. "We had groups of young people coming in off and on all day to just listen. And not only that, this morning we decided to dress the window. We managed to fix a cute window for displaying the album 'Carousel' from the Broadway hit. 'If I loved you' is in it. The window looks like a red tent with awning stripes. Around the ledge we put the little pamphlets telling the story of the musical." The next night, Betty and Rod went to the Hollywood Bowl, and "we both thought it stunk! The Ballet wasn't nearly as colorful as it could have been. They took so long changing the scenery between acts that we didn't get to see any of the 3 acts of the last number. We left at 11:30! I bet people didn't leave until 12:30 or 1! That's ridiculous. When we got home, I packed his things for his trip...he and Mike are leaving at 6 in the morning."

On Friday, Betty had been married to Harvey for nine months, but they had been together for only about six of them. She and Elsie continued to work on the window displays at Stella's, and they had some professional help. "We've spent just about all day dressing the window at the store. We finished the merry-go-round, and while we were working on it this afternoon, one of the fellows from the cartoon department at the studio came in. He did a lot of the work on the dancing scenes in 'Anchors Aweigh.' We needed three horses for our merry-go-round, so he drew them for us. They really look like they are prancing. Elsie and I went out to dinner and then to the movies with the Stellas. We saw Jack Oakie and Peggy Ryan in 'That's the Spirit' and Abbott and Costello in 'The Naughty Nineties.' Both were funny and entertaining, but they still lacked something. On the way home from the show, we stopped at the store and tried the lighting effect in the window.... red and amber. Looks so much better with the colored lights on."

Betty went to the Hollywood Bowl again on Saturday. "It was really good tonight and made up for that last punk performance...they danced 'Swan Lake.'" The next day, some friends from Illinois dropped by. "Daddy went all through school with Art Rosine, who is now Manager of the Chicago Tribune. They live in a beautiful apartment on Lake Shore Drive. If we go through Chicago, they want us to be sure to see them."

When Betty sent records to Harvey, she packed them in tins given to her by an Army Air Corps. Sergeant, Bill Binder. Sgt. Binder was a photographer with the First Motion Picture Unit, based at nearby Hal Roach Studios. The F.M.P.U. (or "fum-poo") was established in 1942 as the 18th Air Force Base Unit of the US Army Air Corps and charged with the production of training films, morale films, and propaganda films. It's first film, "Winning Your Wings," produced at the Warner Studios in Burbank, was an attempt to help with much needed enlistments; it was credited with 150,000 new recruits. The unit was later moved to the empty Hal Roach lot, and during the war produced some four hundred films. Several movie stars served in F.M.P.U., including (Sgt.) Lee J. Cobb, (Maj.) Clark Gable, (Capt.) William Holden, (Sgt.) Alan Ladd, (Sgt.) Edmund O'Brien, and (Capt.) Ronald Reagan. By August 1945, F.M.P.U. had over a thousand personnel, not counting combat camera crews in the field. Sgt. Binder came into the music store that Monday and chatted with Betty: "...(he) told me today that a bunch of the fellows of the Roach Studio A.A.F. group were in Guam. They are motion picture Combat Crew cameramen. If you can look them up, try to. One of the group's Lieutenants told Bill he knew you, and that he'd talked with you the last time he was in Guam. I hope you see them, because they will be home really soon and maybe could bring me a picture of you.... a word picture if nothing else."

Betty wrote her letter the next night on the way home from the Hollywood Bowl. "You'd never guess where this note is being started....at the corner of Hollywood and Highland Blvds in a La Brea bus! Elsie and I tore like mad from the Bowl concert to catch the first bus and avoid the crowd, and so tonight the bus decides to wait for the Highland Streetcar. We got on the bus anyway and, of course, it will be so late when we get home that we decided to start our nightly letters. The concert wasn't too good tonight, but the 1000 voices were beautiful. They did the chorale work for Beethoven's 9th Symphony. That melody is a favorite of mine and was very inspiring. The brass was very much out of tune, and Elsie and I would just look at each other and try to smother our laughter. It has been advertised all over that a chorus of 1000 voices would perform tonight. Elsie leaned over and said it doesn't look like there are a thousand people on the stage, and we started counting...1-2-3. I looked at her and said, 'there's really only 986...I just counted,' and that started us laughing all over again. Mary Alyce and Marion didn't appreciate our laughter, until we told them why we were laughing. Another La Brea bus just rolled by!" She finished her letter later at the Irving's that night. "Bill Binder (the Sgt. I told you about yesterday, brought some of the pictures he's taken to show us today. One was a picture of the Caesarian birth of puppies... very adorable puppies. He also brought us chocolate bars from the PX which he has promised to do for months. Now we're pressing for more tins, so I can send more things to you." Mr. Stella asked Sgt. Binder to take some photos of the new window decorations, in the hopes they might wind up in a local magazine. Binder said he would come back the next day with his camera.

Betty and Elsie picked up their friends at the Selznick Studios, and then went to have dinner before heading for the Bowl. "We drove with Marion to Hollywood Blvd. and ate at 'Gorham's' – just a block west of Grauman's Chinese Theatre...I'm in the Bowl now and am writing a bit during the intermission. It is so cold tonight that already the dew is making the tops of the boxes wet as can be. We all have newspapers wrapped around our legs to try to get a little warmer. This intermission lasts so long; the stage crew certainly take their own sweet time. It's pretty good tonight, but everyone is yelling about how cold it is. It'll be late getting home tonight because 'Princess Aurora' in 2 parts and 3 acts hasn't even started yet, and it is 10:45. I just hope we don't miss the last bus and streetcar."

23

JEEP RIDE TO THE
SOUTHERN END OF
THE ISLAND

September didn't start out well. With the war ending, everyone's mind was someplace else, and it was difficult for Harvey to get work done. "No matter what we've tried to do, it has turned out wrong. All the men have either taken it into their heads to take the day off or have decided to do as little work as possible. Most days there are just one or two men like that, but today almost everybody has that attitude. What work they have tried to do has been screwed up in one way or another. The phone has been ringing all day with people wanting everything from a large warehouse building to a two-hole latrine. With the war over and everybody, including the soldiers, getting peace minded, I can't seem to get the men to realize that we've still got a whale of a big job to do yet. The men keep knocking off earlier each day until I jump on them about it, and then they straighten out for a while. But before long they are right back where they started. It's just one of those things that happens, I guess, when a war reaches this stage."

Earl Sexton, Virjeanne's husband in the Marines, was getting ready to ship out as part of the occupation force in Okinawa. Since he wasn't able to communicate directly with Virjeanne or his parents, he asked Harvey to let them know he was okay and might be out of touch for a few weeks. The troops had been issued Japanese currency to use in Okinawa, and Earl gave Harvey some of it to send home. He also gave Harvey some Japanese money and a couple of books of western stories, a small piece of metal from the instrument panel of a Japanese plane (Harvey riveted it to his cigarette lighter), and another small piece of ivory from the same plane with Japanese characters painted on it. Harvey sent some of the currency to Betty and hoped the two couples would see each other once everyone was back in the States. Earl left Guam on the 8th, and on the 13th sent Harvey a letter from Saipan where they were dealing with very bad weather. Their ship was rolling so badly that most of those on board were sick. They were expected to leave Saipan the next day, the 14th, and were due in Japan around the 25th.

On Friday night, Harvey and Mac went to the movies to see *Destry Rides Again*, starring Marlene Dietrich and Jimmy Stewart: "...a bang-up movie with lots of shooting, fist fights, and hard riding cowboys. We hooted and hollered all the way through. It must be an awfully old picture, but I hadn't seen it, so Mac and I sat in the front row with our mouths hanging open. For a western picture, this one wasn't half bad. Everyone whistled at the heroines, booed the villains and had a big time. Tonight, we are supposed to see "Impatient Years" which sounds to me like one I've seen before, but I guess we'll go anyway. Can't afford to lose my standing at the first-nighter set now." Later that night, Harvey shared with Mac for the first time that he and Betty would live in Pittsburgh for a while but would probably settle permanently in California.

On Sunday, it had been exactly nine months since Harvey and Betty had said their goodbyes at the railway station in Hays, Kansas. Harvey was up early and heard the news that the peace agreement had finally been "signed, sealed and delivered." He noted that there was very little excitement as the servicemen listened to the news, only relief that there hadn't been any last-minute glitches in the peace process. After lunch, Mac, Pop and Harvey took an extended ride in the jeep, and they stopped at the Marine base to say goodbye to Earl Sexton. Then they continued their exploration of the island, taking photos as they drove. "We saw lots of big banana trees, but none of the bananas were ready for picking. These bananas, instead of growing long and slim like ours at home, grow short and fat and don't taste nearly as good. If we find ripe ones, we eat them because they are better than nothing. And today, the jeep worked like a charm...my night crew of mechanics aren't very busy except in emergencies, so they spend all their time tinkering with my jeep." On Sunday night, the three of them saw *National Velvet*, with Mickey Rooney and Elizabeth Taylor. Harvey predicted big things for Taylor: "that girl is the sweetest little kid that I've seen for a long time. She should be a big star in no time at all. It rained almost all the way through the show, but no one minded a bit. The race scene had the whole crowd sitting on the edge of their seats, pulling for the right horse to win! I hope we can see some more like that."

Monday was Labor Day back home, a day to take off work to celebrate V-J Day, but for the unit on Guam, it started out like any other workday, and the men were griping. However, at about 10:00 in the morning, a call came in from Wing Headquarters that the day was to be an official holiday, and everyone took off for the rest of the day. Harvey had a few things to do, but he quit early in the afternoon, when the fatigue that had been building finally caught up with him. He slept until suppertime.

Harvey had earlier told Betty about rumors that the Service Groups of the 75th would be going to the Philippines to ferry supplies to the occupation troops in Japan. In his Monday night letter, however, he reassured her, "apparently the rumor was unfounded, or the plans have changed. The next move we'll make now will be back home. At least, that's the situation as it stands now. Everything now points to the Service Groups here sending their personnel home as individuals rather than in groups. The men will leave as they meet the Army's requirements for discharge. We hear all kinds of rumors being circulated about how and when the discharge system will be changed, but there's nothing definite as of now. The number of points needed by enlisted men has been cut from 85 to 80, and now they are working on a deal to discharge all men of 35 years of age who have served 2 years in the Army, any portions of which is overseas service. That's a cut of 3 years in the previous age requirement ... it looks as if they are really working on the problem of getting us all home. The problem is that everything is so indefinite. We have no idea whether we'll stay here one month or twenty. The biggest development so far for us out of the treaty signing is the complete relaxation of censorship regulations. The word came over the radio, so it shouldn't be too long before we have directions, through military channels, to stop censoring enlisted men's mail. We've been doing that right along here, and what a chore it is. It may sound like an interesting job to some people but believe me it isn't. The officers don't like it, and the enlisted men feel frustrated by it, so the sooner it stops the better. In Headquarters Squadron, we divided our officers into three groups, and each group handled censoring our enlisted men's mail from the squadron for two nights in a row, so that each group censored letters two nights out of six. We have almost 300 men in Hq. Sq., which means quite a bit of mail to read. After a while it sort of gets automatic and doesn't take nearly as long as you might imagine...but I'm sure glad that it's all finished."

General Carl Spaatz was Commander of the US Strategic Air Forces in the Pacific, and his headquarters were on Guam. He was scheduled to visit the installation at Northwest Field, and the unit was planning a parade in his honor. Unfortunately, with men gradually being sent home, they were short-handed. "They called me today and asked me to send over a list of the men I'd need to operate and couldn't get along without, so they would know how many men to count on for the parade....so, I sent them my complete roster. That gesture wasn't appreciated, so all afternoon I worked on a list of men that could at least give the appearance of working on something. Then, just a few minutes before five, we got word that the parade had been cancelled because General Spaatz couldn't make it. A lot of work for nothing, but at least now we don't have to worry about the parade." Official word also came through that all censorship was to stop. "It was a huge relief to stop worrying about the enlisted men's mail. It began to rain after supper on Tuesday, so Harvey and Mac decided to skip the evening's movie, *What a Blonde*. Harvey was disappointed because the lead actor, Errol Leon, was one of his favorites.

It was still raining on Wednesday, slowing up the unit's ongoing projects. "We're trying to make a change in our vehicle maintenance setup by building a separate repair shop and grease rack for trucks used to haul water. All water, both for drinking and showers, has to be hauled into the area on 2 1/2 ton trucks with large tanks. Adjacent to all showers and water-using agencies are towers with similar tanks on top. The trucks pull up to a tower and transfer the load of water from the truck to the tower with a gasoline pump. All these trucks are dispatched and maintained in our yard and, because they work on a 24-hour shift, it ties up our maintenance schedule. By putting a non-com in charge of them and giving him his own repair set up, we hope to straighten out the mix-up." That night there was a stage show at the theater, followed by a movie, "a pretty fair double feature. The stage show starred Mary Brian and Charles Ruggles....they had a couple of singers in the cast who were plenty good, one of whom had a terrific figure and got the majority of the encores. Charley Ruggles was his usually super funny self and had us all in stitches. The movie was 'Devotion' with Olivia de Havilland and Ida Lupino and although the acting was fine, I'm still in doubt as to what the point of it all was. A little too deep for me." Although the film had been produced in 1943, it wouldn't actually be released in the States until 1946.

In a September letter, Harvey tried to explain to Betty the complicated arrangement of units at the base. Individual units had been merged together, leadership responsibilities had shifted, and the creation of a unified Officers' Club had become awkward and somewhat contentious. It was confusing for the men, and Harvey knew that it must be even more so for Betty and those at home. "To begin with, when the four Service Groups got here back in the early part of the year, they were consolidated into one large group, consisting of three large Squadrons. That left us with four officers instead of just one for every job that the new group had to perform. So, the best idea was to make the senior officer in each department responsible for that department, with the other officers subordinate to him. The 315th Wing is the Headquarters for the four Service Groups and also four bomb groups, but the Bomb Groups operate separately...so that the Wing has under it four regular-sized Bomb Groups, and one very large Service Group. Colonel Neyer, being the senior of the four Service Group commanding officers, was made C.O. of the consolidated group, but he has since been declared surplus and a new West Point colonel has been shipped in to us for the purpose of being the commanding officer of the consolidated group. A number of officers, myself included, have been put on special duty with the Wing for the purpose of operating functions that are strictly under the Wing itself. The largest of these functions is the Utilities Section, which the four Service Group Utilities Officers operate in conjunction with several Wing officers. This consolidation has lots of advantages in that it gives us four times the power we had before, but there are also disadvantages. It's hard to make a merger like this work since all the men and officers still retain the individual group spirit that they had before the merger. Not only that, but each of the four groups had formed Officers and Enlisted Mens' Clubs back in the States, and now that we are forming a consolidated club, it's a rather ticklish situation because of the varying amounts of property each club brought for itself. Naturally, the new club wants the use of as much of this equipment as it can get, but the officers concerned are reluctant to let them use it because some of groups brought quite a bit more equipment with them than others. But, after months of wrangling, the new C.O. has gotten things pretty well organized in just the few days since he has been here. A bad feature of the new situation is that military discipline will now be enforced to the "n-th" degree, not merely because of the new C.O., but because we are now part of a peace time army. After this new club gets under way, we'll have a swell place to play bridge, a little poker, have a beer or two, write letters, and quite a few other things. One good thing is that those guys who insist on having noisy parties that last all night can at least have a place to hold the parties instead of keeping the rest of us up half the night trying to quiet them down."

Between 1938 and 1943, Columbia Pictures produced twenty-seven movies based on the Chip Young comic strip "Blondie." Harvey had never seen a Blondie picture, and when *Leave it to Blondie* was scheduled for Thursday night, he was excited. Unfortunately, the new C.O. picked that evening to call a meeting. However, Mac and Harvey did make it to the theater on Friday and saw *The Great Stagecoach Robbery* with Bill Elliot and Robert Blake. Elliot had been discovered at the Pasadena Playhouse in the twenties and had been featured in westerns ever since. Robert Blake had been a child actor, winning a role in MGM's *Our Gang* series at the age of five. However, he is probably best remembered now for his later television series, *Baretta*, and for the difficulties in his personal life. Harvey and Mac enjoyed the movie that night: "a story about Red Ryder and Little Beaver. Talk about fights and shooting. But the best part was the Bugs Bunny cartoon.... I'm determined to see a whole program of cartoons when I get home."

Harvey and Bob Yates spent Sunday putting their ideas about the new Officers' Club on paper. They had already acquired two Quonset huts for the project, so they were able to lay out the building site. Then they drove to the site and laid out building corners so that they could start construction as soon as possible. "The two Quonsets placed end to end will give us a building 20' x 112' and putting it right next to our mess hall will give us a pretty good deal. Naturally, it will have a bar and stuff like poker tables and crap tables, but it will also have some lounging chairs and a juke box.... the construction work will all be done by officers in their spare time, and I guess that means that we Utilities Officers will come in for a good share of it. Any grading or clearing on the area will be my job because I have control of that kind of equipment. It'll be lots of fun, though, especially since we'll be doing the work for ourselves. We hope to finish the job in about two or three weeks which means we'll really have to go to town to make the schedule. We're limited as to time because it gets dark about 7:00 p.m., which doesn't give us much time in the evenings."

On Monday, some of the additional equipment arrived that Harvey had requested from the Navy. When he went down to the dock to check on it, he found "six brand new dump trucks. There were International trucks and all of ours are G.M.C.'s or Diamond C's, but we grabbed them even though it will be difficult to get parts. Not only that, but there will also be more stuff coming on Wednesday!" The movie that night was *Song of Bernadette*. Harvey had seen it, and since he felt it wouldn't be as good the second time, he stayed home. Some of the officers in the barracks had found a document describing the *Kota Baroe*, the ship which had brought them to the Marianas in May. Peck duplicated it on a teletype machine, and Harvey sent Betty a copy.

The Tuesday night movie was *Thunderhead, Son of Flicka*, and it was a hit with the men. "The photography was the best I've seen in a long time. The locale was supposed to be Utah, and the scenes of those mountains and canyons really made me want to look at that same scenery with you.... for a city bred guy, I've got a lot of that 'wide open spaces' blood in me. Maybe we should have a ranch and raise horses or something? ... or maybe the best idea would be for me to stop seeing all these western pictures?" On Wednesday, more equipment came in for the Section: two big bulldozers along with a roller, a steam shovel, a ditching machine, and a concrete mixer. Harvey estimated all the equipment in the yard would cost at least three quarters of a million dollars. In the afternoon, Harvey, Mac, and Pop worked on the Officers' Club until they were driven inside by heavy rain. They had been hoping to see the evening's picture, *Without Love*, with Spencer Tracy, Katherine Hepburn, and Lucille Ball, but because of the downpour, they weren't able to get their machinery back to the motor pool until after 8:30. It was still raining heavily on Thursday, and jeeps and trucks were stuck in deep water and thick mud. Even trips to the latrine were an adventure, especially at night. While work in other sections of the Wing had slacked off, in Harvey's section they were as busy as ever. Rumors were still flying around, and Harvey passed on the latest one to Betty. "One of the more persistent rumors is that we will be one of the occupational wings in the 20th Air Force and will be stationed either in Manila or Hawaii. If it should happen that we go to Hawaii, I'll be sending for you as soon as it is humanly possible for you to come, but as I say, that's just one more rumor." In his Thursday letter, he also provided some details about the bathroom arrangements at the camp. "Incidentally, you'd get a big kick out of seeing the latrines we have here. Of course, the sitter-downers are the usual country variety, but the stander-uppers are just a piece of pipe in the ground with a funnel stuck in the top!! Rather a ticklish situation at night when there is no moon. A man has to have good aim. I'll swear they haven't made those funnels large enough."

On Friday the 14th, Harvey received Betty's letter, written a week earlier, in which she shared that her brother would likely be entering the service soon. He wrote back trying to reassure her, and he shared how his own family had reacted when he told them he was joining the army. "I know how you feel about Rod's going into the service. I can still see my mother's face, almost four years ago, when I told her I was leaving. I'm glad it's not happening so suddenly in Rod's case, because I left within 24 hours of the time I told my folks, and I know it was really hard on them. It's really hard to realize it at a time like this, with all your mixed feelings inside, but it will really do a world of good for Rod. Actually, it's a pretty rough life, but it's one of the few times in a man's life when he can allow some of himself to come out that can't be brought out at any other time. A guy really learns to take care of himself in every way. He'll take lots of knocks, but he'll come back a better guy. It's a tough break that he has to drop out of U.S.C., but there must be something better than U.S.C. around the corner for Rod. I sure hope that the West Point business comes thru before long."

One of Harvey's favorite journalists was Bill Henry, whose column "By the Way" appeared regularly in the *Los Angeles Times* and was available to servicemen in the Pacific. Henry wrote on a variety of topics, ranging from politics to sports to the theater. In his September 7th column, he described an experience at the Adelphi Theater in Manhattan, and Harvey enclosed the column with his letter that night. He knew she would enjoy this peek behind the scenes: "Perhaps you have never had the experience of standing in the darkened wings of a theater watching a preliminary rehearsal of a big musical show, so here's a little something about it." The show was the musical *Spring in Brazil*, starring Milton Berle with Carmen Miranda and Frick and Frack, and this was the first time the cast, complete with singers and dancers, had gathered on stage. The purpose was to acquaint the cast, who were grouped on chairs and benches around an ancient piano, with the music. "[Robert] Wright apparently is the lyricist, [George] Forrest is the music man. Wright sings about as well as I do after a bad cold and so does Forrest but that isn't the idea. They ran through a couple of the songs – Forrest rocking the whole stage with his enthusiastic thumping, Wright trying to make up in expression for his lack of voice...the stage manager says the show is seven or eight weeks away from its Broadway opening. Five or six weeks of rehearsals, then a couple of weeks to polish it at Boston – and then the big splash with Berle as star." Unfortunately, the "splash" never happened, due to "creative differences." Berle was later replaced, and the musical closed soon after opening "because it's comedy star wasn't suited to it."

Along with Mac and Pop, Harvey was planning a busy Sunday. In the morning, they would work on the new Officers' Club (which was progressing nicely), and in the afternoon they planned an excursion: "...in the afternoon we're going to take a long ride to the southern end of the island into what is known as the 'restricted area.' That portion of the island is almost devoid of military installations, and there are several native villages here and there along the road. It is kept under a restriction to keep the soldiers from overrunning the place. We've arranged for a pass from the island Provost Marshall, and we'll have a whole afternoon of sightseeing." With the relaxation of censorship regulations, Harvey was able to be more specific with Betty this time about his surroundings. "...I can tell you now that we are located on the extreme northern tip of the island. Our field is called Northwest Field. There aren't any native villages near us except for two or three little huts which are owned by a couple of natives that operate a sawmill. We are connected with the rest of the island by a long, paved, three lane road that runs the whole length of the island on the western side. The traffic on that road would put Wilshire Blvd. to shame. There are M.P.'s at intersections to direct traffic, and they have no easy job, especially on a day like Sunday when most everyone is out trying to get some air and relax." They hadn't realized that it was such a long trip. "We intended to visit three villages, Inarajan, Merizo, and Umatac, but didn't have time to see the last one. We're going to take another trip down there as soon as we can and see the rest. The trip wasn't as exciting as you would imagine, but it was really a big relief to get away from the scenery that we had seen so often before. The natives there are much more natural than they are on the parts of the island being used by the Army, Navy, Marines, See Bees and Coast Guard. Lots of them live in very nice houses, lots better than the thatched huts that we see close to us. A few have built houses out of some kind of concrete they make themselves. The village of Inarajan has a pretty nice church that I got a picture of. Didn't take very many pictures because the day was cloudy, and we intend to go back again. Funny thing about the churches, we haven't seen one yet that wasn't Catholic. About 95% of the people on the island (natives) are Catholic, and it seems as if the other 5% don't build churches. Another odd thing is that there doesn't seem to be any girls between the ages of 16 and 30. We passed lots and lots of banana trees and coconut trees, but the road was so rough we couldn't really stop. The roads are full of natives riding bullocks or riding in carts pulled by bullocks. These animals look like water buffaloes, although they aren't by any means small. Most of them have long curving horns that they toss angrily when the natives try to hurry them faster than their slow, ambling gait. They are the only means of transportation for the natives except for a very infrequent bus which is provided by the Navy. This is just a truck with 'Guam Bus Lines' painted on the sides. There can't be more than five of them on the whole island. The roads near us aren't bad at all, but in that restricted area they are worse than terrible.... not paved at all and many places are under water from these heavy rains. Once we came upon a truck that was stuck in a ditch and because the road was so narrow, he had traffic lined up in a half mile in both directions. Lots of cussing, sweating, and splashed mud before he got out."

Harvey was enthusiastic about the new equipment that had arrived from Navy surplus. It had taken a couple of days to get it all assembled, but it was now ready for use. "Our new bulldozers are Allis and Chalmers' model HD-14's and are as smooth running as a new car. We've been accustomed to Caterpillar dozers, so these are a little new, and strange to us, but I believe I like them just as well, if not better. Our new shovel is a Northwest 3/4 yard job and works like a dream. It's not as big a shovel as I'd like to have, but it's plenty good just the same. The dump trucks are Internationals instead of General Motors and are lots more efficient than ours. This is all Navy equipment, which is the reason for it being different from our old stuff."

Harvey heard from his new Marine friend, Earl Sexton, who reported that he was to be stationed in the Nagasaki area, so he asked Betty to pass this on to Virjeanne when they spoke.

The new club was coming along well, and the team expected to have it finished in about two weeks. The floor was almost finished, and about half of the roof arches were ready to put in place. They were building a big screened-in porch along one side, resulting in a fairly big club. In his Sunday letter, Harvey included a sketch of the layout. "Pretty swanky joint when we get it finished. I'd just as soon not be here to use it, but that's too much to hope for." He was referring to the news that captains would now need eighty-five points before they would be discharged. He had fifty.

Ralph Haver wrote again, this time from Okinawa. "We left Seattle on 17 July and got here the 5th of this month. It took us _50_ days of which more than half were spent sitting in ports. We stopped at Pearl Harbor for one week, Eniwetok one week and Ulithi for two weeks. God, was that a monotonous trip? We were 25% overloaded and consequently we junior Officers were quartered in troop space – 5 bunks high. By the time we arrived here we were ready to murder each other, especially the Navy Officers – the snooty bastards. We no sooner landed than our outfit was deactivated, and all our personnel made available to the 8th Air Force units on the island. Fortunately, I got a good assignment in the Staff Engineer's Office. I'm replacing a Major who was in charge of designing. As long as I'm stuck here for a while, I couldn't get a better assignment. How are your points adding up these days? I've got 55 as of the Feb count and being as how I ain't got promoted (thank the Lord) I only need 58, and from the way they are sending high point men home around here I don't believe that I'll be here six months."

Before the movie that night, there was a concert at the Gecko. Harvey and Mac worked on the flooring of the new club until dark, and by the time they got to the theater they had missed the first half of the concert. "It was a band concert given by the 315th Wing Band. They call themselves "Armstrong's All Americans" (General Armstrong is the Wing C.O.) and they are pretty darn good. When they first started practicing, we could hardly stand to listen to them, but they've certainly improved. They used to practice by playing 'Sentimental Journey,' until now we can't stand to hear that tune at all. But tonight, they played like big time stars." They did see the featured movie, though, and Harvey loved it. It was ".... a swell show – 'The Adventures of Robin Hood.' Gosh, I hadn't seen that for years and it seemed as fresh and new to me as the latest picture out. The color was beautiful and the photography much better than most of the stuff that comes out now."

By Tuesday, the Utilities Section was getting more comfortable with the new equipment. "It's been a pleasure for the operators to handle this new stuff after fooling around with the equipment they've been using ever since we first got here. It was new when we started, but it was too small to handle the jobs that we had been forced to do with it, consequently it's been wearing out lots faster than it ordinarily would. I hope that now we can assign equipment to jobs in proportion to the size of the job, and still keep equipment in a fair state of repair. We have inspectors that come around periodically to look at everything we've got, and believe me, those guys don't miss a single trick." The morning started slowly, and a sudden rainstorm came up and stopped work completely for a while, "...only lasted for about ten minutes, but it sure did a good job of soaking things while it lasted. The roads and area have been muddy for so long I'm beginning to forget what it feels like to have clean shoes. The mud on my floor at the BOQ is about four inches deep and is getting packed down so well that it will be hard to tell just where the mud stops, and the wood begins." He was able to quit at about 3:30 in the afternoon so he could help on the Officers' Club project. Some officers had little to do in their sections, and they had been working long hours trying to get the club finished. The flooring was all laid out, all of the roof arches were up, and the siding was ready to be nailed on. As Harvey noted, "it sounds silly to be nailing steel sides to steel arches but that's the way these Quonset huts are built."

B29 on runway, Northwest Field, Guam, 1945

The movie that night was *God Is My Co-Pilot*, with Dennis Morgan and Raymond Massey. "One of the best war films I've seen. The story is that of Col. Robert L. Scott from Macon, Georgia, who cut a rather wide swath with Chennault's Flying Tigers in China. I remember seeing a 6 by 8-foot picture of him hanging in the lobby of the Dempsey Hotel in Macon, but this is the first time I've heard his story." The Flying Tigers was an American Volunteer Group that had helped the Chinese Army defend itself against Japan in the early days of the war, and Scott, a Brigadier General, was an ace pilot credited with shooting down thirteen enemy aircraft.

Harvey had borrowed a couple of books and planned to do some reading after finishing his letter that night. "'Lost in the Horse Latitudes,' and 'Blood Money.' This latter one is one of many blood and thunder mystery stories that are making all the rounds here. Almost everyone is reading one at one time or another. A man gets pretty hungry for reading material and will grab almost anything in sight no matter what the title is." Harvey enjoyed reading books that had been turned into motion pictures, especially to see the differences between the two. "After reading the sequences in some books, it is a kick to see the movie and notice how the director has handled some of the passages." He was able to read some of the H. Allen Smith book (*Lost in the Horse Latitude*) after finishing his letter. He had read a couple of Smith's other books, *Low Man on the Totem Pole* and *Life in a Puddy Knife Factory*, and though they were silly, he enjoyed them. "It's the craziest book I ever heard of. To write like this, a man has to be either an idiot or a genius – and this doesn't sound like the doings of a genius. He writes with a complete abandon of rhyme or reason and doesn't mince words when he describes anything – actually, it's really funny!"

Work on the club was progressing nicely, partly because so many officers were pitching in. "We've got a system of lights rigged up so now we can work after dark, so tonight we all worked until around 9:30. We've got all the roof arches in now and all the rafters up for the roof. Tomorrow we start with the siding and roofing. It's actually going faster than most of us thought at first, mainly because there are more officers turning out to help with it than we had counted on. There are about 10 or 15 of us who are out there every night, and then there are always a few who come now and then."

Ever since arriving on Guam, the servicemen had been producing their own little newspaper. It was a one-sheet (back and front) mimeographed handout called the *Pacific Courant* and was distributed through the camps. Harvey noted that copies of the newsletter were not allowed to be sent off the island during the censorship period. "I don't know why it has been kept secret, because there isn't anything in it that you don't already know about. They used to print right across the top... 'NOT TO BE MAILED OFF THE ISLAND,' but it's not there now so I guess it's okay to send this." He sent her a copy of the Sept. 19, 1945, issue, which contained this article:

OCCUPATION TO REQUIRE SMALL FORCE

Tokyo (UP) - Gen. Douglas MacArthur announces that the occupation of Japan was proceeding so smoothly that all "citizen soldiers" (draftees) in the Pacific probably can be demobilized within six months, leaving the garrisoning of the enemy homeland to 200,000 regular army troops.

By using the Japanese government structure, he said, he was enforcing the surrender terms with only a small fraction of the millions of men, billions of dollars and years of time that would have been necessary if an Allied military government had been established. MacArthur said that the original landings involved "grave risk" but added that the subsequent progress already has assured the success of the occupation. He also said, "Probably no greater gamble in history has been taken than the initial landings, in which our ground forces were outnumbered 1,000 to one, but the stakes were worth it."

The newsletter also contained stories about the death of the famous Irish tenor, John McCormack; the end-of-the-world prediction by a Pasadena minister (Betty had sent a clipping about this), a baby who was named "Gale" after being born in North Carolina during a hurricane, and a man in Colorado who had survived despite being run over by an entire freight train. The entire back page included sports news about baseball, football, and horse racing.

Thursday started on a bittersweet note. At 2:30 in the morning, Pop Bristow left for home. "He's been sweating it out for a couple of weeks now, so he had his stuff just about all packed up. Lucky he did because I don't think he had more than half an hour's notice before he was supposed to go. He woke me up to shake hands and say goodbye when he left. I think he was lucky enough to get a plane ride on A.T.C. (Air Transport Command) all the way through. I sure hated to see him leave 'cause he and Mac and I had gotten to be pretty good buddies." There was another double feature that night for Harvey and Mac. "What corn they were dishing out. The first production was put out by P.R.C. pictures called 'The Great Mike'. It actually stunk out loud!!" P.R.C. Pictures (Producers Distributing Corporation) was one of the less prestigious of the Hollywood film studios, located in the "Poverty Row" section of Gower Street. P.R.C. put out mainly poor quality, low-budget, B-movies that usually took a week or less to film. This one starred Carl Switzer, the highlight of whose career was the role of Alfalfa in the *Our Gang* series. The second film that night, a twenties-themed movie with Joan Davis *(Note: Harvey didn't name the film, but it was probably Show Business)* was better. "She was fairly funny, but coming after that other stinkeroo I guess we weren't really in the mood for it. Not only that, but it rained almost the whole way through. We were just stubborn enough to sit through the whole mess."

The Utilities Section was putting up a Red Cross building for one of the bomb groups and a chapel for one of the others, and those projects kept the unit busy on Thursday. That evening, after a shower and a quick beer, Harvey and Mac hurried back to the movies. "I didn't want to miss tonight's picture, 'The Unseen,' with Joel McCrea and Gail Russell. And then after getting there I found that I had seen the picture before! In fact, I think we saw it together in Hays if I remember correctly. It was pretty good, though, so I sat through it a second time. Tomorrow night we have 'The Clock,' with Judy Garland and Robert Walker. That's the one you told me to see, wasn't it?" He did manage to see the movie the next night, "and could hardly see the screen for your face. The picture was a full and complete replica of what our marriage would have been if we had been married in Spokane... When I looked at Judy Garland, I saw you and in Robert Walker I saw myself...I think that picture has hit me closer to my heart than any I've seen since we parted in Hays."

In his letter that night, Harvey used Pop's departure to describe the BOQ's setup to Betty. "The far corner of our room looks kind of bare without all of Pop's stuff strung around. There are just two of us now, Lt. Leonard and I in this end of the building. Between our room and the next room, the partition is not built all the way across so that Mac, sleeping in the next room with Lt. Peck, seems to be in our room too. One of these fine days we'll finish the partition, but I'll leave a door so that Mac and I won't have to go outside the building to visit. With only two of us in here now, Leonard and I can really arrange our stuff so we'll have lots of spare room. Maybe we can even rig up a combination living room and bedroom effect. I don't want to make it anything permanent, though, because I'm not figuring on staying any longer than I have to."

On Sunday, Harvey and Lt. Leonard rearranged the Bachelor Officer Quarters. "First we knocked out a 4 x 8-foot panel on each side of the room, covered the openings with screen and then replaced the panels with hinges at the top so we can swing them open to allow a lot more air to come through the room. Then we went out to hunt for material for the partition between our room and Mac's room. We found some 2 x 4's for studs and five big pieces of plywood for the panels. After we get that put up, we're going to put in a cloth ceiling, so we'll have an air space above the room to help cool it off. Then when we get all of that finished, we intend to paint the whole room. We don't know yet what color we'll find, but almost any color will do I guess. We managed to get all the studding put up for our partition, but the plywood will have to wait until tomorrow night. I found a piece of Masonite just the right size, so I made myself a desk top. The plywood top that I had before was getting pretty well beat up, and I had to do something with it. I also found a piece of acetone about 18" x 12", so now I have that on the top of the desk with adhesive tape around the edges and five of your pictures underneath it." Harvey wrote that he was pleased Betty had been able to see Jacques Dangers and his family. "Everyone here liked Jacques a whole lot and were pleased to hear today that he had gotten such a quick trip home!" He asked her to call Pop Bristow when he got home, and he enclosed a letter he had received from Earl Sexton's parents in North Carolina, thanking him for letting them know their son was okay.

Another night at the Gecko theater on Monday, and as the picture was about Pittsburgh, Harvey was especially interested. "We saw 'The Valley of

Decision' with Greer Garson and Gregory Peck. I had read the book quite a while ago and was pretty anxious to see how closely the movie followed it. Surprisingly enough, they were almost exactly alike. It's the story of Pittsburgh back in the early steel mill days around the 1870's. Lots of the scenes looked familiar but not very much like present day Pgh."

The only mail that Harvey received that day was his September issue of *Capitol* magazine (published by Capitol Records). An article about Mickey Scrima caught his eye, and he sent the clipping to Betty. Scrima was playing drums with the Johnny White combo at the Palladium on Monday nights and had played with many of the best-known bands of the era, including the Charlie Barnett band and the Harry James Band. He and Frank Sinatra had joined Harry James at the same time in 1939 and had been roommates on the road. Scrima had appeared in a number of movies, including *Springtime in the Rockies* and *Private Buckaroo* in 1942 and *Bathing Beauty* in 1944. His music career though, while interesting, wasn't the only reason that Harvey and Betty knew of him; they had eaten at his restaurant, Mickey's Spaghetti House, during their brief time together in California.

Harvey spent a lot of time in his Tuesday letter talking about, and grousing about, the heat, the rain, and the ever-present dust – mud – dust. It wasn't an exciting topic, but since these were constant issues for the men, he tried to give Betty a feel for what life was like on Guam. "Today is so hot and sultry that a man can hardly stand it. It's one of those days that seems to threaten rain every minute, but never quite gets around to it. The clouds are pressing down almost to the ground. It hardly leaves a man enough room to breathe. Right now, I'm wringing wet although it's not really hot, just sultry. We had lots of rain last night, so our yard is all soaked up again as per usual. I guess we'll never get the blamed thing (the officers' club) done until this rainy season is all through and done with. The natives around here say that we still have a good two or three months of rainy weather yet, but I'm hoping that it clears up before that. Another problem that the rain brings is the fact that we are getting wash service from the laundry, and we have a hell of a time finding enough dry weather to hang our clothes out to dry...Now this darn typewriter is acting up again. It's been at least two months since we had it checked and cleaned up, so I guess it's high time we did it again. In this climate, the darn thing collects lots of dust and seems to corrode quite a bit faster than it ordinarily would. It's funny how this climate affects metal objects like that. Weapons and everything else made of metal have to be cleaned and oiled about four or five times as often as back in the States, or they start rusting."

Often Harvey began his letters at suppertime before going to the movie theater, and then wrote again when they returned to the BOQ. This letter was no exception... "Tonight at the movie we are going to have a stage show of some kind followed by a movie, 'Boom Town.' I'm sure I must have seen the picture before, but I want to see the stage show and I'll probably stay to see the picture again. Clark Gable is in it, so it might be worth seeing again. Hope so, anyway." and then later: "Back again, and the show was swell! It was a G.I. stage show put on by guys right here on the island, but they were plenty good. Lots of real professional talent. The singer, who used to yodel for Jan Garber, sounded like a cross between Frankie Sinatra and Morton Downey – but good! 'Boom Town' was swell, and I hadn't seen it before. The picture must be an awfully old one because the film we had was a reprint." Harvey had mentioned Jan Garber. Garber was an actor and violin-playing orchestra leader who recorded primarily for the RCA Victor and Decca labels. He was a regular on the George Burns-Gracie Allen radio program. Downey was a popular composer, songwriter, pianist, and singer who in 1930 had opened Delmonico's night club in New York City.

On Wednesday, Harvey had to deal with some staff issues. Early in the morning, one of his officers, Lt. Milleville, called to report he was in the hospital. He had cut off a piece of his middle finger while using a jointer in the wood shop, and doctors wanted to keep him in the hospital for about three weeks. Harvey was glad that the injury hadn't been worse. Then, a little later, a couple of vehicle inspectors came to check the motor pool and found the maintenance records to be in pretty bad shape. "The vehicles were all in a pretty good state of repair, but the records for that maintenance hadn't been kept up to date at all. That's Milleville's job, and naturally I didn't feel too good about it. I put a couple of men on the job right away to try to get things in some kind of order before we have a real serious investigation, but I'm sure disappointed in the way Milleville has been doing his job. My job is to handle the operation of the equipment and his is to handle maintenance so that vehicles will be in shape to do the job...Actually, since Milleville is working for me, it's my responsibility to see that he does his job, but I gave him credit for doing his job and haven't been checking in on him too closely. But things will be different from now on."

That night, the movie at the Gecko was *Circumstantial Evidence* (a Class-B movie) and a Bugs Bunny cartoon. Harvey was glad for the diversion. With his letter to Betty that evening, he enclosed a small piece of ivory from the instrument panel of a Japanese plane.

The uncertainty about when they would be going home was beginning to get to the men—and to Harvey. "I wonder when this being apart is going to be over and done with. I don't see how it can go on much longer, and yet it keeps dragging on with no one seeming to do very much about it. The soldiers here are really on edge waiting for their chance to go back to the States – hoping that some regulation will be passed, making men in their particular category eligible for discharge. The first of the year seems to be the time when length of service will begin to count so I'm sweating it out till then."

Harvey got up early Friday and, after a breakfast of hotcakes and bacon, worked for most of the morning on a report that had to be turned in on a truck that had been wrecked. Men were gradually being discharged, and additional personnel reported on Friday to help bolster the Section's roster. "Lots of zebra's (officers with stripes) among them... 1 1st lieutenant, 5 staff sergeants, 2 sergeants and 3 corporals. That's a lot of rank to come reporting in at one time. We can use them, though."

There was an A.A.F. (Army Air Forces) stage show, and a movie planned at the theater that night. The movie was *Hangover Square*, with Laird Cregar, Linda Darnell, and George Sanders. At the last minute, however, the Colonel called a 6:30 meeting, and Harvey missed the first part of the show. "The Col. called a meeting of all the officers of the combined Service Groups. The purpose of the meeting was to organize our Officers' Club and to elect officers for it. Our new building should be ready for use in less than a week, so we want to be ready to start operation as soon as we can. Damned if these crazy guys didn't elect me president of the blamed thing, so I guess quite a few of my evenings now will be taken up with that. I think I had told you that I had been made president of the 75th Officers Club (our old one), so now I've got a real job on my hands trying to organize the Consolidated Club from the four Group clubs and liquidate the 75th Club at the same time. To form a Consolidated Club, the four Service Group Clubs have to be disbanded and the assets and equipment disposed of. I guess for a while now I won't have much time to worry about point systems and discharges. These officers have no idea what they're letting themselves in for. I hope I can make a little headway with both clubs.... this afternoon I had already done a lot of running around with Dick Skinner (he's Secretary-Treasurer of the 75th Officer Club) trying to dig up the proper regulations and authority for disbanding the club. Didn't make much headway, either. Dick is really a go getter and makes a fine club man. Especially at a time like this when there is so much research and book work to do on the darn thing."

If all that weren't enough for one day, there was an incident with the urinal system Harvey has described to Betty in an earlier letter. "The inevitable finally happened tonight. Dick Skinner and I both headed for the place. I got there first and picked the funnel in the lower left-hand corner of the urinal.... Dick came into the little enclosure, and he picked what he thought was the one next to me....to my left (it was as dark in there as the inside of a cat), but the one he picked.... didn't exist. When he realized what he had done, I thought the two of us would die laughing." Betty received the letter describing this incident a week later, and it reminded her of something that had happened at the USO. "That reminds me of that little sign they finally had to put up in the men's room at the U.S.O. They had such a time trying to keep it presentable that one day this little sign appeared. 'We aim to please – You aim too, please!!' Maybe you should make a little sign for your new officers' club! I'll never forget the Jr. Council meeting when the girls made a report about that!"

Sunday was a work day on the new club. "Any club on the island that is going to cater to lady customers (Red Cross Workers, nurses, etc.) has to be equipped with a ladies room of sorts. Also, we are going to need a soakage pit for the waste liquids from our bar. Both these installations will require a lot of excavation in this hard coral, so I'll have to bring a couple of jack hammers tomorrow to start work on them. If we hit some extra hard places in the coral, we'll probably have to blast a little bit, but that won't be too bad. A little ticklish because it's so close to the building, but I think it can be done.

"We really put in a day of manual labor at our club site today. We started that latrine pit this morning around nine and kept it up all day until five, with about half an hour out for reading your letter and a little bit of lunch. We kept two jack hammers going all day, along with four or five shovels, but in the hard coral we didn't make much headway. It'll probably take us several more days to finish it. I don't expect to be able to open the club until maybe a week from tomorrow. Maybe later than that."

The Sunday night movie was Betty Grable's *Diamond Horseshoe*. "The high notes of the show for me were songs by Dick Haymes and a piano piece by Carmen Cavallero!! Grable confined herself to bumping, grinding, posing and making sounds that could have been singing. All in all, not too bad."

STUDIO AUDIENCE FOR

BURNS AND ALLEN

Saturday was the last night of the Hollywood Bowl season, and Betty really enjoyed it. "We were really busy at the store today and worked from 9:30 till 6 when we had to leave for the Bowl. It was the last night and was just about the best night of all. It was ballet again – but the whole atmosphere of the place was just perfect...lighting effects, scenery, and the dancing was so good! On the way home, I passed a liquor store and heard on the radio that Truman was making his V-J Day speech. So, it is to be Sept. 2nd!"

Betty and the girls were staying at the Irvings' house, and on Sunday they listened to a special V-J Day broadcast featuring Bing Crosby and President Truman. Harvey's mother was listening too, and later wrote to Harvey about the broadcast. "Bing Crosby was M.C., and Dinah Shore sang and Frances Langford too. Bob Hope read a poem, and Orson Welles spoke. The President was introduced by a Pfc. just returned from the Pacific. I hope you heard it for it was sure good."

That night, Betty and her friends went to the movies and saw *1,000 and one Nights* and *Picture of Dorian Gray*: "the most horrible picture I've seen in a long time. Have you seen it? Eddie Wright told us about it when they were making it. The whole picture was so filthy that it made my skin crawl. It shows the marks of sin and immorality while he, in real life, remains young. It makes me ill to even think about it, but I hope you see it just to hear what you say about it."

Edna went to a studio in Palms on Wednesday to have some formal photos taken, and Betty went with her. While they were there, the photographer's dog was hit by a car, and Morris (the photographer) and his assistant, Ben, took the dog to a vet, leaving Betty and Edna to look after the studio. Betty used her time to start another letter, and she told Harvey about the day's headlines which detailed a Santa Fe passenger train derailment near Arcadia.

Rail Wreck at Santa Anita Injures 50
Four Known Dead in Derailment of Santa Fe California Limited

The second section of the Santa Fe's eastbound California Limited was derailed at the old Santa Anita Station, one mile west of Santa Anita race-track, last night with four known dead, more than 50 injured and a number trapped in smashed coaches. Of the 16-car train, two baggage cars imme-diately behind the two locomotives and two coaches following the bag-gage cars were worst damaged. Hospitals in all surrounding communities - Arcadia, Pasadena, Temple City and Alhambra, as well as Los Angeles General Hospital - were requested to stand by to receive injured victims.

"I found some more little Penguin books for you today ('Mr. Littlejohn,' 'Boomerang,' 'Young Man with a Horn,' and 'The House without a door'.) I will send them on right away. They don't make 'For Whom the Bell Tolls' in that edition. The movie is playing at the little theater down the street, and we thought we might have time to see it after those pictures were finished. Ben said the movie was cut, and we wouldn't even recognize it...I enjoyed it so much the first time that I'd hate to be disappointed in it this time. I'm listening to the radio as I write, and they are playing a whole series of senti-mental ballads. 'I've Got You Under My Skin,' 'Falling in Love with Love' etc. A fellow from the studio came into the store today and told me not to buy any records from the new R.K.O. picture 'Spellbound' because he had extras at the studio and was saving an album for me! I'll have to save some more records for him. He came in a few days ago and picked up several albums costing about $25.00 for David O. Selznick, who was going to use them for a birthday gift!"

On Friday, there was bad news from Rod—he'd been drafted! He called home, and after talking to his mother for a while, he asked to speak with Betty. "Rod wanted to talk to me. He comes on the phone and says, 'Just call me Pvt. Lundin.' I could feel my stomach turn right over. He had gone into Los Angeles for his physical – he and Mike both passed, and from what I gather, he will be in the service in about three weeks. It's going to be quite an experience for him, but it seems so sudden. I hung up, and the tears started to fall. He is going down to U.S.C. tomorrow to return his football uniform. At least he played with the Trojans for a week. Sessions don't start until Nov. 1, and he'll be gone by then, I guess. I wish we'd hear from West Point soon, so we'd know about that deal. It might make a difference in what would happen now. He and Mike are putting in for Army post office work- and overseas, so they might leave right away as they would need no further training than what they already have. That would be just about all we'd need. God, give me the strength I'll need to help the folks over the first rough weeks away, and the last weeks home." The next day, Rod's parents convinced him to wait before withdrawing from SC. Their feeling was that something, maybe the West Point appointment, might still come through, and it would be unwise to have already forfeited his scholarship.

With her Monday letter, Betty sent Harvey an article describing the end of war-time meat and shoe rationing.

End Meat Rationing on Oct. 1

Meat rationing will end Oct. 1 and shoe rationing will soon after it was learned today. Secretary of Agriculture Clinton Anderson favored lifting meat rationing on Sept. 1, it was learned, but Price Administrator Chester Bowles requested that no action be taken until O.P.A. had cut down its paid field personnel.

Having laid off most of its paid field employees, O.P.A. has agreed that meat rationing will go Oct. 1 and the two agencies have drawn up blue-prints heralding the end. There is a good supply of beef, lamb, mutton and poultry on the market, although there is still a pork shortage. Fats and oils will continue to be rationed, as will sugar. Shoe rationing, it was learned, will probably end between Oct. 15 and Nov. 1.

President Truman notified war agencies on Aug. 15 at the time of the Japanese surrender that as many controls as possible should be lifted within 60 days - all if possible. Already rationing of processed foods, fuel oil and gasoline has ended. Most War Production Board controls have been eliminated. The O.P.A. believes most rationing will end this year - including rationing of automobiles and tires.

Now that the fighting was over, Harvey's return to the States was always on both of their minds. Betty saw an article in the *Herald-Express* and forwarded it to Guam.

Releases Before July 1

Undersecretary of War Robert P. Patterson promised the Senate Military Affairs Committee today that six million soldiers will be discharged by next July 1. "From an army of eight million, we will be down to two million, five hundred thousand by that time," he said. "The point system is the means by which we determine who shall be discharged."

Beyond this, he said, it is up to Congress to say what the size of the army shall be. The army, he said, has only the short-range plan of cutting to two and a half million. Patterson appeared before the committee as a result of wide-spread demands on senators from parents and men in the service for their prompt discharge.

Because Secretary of War Stimson, and Gen. George C. Marshall, Chief of Staff, were unable to be present, Patterson and three generals actively in charge of demobilization testified. The army, Patterson told the committee, plans to retain the point system. He said sampling of opinion of troops shows that soldiers themselves approve it.

Asked to state the policy of the War Department on sending men who were in combat in Europe to the Pacific, Patterson answered: "No men with over 45 points will be sent to the Pacific if they have been in combat in Europe. It is possible that a few who were in combat a short time in Europe would not have the points."

Stella's was busy on Friday, and in addition to working the counter, Betty helped Mr. Stella with some instrument repairs. "I helped Stella put a new head on a banjo. Do they ever smell bad when wet! It reminded me of the time I had to take a smelly frog to pieces when at the J.C.!" On Saturday, Stella's was less smelly, but even busier! "Have we been busy at the store. The average sale I made today was $8.00 which is pretty good considering how many single records I sold. I get tired on days like this, but I like it so much when we are busy. It's evening now as I write this, and on the radio I'm listening to Tchaikovsky's 6th Symphony – the particular theme is 'Story of a Starry Night.' I like it so much."

On Sunday, Betty and Rod drove to Glendale to visit with the family of one of Harvey's friends from Guam. Harvey and Jacques Dangers had been stationed together in Spokane, and Jacques was eager for Betty to meet his children. "Coming home, we drove all over; to Sunland, San Fernando Valley – we didn't get home until 6:30."

Betty had just received the description Harvey had sent of the troop ship he had taken to the Pacific. "The description of the Kota Baroe certainly is interesting – I can almost see all of you boys crowded together on it. I hope you come back on something more comfortable, like the 'luxurious Lurline' or something? Too bad you didn't get to see 'Without Love' because it was really good.... Helen Hunt came by the store today. Her new husband, Jack Hunt, left the States today for Saipan. They were married on September 7th and had only 1 1/2 day together. She came on home with me and had dinner with us. Then we went to a show in Beverly Hills and saw 'Guest Wife,' with Don Ameche and Claudette Colbert...you positively have to see that picture. We stayed and saw it twice, and I laughed all the way through it."

Harvey and Betty were only one of countless couples dealing with war-related separations. There were millions of American marriages during the war years, many of them involving people in the service. The big news in Hollywood that week was the marriage of former child star Shirley Temple and Sergeant John A. Agar, an Army Aviation engineer stationed at Geiger Field in Spokane (where Harvey had been based). Sgt. Agar was on a seven-day furlough (plus eight days travel time) after which he expected an overseas assignment. The wedding took place at the Wilshire Methodist Church on Wilshire Boulevard, and the reception was held at her parents' home in Brentwood. Betty sent three clippings to Harvey from the September 18th issue of the *Herald-Express*, one of them about the Temple-Agar wedding, another about Truman's plans to end the Draft, and a third about a Pasadena pastor, Rev. Charles Long, who was predicting that the world (not the war, the actual world) would end on Friday, September 20th, at exactly 5:33 p.m. "He wasn't sure whether that would be Jerusalem or California time."

On Wednesday: "Madge came over and we had lunch. We called Helen when she got home from work, and the three of us went to the Dome in Ocean Park to see 'Incendiary Blonde' with Betty Hutton and 'Midnight Manhunt.' Betty Hutton surely knocks herself out in this picture. Did you know she was married the first part of this month to a Chicago businessman?"

Betty sent Harvey two envelopes on Thursday, one with her daily letter and the other loaded with clippings. "Helen called to see if I wanted to go to a studio broadcast! I don't ever remember going to one before, so I said I'd love to. We had such a good time. It was the George Burns & Gracie Allen show at

N.B.C. – that's on Sunset, at the corner near the Palladium, remember? Bill Goodwin was M.C. – he's the one who marries Betty Hutton in 'Incendiary Blond.' I got a bigger kick out of him than I did all the rest. Meredith Wilson's orchestra played, and there was a small combo that was terrific. Piano, bass, drums and electric guitar. I don't remember the name...something about 'Paul.' [It was the Les Paul Trio.] We stopped by the Strip and had a bite to eat. I've felt so good today, even though Elsie and I worked like sons of guns all day!" Notes from that day's broadcast are filed in the Paley Center for Media:

MAXWELL HOUSE COFFEE TIME STARRING BURNS AND ALLEN (RADIO)

Summary

One in this series of comedy programs starring the husband-and-wife comedy team of George Burns and Gracie Allen. In this episode, George and Gracie are moving to a new home. Bill Goodwin arrives, and Gracie tells him why they are moving. Then Bill explains why he will not be working on the show, but when he hears who the new sponsor is, he changes his mind. As George and Gracie are preparing to leave, the postman arrives with the mail and is dismayed to learn they are moving. Next, Gracie meets their new neighbor, Meredith Wilson, and learns that he has his own orchestra. She decides to ask him to appear on their show. However, in order to convince George that he should hire Meredith, she asks the orchestra leader to rid their new home of its old tenant. Unfortunately, he mistakes George for the old tenant and hits him on the head with a flute. In addition, Les Paul and his Trio perform "Out of Nowhere," and Meredith Willson and his Orchestra play a musical piece. Includes commercials.

Details
NETWORK: NBC
DATE: September 20, 1945, Thursday 8:00 PM
RUNNING TIME: 0:29:33
GENRE: Radio - Comedy/Variety
SUBJECT HEADING: Comedy
SERIES RUN: NBC - Radio series, 1937-1938, 1940-1942, 1945-1949
COMMERCIALS: Maxwell House coffee, Jell-O pudding

Credits

Meredith Willson... Conductor, Orchestra leader, Cast, himself

Les Paul Trio, the...Music Group

Bill Goodwin...Announcer, Cast, himself

George Burns...Cast, himself

Gracie Allen...Cast, herself

Paul Whiteman...Cast, himself

Mel Blanc...Cast, the Happy Postman

Among the clippings that Betty forwarded was a full-page piece (with photos) about the Shirley Temple wedding, and, more importantly to her, another update on the status of discharge plans for servicemen:

CUT ARMY PTS. TO 70 ON OCT. 1: 2-Yr. Men Out This Winter

Gen. George C. Marshall told Congress today that the army point discharge system would be reduced to 70 points on Oct. 1, 60 points on Nov. 1, and that it would be abolished altogether in "late winter." The chief of staff, in an hour-long session at a joint meeting of senators and congressmen, said that the War Department proposed to release all men with two years of service or more in the army, on their application as soon as the point system is abolished.

TWO-YEAR PLAN: Discussing the coming end of the point system, Marshall said "By late winter we will reach the point in the army point system, where in effect the point system will cease, and two years' service will govern the men wherever they are. At the same time, Marshall asserted that the War Dept. has received an official communication from General Douglas MacArthur confirming his estimate that 200,000 could safely occupy Japan and Korea by March.

Rod played his first JV football game for SC on Friday, and Betty and her parents were there. "Just got home from the football game. Such a mob of people. Must have been a crowd of 85,000. I've never seen so many people in the Coliseum. Rod did well – as we knew he would. He played three quarters of the game, and the final score was 6-6. They were all over the field. The Varsity game was a humdinger, 13-6, U.S.C. over U.C.L.A. I think U.C.L.A. looked like a more finished ball team, but we got the points, and that's what counts. We had seats on the 50-yard line – halfway up- after this I want to sit on the 50-yard line whenever we go to a game! During the halftime, the bands and both cheering sections did some animated card stunts – they had huge spotlights on them, and all the rest of the Coliseum was blacked out. As soon as they were through, they asked everyone to light a match at the same time, and what a sight that was."

Mr. Stella had to attend a funeral on Saturday, and Betty volunteered to work late and close up the store at 9:00. "I paid the girls and closed up shop. Remember I told you we had been so busy this week – well I took the reading of the cash register tonight, and it was the largest since Christmas Day. This week, we took in about $525.00...what a business, this music racket! Elsie called this evening to tell me she wouldn't be at work on Monday because she was driving to San Francisco with a couple of friends. The boyfriend of one of them had wired he had just arrived there after being liberated from a Japanese prison camp in the Philippines. June had just about given up hope of his being safe and alive when she got a cable a couple of weeks ago."

In late September of 1945, three and a half years since Betty and Harvey had met, she thought about the role letters and post cards had played in their relationship. "A separation from one you love is a funny thing. I find myself almost at a loss to explain what I mean. Even our case is different than all the rest. The actual time together has been rather short, but look at the years in between that we have been cementing our love through letters! In fact, it has been going on since 1942! It's eleven-thirty now, and Rod and I just got home from the show. Neither of us had been to the Meralta Theatre in Culver City since it recently opened, so we decided to go there. After seeing what was playing, I could see why Rod was so anxious to go. Betty Grable in 'Million Dollar Legs' and also Claudette Colbert and Joel McCrea in 'The Palm Beach Story.' They really dug deep for those two pictures! And did I have to laugh when it turned out that the legs weren't really Betty Grable's......but a horse. A long shot who paid off 20-1 and saved the dear old college. Donald O'Connor was in it, and he couldn't have been more than 10 or 12, so you can see just how old the picture really was.

"Bob Hope just came on the radio and maybe he can cheer me up. I came as close to fainting at 2 today as I have in years. Rod checked out of U.S.C. today and will be winding up his civilian activities in the next few weeks.

"I heard today on the radio today that Guam was definitely Navy now, and wonder what is cooking for the 20th now? ...pardon me for a minute while I change the radio to something besides 'Hildegarde'...can't stand her. Just turned on the strangest show I've ever heard! Bob Hope, Bing Crosby, Frank

Sinatra, Linda Darnell....all just ad-libbing. Finally, the announcer came on and said it was a special transcription celebrating Bing's first picture that he has produced...'The Great John L.' What that man does have a finger in. Horses – Decca Records – pictures – he'll be made of money! Lots of planes are flying over just now, and the noise is terrific."

With Rod entering the service, Harvey's mother wrote to the Lundins expressing her sympathy. "I can just imagine how Betty's folks feel about him going. But it is something that no one can do anything about. I'll never forget when you went, we had no one left, and it was just like the bottom had dropped out of everything."

On Wednesday, Betty and Elsie had a full day at the store. "We got stacks of records in, and also spent all afternoon filling out orders for Victor records. Eddie was helping E.A. on the record order, but he got so tired after the first half hour that he gave up and went home. He borrowed Elsie's accordion to practice on while he was home. They had some good programs on the radio tonight. Jack Carson started his new show and he, with his nephew 'Tugwell' really slay me. Such crazy guys. Ellery Queen had a good mystery on too. I didn't use to care for them but enjoy them a lot lately." Betty enclosed the program guide for LA's radio station, WMPC. The guide contained a note about Fred Haney, former manager of the St. Louis Browns, who did play-by-play broadcasts of home games for the Los Angeles Angels and Hollywood Stars of the Pacific Coast League. On Thursday, Betty had lunch with Mary Alyce at the RKO studio. "We ate in the commissary and hob-nobbed with some of the stars. Such a thrill! Dorothy McGuire (who played in 'Claudia') and Pierre Aumont, Maria Montez' husband, were sitting at tables near us. It was sort of fun, and I hope to do it again.

"The Stellas have gone to Lytle Creek, and will be there until Monday, so we gals have the store to ourselves. I'll have to be there all day tomorrow to see that everything goes as it should. This is the last weekend Harry James is to be at the Casino, so we went over for a little while. It is the first dance I've been to since I came back. Talk about getting rusty when it comes to dancing! You should have seen me when Rod pulled some of his fancy stuff.... I just stood there watching him. I figured I'd be watching and listening most of the time, but none of Rod's friends were there so he and I danced all evening. I must be getting old for I just can't take it anymore. James' band looks so much better than it did. They really were well dressed and sounded good. The Casino has two bars now, where before they just had soft drink stands – it has changed the type of crowd considerably.... can't say I care for it. Dancing to Harry James brought back such vivid memories.

"Billy Riddle, the make-up man from the studio, was in late yesterday afternoon and was showing Elsie how to paint her lips with a brush. He had his hand on her shoulder and her chin rested on his arm so he could keep her head steady... when who should walk in but her mother, with a gleam in her eye demanding 'What are you doing with my daughter?' We all about died laughing."

25

OPENING NIGHT

AT THE NEW

OFFICERS' CLUB

Harvey and his fellow officers were trying to have their new Consolidated Officers' Club ready as soon as possible. On Sunday, the 1st, there were two planning meetings, followed by three hours of work on the club after supper. "I helped to lay some flooring on the club itself. After working that jackhammer yesterday, and then pounding nails for over three hours tonight, you can imagine how my hands look. We're trying to have our opening on the 18th, which is going to mean a lot of hard work getting ready but if everything goes right, I think we'll make it." He had received word earlier in the day he would be moving out of his job with the Heavy Equipment Section and up into the Main Utilities Office, and he had mixed feelings about the change. "Won't mean a promotion or anything but it probably will mean a lot more to do and more boiling pots to watch. I hate to leave my other job because it was just the kind of work I like, and I was with lots of the men that came overseas in my Section. I'll hate getting away from them, but that's the way things go. Naturally, I'll still be in the Utilities Section of the Wing, but I won't be directly connected with the Heavy Equipment Section. A Capt. Nielson will take my job, and I've had about a week or so to break him in."

On Monday, there was a new typewriter in Harvey's Office, and he used it to type this at the top of his letter to Betty. "Exactly 6 months today since you climbed on that d___ train. I won't ride another one except in your direction!!!" At noon, Harvey and Leonard painted the partition they had put up in their quarters. They could find only two colors of paint, white and blue, and there wasn't enough of either for their project. So, they mixed the two, and the partition ended up a light blue. There hadn't been any fresh rumors about the point system and timing of discharges, but Harvey was upset by some other news. "The biggest gripe now is about this battle star stuff that is going around. In our Wing, we have four Bomb Groups and four Service Groups along with a Wing Headquarters. Naturally, the Wing headquarters handles the operations of the service groups and the bomb groups, and any decisions that have to be made are made there and then passed down to the lower units. Well, the bomb groups are composed of flying personnel and ground crews, while the service groups are made up of technical men and administrative men. The flying personnel of the bomb groups have been awarded three battle stars to wear on their theater ribbons and wing headquarters has construed the order to include all personnel of the bomb groups and wing personnel. Those battle stars mean five points each, which means that men receiving battle stars are now fifteen points closer to going home than the service group personnel. It's the most unfair system of issuing awards that I have ever seen in my life. There have been quite a few bronze star awards along with a few Legion of Merits that went almost exclusively to Wing Headquarters personnel. The flying men of the bomb groups are getting most of the Air Medals, which is only right. Those guys really deserve anything they get. But when the rest of these guys start pulling ahead of us in the race to go home, merely because of someone's discrimination, that's going a little bit too far!! The men in Service Groups are truly the 'forgotten men' of this war. And it had to be my luck to be assigned to one of them. At least I'll know better the next war. I got into this one on my own hook, so can't afford to complain too much, but most of the rest of these guys really have a legitimate gripe. 'The time has come, the walrus said, to....' aw nuts!"

Harvey was busy helping Captain Neilson with the transition into Harvey's job with the Heavy Equipment Section. "It will probably take at least ten days or more before we can get all of the property transferred to him and get him in shape to start operations on his own. There must be at least 8 or 9 hundred thousand dollars' worth of equipment in the yard now, and it will take some time to check and transfer the accountability. At least I'll have that off my hands! Wouldn't it be rough if I had to pay for some of it? Egad!" It was raining heavily, so they skipped the movies that night. Instead, Harvey played bridge, a game in which he was becoming more and more interested. He teamed with Col. Turner, and they beat Mac and Capt. Lander "again!"

On Saturday, a new policy was put in place in Harvey's Section....Saturday afternoons off! In addition, the PX had increased the beer ration so that every man would get twelve bottles, instead of six. "I don't know what the idea is, but the deal has been a big hit with all the men. I don't drink more than two or three bottles a week, so the increase doesn't make much difference to me. Some of these guys, though, just lap up all they can get." Another change involved the laundry service, with a new laundry opening up that returned the clothes—DRY! "Send my first bundle in today. That's really a big improvement over this wet wash stuff, especially in this wet weather. I've had laundry on the line for the last five days. Probably never will get it dry unless I build a fire in my room, and I don't think Lt. Leonard would appreciate that."

That night, Harvey and Mac saw Gary Cooper's *Northwest Mounted Police* at El Gecko. "Really liked it. It must be as old as the hills (1940!), but neither of us has seen it before."

It rained heavily on Friday. "Everything is absolutely saturated. The rain never stops – sometimes it slackens off and sometimes it just pours, but it never stops. I can't imagine where all the water is coming from. Another thing about the rainy weather, the moisture in the air gets to all the envelopes and stamps and sticks them all together. I've lost almost all my envelopes and every one of my stamps in the last three days. If things keep up this way, I'll be writing all my letters on wrapping paper and sealing them shut with flour paste!" The men in the Section were now required to wear their khakis to supper and to the theater, and "all my three uniforms didn't hold up very long under all that wear, especially the wear that our GI laundry gives them. So, this morning Col. Turner and I went down to the Quartermaster Officer Sales Warehouse, and each bought two suits of khakis. Now I should be able to hold out until the end of this business. I also bought a poncho because my old raincoat is about shot. This new poncho has a draw string around the neck and snaps down both sides so that no rain at all can get to your clothes except down below the knees. It's made out of some kind of treated cloth and should be good for football games and stuff like that when I get home." He wanted to send Betty a sample of the cloth but couldn't find one. He did, however, send her something he thought she might find interesting—a thin strip of metallic foil paper. "It's a piece of the 'radar ribbon' our bombers have dropped over

Japan so the Japanese radar stations can't detect our planes in the air. They dropped this stuff by the thousands of yards, and with the Japanese stations picking up every little piece of it on their instruments, you can imagine the confusion it causes." He gave away his high-top combat boots to Technical Sgt. Sam Wylan, the motor sergeant in the heavy equipment yard. He'd had the boots since his days at Walker field but hadn't needed them in Guam. Since Sgt. Wylan spent most of his time in the muddy yard, Harvey thought he needed them more.

Because of the rain that day, not much work was done by the Heavy Equipment Section. Harvey felt Capt. Neilson, his replacement, was learning quickly. "He seems to be a pretty nice guy and apparently likes his new job very much. He's catching on to things fast enough, and I should be able to start my new job in less than a week. The main problem now is to get all the property transferred from my account to his, and then leave him to worry about the things that I've been worrying about for the last six months. Maybe I'm going to like this change better than I thought I would. Bob Yates and I will be working together on this new job and that, in itself, is a good thing." Harvey skipped the movie (*Utah*, with Roy Rogers and Dale Evans) and spent the evening playing bridge and reading; Betty had sent him a box of books, and he was especially enjoying *Young Man with a Horn*: "really well written. I wonder who the author had in mind when she wrote the story? The story sounds familiar to me as if I had heard of a trumpet player with practically the same life story." The novel, written in 1938 by Dorothy Baker, was loosely based on the life of jazz cornet player, Bix Beiderbecke, and was later (1950) adapted for a movie with the same name starring Kirk Douglas, Doris Day and Lauren Bacall.

Harvey closed his letter that night with something he had been thinking about all day. "This morning there was a notice on the bulletin board asking for volunteers for 90-day duty in the Japanese Islands. If I was sure that it was only for 90 days, and not a come on for some other scheme, I'd snap it up in a minute, but I know how the Army works on that kind of a deal. They'll get a crew of men stationed up there and then keep finding jobs for them to do to for two years. And that's not for me! Ninety days would be alright and would be an experience that wouldn't come along every day, but I don't want any of this long-term stuff. Not when there is a chance of getting home in the next six to ten months." Clearly, Harvey's optimism about a quick discharge after V-J Day was fading. Betty in California, and his family in Pittsburgh, were still holding out hope for his return home by Christmas, but Harvey now was considering a three-month term with occupation forces in Japan as perhaps the quickest path back to California.

When Harvey received Betty's letter about Harry James playing at the Casino, and the memories his music brought back to her, he wrote: "It does the same thing to me. There are three or four tunes that I always associate with those wonderful weeks in California in 1942, and his 'You Made Me Love You' is one of them. 'Jersey Bounce' and 'Who Wouldn't Love You' are two more. As far as I'm concerned, they are the all-time high spots on my Hit Parade. I guess there are better songs, but those three are tops for my money. Irving Berlin and all those other guys might just as well close up shop because the best tunes have already been written. I wonder why the Casino did away with their soft drink stands? Maybe they feel that they'll do a lot more business selling hard liquor, but I doubt it. Sounds like they are setting up a carbon copy of the Palladium, doesn't it?" Harvey found the movie that night, *Escape in the Desert* with Jean Sullivan and Philip Dorn, to be a bit corny, but he enjoyed it. The picture was a short one, so he was able to write to Betty and still turn in fairly early.

By Wednesday, the work on the Officers' Club was nearing completion. They had been working on it after working hours and at night and "we've finished it to the point where all that is left to do is a small list of items like furniture and inside decorations. We've got our bar all made and ready to set up and all the easy chairs finished and ready to varnish. We've made twenty big easy chairs and large divans for inside the club as well as a few items of porch furniture for the patio outside. One of the Majors has been working to procure all the floral decorations for the outside of the building, and he's been scouring the island for banana trees and coconut palms so we can really have a good-looking patio outside our porch. We managed to get hold of a big walk-in refrigerator and a fair-sized ice making machine so we should be able to turn out almost any kind of food or drink. The patio will be a large square area about 75 feet square with coral flooring and easy chairs and porch furniture around with tables, etc., so even when the club isn't in full operation, we can have a nice place to lounge around in and read out in the open air where it is coolest. The floor of the club and porch are covered with tongue and groove flooring that somebody was lucky enough to find somewhere on the island. Really, it should be one of the best, if not the best on the entire island. But this job of being president is a pretty rough deal at best. I've got more darn worrying to do than enough, what with all the details of officers I've got working on every little project. Fortunately, a good percentage of them are fairly cooperative, so I don't have to go begging for help on anything that comes up. Someone turned up some leather and we're using it, along with the stuffing from of old mattresses to make seats for our new furniture."

Harvey felt that Capt. Neilson would be ready to take over the Heavy Equipment Section by the end of the week, but he was still having some trouble getting all the property sorted out so that Neilson could sign for it. Harvey had over 140 men working for him, and with all of them using the equipment and tools, it was tough to keep track of it all. Harvey had been reading a lot since leaving the States, and one of the men brought him two more books that day, *Mrs. Egg* and *Bugles in the Afternoon*. He hadn't heard of them but told Betty he would read anything he could get his hands on. Lt. Leonard's wife had sent him quite a few books, and he would always pass them on to Harvey. Leonard's preference tended to run toward "bloody murder mysteries and gun-shooting westerns," and Harvey would read those as well. One of the latest was *Pistol Passport*, and it was "as bloody as they come. More cowboy gun battles per page than any book I've ever read. Maybe being from Texas has affected him that way?" The next two books on Harvey's list were Martin Flavin's *Mr. Littlejohn* and *Lost Horizon* by James Hilton.

With the fighting over, men and women in the service, including those on Guam, were thinking about their post-war lives, and Harvey and Betty were allowing themselves to consider the details of their future family life. "Thoughts of when this business will all be over, and we'll be back together again in our own little home with our own little family of two or three or four or---what am I saying? Those will be wonderful days. That letter of yours today asking about the names for any of our prospective children *[Note: this letter has not yet surfaced!]* really started the ball rolling and I've been thinking all afternoon about whether we would have boys or girls and whether they would look like me or you. Please make them look like you, because it would be an awful handicap if they had to go through life looking like their father. And say, that name you suggested sounds pretty good! For a girl, of course. But I just couldn't go along on having a boy named after me. I still think that part of his name should be Lee. Don't know why I'm so stuck on that particular name, but it has always sounded good to me. Gosh, we are going to have a world of fun growing up with our children, aren't we!! But, if we don't ever have any, I wouldn't be disappointed. Sounds like I'm talking at cross purposes, but you know what I mean. All I'll ever want is you, and anything else will be 'in addition to', and not 'instead of.'"

Clearly, everyone on Guam wanted to know when they would be heading home. Harvey's letter of October 11th had to be confusing for Betty. He spent the first half of the letter laying out possible scenarios for his discharge process, making it sound like it might happen soon. "It is really lucky that we can be together so soon after I hit the West Coast. There won't be any long trips involved unless we make them together. On my official papers, I've got your address listed as my address which should mean, as far as I can figure, that I'll be discharged as close as possible to that address. It's possible that the government may insist on discharging me at the post closest to where I enlisted which would be in Pennsylvania, but I rather doubt that. Actually, I can't quite make up my mind as to which way would be most advantageous for us. If I'm discharged in Pennsylvania, I could possibly spend my terminal leave in California and then take you east with me when I go to report for discharge. In that case, the gov't would pay my transportation across the country. I figure that I'll have about 3 months terminal leave coming to me by the time I get home, which would mean a pretty fair vacation before I start back to work, but I guess we can't count on anything too much because regulations are being changed right and left to meet the emergency. I hope we can turn things to our best advantage when our time comes." After all of that, he went on to say he probably wouldn't be home for quite a while. "At the rate things are going now, I can't see much hope of me getting discharged before April or May of next year. Possibly later. I don't have much to base my assumptions on, so I could be way off either way. I'm certainly not planning on getting home much sooner than that."

On Friday, Harvey lost another roommate. "Late last night, Lt. Leonard received word that he was to be put aboard a boat at 10:30 this morning, and after staying up most of the night packing, he made it just in time. So now, I'm in a room all by myself. I sure hated to see Leonard leave because he's a pretty swell guy, but it's nice that he got a break and could go. I guess that Mac will move in with me now that the room is just singly occupied. The room he's in has four in it, and that's pretty much of a crowd. He likes it pretty well where he is, though, and may not want to move...I'll let you know what the score is later." Lt. Leonard's sudden departure was ironic, since he and Harvey had just finished rearranging their room in the BOQ. The unit was now working only half days on Saturdays, and after running errands in the morning, all of the officers "pitched in to work on the club all afternoon. I took a large bulldozer over to smooth down the coral we've got in our patio and parking lot, and I spent about 3 hours on that in the hot sun and then another 2 hours digging holes for the trees and shrubbery that we are planting. Our opening date is next Thursday, the 18th, and that's not very much time for all we've got to do. It's going to be a close race to have every little thing in order for that night. We're painting the inside white on the ceiling and halfway down the walls, with a blue gray below that to the floor. Our furniture is almost all done, and the bar should be finished tomorrow. The food and liquor has all been arranged for that night, and we are going to have the band from the 314th Wing at North Field." The officers were expecting a large crowd from all over the island, including all of the nurses and Red Cross workers that could make it. They were all looking forward to the big opening and hoping everything worked out well. That night, Harvey received three letters from Betty (numbers 179, 180, and 181), one from his mother, and one from Elsie, Betty's friend at the record store. Betty had also sent him a "care package" which included soap, candy, cigarettes, gauze bandages, and a book titled *You Know Me, Al*. The book, published in 1916 and Ring Lardner's only novel, was considered a century later (in 2013 by NPR's Colin Fleming) as "the finest piece of baseball fiction ever composed."

Harvey's mother had been hearing reports about the typhoon that had hit Okinawa, and she was wondering about the possible effects on her son. "We heard on the radio that tons of food and other necessities were sent to them from Guam. Maybe if their airfields have all been destroyed you might be sent there?...I see by the Wilkinsburg paper where Frank Thomas (from up in back of us, on the corner" is back in the States after 10 months overseas and is due here next week with his wife and baby, born while he was over there. He is a major now. I hope they make you a major... that's the least they can do if they are going to keep you over there for a while longer." She also read that discharge points might be lowered to fifty by December 1st, partly because of a significant increase in voluntary enlistments. She was noticing a lot of soldiers in town wearing "discharge emblems."

She told Harvey that she and his father had gone to the movies and had seen Hedy Lamar in *Her Highness and the Bellboy*. "Not bad. She sure is pretty, isn't she?" She noted that many stores were doing a good business. Because of the stream of soldiers coming home, men's wear shops were particularly busy. "Everywhere you looked you saw service men with suit boxes, shoe boxes, or hat boxes under their arms. I hadn't really realized how many there were being discharged. I was sure wishing one of them was you. I hear the Navy's points are being lowered again and each month will be lowered more. Is the Army doing that too?"

His mother sent Harvey some books to read, and she told him she was planning to attend some of the book reviews being offered by a local Rabbi, Rabbi Freehof. "I can get more out of his reviews than if I read it myself. Some of them are over my head but he can bring them down to my size. The eight he will review are – 'A Lion in the Street' (The Beloved Demagogue), 'Young Jefferson' (The Statesman Scholar), 'Immortal Wife' (the Explorers' Partner), 'War I Have Seen' (The Homesick American), 'A. Woolscott' (The Twisted Talent), 'Rickshaw Boy' (The Good Pavement), 'The White Tower' (The Beckoning Peak), 'So Well Remembered' (The Prosaic Saint). If any of them sound good to you and you think you'd like to have them, let me know and I'll get them for you. From the sublime to the ridiculous, we went to see 'Duffy's Tavern' last night. Usually, those pictures with lots of stars aren't very good but this one was pretty good."

On Sunday, about a dozen officers, including Harvey, worked all day on their club, installing the bar, painting furniture, and planting palm trees and other greenery around the outside of the building. After lunch, Harvey relaxed for half an hour while he finished the last two chapters of *Bugles in the Afternoon*, a story he enjoyed about the life of a soldier serving under George Custer. Later, some of them went to dinner. "Jay and Bob Yates and I went down to the 103rd Seabees for dinner with an officer we know down there. Their mess is advanced to the stage where they have tablecloths and use napkins. They had fried chicken with ice cream for dessert...not bad at all. Then we sat around their club and talked over a couple of drinks until after 10. It's past eleven now, and after that fast ride back with the wind blowing in my eyes, I'm plenty sleepy. I wanted to start on that book you sent me, but I guess it will have to wait until tomorrow night." He realized his daily sched-ule had changed over the past few weeks. "Funny how I've gotten out of the habit of going to the movies in the evenings lately. I've either been reading, working on the club, or playing bridge. We're supposed to have some pretty good shows coming up, though, so I guess I'll watch for them."

Since the end of hostilities, many of Harvey's letters opened with the date and some version of "Still on the Rock!" On Monday, October 15th, he wrote that he was still stuck in the heavy equipment pool, "but only because my jeep has been in the shop waiting for some new parts, and I can't get around to the various supply agencies to get all my property signed over to Capt. Neilson. Replacement parts are very hard to get here, so sometimes it means waiting for three or four days, sometimes longer, before a vehicle can be repaired. Two of the hydraulic cylinders on my brake system went bad at the same time, and it's plenty hard to get one, let along two. But the jeep has been deadlined for four days now, and I guess it won't be very long before the parts come in. I'm anxious to get all this property cleaned up. We recently got another bunch of equipment shipped in to us, so now the value of the property assigned to me must be well over a million and a half dollars. That's really a lot of property!!!" *(Note: "A million and a half dollars" in 1945 would be over twenty million dollars today.)*

The scheduled opening of the new Officers' Club was quickly approaching, and Harvey was worrying that it wouldn't be ready in time. "This is the week that our club is supposed to open, and I'm having a little bit of trouble getting enough officers to volunteer their services at night to help finish the job. So today at lunch time, I got the Colonel's permission to publish a roster of men for each night this week, so we'll be sure of having enough help. Nobody likes the deal, but it's the only way I can be sure of finishing on time. I've designated different officers to take care of the jobs that specifically pertain to opening night such as: food, drinks, transportation for nurses, etc., and tonight we are having a meeting of all the officer committees to make sure they are going to be able to complete their specific jobs. We may run into a couple of snags at the last minute, but so far things look as if they are going pretty smoothly. There should be a crowd of more than 500, but I can't be sure until the officer in charge of invitations makes a last-minute check. At least, we'll be prepared for that many."

Harvey was getting increasingly anxious to get home to Betty, and many of his men were also itching to get back to the wives and girlfriends they loved. Others, though, were struggling. "Two boys in my section recently got 'Dear John' letters, and the poor guys are really suffering. One of them asked me to get him get assigned to duty in Japan or China so he wouldn't have to go back to a life without his wife, whom he loves very much. One of the boys is having trouble with his wife's parents, and the other one's wife has apparently found someone she likes better than him. Both of them seem to love their wives, and neither can understand why the situation has come up. One guy has been hearing from his wife every day or so, and all the letters have been full of love and so forth. Until the one he got the other day which told him about the other guy and asked him for her freedom. Boy, wouldn't that be a slap in the face. Even if a woman does fall out of love, which is certainly possible, she should have the decency and common sense to wait until he comes home to give the guy a chance to get the bad news gradually. When I hear things like that, I'm so darn thankful for our wonderful marriage that I don't know what to do." Hearing about these "Dear John" letters had clearly shaken up several other men in the unit.

Harvey closed his letter that night with news about the recent typhoon and its impact on those stationed on Guam. "Our food has really been lousy lately. Okinawa was the victim of a pretty rough typhoon. Almost all of their food supply was destroyed, and now all food that is available is being shipped up to them. Don't get the idea that we haven't been eating three meals a day, but they just haven't been as good, nor with as much fresh meat, as before. After the emergency is over, our meals will no doubt get back to their old standards but right now 'them's the conditions what prevail.' We haven't had fresh meat more than twice in the last two weeks, with one of those being lamb. In civilian life I could eat lamb, but this stuff we're getting now is awful. Don't know how the cooks manage to make such a mess out of it. I'm sure it isn't easy!"

Harvey hadn't been to El Gecko for a while, but on Tuesday he, Mac, and Lt. Yarnas took a break from working on the club so they could go. "The movie tonight was 'The Corn is Green,' with Bette Davis and a new fellow by the name of John Dall. Both were really good, and the picture is among the better ones. I don't know whether it's a new picture or not, but don't miss it if you have a chance to see it." After the movie, they went back to the club to relieve the officers who had been stuffing the leather cushions for the divans and easy chairs. It was only two days before the opening on Thursday evening, and it was beginning to look more and more like they would make it after all. "I'll sure be glad when it's all over so we can all settle down to enjoy life again and have our evenings to ourselves. I guess, though, that it has given us something to do when the time may have really dragged otherwise."

On Wednesday, a new Wing regulation was announced, giving everyone Wednesday afternoons off in addition to Saturday afternoons. The officers used the opportunity to spend the whole afternoon working on the club, but Harvey hoped that he would also get some relaxation time after the grand opening. He had a new roommate. Mac had moved into Lt. Leonard's spot in the BOQ. "For a while there, I was all by myself with no one else to consider when it came to leaving lights on, etc., but Mac's a good guy and I know we'll have a h___ of a good time. We managed to get a supply parachute today, a small yellow one, so we put it up as a ceiling in the room...you should see it! With pale blue walls and a bright yellow ceiling – what a combination! These parachutes are pretty heavy stuff, so I don't believe you'd want any of the cloth sent home to you, but I'll enclose a sample just in case you might want me to dig up a few pieces for you. Yellow is the only color I can get but if you like the material, I guess it could be dyed pretty easily. I haven't had an opportunity to get any of that fine parachute material, but I'll snag it if I find out there is some available. Lt. Ridgeway (77 points) just got news about an hour ago that he is to leave for home at 8:30 in the morning, and he's well on his way toward getting stinko. There's a bridge game going on next door, and he's in there raising hell and almost breaking up the bridge game...I'm glad he won't be there to foul up the party tomorrow night."

Thursday was opening night at the club. Harvey figured he wouldn't be back to the BOQ until very late, so he wrote a quick letter to Betty in the morning. He went in to his office, and his request was granted to use the rest of the day preparing for the event. "I've had some contacts with the Island Command outfits on the other end of the island, and I think I've gotten arrangements started for the procurement of flowers for the tables tonight. I haven't any idea what kind of flowers they will be, but I'm sure they will be pretty because that's one thing that this island has lots of — colorful flowers. After that was taken care of, there wasn't a single arrangement to be made, and all that remained for me to do was to shag it down to the club and get things fixed up there. This morning our week's liquor ration came in, and now we have about thirteen cases of liquor to dispense across the bar besides better than a hundred cases of beer. Believe me, that's a lot of beer and liquor to be consumed! But I haven't the slightest doubt that most of it will be gone before tomorrow morning. I'm just thankful we were able to get enough to make some kind of showing.

"We've completed all the construction on the club with the exception of oiling the floor and finishing the parking area out front. Those two things won't hold up our opening and can be done at any time after the club is officially open. It really looks pretty good inside, with the super paint job that we put on it. It's all in a combination of white and a light blue with all the furniture being either varnished or painted a dark blue.... that's all the time I'll have today, but I'll be back tomorrow to tell you all about the big doings at the Officers Club."

Just as the club opened that evening, Harvey received a telegram from Betty: "DEAR HARVEY CONGRATULATIONS ON OPENING CLUB THINKING OF YOU DARLING AND MISSING YOU WITH LOVE BETTY."

The club opening was a success, and Harvey sent details the next day. "We finally got our club officially opened, and it really was a howling success, no kidding!! We had about 400 guests, and everyone seemed to have a whale of a good time. And, your wonderful cablegram came just before the club opened – thanks loads…I'll enclose it here so you can see how it looked when it got here. We worked all yesterday afternoon getting the place in shape, and I was still inside, in my underwear, putting some finishing touches on a few things when a couple of the lady guests started to come. I got out just in time, but it just goes to show you how close we came to not being ready in time. There were about 35 or 40 women from units all over the island, mostly nurses but quite a few Red Cross workers too. The music was furnished by a 7-piece band from the 314th Wing at North Field, and they played good music of all kinds, sweet and hot. All women have to be back in their quarters by 10:30, so we opened the bar at 6:30 and the dancing began at 7:30. Among the guests were two brigadier generals and fourteen full colonels. There was a hospital ship in port overnight, so we had all the medical personnel up for the party. The bunch got a little rough after the women left, but no one gave us any real trouble. What with all the free drinks, I was surprised we didn't have more trouble than we did. We closed the club at one in the morning and had to actually force a lot of officers out so that we could close. There was a terrific mess to clean up this morning, but the club was back to normal again this evening and I really think we'll be able to make a go of it. There is still an awful lot of work to be done before we can call it finished, but that can be done more slowly." With his letter, Harvey enclosed a copy of the invitation to the grand opening that the 315th had sent out.

The OFFICERS CLUB of the 315th SERVICE CENTERS…

The Officers of the Service Groups, 315th Bomb Wing cordially invite you to attend the opening of their Officer's Club on Thursday, eighteenth of October nineteen hundred and forty-five.

Music,
Entertainment &
Refreshments guarantee
an enjoyable evening at the
newest and coolest
Club on Guam

Harvey started his new job on Friday, and he wrote his Saturday letter to Betty from his new office. "I haven't very much to do on my new job as yet outside of a lot of running around to check on a few different jobs. The office has a lot of coordinating to do as far as arranging for delivery of materials etc. Every new job to be done in the Wing area comes across our desks here, and priorities for construction are assigned to the jobs after we investigate the requirements and necessary materials. It's really a lot of fun getting a job request and then going out on the job to investigate the thing. For one thing, it's the first time I've been able to get out on a variety of jobs, instead of being confined to heavy equipment jobs. I'm getting experience with all kinds of building work and plumbing, electrical, and refrigeration work, as well as the same old heavy equipment stuff that I've always done. But now, instead of actually performing the work, I'm estimating and recommending work. I think I'll like it even better after I get into it a little further. I guess I'm getting to be one of the 'big wheels' in this outfit. The only thing that I don't like about it is that the new job doesn't call for a promotion. Oh well, I didn't want to be a general anyway." With his letter, Harvey enclosed the most recent issue of *Navy News* in which there was an article about troop movements coming home from the Pacific. Navy Secretary James Forrestal noted that the return of scores of warships for the Navy Day celebration would not slow down homeward movements of the armed forces. "Explaining that Navy Day, Oct. 27, was designed to pay tribute to the Navy's achievement, Forrestal declared: 'I would not have such an event marred by an erroneous belief that it is slowing down demobilization. Therefore, I hope everyone will understand that no vessel which could carry men is being held in port merely to celebrate Navy Day.' The Navy announced that 750,000 men would come home from the Pacific in warships alone in the next 11 months. This is exclusive of the hundreds of thousands who will return on Navy transports."

All of Harvey's letters to Betty contained expressions of his strong feelings for her, but usually there was also some description of his daily life on Guam. Not in this Sunday's note, though. He was missing her terribly and only talked about his feelings for her and memories of times they had shared together. He remembered the night they had met three and a half years earlier. "He (God) sure had something special in mind when he brought me to Los Angeles from Pittsburgh, almost 3000 miles. And I wouldn't change a minute of it except that maybe I'd kiss you twice instead of once that first night at your front door. You know, when I went down to the 'trolley' that night after leaving your house, I felt I had suddenly come out of the rain into the sunshine...."

On Monday, it was back to work at his new job. "Quite a few of our jobs are recreational projects, and it doesn't help the morale of our guys to be working on baseball fields and basketball courts for men who do little but watch us work. But the very fact that so many men are being discharged right now keeps them from minding too much. They're always hoping that, for some reason, they'll be next in line. And, believe me, I'm hoping the same thing! There was some encouraging news on the radio tonight about discharges. Apparently, Congress is about to pass legislation that will greatly speed up the flow of men being returned to the States for Discharge. I hope that the plan they dream up this time will include me."

That night at dinner Mac and Peck mentioned that their wives were dealing with medical issues...one was having an operation that could result in a mastectomy, and the other had just been diagnosed with a possible tumor. This worried Harvey, and he encouraged Betty to follow through with routine examinations. He was playing a lot of bridge and was encouraging Betty to learn so they could play when he came home. On Tuesday, he and Colonel Turner played against Mac and Peck, and "were beaten after a long, hard struggle, by the fairly close score of 800 points. Considering the bad cards that the colonel and I had, we did very well!! I sure am getting to like this game!"

Wednesday was Betty and Harvey's eleven-month anniversary, and as Harvey noted, they had been apart for more than half of that time. On a much more mundane note, Wednesday was also a big day for Harvey on Guam—slot machines for the Officers' Club!! "Today we added a new fixture to the club. Three slot machines, two nickel ones and one dime one. The well-known 'one armed bandits.' Remember me knocking myself out with them at Walker and in the basement of the Lerner Hotel (sp?). We even had our pictures taken by one of them, the night of the colonel's party. These machines were sold to us by a club at North Field that is closing up in a few days. We bought them for $150.00 and expect to have our money back within a month. After that, any receipts from them will be clear profit. We're operating pretty close to the line right at the moment, so I hope they come through for us. The furnishings in the club and the expenses for our opening night pushed us pretty far under, but we are gradually getting our heads above water and once we reach an even keel, we shouldn't have any trouble."

Harvey received another letter from Virjeanne's husband, Earl Sexton. He was now stationed in Sasebo, Japan, and did the mail and message run between there and the town of Saga. "I was going to write a few days ago, but I was called to make a run to Saga, 50 km up north. We arrived at Kyushu on the 23rd of September, and I sure was surprised when I arrived. Everything was so different. I didn't think we would be able to go anywhere, but we do. At the present time we are going toward the city that was bombed with that atom bomb [Nagasaki]...already we have repaired 50 miles of road good enough to make 45 to 50 miles per hour. I leave Saga at 16:00 and go to Sasebo tomorrow evening. I leave there at 7:00. 2 trips a day and one round trip... it's some life here. There are so many MPs here you can't turn around without seeing 3 different ones. That is in Sasebo. Well, we are 50 miles further on down, and in between these towns there are no MPs. I guess you know, I'm not supposed to stop but no one ever knows.... [Written later:] I didn't get to finish this last night. It was almost 1:00 p.m. when I started, and so this morning when roll came, there were 3 boys locked up, 2 corporals and one staff sergeant. You can bet they are in for trouble, and I hope they get out OK."

Harvey started his Thursday letter at 7:30 in the morning, before the rest of the officers came in to the office. He was using a Remington Noiseless typewriter, and it was taking some time to get used to. "This Remington is a pretty good machine, but it doesn't seem to make enough noise to suit me. Typing should be accompanied by a lot of clatter and racket, but this darn thing just goes along without making the slightest sound, and it doesn't seem right. Can't tell when I make a mistake or anything!" He didn't expect the others to come in for a while because of their partying the night before. "We are supposed to start working at 7:30, but hardly anyone gets going before 8 or after. Especially some of the officers in the barracks across from me. Those guys probably won't get going before supper time, if they are even conscious by that time. They threw a party in their room last night and kept it up until almost breakfast. They made enough noise to keep everyone awake in the whole area. They must have got hold of some extra liquor somewhere, and that's what prompted the party. They were all pretty sloppy drunk...but I guess that after spending some length of time in these darn islands away from civilization and everything, a guy can't be too responsible for these actions, especially for when he doesn't have too much waiting for him when he gets back to the States. I was thinking about 11 months ago this morning. The two of us were in our "honeymoon cottage" on the beach above Santa Monica... then that wonderful drive and breakfast further up the beach! When I get back, we want to get reservations at Los Tunas for about a week!"

That morning, Harvey learned he'd be losing another roommate—this time it was Peck. "Remember me telling you about Peck's wife, Marie, needing an operation? Well, she's going to have it on the 31st, and she went through the Red Cross to try and have Peck come home for it. And believe it or not, it worked!! A teletype came through this morning, and Peck is to leave for home in a day or two. That is really a lucky break for both of them. It's too bad it has to be for a reason like that, but if everything works out, it'll be a good deal. At any rate, he'll be leaving tomorrow or the next day. I sure hate to see him go, but I'm glad he'll be getting the opportunity. I'm sure sweating out my turn to come home, but I don't want it to come for that kind of reason.... I don't want you to be sick in order for me to come home! Mac was sure down in the dumps today when he heard that Peck was leaving. He's been so homesick himself that any mention of going home brings tears to his eyes...I really feel sorry for him. He'll really be downhearted when Peck leaves because the three of us have been pretty close to each other right along." Harvey was feeling homesick as well, and at the end of his letter, he finally admitted it. "You know I talked about Mac getting homesick when he hears about Peck going home? Well, darling, I've got to admit that I also got a little that way myself down deep inside of me. Thoughts of him being stateside before long brought on thoughts of you....so far, I've been able to keep busy enough to have very little time to become depressed, but it's hard to fill up the few minutes in bed before you go to sleep with anything but thoughts of home."

Harvey started Friday's letter in the office. "This machine I'm using now is a noisy old Woodstock, and it must have been used in George Washington's utility office. I'm afraid to pound on it too heavily because I'm liable to get a faceful of keys. Boy, I really put the miles on that old jeep of mine today. It seems that every time the phone rang, I had to attend to a job across the runway from the office. We are pouring a lot of concrete on the other side, and the guys we've got setting up forms and stuff are pretty darn inexperienced. It keeps us hopping to make sure there aren't any hitches developing. There must be at least ten or twelve jobs requiring from 50 to 150 cubic yards of concrete each, and that adds up to a sizeable job. The coral we are using to make our concrete isn't as fine as it really should be, but we just have to make it do. Sometimes there are big lumps in it which have to be taken out before the stuff can be smoothed down, and that is plenty messy. The concrete floors and slabs we have already poured, though, don't look half bad considering... What the hell, these are field conditions anyway, what do these guys expect?

"Last night we had an officers' club meeting to try and get the members to vote us another appropriation in order to meet the debts we incurred on the opening night and the expenses that we had to make for some of the furniture and the beer and liquor etc. You never heard such haggling and bitching in all your life. You'd think that we were asking them to give us one of their eye teeth or something. The d___ guys want a club and want all the modern conveniences in it, but they want it all for nothing. We presented them with a complete itemized list of our expenditures, which I'm afraid was a big mistake because they took apart every item and demanded a complete explanation of every little nickel's worth. The meeting lasted for over two hours and, when I finished, I was wringing wet with sweat. I hope we don't ever have any more large expenses, because I'd resign my job rather go through a mess like that again. But we finally got our loan of $4.00 per officer which we hope to be able to pay back someday. If the bar receipts and the 'take' from the slot machines is large enough, it's possible we may be able to cut out all our dues.

"Peck finally got away this morning about eleven o'clock. His orders came through, and he took off within a few minutes. He's not going to be able to fly all the way home, so he caught a B-24 out of here to Saipan and from there he'll get the fastest water transport available. Probably it will be well into November before he gets Stateside, but at least he'll be getting there. I imagine he'll make it sometime around the 15th of the month, or even earlier if he is lucky. Sure was a lucky break that the Red Cross saw eye to eye with his wife on the necessity of his being there when she has her operation."

Mac, who was the unit's Supply officer, had been urging Harvey for some time to turn in his Army carbine, and he finally got around to it on Saturday. "Right after lunch I dug it out of my footlocker and cleaned it up so that I could give it to him. I was really surprised at the good shape it was in – didn't take me more than twenty minutes to put it in tip top shape. I hadn't even looked at it since we got over here, and I expected it to be almost all rusted away. But not a spot on it."

On Sunday, Harvey typed his letter to Betty on his "own typewriter." "Mac found me a portable job in the supply room that no one was using, so he brought it down for me to use on my letters to you. It doesn't have the best type in the world, but it still is better than that old handwriting of mine. It seems funny, but I seem to be able to think better when I'm using a typewriter. Can't imagine why that is, but I always find a lot more things to tell you when I'm beating out the word on a machine than when I'm struggling with a pen. Today was the laziest day possible. This morning, Mac and I just laid in bed and either read or slept. For the main meal of the day, we actually had roast turkey with mashed potatoes and green peas. This afternoon the weather was hot, but cloudy and uncomfortable...we started to play horseshoes around one o'clock and before the afternoon was over, we had played 17 complete games!! That's a lot of exercise for one day. Col. Turner is an old horseshoe pitcher from way back when, and he really made the rest of us get on the ball to keep up with him. Mac and I were pitching against Col. Turner and Jimmy Ray. They beat us more times than we beat them, but it was fun just the same. Apparently Col. Turner had pitched a few games in practice with the state champions of his home state of Vermont. After supper, the four horseshoe pitchers went to the show and saw "Medal for Benny." I still don't know what to make of the blamed picture. One of the oddest films that I have ever seen. J. Carroll Nash plays a super role as Papa Martin, and Dorothy Lamour is even more sensuous than she has been in some of her other pictures. She wears lots of filmy blouses that really must have been hidden to get past the Hays office. The picture ends and leaves you up in the air. It just doesn't seem to be the proper place to end it. Maybe it's just that I'm too discriminating. Pretty good show, though."

At the top of his October 29th letter Harvey replaced his usual "Still on Guam!" with "Still on a very wet and sloppy Guam." "Sitting here in my room tonight I'm really feeling better than I have for a long time. Tonight, Mac and I went to the movie and saw 'Pillow to Post' and along with the weather, we had a circus. No kidding, we just roared all the way through. About six o'clock, it started to rain like a broken water main, and when it stopped about at about 6:45, we were plenty pleased since we badly wanted to see the show everyone had been talking about. Well, we no sooner got seated than it started raining again, and really in earnest this time. But already being there, we wouldn't have left in the middle of the movie for anything. The show was one of the best comedies I have ever seen. Mac and I had to almost hold on to each other to keep from falling off the seat. Ida Lupino and Sydney Greenstreet were exceptionally good, and the rest of the cast just filled it in right. We could hardly see the screen for the rain, and the noise it made splashing all over everything made it plenty hard for us to hear what was being said on the screen. No one seemed to mind too much. Just so long as they got the general idea of the picture. Darling, if you can possibly do it, see that picture. And while you're watching it, think of Mac and I (on second thought, just think of me!) sitting out in the hardest rain you can imagine just laughing like a couple of idiots. It was a riot!! I had on my nice new poncho, but the darn thing leaked a little around the drawstring at the neck and I might as well not have had it on. Every stitch I had on was soaking wet. Mac just had on a regular gabardine raincoat which didn't even slow down the rain as it hit him. My moccasins were just floating with water and mud, so I guess it will be at least a week before I get them clean enough that I can wear them without socks the way I like to. Today was such an ordinary day that I was beginning to wonder if I had anything interesting to say to you. But after being to the show, the whole situation has been changed. I really wish you had been with us tonight, 'cause you would have had the time of your life!!...this will provide conversation for a whole day tomorrow." The movie the next night was *Hitchhike to Happiness* with Al Pearce and Dale Evans. Everyone was saying it was just a mediocre picture, but Harvey and Mac still intended to go—that is, until they saw that it was still raining!

On Tuesday, Harvey noticed that the incoming mail from Betty was piling up in his footlocker. "Holy smokes, in another three days, I'll have No. 200!!! Can you imagine that? If worst should come to worst, and I have to stay overseas for a year, I'll have gotten 365 letters from you in succession. Boy, that's a lot of writing...Just for the fun of it, I did a little figuring on the deal and came up with these figures. If you wrote a letter every day for a solid year, you would use 365 envelopes and about 1095 sheets of paper. The postage alone would cost $21.90, and there would be about 191,625 words crowded on those 1095 sheets of paper, not including the addresses or return addresses. In the process you would use up around four bottles of ink and about a quart and a half of witch hazel for your sore arm and hand.....silly, isn't it?"

Harvey and the others had the afternoon off on Halloween, and they spent time working on the club. "We were making some of the finer improvements that it badly needs. Some of the officers worked on shrubbery, and some were on a general clean-up detail. My work was to take a dump truck and, with three other officers, pick up enough larger pieces of coral to make a borderline for a walk in front of the club. After we had enough of the large pieces, we got some of the fine coral and filled the walk in with that. It's kind of soft as yet, but after the first rain, it will pack down and will be as hard as concrete.... We still have a lot of fine coral to haul in for the parking lot, but that can be done next Saturday afternoon if we can find enough officers that aren't too busy with their duties to help. Before long, we'll have a club that will do justice to any air base in the states...no kidding.

"Went to the show tonight with Mac and saw a real old one. 'The Cowboy and the Lady', with Gary Cooper and Merle Oberon. It must have been filmed about five or six years ago, but it still was plenty good. Especially since I hadn't seen it before. I noticed for the first time tonight that Merle Oberon is pretty good looking. I really never paid much attention to her before. *(Note: the picture had been released in 1938. Betty had seen Merle Oberon in July, sitting in the next car at a drive-in restaurant on Sunset Boulevard. —DB.)*

LOS ANGELES PARADE
FOR ADMIRAL HALSEY

As October began, Southern Californians were experiencing a heat wave with near record temperatures. Betty sent Harvey a clipping from Monday afternoon's *Herald-Express*: "The mercury here today was pushing hard on the heels of an October record. It had already tied the Sept. 3 record for the hottest day this year with a 100-degree temperature, recorded at 2 p.m. Hottest day was Oct. 3, 1885, with a sizzling 102 recorded. Any breezes you may be lucky enough to encounter will be strictly desert variety on account of very high pressure inland blowing air this way." On Tuesday, the temperature hit 101, the hottest day in sixty years. Everything in the record store was covered with dust because of the hot desert air, and Betty and Elsie spent the day mopping the floor. Even though Christmas was still almost three months away, they were starting to put up holiday displays in the store window to highlight gifts for overseas mailing. Marion came into the store to tell Betty that Mary Alyce's husband, Will, was home from the Pacific. He had flown non-stop from Guam to Hamilton Air Base in San Francisco and had called Mary Alyce from there. He was to report to Fort McArthur on Friday for discharge. In his last letter, he had predicted he would be in Guam for at least another month!

That evening, Rod let the family know he would be leaving in three weeks. "He told us he had stopped by the ration board today and had learned he is to leave Oct. 22nd. He goes to Mac Arthur for about three days and then is home for a week before he is assigned. I'm glad he has something definite to plan on because this uncertainty has been driving him crazy…not to speak of the whole family." Rod hadn't heard anything about the possible West Point appointment for several weeks and had given up hope that it might come through.

Betty enjoyed hearing about the progress on the Officers' Club and hoped it would be done soon enough so he could enjoy it a bit before heading back to the States. The constant changes and updates in the discharge point system were confusing her, and she asked Harvey to explain it one more time.

Mary Alyce stopped by the music store on Saturday morning for a visit with Betty. Her husband was at Mac Arthur and was to be discharged the next day. They would live with her parents until they could find a place of their own; she'd continue working at the studio, and he would continue his studies. He had been in Guam for three days but hadn't had a chance to contact Harvey. "He didn't sleep at all the whole time he was there since the boys stayed right by the card file that determined their place in line for a plane ride home. He put his card, and those of several friends, at the front of the list when the fellow wasn't looking, which is how he got home in such a rush. Will said they kept putting names up ahead of his right along, and he wanted to get home just as badly as anyone, so he was tempted…and did it. He told Mary Alyce that it seemed a lot hotter in Guam than it was in Tinian."

Workers at the Warner Bros. Burbank studio were on strike, and Betty sent a clipping from the *Herald Express* (Los Angeles' afternoon daily) with an article and photos about the violence that morning.

Early morning fighting on the picket line, followed by comparatively peaceful picketing which kept workers off their jobs and halted all film production, highlighted today's events at Warner Brothers Burbank studio as strikers, equipped with gas masks as a protection against a second barrage of tear gas, continued their blockade at studio gates.

Meanwhile, virtual certainty that mass picketing soon will end came when Superior Judge Joseph Vickers issued a temporary restraining order at Warner Brothers' request for an injunction against the strikers, stipulating that no more than four pickets may form a line at the main gates and no more than three at any of the seven other studio entrances.

PROHIBITS VIOLENCE

The order, made returnable on Oct. 15, also prohibits any violence in the picketing. In effect, the order makes illegal the presence of more than

25 pickets at the studio at any time. A loud chorus of jeers and snorts from the crowds of strikers drowned out the words of a court attaché, Deputy Sheriff Frank Reap, late today when he attempted to read the restraining order over a loud-speaker inside the main studio gates.

Brief fistfights between policemen and pickets began this morning when the officers attempted to escort an employee, a doorman identified as Max Friebraum, through the main gates. The disturbance was eased immediately after the man gave up attempts to enter the studio and took his place among almost 500 would-be workers standing across the street from more than 1000 pickets.

On Sunday, Betty went with Rod to a Post Office picnic at the beach. About twenty people had planned to attend, but in the end only four showed up. Nevertheless, it was a good afternoon with enough food that all four of them took some home. They played basketball and volleyball and also some catch with a football. Afterward, they went to a matinee at the Dome Theater on the pier. "'A Bell for Adano'- did you see it? If you haven't, be sure to see it when it hits Guam...I know you'll like it. I thought it was really swell – with it was a Class B Universal musical, 'Swing Out Sister.'"

On Wednesday, after everyone else at Stella's had gone home, Betty started typing a letter to Harvey. It was 5:00 p.m., and "E.A. [Mr. Stella] has some crazy fool idea that one of us girls should come at 8:30 and work until 5, while the other comes at 9:30 and works until six. Maybe he figures that he'll make 3 cents more a day that way?" As she typed, a workman was spraying varnish on one of the pianos, and the spray hit her in the face... "the darn stuff makes my throat hurt. At least the piano will look good when he is finished." Perhaps Mr. Stella was right after all, though, as the store became "a bee-hive of activity" at about 5:15. In addition to multiple customers, a shipment of records came in. "Some cute GI records came in today, and I brought them home to send on to you. Every one of them reminded me of little things you've said in your letter."

That evening, Betty, Elsie, and Bev went to the Pantages Theater on Hollywood Boulevard and saw Danny Kaye in *Wonder Man*. "He is the funniest thing I've ever seen – and so very clever. You and Rod will sure get a kick out of it. Speaking of Rod – now that the date is certain when he leaves (a week from next Monday), he feels much better about the whole setup. He's surely keeping busy all the time seeing everybody and going places. Hard to try and keep track of him. The folks are taking it all swell, and me too, though

I get that funny feeling in my stomach when I think of him going." That night, after Rod came back from skating, he and Betty sat in the kitchen while he ate his dinner. "Finally he finished, and I came into the bedroom to finish this letter. He kissed me good night and made some crack about how many years it would be before we saw each other again. That did it! - started the tears that had been stored away for so long now. Now that they're started, I'm having one heck of a time stopping them. Guess I'll just have to cry them out of my system tonight, for it won't make it any easier for my folks to see me carry on, after I put up so many arguments about the opportunities for Rod in going away now."

While Betty was writing to Harvey on the 10th, his mother was writing to Betty. She shared the usual family updates and vented about the constant delays in Harvey's discharge from the service. She noted that he had been in the army for forty-six months and wondered if, perhaps, a promotion to Major might occur if his discharge were delayed much longer. Every morning, she listened to Tom Breneman on the radio, and this morning he had reported it was 101 degrees in Hollywood—it was just 39 degrees in Pittsburgh that day. Some fifteen years earlier, Breneman had been program director at station KFVD in Culver City, and his current show, *Breakfast in Hollywood*, aired on the Blue Network, ABC, NBC, and the Mutual Network. It reportedly had ten million listeners across the country. The previous March, he had opened his own restaurant, aptly named Tom Breneman's Restaurant, on Vine Street off of Sunset Boulevard, and was broadcasting his radio program from the restaurant.

On Friday, the same day that Harvey's roommate, Lt. Leonard, had boarded a ship for the States, Betty received a telephone call from another of the Guam group—Pop Bristow! "This afternoon I had a call at the store. It was Mr. Bristow. He surely is a nice fellow to talk to. He said he had just gotten back to L.A. a couple of days ago and called right away in answer to my note. Said he hadn't written you or heard from you since he said good-bye. It's rather hard getting anything definite said in such a short time on the phone, and there are lots of things I want to ask him about when I see him. He's going to call Monday, and we'll set a date for one night next week to meet in L.A. for dinner. His wife, his boy and me. I'm looking forward to meeting them. From what he said today he seems very sure that the 315th is going to the Philippines or China. Have you heard any more news along that line? Guess I'll find out more when I see them.... I was so excited hearing from someone who had seen you recently." On Saturday, after a busy day at

Stella's, she went to the wedding of some friends (June and Wally) and then to the reception. She finally got home after one o'clock in the morning, and was too tired to write a long letter, but she did enclose two clippings from the *Herald-Express* that she had been saving since August. One was a teasing reference to the new Officers' Club in Guam. It was a "Private Buck" cartoon showing two soldiers in a life raft in the South Pacific. One of them was reading a menu for an Officers' Grill that had floated by: "It says, 'choice of sea food – lobster thermidor, baked shad a la something or other____.'" The second clipping was an article, with photographs, about the two million-dollar antisubmarine net the Navy had installed to protect the California coastline. "One of the anti-submarine nets stretches from Rainbow Pier at Long Beach to the breakwater, with a gate to permit small craft to pass through. Another net stretches across the main channel with a gate for larger vessels. Nearly 300,000 ships have gone through the nets without damage. The net curtain is anchored with eight-ton weights. It is being removed by tenders 300 feet at a time and the metal is being taken to the net depot at Seal Beach."

Betty's mother wasn't much of a correspondent, but on the 15th, she sent a letter to Harvey in Guam. She and Betty's dad were struggling with many of the same issues confronting countless families in the States. "I have said at the beginning of each week that I would get a letter off to you; but Saturday would always find me with no letter written. The last few months we have, more or less, been going in circles. It has been hard for Rod to know just what was best or right for him to do regarding the Service, and it's been equally hard for us – loving him as we do- and not being able to help him decide. Once again this old war seems to be placing loved ones away from Home where they belong. We are thankful that the time is drawing nearer when you will be on your way back – even though it may yet be months, it is still nearer than before the Surrender. The card you send Daddie and me for our anniversary was mighty sweet, but the message you wrote on it was worth more than words can say. Thanks from both of us. How we wished you could have been here for Rod's Graduation! I know you would have been very proud of him, too. Will try to write oftener from now on – but you know we are sending love and good wishes out your way always. Love from us all – Mother, Dad and Rod."

Betty also wrote to Harvey that evening. "I've got the 'weeps' tonight – just when I thought I could behave myself. Rod is leaving Friday instead of Monday because he is going to enlist. I know it is a good opportunity for him, still I can't help feeling a sense of loss already. I got up from the dinner table early and came into my room so he wouldn't know I was crying." She was on the early shift at Stella's and had been at work since 8:30 a.m. It was a diffi-cult day—not only was the weather bad, but Rod had stopped in to give her the news about his enlistment. A photographer had asked Rod to do some "experimental modeling" and, after work, he and Betty went into Culver City to have his picture taken. "Took 24 poses. There certainly should be some good ones out of that!"

The next morning, Rod went in for his physical. Betty wasn't working that day, and after doing odd jobs around the house, she picked up Rod's photos from the day before. "You'll have to see 'the body beautiful!' Plenty good! Morris is planning on using the pictures for the display of his price book. So now, among everything else, our brother is a model. Your club should be opened by now, and I surely hope it helps you all pass the time more quickly. Be sure to take some pictures of the 'super structure' for our book. This eve-ning I put in the photos you sent me, so it is up to date again." Rod's plans had changed again: "He thought he would be going Friday since he was enlist-ing in the regular army, and so he, Daddy and Carl called off the fishing trip they were going on in the Sierras. Now, when Rod came in this afternoon he said he didn't have to go until Monday after all. Daddy wasn't too keen about going up to the mountains since it has turned so cold, but the boys still wanted to go so they packed up and left tonight. Nothing like leaving in the spur of the moment. They had the car packed so full, you'd think they were going for a week instead of a couple of days."

Betty heard from Pop Bristow that day, and he offered to take her out to dinner at the Biltmore Hotel on Friday with his family.

In October, the Navy's Third Fleet was in Los Angeles and also along the California coast. The fleet had originally been formed in March of 1943 under the command of Admiral William Halsey, and it formed the basis of Admiral Raymond Spruance's Fifth Fleet, established in April 1944. The fleet designa-tion flipped back and forth between "Third" and "Fifth", with active command alternating between Halsey and Spruance. This allowed one of the admirals and his staff to always have time to plan subsequent operations, and it served to confuse the Japanese into thinking there were two fleets, rather than one, in the Pacific. The Third Fleet operated in and around the Philippines, the Solomon Islands, Formosa, Okinawa, the Ryukyu Islands, and the Japanese home islands. It had taken part in the Palau Islands campaign (September–November 1944), the Philippines Campaign (1944–1945), and the Battle of Leyte Gulf (October 1944). It had been active in the war's final operations in Japanese waters, launching air attacks on Tokyo, the Kure naval base and the island of Hokkaidō. At the end of the war, Admiral Halsey led the fleet into Tokyo Bay on August 29th, and the signed the documents finalizing the Japanese surrender on the deck of the USS *Missouri*. After the war, the Third Fleet was decommissioned and returned to the States.

On October 17th, there was a parade in Los Angeles for Admiral Halsey and his officers:

> Truly a hero's welcome went out yesterday to Adm. William F. Halsey, who took every opportunity during his hasty visit to Los Angeles to share his glory with all of the officers and men of his famed 3rd Fleet. He was spun from Mines Field over roads lined with cheering crowds, through a city that echoed with his praises, to the City Hall for an official welcome from Mayor Bowron. Holding to a tight, crammed schedule...he was rushed to a luncheon at the Biltmore...and was presented with a fluffy toy white horse by a cub scout. 'I know you mean this welcome not for me, but for every officer and every man of the 3rd Fleet.'

Art Greengard, who sometimes did radio repairs at Stella's, had a son on the USS *South Dakota*, one of the Third Fleet ships anchored in San Francisco Bay. The son was given some leave time in the city, and his family joined him there for a celebration. Evidently, he had spent some time in Guam in June when his ship had stopped there for repairs.

Stella's was busy Friday afternoon, with Betty and Elsie selling fifty dollars-worth of records in one hour. Rod came to visit and have lunch. "I left work at 5 and waited at the bus stop until 5:30 for the P.E. (Pacific Electric train). Of course, it would be late when I was in a hurry. At Vernon, we got in a terrific tie-up and that delayed me a bit. Finally, I got down to the Biltmore Hotel at 6:15 to meet the Bristow's. I was really pleased with the whole family. He is very nice and talked about such interesting things all evening. He sort of reminded me of Major Bennett, the way he acts. His wife, Millie, is very sweet. And—that boy of theirs. He reminds me of a young 'Quiz Kid.' Every time he talks, he says 'excuse me' first. He is a sweet boy and so proud of his dad. His eyes just about pop out of his head when he watches his dad talk. It was so packed in all the eating sections of the Biltmore that we decided to go someplace else. We went across the street to get the car and drove out Wilshire to La Cienega and had dinner at Laury's Prime Rib place. I haven't eaten there in a long time, and I really enjoyed myself. They are very easy to talk to and we talked, talked, talked!! I took the pictures you sent me, and he enjoyed looking at them and telling us about them. He asked me if you had written about some of your adventures, and of course you had. Specially that ride in the jeep, when it sputtered so. That really tickled him. Millie and I just about died laughing at him talking about his getting rid of his clothes on his way here. At every stop he would take a shower with his clothes on, and just leave that complete set of clothes in the shower and put clean ones on. This he did on his four stops – so he had less to carry and clean clothes all the time! Took him 3 days to get home. Had trouble with a feathered propeller all the way to Hawaii. They finally put a new engine in. He seems to think the 315th will go to Japan and will be used as a striking unit for the China Sea and the coasts of China and Japan. Or a portion will go to the Philippines. Said if you were still with Heavy Equipment, you'd be about the first ones to go – in the advance group. At least now you won't have to do that—maybe? I hope you get to stay on Guam long enough to enjoy your club – he said he helped build it. I told him the formal opening was last night and that I had sent you a cable. He thinks a lot of you and said to tell you hello and to write him when you find time."

Mr. Stella's son, Eddie, was on furlough from the army and had been helping out in the store for a few days. He came in on Saturday "not quite as cocky as he has been for the past few weeks. When he got back to camp from his furlough, he had orders to move to Kansas! At a staging area in Topeka. From there he'll either get out or be sent overseas...so he is kind of down in the dumps."

That night after dinner, Rod and Betty went to Hollywood, intending to see Harry "the Hipster" Gibson play piano at Billy Berg's jazz club on Vine Street. Gibson had been the intermission pianist for Fats Waller in New York. His first album, 1944's "Boogie Woogie in Blue" led to an invitation at Billy Berg's jazz club in 1945, where he broadcast shows on live radio and recorded V-Discs. He composed a number of comedy jazz numbers, his most famous being "Who Put the Benzedrine in Mrs. Murphy's Ovaltine?" Billy Berg's was *the* place to go in Hollywood. "All the top musicians and entertainers worked in there. Every Sunday they would have concerts where different up-and-coming singers would come out and sing, people like Kay Starr and Frankie Laine. Can you imagine Berg's never charged admission? They opened at two o'clock in the afternoon on Sundays and people would line up clear down Vine Street from Hollywood and Vine to Sunset and Vine. Louis played there, Billie Holiday, all the big names.

"On the way over we decided to go to the Pantages to see 'Kiss & Tell' with Shirley Temple first. It was really good. Hope you get to see it. Also saw some horrible, captured German films. Plenty Gruesome. After the show we walked over to Billie Bergs' and stood in line for a while. Finally, we decided that it would take all night to get in – so we came on home." Their parents hadn't been interested in going to the Club, so they had taken the bus to the movies on their own and saw *Guest Wife*, with Claudette Colbert and Don Ameche.

Rod was leaving for the Army on Monday, so on Sunday evening the family decided to go to the movies. "The four of us went over to the Fox Wilshire at Wilshire and La Brea – across the street from the jewelry store where you and I stood years ago, remember? Had to stand in line for about a half hour! Saw 'Weekend at the Walldorf.' It was really fine. We all enjoyed it so. Virjeanne is an usherette there, so we had extra special seats. You'll like the show, I'm sure. Rod has a secret passion for Lana Turner, so naturally he liked the picture! We came home and had a chicken dinner. We laughed and cried during dinner – hope the food will digest!! After dinner, Rod went over to tell Grandma goodbye and a couple others, and the rest of the evening we sat around the living room listening to the evening programs with the lights off. Sort of peaceful and restful after all the commotion we have all felt. Listened to Bergen, Baby Snooks (a cute new show), the Great Gildersleeve, Fred Allen, and some musicals. It's only a little after nine, and Rod has already hit the sack for he has to leave pretty early."

Having a family member leave for military service was always tough for those staying behind. Rod was up early on Monday and was at the train station by 8:30. Their mother was in tears, and Betty tried to comfort her after he had gone. "Seemed so funny coming home in the evening and not finding Rod here. All three of us kept up a silly patter about nothing, as families have a habit of doing to cover up feelings. It didn't matter too much tonight if our tears fell in our soup – and a few did. About 7:30, Rod called from MacArthur, and you never saw such a relieved look on anyone's face as on Mother's. That was just what she needed. We all talked to him. They kept the boys waiting around all day in the station, and he didn't get down there until about 5 or so. Had dinner there and was issued blankets and a bed. He sounded perfectly contented now that he was actually on his way. After we had hung up we all looked at each other and laughed and cried over absolutely nothing. I think Mother and Dad relaxed for the first time today. And I felt better because they did. Such is life at 12724 Caswell on this important day!" On

Tuesday, Harvey wrote to her, knowing well it would be several days before she received the letter. "By the time you get this letter, Rod will have been gone over a week, and you've no doubt got yourself pretty well wrapped up in waiting for his letters to come. I wish I could write something here to make you feel a lot better about his going, but I'm too poor at handling my limited vocabulary. Just keep relaxed, it's bound to turn out for the best. Be sure to have him let me know just where he's going because he may be somewhere that I'll have a chance to visit."

President Truman gave a speech on Wednesday morning, and Betty and her parents heard the radio broadcast. In his address, Truman urged universal military training for everyone between the ages of eighteen and twenty. Training would be for one year, after which trainees would enter the reserves for six years. Betty asked Harvey if he was at all interested in staying in the army for a longer period of time. "Looks as if the U.S. Army is to be 'the thing'– might be a good idea to stay in – they'll need some good leaders, and you are the best one I know. Seriously, what do you think of it?"

For her part, Betty had been thinking of going back for further education. "We went out to Westwood in the bus. I wanted to see what they were offering at night school at U.C.L.A. – got the bug to go back. Their classes started last month, and anyway, all they offer this term is Physics, Psychology, and Chemistry – they aren't for me! I'm going to call the Extension Branch in L.A. and see what they have to offer while I'm still in the mood. The colleges are overflowing this semester. Everybody has decided to go back to school, I think. I had to wait 2 hours in line just to see a counsellor. Mother and I went back to the Village and ate at Albert Sheetz [the Albert Sheetz Mission Candy Company was on Canon Drive in Beverly Hills]. Had a good lunch and then shopped around until 5."

Betty's letter on the 24th had the heading: HAPPY ELEVEN! It was their eleventh anniversary. She had misplaced her pen, and this was the first letter she had written in pencil (a bit difficult to read as I write this, some seventy-five years later! —DB). It was a busy day at the music store, and the temperature hit 90 degrees, with bright sunshine. After work, she went to visit Virjeanne, and the two realized it had been over a year since they had spent an evening together. "Had a nice dinner and then Elsie drove by and the three of us went to a show. Saw "Love Letters" with Jennifer Jones and Joseph Cotton. Really outstanding, I thought. Hope you get to see it soon. Very emotional picture and showed how much you can get to love a person through letters. As if we needed anyone to tell us that! Silly people. Lots of news and cartoons also at the Paramount tonight. Stopped in at a drive-in and had some hot chocolate on the way home. Right now, we are in Virjeanne's room, and she is looking through our epic album. First time she's seen our wedding pictures even. How about that – and here it is <u>11</u> months we've been married today. Such happy months, even though we've been apart too many of them. Virjeanne showed me the letters Earl wrote to her about you. He thinks you are grand and wished he worked under you." She enclosed an article from the *Herald-Examiner* about the impending end to more rationing restrictions:

> Tentative plans call for an end of shoe rationing, either Oct. 28 or Nov. 1, it was learned today. Government officials also have considered the possibility of terminating the program earlier if these plans become generally known. There are other developments and prospects on the rationing front:
>
> 1. OPA has decided to cut butter ration values from 12 points a pound to eight. It will be announced tomorrow.
> 2. Passenger tire rationing may be ended late in December.
> 3. Truck tires are slated to come off the list by late November.
>
> Choice of a date for ending shoe rationing is expected to be made today or tomorrow by OPA and War Production Board officials.

Thursday was Betty's turn to stay late and close up at 6:00 at Stella's. As luck would have it, that last hour was incredibly busy: a man came by to pick up his Philco radio but forgot to bring cash, and she finally allowed him to use a personal check (against normal store policy); a little kid played twenty or thirty records before remembering he had only brought thirty cents with him; and a woman came by to pick up sheet music she had ordered weeks earlier, but she couldn't remember the tune's name. As soon as Betty walked in the door at home, the telephone rang, and it was Rod. "He's been issued all his clothes and had his exams – all he needs now is his shots. He doesn't think he'll be home this weekend as he first thought he would. Said he may ship out even before he can get home. If they have 8 weeks basic, he should be home for Christmas...if not it will be a while longer before he'll get home. Then again, he may have a 24-hour pass before he ships. He sounds fine. Wrote us all today and said he was going to write to you tomorrow." Rod did write to Harvey to fill him in on his situation. "How's everything in Guam? I guess Betty has told you that I enlisted and left Oct. 22. This is my first day here at Fort MacArthur. Have you ever been here? It's not bad, and in fact I like it pretty well. I've been pretty lucky about details so far. No K.P. – so far. Had a detail last night and went into the San Pedro Y.M.C.A. to move some beds and then watch a basketball game. We got our full issue of clothing yesterday. Never saw so many clothes in all my life. I enlisted for 18 months in the Regular Army. I don't get a chance for any choices, but I'm trying to get in E.T.O. Slim chances though. Anything is better than what I'd get if I was drafted. Don't you think so? Food is swell here, but I don't like the waiting-in-line part. Write soon. I probably won't be here when the letter gets here, but they will forward it. Bye for now, 'Sir' ha! ha! Rod."

Harvey's mother wrote to Betty to express her sympathy. "I have been thinking about you and your folks so much lately, and really understanding just what you are going through. Separation at its best is never easy, but Rodney seems so young to have to go into the Army. I'll never forget, if I live to be 100, the day Buddy left. That's just one of the things you never forget. Your situation has been doubly hard, Betty, to have Buddy go and now Rod. I hope the time will pass quickly, and all these separations will have become history. That was a brave letter you wrote us the day Rod left. I couldn't keep the tears from spilling over myself when I read it. I just wished you were close enough that I could put my arms around you.... I hope Rod likes the army, because it is so much easier to do something you like, and the time will pass quicker. I hadn't heard about being able to enlist for a year and a half. That sounds like a good idea to me. Did he go to Camp MacArthur? Is it in California? I hope they haven't taken him too far away." Later that day, she and Harvey's father went into Pittsburgh to see *Our Vines Have Tender Grapes* at the Loew's Penn Theatre on Sixth Street.

The mail between Guam and California had been sporadic since the war's end. Even though both Betty and Harvey wrote almost every day, delivery time in both directions was unpredictable. Sometimes Betty wouldn't receive a letter for several days in a row, while at others, she would get two or three in the same day's delivery. On Friday, she hit the jackpot and received six letters! "I was so excited when Mom called this afternoon to tell me, I could have cried. Mail has been so slow coming the last few weeks. All day everything has seemed to go wrong.... You know that check I received last night on the Philco? – when E.A. went over to the bank this morning, there were insufficient funds in the bank account to cover the check! He called the fellow and got it straightened out, but all day things went out of the ordinary... like, a little girl grabbed an album off the rack and broke the records, with her mother having to pay for the album...and the record order came in via

Railway Express instead of 'specified Parcel delivery' and it cost us 79 cents more than it should have...etc. But then Mom called and there was sunshine again. This evening Elsie and I went over to Stella's for dinner after work. Sort of a party for Eddie because he leaves tomorrow for Topeka, Kansas. From there.... who knows? Then E.A. stayed home, and the four of us went to a show. Saw 'Mildred Pierce' at the Wiltern (at Wilshire and Western). That is really a good picture, and the last few I've seen I've enjoyed so much. I know you'll like this one. Joan Crawford, Zackary Scott, Eve Arden, Jack Carson and Ann Blythe." She enclosed an ad for the movie from the local paper: "We must tell you what 'Mildred Pierce' did! Broke every Existing House Record at Warner's 3 First-Run Theaters! Earned the Critical Acclaim of Every Outstanding Reviewer in the Nation! Took L.A. by Storm with One of the Most Unusual and Engrossing Pictures Ever Produced! Join the Throngs!! See for Yourself!" The movie won three Academy Awards: Best Picture, Best Actress in a Leading Role (Joan Crawford), and Best Actress in a Supporting Role (Eve Arden)—and was nominated for three others.

On Saturday, Betty received a surprise visitor at the store. "Pvt. Lundin is home on a 24-hour pass. He got in about 5 and surprised the folks, and then came to the store about 7:30 and surprised me! I just about fell over, even though we sort of expected him. He looks so good in his uniform, and he got one that fits him! ... He waited around, saw a lot of folks in Culver, and then brought me home. He's gone on now to the dance at the Casino. He has to report back to Ft. Mac Arthur at 9 tomorrow night – expects to ship Tuesday but doesn't know where yet." With her letter, she enclosed the front page of the *Herald-Express*, which featured the headline... "500,000 Cheer Great Navy Day Parade." The parade through downtown Los Angeles was followed by a program at City Hall, with an evening celebration scheduled for the LA Coliseum. The paper included the program for the Coliseum event:

6:00 p.m.	Doors open at Coliseum
7:00	Massed bands, light display and arrival of Purple Heart groups
8:00	Arrival official entourage. Formal program begins
8:15	Mayor's address of welcome
8:20	"Pearl Harbor"
8:35	"Fall of Corregidor"
8:45	"Cemetery at Saipan"
9:00	"Flag Raising Iwo Jima"

9:12	"Kamikaze Attack on Aircraft Carrier"
9:19	"General Le May's Decision"
9:25	"Atomic Bomb"
9:31	"Surrender Scene Aboard USS Missouri"
9:45	Address by Rear Admiral Robert C. Carney
9:55	"Tribute to Victory" Parade
10:30	Fireworks display and end of spectacle

The newspaper that Betty sent also described the Navy Day Parade in New York, which featured an address by President Truman in Central Park: "President Truman declared today that the United States will maintain the world's greatest naval and air forces to enforce the peace and withhold the secret of the atomic bomb until its use is outlawed. The President, in a speech in Central Park, gave a 12-point program to chart American foreign policy after commissioning the super-aircraft carrier [USS] *Franklin D. Roosevelt* and shortly before he reviewed the fleet in Navy Day ceremonies in New York."

Betty and Rod had a good visit, but the impending "goodbye" was just below the surface. "Rod went over to the Post Office to see several of the fellows, especially Mike. He told them all goodbye, and then we left for Fort Mac Arthur. On the way down, we picked up a young marine who was on his way back to Oceanside. It helped him quite a bit to get a lift, and sort of helped us too, as we drove Rod to camp. I've felt swell all day – we've acted foolish like we always did – danced to records, laughed as we teased and kidded back and forth. But when we stopped in front of the camp, all the laughter stuck in my throat. It was all I could do to smile and kiss him goodbye. He is to leave for the basic training camp on Tuesday – as far as he knows now. We said very little on the way home, but I know we were all thinking a lot. Remembering lots of years of 'growing up days.' They were wonderful days too. We got back home about 9:30 and whether you know it or not, you held my hand all the way home!"

On Monday, while Harvey was watching a movie in pouring rain, it was also raining in Southern California. Betty was reading about his growing obsession with the game of bridge: "...you are getting to 'adore' bridge, and I don't know the first thing about it. 'Fraid I'll never be a card shark, do you mind awfully. If you really want me to play cards, I'll learn but confidentially it will be an effort. Rod just called, and we had a last chance to talk to him while he is at Mac Arthur. They ship tomorrow, and of course he doesn't know where he is going. He called late because he's been to a show all evening, and then they also had a surprise U.S.O. show. He could hardly talk because they've laughed and yelled so much at the show. Nothing happened of importance because of the rain all day. Yes – we're finally getting our rain, and I like it. This morning when I woke up I heard the rain falling so gently that it practically lulled me back to sleep...but I dragged myself out of bed and went to work. It has rained all day, but even so we've had the same people wandering in and out of the store. Daddy stopped by to pick me up at 5 on his way home from City Hall."

With her letter that night, Betty enclosed a clipping about a man on Attu Island in the Aleutians: "Willie Golodoff's wife sent him out to catch some fish in June 1942, and Willie never came back. Reason was that the Japanese landed that day, captured him. He was imprisoned in Korea, now is recuperating in a Marine hospital in San Francisco. He's afraid his wife, Julia, will be angry when he goes home without the fish he promised to get her when he stepped out long ago."

Betty had the day off on Tuesday, and she slept in till 10:00. She and her mother went into LA and did some shopping. Betty then went to Schirmer's Music Store on South Hill Street to take some music to their wholesale music department and to order Christmas music books for Stella's. Their thoughts were on Rod, "he is on his way somewhere.....wonder where?"

Halloween was a busy day at Stella's: "had a nice day at work today. E.A. didn't come down until 5, and I left then. Allene is working part time at the bakery now, and she came over to have lunch with me. That evening 35 or 40 kids stopped by the house for trick-or-treat. "They were all so cute, though. Couple of them were practically babies. I surely remember going around like that with Rod years ago. We used to make so much of holidays. Elsie and a couple of friends stopped by too. She was all dolled up in a clown suit...a rather abbreviated one!...

"I called Peggy Paulson this evening, because today is their second anniversary. She wrote to us several times in Hays...she's the one I borrowed my wedding veil from. Even though they were in the midst of a party, she and I had a good visit and got caught up on a lot of gossip."

27

POINT SYSTEM

FOR DISCHARGE

Thursday was November 1st, and Harvey had been on Guam for almost six months. To "celebrate," he and Mac went to see the movie at the outdoor theater. "Just got back from one of the best movies I have seen in years – 'Weekend at the Waldorf' with Ginger Rogers, Lana Turner, and Walter Pidgeon. It was really a riot, and as true to life as can be. I've never stayed at the Waldorf-Astoria, but from what little I've seen of the place, all that the picture portrayed is possible. When we go back east, we'll have to stay there and see what kind of a set-up they actually have. I can see what Rod means about Lana Turner, and I must admit that she holds a warm place in my heart...but it's the third place. First comes you and that naturally doesn't leave room for anyone else, so the other places are honorary. First honorary place goes to Loretta Young and second place to Maureen O'Hara and then comes Lana Turner. The tide really swung in favor of Lana Turner tonight because before this picture, she was about no. 14 on my list, but she rose to third place tonight. Bet she's thrilled about that!!"

That morning Harvey had noticed an article in the daily mimeographed paper published on the island. The article was titled "Police Seek Sailor on Rape Charge," and it described a sexual assault in the 'women's lounge' of the Southern Pacific train station in San Francisco. "I very rarely read items of this nature, but this one caught my eye when I noticed that the girl involved came from Venice. Gosh, darling, I hope it wasn't anyone you know. An experience like that must be tough on a girl." He enclosed the clipping with his letter that night, along with two photos from the Duquesne Light newsletter he had just received. "The other two pictures I'm enclosing are of people you have seen or met in Pittsburgh. Mr. Robinson was the guy that you met downtown in the department store. He was the one who brought his wife and daughter, Jean, out to the house the night when Mother had the gang out there for the get-together. Remember? Jean's husband is the one that was lost in the South Pacific. The other picture shows Mary Martha Briney, who sang at the William Penn Hotel the night we were there for dinner. She's the best of the local Pittsburgh talent. Thought you might like to see some of your 'old acquaintances'!" The second photo had the caption: "Since August 1936, Bernie Armstrong (right) has been on the air for the Duquesne Light Company. He is shown here with Mary Martha Briney and Bob Carter, two of the well-known stars who appeared on the program. Paul Shannon is the announcer."

Harvey was in a lazy mood on Friday, too lazy even to go to supper. Instead, he went over to the club to talk for a little while with some friends, and the "little while" became a whole evening. "Finally managed to drag myself back to the sack after spending all evening over in the club talking and chewing the fat with a whole bunch of guys. We didn't have too much to talk about except the fine meals we were going to have back in the states and a few things like that. A couple of guys got started on stories about their college days, and before we knew it, the thing had developed into a good, old fashioned bull session!"

On Saturday, Harvey played horseshoes all afternoon, right up until dinnertime. "You know, a guy should have better sense than to look forward to an afternoon off for three days, and then to knock himself out when it finally comes. Mac and Col. Turner and I went to the show tonight to see 'Out of this World' with Eddie Bracken and Veronica Lake. Kind of a silly picture but not too bad. Eddie Bracken singing with Bing Crosby's voice just about floored me. There really were some of the screwiest situations that I ever heard of. Especially when they were trying to make Eddie catch cold so he wouldn't be able to sing at one of those benefits. And Cass Daley was busy as usual, splashing her mouthful of teeth all over the place. As a singer, she would make a fine bricklayer."

Later that night, several of the officers partied at the new club—perhaps a little too much. "Last night at the club a few of the guys (the same old ones), had quite a few too many drinks again, as is usual on a Saturday night, and they raised h____ until the wee small hours this morning. I never saw such a bunch of goofs in my whole life. They seem to have nothing on their minds but to get spiflicated (?) and to be as thoroughly obnoxious as possible. Apparently they enjoy themselves, and I certainly hope they do because no one else enjoys their condition. Their usual procedure is to start in at about seven o'clock in the evening and get as many fast drinks under their belts as they can. Then they pour them down more slowly for the rest of the evening, getting louder and louder all the time and favoring everyone with a variety of crude songs etc. Most everybody else is sitting around either playing poker, craps, bridge or reading a book, and just drinking enough to enjoy themselves. Some of the single men, and a few of the married ones, have dates now and then with some of the nurses or the Red Cross workers. You can imagine what kind of an atmosphere exists in the club for the ladies with all that noise going on. The longer I stay in the Army, the more of an insight I get into the male human nature, and the more disgusted I get with it. Some people certainly let themselves go completely...but I guess if I didn't have that to gripe about, I'd find something else I didn't like. I'm sorry to ramble on. I'm probably just getting the slightest bit 'rock-happy.'" He was having an increasingly tough time dealing with all the letters he was saving:"...with all your letters piling up on me the way they are, I'm afraid I'm not going to be able to save them the way I wanted to do in the first place. I've got six big bundles of them now in my footlocker, and I've got another bundle to put away as soon as I can get to it. I'd like very much to keep them, but I don't see how I can do it. OOPS, the mail man just brought me <u>three</u> more letters from you and one from Dad. Just give me a second while I read them, and I'll be right back again. There may be something in them I'll want to talk to you about.... Here I am again, and I'm glad I read all those letters before I sealed this one up. Your letters always make me feel as if I were talking to an angel!"

At about that time a letter arrived for Harvey from Ralph Haver in Okinawa, the first time he had heard from his friend in six weeks. The envelope was marked: <u>Inter Island</u>. "Hi Harvey – For gosh sakes, warn me next time before you write because unexpected things like that startle me. I shore were glad to be a hearin' from you, tho. It sounds as tho' things are going well there with you. I wish we could say the same for this place. This island is p___ poor as far as supply goes. There just ain't nothing on this island – no lumber, no Quonsets or prefabs, no hardware, no beer to speak of and whisky is really scarce. Food ain't so good either. Most of the time we eat "B" rations, occasionally we get fresh bread, a few fresh vegetables and sometimes fresh meat. Mostly "B" rations tho, and it gets mighty monotonous. The typhoon made things interesting up this way. My pyramidal tent took off and left me high but not so dry, as did about 50% of the other guys' tents. Things were really messed up for a while. The Quonsets were moved around and tossed through the air, and it was lucky we were in tents. When it finally wound up, we were short of tents, gas and food. We ate "K" rations for one day, "C" rations for 2 days, and finally got some of the stuff from you guys which was the best we'd eaten yet. The trouble with this place is that it has no harbor, and all ships have to be unloaded by lighters. Most Army units are pulling out of this place, and the Navy ain't going to have nothing here at all. I guess that's enough bitching, so I'll tell you about my job. I've got a damned interesting job working as Assistant Staff Engineer here in Headquarters. I work under Colonel Hall, a West Pointer, who is a helluva nice guy and easy to get along with. My job as engineering officer consists of doing all the design work – it's a good deal except, as you say, these guys can't make up their minds. I keep busy as the devil and consequently time really passes quickly. I'm really glad to hear Jack got out and back to his family. That's my main objective nowadays – give me that 'happy home life', and you can take the whole Army and you know what with it. I'm sitting here with 55 points, and from the way things look I'll be getting out of here about February sometime. That's just a guess, but I'm optimistic – and I hope justly so. I hope you're wrong in your estimate of June or July – that's <u>too</u> damned long. The family is doing fine. Where are you and Betty going to settle? Keep me posted as to how things go with you and Betty and be sure to give Betty my regards. Also, give my best to Yates." Harvey was clearly writing letters from Guam to friends in the Army and to others at Duquesne Light Company in Pittsburgh. None of these letters have been found (unlike those to Betty), but there are clues to their content in this letter from Ralph. Harvey clearly had written about his pessimism regarding an early return to the States as well as about his plans with Betty to start a family as soon as he got home.

The references in the Okinawa letter to *B*, *C*, and *K* rations meant nothing to me, so I had to do a little research. According to the Defense Department: "C-Rations were developed in 1938 as a replacement for reserve rations, which sustained troops during World War I, and consisted chiefly of canned corned beef or bacon and cans of hardtack biscuits, as well as ground coffee, sugar, salt, and tobacco with rolling paper—not much in the way of variety. Researchers at the Quartermaster Subsistence Research and Development Lab in Chicago went to work to design food products that could be kept for long time periods and were more delicious than reserve rations. The design they came up with consisted of 12-ounce tin plate cans that were opened with a key. At first, the meals were stews, and more varieties were added as the war went on, including meat and spaghetti in tomato sauce, chopped ham, eggs and potatoes, meat and noodles, pork and beans, ham and lima beans, and chicken and vegetables. Besides these main courses, chocolate or other candies, gum, biscuits and cigarettes were added.... K-Rations (short for "kommando") were lighter than C-Rations ("combat"), but soldiers complained about the taste and lack of calories." K-Rations were designed for short-term use for troops on the move in combat. Meals served in mess halls were designated either as A-Rations (fresh food) or B-Rations (packaged, unprepared food).

By this time the Army was trying to get servicemen and servicewomen to reenlist, and the offers were getting more and more attractive. "I thought after the time that these men had been over here, and the long time they have spent dreaming of going home, there wouldn't be any reenlistments, but the number is really astonishing. As for myself, the offer hasn't been made yet that is attractive enough to keep me in the Service. The Army is offering an immediate 90-day furlough in the States, with all mustering out pay and so forth, but they do not allow a man to choose his branch of service or the theater of operations in which he will serve. The enlistments are for periods of two or three years, and the rank becomes permanent in the Regular Army. All this applies to enlisted men, and there will be a different deal for officers but so far I haven't heard it. Don't worry about me staying in, because there isn't one chance in a million that such will be the case. I want too much to have a simple home life with my beautiful wife. Being in the Army is not very inducive to bringing up a family, and I know that's what you and I both want. My only interest in the Army at present is to get out of it as soon as possible so I can get home to you." His family in Pittsburgh was also reading about the re-enlistment incentives, and they were concerned he might decide to stay in the service. "Are there many in Guam being returned to the States? The army is really holding out some very attractive bait."

Rod wrote again to Harvey, this time from Aberdeen Training Grounds in Maryland. "Well, we finally shipped. We left last Tuesday and arrived here Sunday. What a trip. It wasn't too bad because we had a Pullman most of the way. We went through Washington D.C. and had a chance to see a little of the Capitol. It is really beautiful. Have you ever been there? We are to receive our 10 weeks of basic training here. After that we have some specialist training. When you write, tell me where you had your training and what it consists of so I can have an idea of what I'm getting into. I like the Army quite well so far, but I'll be glad to get back in my old 'civies.' If I get out when I'm supposed to, it will be April 22, 1947. Looks good, doesn't it?"

Soon after Harvey and Mac had redesigned their room in the BOQ, they were assigned another roommate! "He's from the 73rd Bomb Wing in Saipan. The 73rd has been overseas quite a while and is shipping back to the States as a unit. So, they got rid of all their men who didn't have enough points for discharge and took in men with high points from all the other units on Saipan, Tinian and Guam. Some of the men who left our Wing are going home with the 73rd. This captain's name is Amason, and he hails from Pendleton, Oregon. Not a bad guy at all. Mac and I had our room all fixed up for two men, but we made room for Amason without much trouble. Tomorrow is our first half day this week, and it looks as if we'll spend the afternoon working on the club again. We still have lots of beautification work to do before the club is finished. We've even got some construction to do. Maybe by the time I'm ready to go home, we'll have it finished. The last two evenings now, we've played volleyball and in this hot weather it really brings out the perspiration."

Wednesday night: "Both Mac and Capt. Amason are in bed asleep, so I guess I'll have to be at least a little quiet. I've been over at the club playing cards until just a minute ago, and when I got back both roommates had hit the sack. Today was a half day for us, so we knocked ourselves out on the volleyball court for about two hours and then pitched horseshoes for another hour or so. That volleyball can really be a strenuous game!! Especially the way we play it. I haven't had any cause to bitch about our meals lately, because they have been lots better than the ones we had while food was being shipped to Okinawa. I guess they must be okay up there now. Tonight, we had some of the best roast beef I've tasted in a long time."

There were still pockets of Japanese soldiers hiding in Guam jungles and caves some fifteen months after the island had been recaptured by the Americans, five months after Harvey's unit had arrived, and over two months since Japan had finally surrendered. Harvey wrote on November 7th that, "Last Monday, 23 Japanese surrendered here on the island just about a quarter of a mile from here. Their story is that they had just found out about the war being over. Included in the 23 was a small boy and a Geisha girl. A lot of Japanese women were captured when the Island was first re-taken. Yesterday's Navy News carried the article, so I'll cut it out for you. I missed a good show at the theater tonight – Fred MacMurray in 'Murder he Says.' Maybe I can catch it at one of the other theaters."

Harvey wrote his Thursday letter at a bridge table in the Officers' Club. "Captain Amason is already asleep so I thought it would be better if I took my little typewriter and came over to the club. That way the noise the thing makes wouldn't keep him awake. It's not a bad deal, either, because I can have the table waiter bring me a coke or a beer if I get dry while I'm writing. Not only that, but the juke box keeps giving out with sweet music and stuff. The only disadvantage is that everybody and his brother comes over to pass the time of day and take my mind away from what I'm trying to say. Sol Mayer was just here to talk for a few minutes, but he didn't stay long because he has sense enough to know my mind is on you. Jimmy Ray is sure a happy boy this evening!! He got a cablegram this morning from home saying he is now the proud father of a boy! The cablegram said, 'Son is born, both well, please don't worry.' At suppertime tonight, and over our cups of coffee after supper, he passed out cigars in wholesale fashion. We all had them lit, and the mess hall looked like there had been an explosion, with all the smoke. He had his bottle of liquor out after supper, so we all had to have a drink to toast the new son. I'm watching him pretty closely, because I want to know how I'm supposed to act when we have our first baby. That will be a wonderful day, sweetheart, and it's a day closer tonight than it was last night. The latest rumor is that officers' points will be lowered to 70 on the 15th of this month. That's coming down pretty slowly, but maybe it will speed up as soon as they get the 70 pointers out of the way. We are also hearing more rumors about the Wing moving to the Philippines. Even if that happens, it shouldn't affect our stay overseas as far as heading home when our points come due. The correct number of points gets you home no matter what theater you are in, so I'm not worried on that score. Remember me telling you about the reenlistment program the Army is sponsoring now? Well, we have had quite a few men apply for the idea, including a number of married men. Boy, I sure can't understand that. Doesn't make sense to me. The guys that sign up for the regular Army have no idea where they may be sent or anything else. Most of them are so taken up with the idea of getting an immediate 90 day leave that they can't see anything else. And, of course, on top of that they get a bonus of $50 for every 12 months of service, plus all of his mustering-out pay. For a single man, it really is a rather good deal, but not for a guy that has a wife waiting for him at home. If being in the Army means staying away from you, I don't want any part of it. I knocked off work today a few minutes after 4 so I could get down to the volleyball court for the nightly game. Boy, the way we go at the game is a caution. But it's fun and lots of good exercise, which I can use. We've got the two teams pretty well divided so every game we play is a tough battle. There are about ten of us that show up every night and, believe me, every one of them has blood in his eye when he steps on the court. Tonight our team won two out of three, but not until after we had to sweat blood to do it.

"The men in charge of the theater have been working on a new projection booth with new equipment of all kinds. Tonight was the grand opening of our theater with its new face lift. The picture was a good one...'Nob Hill' in technicolor with Joan Bennett and George Raft. Don't know if you have seen it yet or not, but if you haven't, don't miss it. There was a singer in it that was darn good, but I can't think of her name to save me. I've seen her before in a couple of films, but still can't place her." *[Note: Harvey is referring to the singer Vivian Blaine.]*

Harvey had received Christmas packages from Betty and his folks at the beginning of November. His willpower gave out on Friday the 9th, and he opened them. Betty had sent a drinking cup and a small stove, but Harvey's favorite was a small soap packet she had "borrowed" when they became engaged in Spokane on the Fourth of July in 1944. "The little cake of soap from the Spokane Hotel hit me right in the heart. I sat here on my bunk for at least an hour, just reliving the wonderful hours we spent there. What a sweet and wonderful way to begin a life together!! I'm sending back the wrapper with a rather feeble attempt at expressing how I feel." Harvey's "feeble attempt" read, "Betty dear – At this hotel, almost a year and a half ago, we formed a corporation that will be the making of the biggest success we two could ever know. Your love means the world to me – as it always will. Just being near you has made me the happiest man alive." That day Harvey played more volleyball in the afternoon, and more bridge in the evening. "Did much better at volleyball, and at least our downfall at bridge wasn't due to any lack of trying. We just couldn't get ourselves a good hand to save us. I'm going to start reading 'April Afternoon' tomorrow afternoon if it isn't too hot. All these books look really good!"

On Saturday, Harvey took his typewriter to the club, planning on writing Betty after playing a little bit of bridge with Mac, Col. Turner, and Dick Skinner. "When we got through, it was ten minutes after twelve, and we had played six rubbers altogether. Darn near fell off the chair when I found out what time it was, I never dreamed that it was any later than about ten o'clock....so, I brought the machine back to the room with me and am starting to write now.

"Tomorrow is the 11th, and that means Armistice Day. We are having our holiday on the day following, which will give us two and a half days of sack time. I probably will knock myself out playing volleyball or something, so the time off won't really do me any good! One thing I want to do is to finish that book, 'Land Below the Wind' by Agnes Newton Keith. Never cared much for travel stories, but this one is plenty good. I finished Wylie's 'April Afternoon' yesterday and really liked it a lot. I've got another one that I'm about halfway through called 'Deep River', but it's so long and dry I don't think that I'll be able to finish it."

Sunday was another hot, lazy day in Guam. Harvey sat in the club's screened-in porch in an attempt to take advantage of any slight breeze. There was a volleyball game going on, and Mac and Col. Turner were hoping to start another bridge game, but Harvey was feeling he might prefer just to read quietly in the BOQ. His thoughts kept going back to the previous November 18th, when he caught a ride from Oklahoma City to LA to marry Betty. While writing his letter, he listened to the radio. "The Army – Notre Dame game is on the radio at the bar right now. My rooting is all for Army, although I'd root for any team against Notre Dame. So far, the score is 41 to nothing against the Fightin' Irish which naturally is making me plenty happy. It's a rebroadcast, of course, but it's as realistic as if it was the real game. Must be a recording."

Harvey's unit didn't work on Monday, making two and a half days in a row that they'd had off. He was surprised to find that he was actually look-ing forward to getting back to work! "...the first time I've felt like that for a long time. This morning we had a game of touch football with the enlisted men, the same team we played back at Walker, and they beat us 25-18. Pretty close score for us old men, eh? Was loads of fun and plenty of exercise. Then four of us played bridge for most of the afternoon. It's funny, before I came overseas, I never thought that I'd like to play bridge, but it is really proving fascinating now." Unfortunately, Harvey's usual bridge partner left that day for the States. "Col. Turner finally left to go home today, after sweating out his orders for about a month and a half. He caught an A.T.C. plane about six this evening and was called so fast that he didn't have time to say goodbye to us. It usually happens like that. He has 79 points and has been ready to go for a long time."

There was a notice on the office bulletin board on Thursday instructing all officers and enlisted men to report to the dispensary for an influenza shot, and he wrote to Betty, "When I got there I found that I had two other shots due, a typhoid and a smallpox, so I took all three of them at the same time to get it over and done with. I guess the three of them don't mix too well, because I've got a headache and feel a bit feverish. But it should be all over in the morning and that's very little to pay for the protection they afford. Rod no doubt went through quite a series of shots when he went to Fort Mac Arthur, so he'll know what I mean. To date, I've had somewhere in the neighborhood of 25 shots since I came into the Army, but that includes periodic booster shots and those I took in the States for this particular overseas theater. Bubonic plague, etc. There has been a small flu epidemic in this area, so the Army thought they had better forestall the thing by giving flu shots to everyone." As I write this in the midst of the current Covid-19 pandemic, it's a little eerie to read about these wartime worries about epidemics. Flu? Typhoid? Smallpox? Bubonic plague? Pittsburgh, where Harvey had been born in 1918, had experienced the highest mortality rate in the country during the influenza epidemic that year. And now he, not to mention his parents, had to worry about Smallpox and the Bubonic plague? The next day he was feeling better, though his arm was fairly sore. He still had a scar on that arm from the "mustard gas" shot he had received back at Walker Field in Kansas. "Wasn't nearly as bad as I thought at first. Some of these officers really had some bad effects from it. Dick Williams and Sol Mayer and Boy Yates were in pretty bad shape last night for a while. And many others didn't get much sleep. But it's just about over now, and we shouldn't have to take any more shots until it's time for us to go home."

That night, Harvey went to the movies with Mac and Jimmy Ray. "The picture was 'The Fighting Guardsman' with Faye Emerson, Anita Louise and a new male star that I haven't seen before. Strictly a Class B picture, but it was fairly good in spots. Faye Emerson played the role of a voluptuous inn keeper's daughter and caused many an 'ooh' and 'ah' when she first appeared in a dress with a neckline down to her navel. I heard lots of remarks that expressed envy for Elliott Roosevelt [Note: FDR's son], her real-life husband. She certainly isn't bad to look at, but her voice was never meant for the movies. Too harsh and loud. But I guess the guys in the audience didn't care whether she even spoke one word..." The male lead that Harvey didn't recognize was Willard Parker. Interestingly, the actress in the film wasn't Faye Emerson at all, but an Emerson look-alike named Janis Carter. My guess is that either Faye Emerson was wrongly listed in handouts for the show, or that a rumor started at the theater and soon had a life of its own. Additionally, although the International Movie data base (IMdb.com) shows a 1946 release date for the movie, it was already being shown in theaters across the US as early as October 1945, at about the same time as it was shown at El Gecko.

Several of the different units on the island operated their own movie theaters, and occasionally Harvey and his buddies went somewhere other than El Gecko. "We just came back from the show, and it was better than usual. The picture at our own theater was one of Gloria Jean's fiascos, so we all went up to the 16th Bomb Group to see what they had to offer. It was 'Over 21' with Irene Dunne. All about a newspaper editor that joined the Army and went to OCS. Boy, some of the scenes really struck a familiar chord in my mind. And believe it or not, the fellow that drove me from Oklahoma City to Los Angeles was in it. He didn't have much of a part, but at least I can now say that I know somebody personally who is in the movies. If you go to see the picture, and I know you would really like it, he's the officer that is just leaving the little cottage as Irene Dunne and her husband are moving in. He only appears for about five minutes on the screen, but he doesn't do too bad." The previous November, Harvey and another serviceman had answered an ad on a bulletin board at Tinker Field in Oklahoma City and had hitched a ride to Los Angeles with Loren Tindall, the actor he had just recognized in *Over 21*. Harvey had been heading to California to marry Betty, and Loren was going out to see a starlet he was dating. Some weeks after their drive to Los Angeles, Tindall had been giving a speech at the launching of the USS *Oklahoma City* in Philadelphia, and had been "discovered" by Max Arnow, the head of Columbia Studio's Talent division. *Over 21* was his third film for Columbia.

"Do you remember Warrant Officer Rawson? He's that fellow who rode part of the way down to Colorado Springs with us that weekend. Well, he's acquired himself a pet. It's a little pint-sized monkey that he got from some guy that came in from India. It rides around on his shoulder everywhere he goes and is really a cute little pet. He intends to take it back to the States with him when he goes, so he's had it treated at the dispensary to eliminate any tropical diseases that it might transmit. And even though it's a little bit untidy in his room every now and then with its personal habits, he seems to like it a lot. He keeps it on a leash all the time, but in the theater the other night it got away and raced back and forth, hopping from one head to another. Caused quite a bit of confusion for a while, but finally it came back to him and perched on his shoulder. Quite a deal!"

There was an announcement at the theater that all men with fifty points or more should report to their orderly rooms at their earliest convenience, and

Harvey was beginning to lose patience with the way the situation was being handled. "That means enlisted men, of course. That bunch of greybeards in Washington will just have to start doing something about getting the officers home before very long. The guys are really beginning to get teed off about the thing, and although they are at pretty much of a disadvantage way over here, I think they'll start to make a pretty good-sized stink about the whole thing. It's beginning to look as if we suffer a penalty just for being an officer. But I guess I'm just starting to get a little selfish about it now. The situation does look a little black, though, when I stop to consider that I'm no nearer to getting home now than I was a year ago today. We are expecting to have officers' points reduced to 70 in the next couple of days, and that is making a few guys happy, but to affect the rest of us, the points have got to drop about 20 more points. And it doesn't look like that will happen for another five months or so. That's a long time to serve in an Army, when there isn't a war to fight or even any reason to be mad at another country.... I guess the whole reason for me being blue tonight is that I'm teed off at the Army for keeping us apart."

Back to the movies at El Gecko on Thursday: ".... saw my favorite actress in 'Along Came Jones' with Gary Cooper and Wm Demarest. Wasn't nearly as good as I had expected but I didn't mind it too much so long as Loretta Young was in it. Actually, I was a little disappointed in her, too, but I wouldn't admit it to anyone. It was the silliest darn picture I've seen for a long time. The latest dope on discharges now is that officers' points will be lowered 5 points a month from now on. It hasn't been announced officially yet, but it looks fairly certain. I hope it doesn't fall through like most of the other stuff. At any rate I should be eligible to come home in March or April. There still are strong rumors that we'll move out before then, but that shouldn't have any effect on my discharge. It'll be effective no matter where I am. I hear that Jacques Dangers got himself a pretty good job in Santa Barbara and is having trouble finding a place up there to live. Sure was lucky for him to find a spot so quickly.

"The shots I got the other day have calmed down, except for the vaccination which is starting to puff up and get awfully itchy. It's a wonder the blood doesn't leak out of my arm by this time. The Army sure does try to put plenty of leaks in a man's plumbing!"

The mid-November heat on the island was beginning to wear on the men. "The last few days have really been blazers. I think this is the hottest weather we've had so far. We had a good-sized storm late last night and early this morning, but here it is 2:00 in the afternoon and everything is all dried up already. All of us are drinking water by the gallon just to keep up with the amount of perspiration we shed. Just sitting here in the office, the sweat rolls down my arms, and off the point of my chin. So far, I've been more or less chuckling to myself about how easy it was to stand this tropical weather, but now the things that people have said about it are starting to show." The men were setting up a new office, and they hoped the new space would provide some relief from the heat. "We're going to move our Utilities office sometime next week, I think. Up until now we've had things set up in two large tents, with wooden floors and screened insides. Our new buildings will be 20' x 56' Quonset huts which should be much cooler and much more spacious. We are laying asphalt floors for them today, and we should be all fixed up by next week." The movie that night was *House of Fear* with Basil Rathbone and Nigel Bruce. Not really a Sherlock Holmes fan, Harvey opted for a return bridge match with Lt. Herrick against Mac and Lt. Weingartner. "This game tonight is going to be a blood and thunder match because the last time we played, we really gave them a shellacking. Hope they don't swamp us tonight or we'll never hear the end of it."

The heat continued on Saturday. "Kind of a slow, hot day today with nothing much doing at the office. We had a baseball game this afternoon with the Hq. Sq. playing the 19th Bomb Group from North Field. There wasn't anything else to do, and I went over to see it. The 19th won, 3-2, but it was a pretty good game anyway.

"The latest dope on discharge now is a little better than it has been, and the future is just a shade brighter. The radio announced today that all men with 51 months service as of Dec. 1st would be let out then, with the idea of dropping the requirement 3 months every week after that. It should drop to 48 months on the 1st of January, which would put me right in line. As usual, nothing is official yet, but at least it's good to think about. Mac has his 51 months in already, and he should be in line in December, putting him just a month ahead of me. Not a bad deal, if this stuff is on the level. Sure am hoping."

On Sunday, Harvey and the officers played another touch football game. "This morning our team played the enlisted men another game and, by golly, we won! Rain came down in a light drizzle all through the game, so you can imagine how slippery the field was. All of us were covered with mud by the time we had played five minutes. The only injuries were a skinned nose for Dick Williams, and a charley horse for me, the worst one I've ever had. Can't hardly move my leg. That makes it a game apiece now in the series we've played, and next Wednesday we'll play the rubber game. Next Thursday is Thanksgiving, and we have a game scheduled for that morning with a team of officers from the 314th Wing at North West Field. It will be a tough one.

"The discharge craziness took another twist for the better this morning when someone started a rumor that months overseas would count time-and-a-half or double-time on the system I told you about yesterday. Apparently that system is really going to go through, although we haven't seen anything official yet. Now, if the rumor about time and a half for overseas time is true, I should have 51 months, just by the skin of my teeth, by the first of December. And if it turns out to be double time for overseas time, I'll be in like Flynn. My fingers are getting awfully stiff from keeping them crossed for so long. Actually, I'm not letting myself get too excited about it yet, since there hasn't been anything posted. I hate to keep going on assumptions like 'if this happens' or 'if that happens' or 'if they lower the points so XX', because all it does is get you up in the air. You can imagine the state that Mac is in right now."

Monday was a busy day for Harvey, chasing down materials for a big Red Cross building they were putting up. The woman in charge was a long time Red Cross worker named Lillian Greenberg who, although rather young, had already put in a long time as an overseas worker. The movie that night was *Wonder Man* with Danny Kaye and Virginia Mayo. "What a screwy business!! I thought I'd pop some buttons. It's really the funniest and the silliest picture I've seen in a long time. Hope you don't miss seeing it. And last night we saw 'Bell for Adano' with John Hodiak and Gene Tierney!! It was really good!! Not only that, but on Thursday night, we have 'Christmas in Connecticut' again, and I'm going to see it this time if it kills me. It'll probably rain cats and dogs, but I don't care!"

Harvey typically took a shower before going to the movies at El Gecko, but on Monday he decided to wait until he returned to the BOQ in the evening. This turned out to be a mistake as the water became really cold after dark. The water supply was a large tank sitting in a tower beside the shower room, and the sun beating down on the tank all day kept the water fairly warm. However, as soon as the sun went down, the water quickly became chilly. The later you took a shower, the colder it became. He remarked to Betty that he didn't understand how some of the officers could take showers each morning.

Thanksgiving was approaching for the American troops in Guam, and the men were enjoying a "long holiday" work week: a half day on Wednesday, Thursday off because of Thanksgiving, half days on Friday and Saturday, Sunday off, and another half day on Monday. Harvey found it ironic that the

Army could afford to give them so much free time while still refusing to send them home. On Tuesday, he and five buddies went to the movies, this time at the theater of the 501st Bomb Group at Northwest Field. "The film was 'Dangerous Partners' with James Craig and Signe Hasso. Looked like a genuine Class B production when it started out, but it developed into a pretty good movie. Signe Hasso is pretty good, and I was surprised to see that she almost lived up to the claims the columnists made about her."

By Tuesday, Harvey wasn't optimistic about leaving the island in December. "It looks very much as if the discharge deal won't get me out until January, at the earliest. Men with 51 months can leave on December 1st or as soon as they can get away, and then men with 48 months can leave on January 1st or soon after that. Maybe I'll be able to get away from Guam after the 15th or 20th of January."

On Wednesday, there was a football game, the "warm-up" for the big Thanksgiving Classic the next day. The game was with the Engineering Squadron and "darned if I didn't get my charley horse back again. It was just about well when I started to play, and I must have aggravated it some way because, all of a sudden, there it was, all knotted up again. I played quite a bit of the game and worked some of it out, but it's still a bit sore. We won the game 6-2, but it was a tight squeeze. All the points were scored in the last few minutes. Now tomorrow, we have our big game.... we rested a while, and then somebody started a volleyball game so I got into that too, hoping it would help straighten out my leg...and it did. The movie tonight was 'Blonde from Brooklyn', so we all stayed at the club and played seven or eight rubbers of bridge."

Thursday was the big Thanksgiving Day Classic football game. Harvey had jokingly noted that they expected a huge crowd of at least 10 or 15. "Should be quite a gala affair, don't you think? We were thinking we'd have some of the troops parade on the field at half time, but I think the weather will probably be too hot, and I think we'll dispense with the parade." On Thursday morning, the long-anticipated football "classic" went to the officers' team, 11-10—without Harvey, whose leg was still bothering him. He relaxed until dinner, which was a huge Thanksgiving meal with traditional turkey trimmings. The enlisted man who was serving the turkey had worked for Harvey at Walker when the unit had been packing for the overseas trip, "so you can imagine how much white meat I got! I could hardly see over the top of it. Right now, I'm so full that I could almost write my letter to you on top of my stomach." He wrote that afternoon on monogramed stationary that Betty had sent him for their "paper" anniversary. (His parents had also sent cards to both Harvey and Betty. His read, "We hope this will be the only anniversary you and Betty will ever have to spend apart!") After supper that evening, the men headed over to El Gecko to see *Salome, When She Danced.* Harvey expected there to be a large crowd at the theater as the men were expecting a sensuous performance by Yvonne De Carlo.

As a footnote to his letter, Harvey described an incident at the airfield where a bomber narrowly avoided a disaster. "The pilot took off from our field and damned near didn't make it. He was loaded down so heavy with gasoline that he ran clear off the end of the runway before he could get into the air. Sure glad he made it."

On Friday night, Harvey went to the movies again. "After waiting for months, I finally saw 'Christmas in Connecticut,' and I thought it was swell!! They sure did get into some screwy mix ups. The guy that played the chef is a scream. He has been in a couple pictures I've seen lately, and I just about roll off my seat every time he says or does anything. He, and the fellow who played the father in 'Miracle of Morgan's Creek' are my two favorite comedians. This goof sure knocked me out in the picture tonight...I hope we can have a Christmas in weather like that sometime." [*Note: the two actors that Harvey noted as his favorite comedians were S. Z. Sakall and William Demarest.*]

"I forgot to tell you that we listened to your records yesterday at the club, and before we had even finished playing the first one, there were about 60 officers all crowded around listening. They are really great. And ever since hearing 'Waiting on the Train to Come In,' I haven't been able to get the tune out of my head. That's the best song I have heard in a long, long time. In fact, as I sit here writing, I can hear it playing again over at the club. Everybody is crazy about it. I'll bet it has been played at least 50 times already, and that's just since yesterday evening. It'll be on the Hit Parade, or I miss my guess." This record, by Peggy Lee, was one of those dropped off at Stella's by Capitol Records.

Harvey hadn't heard from Virjeanne's husband, the marine now stationed in Japan, for several weeks, but another letter arrived just after Thanksgiving. Earl was stationed in Saga, north of Nagasaki, and like Harvey, was keeping close track of the discharge rumors. "So far very few of the boys have gone home. But last nite, I heard some talk that the boys with 50 points and over will be on their way home by the 1st of December. I sure hope so, because even though I don't have 50, maybe if they get out, I'll be coming up next. Who knows? If they do go...maybe by the middle of next year I'll be able to go too, so far I've only got 38 points…kind of low. But better than nothing. I guess we will be coming home about the same time. That would sure be nice. I am now the mail man and go from Saga to Sasebo and back every other day. I have another boy, and we go a day on and a day off. So, for the 2 past months, I've learned a lot about how the M.P.'s work. So far, I've been lucky…I haven't been caught at anything and haven't caught anything from the girls…some of the boys haven't been so lucky."

Saturday was Betty and Harvey's anniversary, and he really couldn't focus on anything other than his feelings toward her. He went to the movies with some of the guys, but even that didn't hold his attention. "This evening five of us got into Jimmy Ray's jeep and went down to the theater at the Fleet Hospital. It's a Navy installation, so we thought they'd have a super picture, but it turned out to be a cowboy double feature that wasn't even worthy of the Star theater in Hays. Both movies were stinkaroos." The next day was a hot one on the island, with the officers just trying to keep cool in the club. "I'm sitting over in the club, as per usual, with a coke full of ice sitting on the table at my elbow, but it doesn't help a whole lot. There isn't a bit of breeze blowing, the palm trees are just as still as stone. The sun is just boiling down, and everyone sitting here is just racking his brain for an idea of how to cool off." A slight breeze started to pick up, though, before the evening's entertainment at El Gecko. "Our movie tonight is 'Patrick the Great,' with Donald O'Connor and Peggy Ryan, so I'm making a special effort to see it on your recommendation…so it better be good! We are having some sort of a U.S.O. show along with it, so this will be a gala night for the theatergoers! Lately, when we have had a special show, we've been just about crowded out of our seats by a lot of jokers from the bomb groups who come early and almost fill the theater. So tonight, patrons will only be admitted with a P.X. ration card. We all have one, and it identifies us as being from the service groups. At least we can be fairly sure that we'll have a decent place to sit down." On Monday, they drove back to the Navy theater, only to be disappointed once again. "Just got in from a very lousy show we traveled almost 20 miles to see. First we went back down to the Fleet Hospital hoping there would be a good show, but it turned out to be the same cowboy pictures, so we drove over to the Agaña Bowl and darned if they didn't have a long 'March of Time' documentary instead of a feature picture. We were pretty unhappy by this time so, on the way back we stopped at a small snack bar at the 331st Bomb Group Officers Club. We each had a ham sandwich and a cup of coffee before coming back to our area.… just before a really big rainstorm blew up."

Stars and Stripes is the American military's newspaper that focuses on matters concerning service men and women. The paper was created during the First World War by Harold Ross, who later founded The *New Yorker* magazine. During World War II, the paper was printed in dozens of editions in several operating theaters and, starting in 1945, was published in the Pacific. Harvey read the newspaper in Guam, and occasionally he would send clippings to Betty with articles or opinion pieces that he found interesting. In the November 24th edition, this Letter to the Editor caught his eye and he sent it on to Venice:

Lifetime Caste System

Sitting on the lanai of my luxurious officers' club, sipping a Singapore "Stengah," smoking a 50-cent cigar and watching enlisted men dig latrines, occasionally touching them with a wire whip if they forget to bow to me, I am enboldened to add a few words to the plethora being printed in your excellent paper about the officer vs. enlisted man situation.

I love the Stars and Stripes, I really do. I love the beating of gums, the gnashing of molars, the wonderful rumble of pure bitching that bursts upon me when I open your sheet.

I don't want to take up too much space explaining (with the aid of training films, cartoons and building blocks) the fact that armies by their very nature and purpose are Fascist organizations, always have been, always will be, if they are to function with any degree of efficiency. Nor will I pull the fact that I was an EM (enlisted man) longer (three years longer) than I have been commissioned. Nor will I cluck sympathetically and simper, as some of the officers you've printed have, "You boys should have uniforms just like ours, you really should."

I'm no Regular Army man, but a civilian picked up by the seat and dumped into a khaki uniform. But I believe in the caste system for the Army, can't see how it can function without it.

That doesn't mean I condone its occasional outrages. No officer worth his salt believes in the necessity of the stupid distinctions you've been printing as objections to the caste system.

But the basic idea of 'caste' in the Army is necessary and good. When you don a uniform you relinquish your rights as a civilian. What the hell do you think war is, a game where all the boys on one team get together and vote on what they're going to do next?

As a parting thought, children, I offer this: prior to the war the colored man lived under the 'caste system' not for one year or two or four, but for every minute of his entire life. You who bitch so bitterly about separate beaches and clubs for officers, separate latrines, subservience to men you don't give a damn about, you great bleeding-hearts who drivel on about equality and justice and fraternity - were you so righteous in your treatment of the Negro when you were a civilian? Remember that you're getting out of it with no more than a few years' resentment at being considered an inferior race. The colored man was born into it, lives in all his days, dies in it. Thank God the Army gave you a chance to see the others' point of view, and if equality means any more to you than being allowed to wear a tailor-made shirt, go out of the Army with the idea of living the ideals you've prated about. Don't carry the Army's necessary caste system over into civilian life.

And for God's sake, don't sell your colored brothers short.

Lt. J.G. Humphries, Army

Harvey and Mac were going to the movies almost every night, but not always at the local El Gecko. "Went to the show again tonight at the Agaña Bowl ...we got there after the picture started so I don't know what the name of it was, but I had seen it before. Alice Faye, Sheila Ryan, E.E. Horton, Charlotte Greenwood and Phil Baker were all in it. It was a color film, and I'm sure I saw it at least three or four years ago. Plenty good show." (Note: It was The Gang's All Here, from 1943.)

Mac was getting closer to heading home but was still working out details. "He found out today he'll be ready to go home sometime next week, that is if he gets all his property straightened out before then. Right now, he's got more stuff signed out to him than anyone else in the group. That's the trouble with being a supply officer when it comes time to move. I think he found a replacement today, so now there is someone to take over his job. Now if he can just account for everything he's signed for, he'll be cleared for shipment. He's hoping to get a plane ride back, but I'm afraid he'll have to be satisfied with going back by boat.... most guys are going that way now. My turn should come at the first of the year."

The officers' team had another football game on Wednesday, and it ended in an unsatisfying 2-0 loss. "Tonight, 5 of us climbed into Jimmy Ray's jeep and went to the 501st Bomb Group theater to see 'Of Human Bondage' with

Paul Henreid and Alexis Smith. I haven't seen such an emotional picture in a long time. It really was a character study. This must be a second edition of the same movie because I remember Bette Davis in a film with the same name, although I didn't see it. Don't miss this one if you can help it because I'm pretty sure you'd like it. Ought to be at least a two or three hanky picture." The film was based on the 1915 novel by W. Somerset Maugham and, yes, Bette Davis had starred in an RKO adaptation of the story in 1934. For her performance, she had been nominated for an Academy Award for Best Actress in a Leading Role. The newer version of the film that Harvey and his buddies saw on Guam was evidently a special showing for the military. It wasn't released in the States until 1946 and received lukewarm reviews.

Harvey was getting increasingly anxious about his discharge date and planned to check the next day for updates of scheduled releases for officers. "I'm going down to the personnel office in the morning to check on the list of officers scheduled to leave here in January. I should be included on that list, and I want to make sure there are no mistakes. Wouldn't it be terrible to be left off a shipment list like that by mistake? Mac is still on the list to go next week, and he is still sweating out a replacement for his job. That's one thing I won't have to worry about when the time comes, because there are two officers, neither of which has as much service as I've got, that can assume my small duties."

After a couple of volleyball games on Thursday, Harvey again went to the movies, this time at El Gecko. "It was a pretty good one, 'Her Highness and the Bellboy' with June Allyson, Hedy Lamarr and Robert Walker. Rags Ragland was in it, too, and I thought I'd die laughing at him!! And that crazy drunk that seems to sneak into every picture!! What a character! Sure hope he isn't so dopey in real life."

SELLING RECORDS AT
THE MERALTA THEATRE

As Betty wrote her letter on November 1st, she thought back to the previous November when she and Harvey had been married. "Today started one of our 'magic months.' We were both sweating it out this time last year, weren't we? But we've been so happy, and I wouldn't trade one second of our life together for all the rice in China. This evening I played records in the lobby of the Meralta Theatre. We are working a tie-in with the theater, and Elsie and I are taking turns while 'Rhapsody in Blue' is playing. They put an ad in the store for the picture, and we displayed our records in the lobby. Worked out pretty good for the first time, too. We didn't sell any records at the show, but it has acquainted quite a few new people with Stella's. I was planning to see the show tomorrow night, and Elsie was going to stop at the house tonight and see our wedding gifts. But after I got there, I found that tonight was the last run of the picture because it wasn't drawing the expected crowds. I called the folks, and they came down and the four of us stayed to watch the picture. I sure enjoyed it. Am glad you got to see it over there."

Occasionally, Harvey and Betty were able to see the same pictures, he in the Pacific and she in California. The major studios were releasing new films all the time, often with patriotic or war-time themes, and many of these recent releases were promptly sent overseas to entertain the troops. *Rhapsody in Blue* was actually filmed in the summer and fall of 1943 but was released in 1945. Harvey, in Guam, saw the movie in July, while Betty, just a few miles from the studio, didn't see it until early November.

"No mail from Guam again today. We did get a card from Rod though, and he is certainly getting his wish to travel. He is on his way to Aberdeen, Maryland. He'll be near Washington, D.C., not too far from your folks, so maybe he can drop in to meet them. Was glad to tear another page off the calendar today because it's a month closer to seeing you."

On Saturday, Betty's father went with a friend to a football game at the Coliseum—"U.S.C. vs. St. Mary's. He said it was a terrific game to watch. I listened to it at the store...I wonder if you got short wave on it? 26-0 in favor of St. Mary's. Harvey Adair was supposed to play first string with them today, but he hurt his knee last week. He and Rod played high school ball together." The other girls didn't come into the store that day, and Betty worked late. That night, as she wrote to Harvey, she could see the searchlights from the movie theaters in Hollywood. *Spellbound*, with Ingrid Bergman and Gregory Peck, opened that weekend at Grauman's Chinese Theatre on Hollywood Boulevard.

An article in the Herald-Express about the USS *Missouri*, site of the Japanese surrender, caught her eye and she sent it on to Harvey.

USS MISSOURI 'WRECK' AFTER KID'S VISITS

New York, Nov. 3 - Sixty thousand school kids who visited the battleship Missouri last Monday were disclosed today to have caused more damage to the mighty dreadnaught in one day than the combined efforts of the entire Japanese fleet and air force during the entire war.

"What those kids did to this ship is incredible," said the Missouri's executive officer, Commander Arthur F. Spring. "Hundreds of them came aboard with pliers, screwdrivers and wrenches hidden in their clothing.

The wildest stunt of all was the pulling of a general fire and battle station alarm. It had the crew nuts until we de-energized the circuit and shut off the clatter.

Another kid sprung the safety catch on a two-ton life raft. It almost killed him when it crashed to the deck. He escaped with a lost finger.

But that was only part of it. The kids scratched their initials all over the ship, yanked everything resembling a lever, removed nameplates from guns and bulkheads and walked off with fire nozzles that weighed 10 pounds apiece.

Some people, probably adults, tried to unscrew the surrender plaque. Since then, we've practically had to wire everything down."

Next Monday will be the last visiting day for the general public. So far more than 630,000 persons have been aboard the battleship during its New York stay.

Harvey's mother wrote to him that Saturday. It had been three weeks since she had heard from him, and she was getting increasingly worried. On Halloween she and Harvey Sr. had gone to see the Ice Capades. "It was a good show. Always is. Packed to the roof." The event was held at Duquesne Gardens in Pittsburgh's Oakland district. In 1932, a local entertainment entrepreneur, John Harris, had leased the Gardens, a garage turned ice rink on Craig Street, and began organizing events, including boxing, rodeos, and ice hockey. During the Depression, he had trouble attracting crowds to hockey games, and he hired the Norwegian Olympic figure skater Sonja Henie to skate between periods. The performances were a success, and Harris began plans to produce a skating exhibition on the scale of the song and dance shows that were popular on Broadway. The Ice Capades premiered in 1940, with 150 performers trained by an Olympic skater. By 1945, the show toured for forty-eight weeks of the year with performances in some twenty cities in the US and Canada. The season premiere that year had been held on September 15th and had been a benefit performance: "Draw a red circle around September 15 on your calendar. On that night in Duquesne Gardens the Sun-Telegraph will sponsor the world premiere of the $500,000 Ice Capades of 1946 for the benefit of hospitalized servicemen. The 152 artists of the Ice Capades cast, headed by the glamorous Donna Atwood, are giving their services free. John H. Harris, president, and producer of the famous skating extravaganza, is turning over the Gardens and all equipment without charge.... You will be letting around 2,900 heroes of three wars know that you are interested in their welfare. The veterans are patients in three hospitals: Deshon, with approximately 2,000 wounded overseas veterans of World War II, Veterans Hospital in Aspinwall, with 800 veterans of World Wars I and II and a sprinkling of Spanish-American War vets, and Marine Hospital in Lawrenceville, with 60 to 70 emergency patients, divided between military personnel and merchant seaman." The Browns had been attending the Ice Capades for several years. On Friday, they had gone to see *The House on 92nd Street* "It was pretty good – different. It refers to the atomic bomb and wasn't allowed to be released until after they had been dropped on Japan."

On Monday, Betty and her folks received a long letter from Rod, who was enjoying his train ride across the country and was about to go through a snowstorm. As she wrote to Harvey that evening, she listened to the radio and heard Sam Koki and His Paradise Islanders performing at a club called the Seven Seas, located across from Grauman's Chinese Theatre on Hollywood Boulevard. In addition to owning the Seven Seas, Koki had worked at 20th Century Fox and at Paramount, and his arrangement of "Sweet Leilani" for Bing Crosby in the film *Waikiki Wedding* had won an Academy Award in 1937. During the program, an announcer broke in to say that the composer Jerome Kern was seriously ill. Kern would pass away later that week.

Again on Tuesday, Betty listened to the radio while writing her letter. "I'm going to try the impossible, write you and listen to a murder story at the same time! I find myself sitting, pen in hand, staring into space. You got me this way, you know of course. I never used to like mystery stories before. Guess I'm going to have to wait until the program is over.....Well, the program is over now, so here I go again. Edna is staying here this evening and we have been talking a blue streak. From what you are saying, it sounds like the club is really going well!

The music store was quite busy the next day, and as Mr. Stella was out of the office, Betty had to deal with several record salesmen who came in. One particular recording caught her eye. "There is a new record out by Helen Humes that we are ordering in for our customers. Have you by any chance heard "Be-Baba-Leba"? Pretty good jive, but a little on the dirty side. If I can find some more time, I'll send one for you. The B-side of the record is a stock arrangement that is fine!" Helen Humes had toured as a vocalist with Count Basie's band and in 1945 was living in Los Angeles, recording solo tunes and movie soundtracks.

On Thursday, Betty and Mr. Stella drove into Los Angeles to buy five thousand records from a juke box dealer. "We worked quite a deal. Paid 11 cents each, and we'll sell them for 25 cents. Some are practically new, and a few are collector's items, so we can make some money on those! On the way back to the store, we celebrated by buying two quarts of ice cream and had it when we got back, so Elsie could enjoy it too."

Harvey's Aunt Peggy worked at the VA hospital in Aspinwall, PA. She had just returned home from a trip with her mother to Atlantic City and wrote to both Betty and Harvey from Pittsburgh on November 9th. "Saw plenty of soldiers, and most of the large hotels on the Boardwalk have been turned into hospitals. All the service men seem to be in very good spirits. Our hospital here is filled up with a large number of World War 2 men. General Bradley, our Administrator, wants to have a 1500 bed hospital built at Pitt University and have Aspinwall turned into TB only. I hope to get out before it goes to TB and would like to get to Pitt. The Camp at Greenville is going to be another hospital, and they are digging the foundation now. Quite a few of the employees here are back from the Army and most of them are working down in the Regional Office....Most of the Army and Navy hospitals will be turned over to the Veteran's Administration, because as soon as a soldier is discharged he must be hospitalized in a V.A. hospital. Tomorrow, we just work four hours, that is our first Saturday half day since war was declared." The "General Bradley" that Peggy had mentioned was Omar Bradley, who had commanded the US Army during the Normandy Invasion. He was later appointed Chief of Staff of the Army in 1948 and Chairman of the Joint Chiefs of Staff in 1949.

Betty's letter to Harvey on Friday, November 9th, was written on stationary with the following heading:

Christian Science Service Center
Welcomes Servicemen and Servicewomen

2230 Main Street
Ocean Park (Santa Monica), California

"Wish you were one of the boys who stopped by here this evening! This is the first night I've served at the Center. Mom has several times, and she enjoys it so much. Mr. Russell came for me at 10 to 7 (I got home from work at 6:30 – boy did I rush!) So far tonight, we've had two Lts. – discharged, who are members of a neighboring church, who just wanted to look around. Two sailors from Port Hueneme who had some cake and milk and talked for a while until they had to leave for a date. One was from Montana, and the other from Louisiana. Right now, a very tired discharged service man is curled up asleep on the davenport in the second living room by the fire. Mr. Russell is back in the study reading his lesson, and I'm at the desk by the door; in case anybody comes in, they'll know there is someone here. This is such a peaceful little home. I hope it is still going when you get back, so you can see it. Religion isn't mentioned or forced on the boys in any way, although there is some literature on the tables along with regular books and magazines...they may read it if they like. During the summer is when they are really busy. The house is used all the time for cleaning up after a dip in the ocean, or a day at the beach. There is a shower here – towels, bathing trunks; - kitchen always stocked with cookies, cake, and milk...also oranges for juice. We have a piano and play all evening, but I'm afraid our friend couldn't sleep if I did it tonight. We are here from 7 – 10.

"Had such a busy day today. Did a lot of cleaning at the store and sorting out of record stocks. When Elsie and I finished, the store was clean, but you should have seen us. I was supposed to go to lunch at R.K.O. with Mary Alyce today, but we were right in the mess at noon, so I called her and made a date for next week. Sold about $15 worth of records to a glamour gal just before I left tonight. It was Anita Colby, and she certainly is lovely. Did you ever see her in the East? At present she is under contract at R.K.O. and is a consultant for pictures. When I find a picture of her, I'll send it to you, so you can see who I'm talking about." Anita Colby was the daughter of cartoonist Daniel "Bud" Counihan, the creator of the Betty Boop cartoons, and although she did appear in three films: *Mary of Scotland* (1936), *Cover Girl* (1944), and *Brute Force* (1947), she is best known as one of the country's first super models. After *Brute Force*, she said "I don't want to act. I want to get into the executive end of the film business." She was the first woman executive in the motion picture industry and had refused marriage proposals from both Clark Gable and Jimmy Stewart. When Betty met her in 1945, Colby was working for David O. Selznick at RKO Studios, helping his contract actresses in matters of beauty, poise, and publicity. Selznick had brought her in two years earlier to work with Jennifer Jones who was to star in *The Song of Bernadette*. "He hired an ex-model named Anita Colby to advise him on how his various actresses should dress and behave, and she had to devote special attention to Mrs. Walker [Jennifer Jones's real name]. Miss Colby had to teach her not only what clothes to buy – sending back any wrong choices – but even how to look back into people's eyes when there they were speaking to her." *Bernadette* went on to win four Academy Awards, including Best Actress for Jennifer Jones!

On Sunday, Betty took a trip to the beach with Edna and a couple of her friends. They drove up to Sunset Boulevard, took Sunset all the way to the beach, turned right and then took the Roosevelt Highway up to Topanga Canyon Road. They went for about ten miles up into the canyon before deciding to come back. Back on the coast, they drove by the motel where Betty and Harvey had honeymooned! "It was only 5:30, but dark already. I wish you could have been sitting beside me as we went through the foothills and along the coast. We went on up the coast toward Malibu and, yes, we passed 'our place' at Las Tunas! It looked so cute! The place was all lit up, the vacancy sign out, and several cars out in front, and it looked as if the patio and swimming pool was lit up...I wished I could go right in then and reserve 'our' room. The moon was shining so brightly and made a silver path all the way from 'over there' to the motel. We drove further up the beach and then came back to the Las Tunas Inn and had some fried shrimp before driving home." On Monday, she had dinner at the Irvings' and then went with her friends to the Meralta to see *Our Vines have Tender Grapes*, with Edward G. Robinson and Margaret O'Brien. "Could surely have used your hanky in that picture. It was so sweet and so true to life. A couple of times I looked at James Craig, and he reminded me so much of you. All the way through it, little things struck so close to home. Little Butch in the movie reminded me so much of Rod when he was little. The second feature was 'The Falcon at San Francisco.' Just like those rip-roaring pictures we used to see in Hays. I hope you see the Bugs Bunny cartoon we saw...the rabbit is on an island somewhere in the Pacific when all the fun begins...you and Mac would really howl."

Betty listened to the Jack Carson CBS radio program as she wrote on Wednesday and told Harvey they were playing one of their favorites, "It's Been a Long, Long Time." She and Elsie had had another busy day at Stella's dealing with new stock. "We really earned our money today. 1,500 records from Columbia: 300 from Decca and quite a bit of sheet music. All of the records had to be checked and stacked away. For three hours we stood in one spot and checked records. The stock looks swell now, and you won't know the store when you get back. Best looking one in Culver. Soon as it gets going again (the front window), I'll take some pictures and sent them to you." Eight hundred more records came in on Thursday, keeping Betty busy. She had lunch with Mary Alyce at the RKO Studios where three movies (*Duel in the Sun*, *The Spiral Staircase*, and *The Paradine Case*) were in production. "Lots of fun – we talked about everything and everybody and got all caught up on our gossip. Saw quite a few movie stars, as they are shooting 3 different pictures now. 'Duel' should be good – so try to see it when it hits the island." Much of *Duel in the Sun*, with Jennifer Jones, Joseph Cotton, and Gregory Peck, was filmed in the RKO Studios on Washington Boulevard, but some of it was shot on location in multiple spots in Arizona and California. It was released in 1946, and Jennifer Jones (coached by Anita Colby, whom Betty had met at Stella's) was nominated for an Academy Award. After work, Betty had dinner with her newlywed friend, Florence, and there were two letters from Harvey waiting for her when she finally got home. In one of them, Harvey spoke about Jimmy and Lee's new baby, and Betty's thoughts turned again to their own future family. "Do you think you'll know how to act when you become a father now?"

Betty's twenty-fifth birthday was on December 16th, and Harvey had written to her parents to see if they could buy flowers for her. Her mother didn't write to him often, but on this occasion she sent him a return letter. "Just a few lines to tell you your letter and money arrived O.K., and the flowers are ordered for Betty. They will be roses and beautiful ones too. The same florist who had charge of the wedding is taking care of this order. The little verse you sent will be tucked in with the roses, and I will try to have everything just as you want. It is hard enough to have to spend your first anniversary – or any anniversary for that matter- apart from each other. It just doesn't seem right, and anything that Daddie or I can do to make the day more pleasant, we are most happy to do. Thanks for writing us. Isn't it grand that Rod is stationed reasonably near your folks? We know they will enjoy each other, and it is a comforting feeling to know they are not so very far from Aberdeen. We all miss Rod very much. Lots of Love to you from your mother and dad in California." Betty's father added a quick hello along with the score of the UCLA-St. Mary's game he had attended!

At Stella's on Monday, Betty had a visit from her friend, Helen Hunt, whom she had known since Job's Daughters. Her first husband, Joe Logan, had been killed in India, and she had recently remarried. She told Betty that her new husband, Jack, was now in Guam and would try to look up Harvey. Harvey and Betty would be friends with Helen and Jack for many years.

The Ebell of Los Angeles is an educational and philanthropic non-profit organization founded by six women in 1894. It was inspired by the work of Dr. Adrian Ebell, a prominent doctor, photographer, and proponent of women's education who had died in a steamboat accident in 1877. Its original mission was "to interest women in the study of all branches of literature, art and science and the advancement of women in every branch of culture." The Ebell Art Gallery, Clubhouse, and Theatre, designed by Sumner Hunt, were built on Wilshire Boulevard in 1927, and many high-profile events had been held there. In 1937, Amelia Earhart gave her last public speech in the Ebell Gallery just before leaving on her attempted flight around the world, and in 1930, Judy Garland was discovered by MGM producer George Sidney while performing on the Ebell stage. During war years, Ebell members sold more war bonds than any other women's club. The basement was also used as a bomb shelter, and USO dances were held in the Solarium.

In Wednesday's *Los Angeles Times* a program at the Ebell was advertised in the Drama and Film column:

> Clifford J. Kamen, South American explorer, and cinematographer, is to repeat his colored movie travelogue on Peru tonight at the Wilshire Ebell Theatre under the auspices of the Motion Picture Society of the Americas.

Strangely, just above the article in the *Times* was a note about the actor who had given Harvey a ride from Oklahoma to Los Angeles a year earlier:

> Loren Tindell will be seen as the pal of Guy Madison in "Till the End of Time", which once was known as "The Dream of Home." RKO borrowed him from Columbia Studio.

As a pre-Thanksgiving celebration, Mr. Stella made plans to take Betty and Elsie and his wife out to supper and then to the Peru program at the Ebell Theatre. "Well, Elsie is sick with a cold and Mrs. S came down with the flu. The show was for one night only, and he decided we would go anyway. Went over to his house after work and I talked to Mrs. S while he changed his clothes. She hadn't had anything to eat, so I fixed her some toast and a couple of soft-boiled eggs to go with a baked apple that a friend had brought over. We got her comfortable, and then we stepped out.... the boss and I. We had a delicious dinner at a place on Wilshire Blvd. near Cathay Circle. We still had plenty of time, so we walked down the street and saw Shirley Temple's wedding pictures in the photography studio. Then we drove on down Wilshire to the Ebell Club. I haven't been there in years...it is very, very nice. Tonight, they had a colored picture travelogue on Peru, and the fellow who took the pictures told all about them as they were flashed on the screen. It was the most interesting and entertaining evening I've spent in ages. Friday night, he is showing Chile, and we may go to see it too. Such a beautiful country. The program started at 8:30 and ended at 11!"

As much as Betty enjoyed the program, she was almost as interested in the people sitting around them. "The people sitting behind us had evidently made the trip over the same country and made comments all the way through. The fellow who took all the stills for the 'Inca' series in Life Magazine a few issues ago was in these same pictures. They worked together on the still and motion shots. Cary Grant and some delicious blonde creature sat right in front of us!

Good looking guy he is! … but all I could think of was seeing him in 'Arsenic and Old Lace.'" By Friday, both Elsie and Mrs. Stella were feeling better, and the four of them went back to the Ebell Theatre. "Elsie picked me up, and we met Mr. and Mrs. Stella at the theater to see the moving (technicolor) pictures on Chile. They were fine but I think I liked the series on Peru better. There is one place I'd like to visit in Chile, though, a resort called Vina del Mar (I think) …looks luscious."

Betty wrote a long letter on the 24th, their first anniversary. Her parents told her they had to go shopping before her father took her to work. The "shopping" was a trip to the florist to pick up the roses from Harvey they had ordered. "When I saw the flowers, my heart spilled over. Ruth (the florist) fixed a beautiful box. Had the dozen red roses and a corsage of gardenias for me to wear today. The whole top of the box was covered with amber colored cellophane and a huge cherry colored ribbon. Mother then showed me the letter you sent to her." Betty's thoughts kept drifting back to her wedding day, and she was close to tears all day. "You know, I think I've felt the most alone today of all the days since you went away, and yet you were close to me. Tonight, the folks picked me up at the store at 6, and we had dinner in Culver City and went to a show. We saw "Yolanda and the Thiefs." Don't bother going to it, for it is the worst picture I've seen in a long time. The news and comic were good, but the picture----oh, the more I see Astaire, the less I like him. When we got home, I told mom that I didn't want any coffee, and she said she and Daddy were going to have some anyway. When they were to sit down, Daddy insisted I have some too – so I came out and you should have seen how pretty the table was. They had the vase of red roses and white candles – and cake and ice cream and coffee…They both have been swell all day, and that was all I needed to start crying again. I could see us sitting on Rod's bed opening gifts, with Rod mingling in too. Mother and Dad everyplace at once doing whatever was needed. I could see us cutting the cake as I cut the little one for us tonight. About this time a year ago, you had carried me over our first threshold!"

On Sunday, Betty and her friend Helen Hunt had dinner in town and then went to the movies. "We had passes for the Meralta and couldn't pass up such a good deal. We saw 'Mama Loves Papa' (a stinkeroo) and "Love Letters.' I like that one just as well as I did the first time I saw it. Hope it hits Guam before you leave!"

Stella's was in Christmas shopping mode on Wednesday, and Betty and Elsie were busily decorating the store for holiday shoppers. "We spent almost all morning decorating the inside of the store 'Christmasy'. We used a lot of brick imitation paper, and the single record cabinet looks like a huge fireplace now. All small gifts and instruments are wrapped in cellophane which catches the light."

As usual, there was mail from Guam waiting for her when she got home from work, and Betty thought back of all the letters Harvey had sent over the years. "It reminded of a couple (of letters) you wrote to me, when you first wrote. How you carefully worded them so I wouldn't read too much, or too little, into them. Golly, those letters meant so much to me. Love letters I'll always cherish!! – and they are all tied up with ribbons too!"

29

DYNAMITE EXPLOSION
AT NORTHWEST FIELD
ROCKS ISLAND

Guam—December 1945: Instead of working on Saturday, Harvey's unit had an inspection and a drill period. "These guys are all pretty close to going home, so you can imagine how they bitched and griped about doing some of this basic training stuff. And just like they used to do in the States, they made me the Squadron Commander for the drill period. I took the men out on the asphalt flight apron to drill, and it was a lot better than the dusty areas here in camp. The whole business took us about three hours this morning, so we all are ready for a good night's sleep."

The officers played bridge in the club that afternoon and then headed over to El Gecko to see *Captain Eddie*. "We had heard so much about it, and I really thought it was plenty good. Lyn Bari has long been one of my favorites, and so has Fred MacMurray, so it was like old home night for me. You'd like it, even though it is sort of sad in places. Some of the silly scenes with those old-time automobiles were a scream."

Betty sent several books to Harvey in Guam during the fall of 1945. One of them was *Four Jills in a Jeep*, the story of four American women performers who accompanied Jimmy Dorsey's band on a USO tour entertaining troops overseas. The group, which included Carole Landis, Kay Francis, Martha Raye, and Mitzi Mayfair, was the first all-female USO troupe. As part of the Hollywood Victory Committee tour, they toured Bermuda, Northern Ireland,

England, and Northern Africa for six months in 1942 and 1943, putting on shows for military personnel, often in battle zones. The book was of special interest to both Betty and Harvey because of the romance and marriage of Carole Landis to a soldier she met while performing in London. Landis and ex- Eagle Squadron Captain Thomas Cherry Wallace met during the London leg of the USO tour in December 1942, and, after a "whirlwind romance," they were married on January 5th. Three days later, Carole and the others were ordered to Algiers in North Africa where, twice, they had to seek shelter in foxholes during bombings. Landis starred in a movie adaptation of her book in 1944. Unfortunately, she would separate from Wallace later that year.

After reading the Carole Landis book, Harvey wrote to Betty from Guam: "Plenty good and true to life!! Too bad Carole Landis' marriage had to go bad after having such a good start. All the books you've sent are making the rounds in the BOQ." Harvey and Betty didn't know it, but Carole Landis's life would end even more tragically than her marriage. She committed suicide in 1947 when her lover (Rex Harrison) refused to leave his wife (Lilli Palmer) for her.

On December 3rd, there was a USO stage play, *Junior Miss*, at El Gecko, but Harvey had to miss it. "I didn't get to see it. Just as I was finishing my supper, I got a call from our Hq saying there was someone down there waiting to see me. Sure enough Helen's husband (Jack Hunt) was there with two of his friends. He's a swell guy, and we had a long talk about you and Helen. He had managed to get some transportation, and he grabbed these two other guys and came up. I've got to go down to the other end of the island Thursday afternoon, so I'm going to drop in to see him then. He's stationed with a unit called USASTAF (United States Army Strategic Air Force, which is the next higher headquarters above 20th Air Force of which our Wing is a small part. He's only been overseas about two months, but he's got enough service time so he shouldn't be here more than a couple of months longer. We'll have to see more of them when I get back, because they'd be loads of fun. I don't remember much about Helen, but he had a picture of her, and I seemed to remember seeing her at your church. He also had a little snapshot of you and I that we had taken at the church the day of our wedding. Tell Helen he looks good and is chomping at the bit to get home." Coincidentally, the day before Harvey and Jack had their chat, Betty and Helen had been running together down Hollywood Boulevard. The two couples would be good friends for many years, and I remember meeting them as a boy in Southern California.

The heading on Harvey's Tuesday letter said it all: "Still Here." While he wrote, he listened to some of the records that had come in Betty's latest tin. "The recordings of Dinah Shore are terrific. Right now, as I write, 'Sophisticated Lady' is playing, and it is out of this world!! Boy, she really has a beautiful voice. 'Stardust' has always been one of my favorites, and the way it's done on this record just knocks me out. I'm a sucker for music like that, especially when Dinah Shore sings them." He spent some more time sorting out his property records—"glad I started early. Even now I may have a tough time making a deadline if it (his discharge) should come sooner than I expect. Poor Mac is having an awful time getting his stuff in shape. He's eligible for shipment home right now, but I doubt very much he'll get away inside of two more weeks. That's pretty rough.

"After supper, Herrick and I played bridge again and we held some fairly good hands for a change. The cards fell just right for us. Every now and then we have some luck like that and when we do, we just mow 'em down like ten pins." In her letters, Betty had tried to gently explain she had little interest in card playing, and had even sent him a cartoon with a soldier's wife saying, "I'm pretty good at cards, but what are these little black marks that look like clovers?" Nevertheless, he regularly went into detail about his card games with the officers!

"Tomorrow night we are going to try to get over to one of the Bomb Group theaters to see 'The Big Sleep' with Lauren Bacall and Humphrey Bogart. Everybody says it is really sharp. We just found out that the drilling schedule we had last Saturday will be a regular Saturday morning routine. Brother, what that is going to do to the morale of the enlisted men!! Not to mention how the officers will feel about it. I haven't heard any more about getting home, so I guess it will be some time after the 1st of January before I leave here. I'm still hoping for a lucky break to get me out of here sooner than that, but it doesn't seem likely."

They weren't able to see *The Big Sleep* on Monday, but they had better luck on Wednesday. "Just came in from seeing a pretty good show at the 331st Bomb Group theater. Wanted to see it a couple of nights ago but didn't get around to it until tonight. It was an awfully odd film with almost too many angles to it, but I liked it pretty well. It was the first picture of 'The Look' (Lauren Bacall's nickname) I had seen, and I can't say I was too impressed. Bogart played his usual good part and really held the picture together.

"This was our afternoon off and four of us played bridge almost all afternoon, just quitting in time to squeeze in a couple of pretty fast volleyball games before supper. The volleyball games almost ended in a riot. We usually do play a pretty fast and rough game. When we start, the rule book goes out the window. The rules say that no player is allowed to touch the net, and in our games we almost tear it down!"

There was still no news on the discharge front. ".... I'm still cleaning up my property accounts, so I'll be in shape to leave when they call me. Mac still hasn't left and doesn't seem to be much closer to going home than before." Harvey was beginning to worry about the growing stack of letters he was saving: "...you never said anything when I mentioned throwing away your letters. I sure hate to do it, and I won't if you say not to, but they are taking up an awful lot of room that I need. When you write, give me the dope, will you, huh? Instead of going to see 'The Thin Man' for the third time tonight, four of us had a swell game of bridge.

"I'm still sweating out that 3-day trip to Tokyo, but it doesn't look very promising. I'd hate to go up there and then find out while I was there that there'd been a chance for me to go home."

By the time Harvey sat down to write his letter to Betty on Saturday night, he was much more optimistic about getting home before Christmas. In the morning, he led the squadron through the new, and very unpopular, inspection and drill routines. "What a waste of time that is. These guys want to go home, not drill." That night, they went to the movies at El Gecko and "saw a real stinkeroo. At first, it sounded like it might be pretty good because the characters were Edward Arnold and Frances Rafferty, whose picture has been in the movie magazines quite a bit. It was 'Hidden Eye', a mystery where Edward Arnold plays a blind detective. It was so bad, I almost got up and left...and a movie has to be pretty bad to me to do that."

What Harvey really wanted to share with Betty, though, were his thoughts about coming home. "Jimmy Ray has a couple of months more service than I've got, and he's getting ready to leave right now. His boat is supposed to pull out about the 15th or 18th of the month, and I shouldn't be very far behind him. I don't have any ties here at all now, all my property is taken care of, and with an hour or so to throw my stuff into a footlocker, I could be ready to go. It will no doubt be sometime shortly before the end of the month, and I'll try to get word to you from here before I leave so you'll know nothing is wrong at this end when my letters stop coming. If I go by boat, there probably will be quite some time between my last letter from here and when I see you in the States. We talked about you coming to San Francisco to meet me, but since I'm not sure what kind of transportation I'll get, I don't think that is such a sharp idea now. Even if I get to San Francisco and you want to come up, the trains etc. will probably be so tied up that you wouldn't be able to get on one. As soon as they turn me loose, I'll get to L.A. as fast as possible. Should have pretty good luck in hitching rides. Gosh, it's wonderful to be talking about getting back to the States and you! Thank God, there isn't much more time to put in over here!! Incidentally, there are about five or six places in the States where I might land, depending on how I travel. If I come by plane it will either be Mather Field (Sacramento), March Field (Riverside) or Hammer Field (Fresno), and if by boat, Seattle, San Francisco, or Los Angeles. There's even talk of going by way of the Panama Canal to New Orleans due to transportation tie ups in the States. Will let you know as soon as I can."

On Sunday, Harvey went to the movies again at El Gecko. "At the theater tonight, we had one of those rough and ready Cagney pictures, "Blood on the Sun." Sylvia Sidney played opposite him, and it's the first time I've seen her on the screen in years. She didn't do bad, either. Cagney, as usual, does most of his acting with his fists, and proceeds to turn every set into a shambles. Pretty good entertainment, though." He sent Betty a birthday package, and when he wrapped it... "I used some of that parachute material for packing. I hope there is enough there for you to make something out of if you want to. I also put in a couple of the shroud lines in case you want to incorporate those also."

With his letter, Harvey included an article from one of the Army's Guam publications:

12 Units Slated for Movement by First of Year
By Sgt. D.J. Cross

All 20th personnel who become eligible for re-adjustment as of Jan. 1, 1946, will have been shipped at the time they are eligible for discharge, it is anticipated by A-1 officials of 20th headquarters.

Unforeseen circumstances, however, concerning shipping space may prevent full realization of this movement it is pointed out by Col. A. E. Minton, Deputy Chief of Staff for Administration, and Lt. Col. E. J. Hazeltine, Acting Assistant Chief of Staff, A-1.

Men eligible as of Jan. 1, 1946, are enlisted men with 50 or more points, three and one-half years of active service, 35 years old with 2 years of service, or 38 years of age. Eligible officers are those with 70 points or 4 years of active duty. [The underlining is Harvey's!]

Personnel will be moved to the States with the 12 units scheduled for readiness on or about mid-December, officials point out. If sufficient officer personnel are not available to fill these units to strength, enlisted personnel will be substituted.

A total of 7,745 enlisted men and 1,556 officers will be shipped.

Units alerted this month are 301st and 305th Depot Repair Squadrons, 55th Air Depot Group., 86th and 100th Depot Supply Squadrons, 87th, 805th and 813th Chemical Companies, 347th Air Service Group, 55th Air Material Squadron, 382nd and 383rd Bomb Groups.

Seven B-24s are being readied for the Sunset Project of the 3rd Photo Reconnaissance Squadron. The crews for these aircraft will be selected on the basis of points and the most eligible personnel will be selected for crew positions.

A-1 officials say that as men become eligible for discharge on length of service, they will be shipped out on the first available transportation.

"The units they mention are those that are moving homeward and to which eligible personnel are attached when ready to leave. When my time comes, I'll be transferred to a shipment like that. Heaven only knows what kind of unit I'll come home with. I don't much care, for that matter. I hope to go with one of those outfits listed but I don't know as yet. At any rate, I'll be home in January. Gosh, Sweetheart, I'm really and truly getting close to the time when I'll see you again."

After supper on Monday, there was a meeting at the Officers' Club to elect new officers. According to the constitution, elections were held every three months so vacancies could be filled quickly when men were sent home. "So now, darling, your G.I. husband is no longer president of the club. And it's a big load off my chest. The new president is Lt. Hoyt, and he'll be good at it. He shouldn't have a whole lot of trouble, because there really isn't too much to do now except worry about installing a snack bar." Afterwards, there was a stage show at the 16th Bomb Group called *Bedtime Stories* put on by GIs from the 314th Bomb Wing at North Field. The show was modeled on *This is the Army*, Irving Berlin's traveling all-GI show that had visited Guam in August and featured "talent" from units stationed at North Field. The band was the same one that had played for the Grand Opening of Harvey's Officers' Club. All of the performers were men, many of them dressed as "sexy" women, and as Harvey noted, it was pretty "raw" at times. "One of the best amateur army shows I've seen. It was written strictly for a male audience and some of the stuff was a little raw, but not disgustingly so. After the stage show, there was a movie I had already seen, 'Weekend at the Waldorf' but the two guys I was with hadn't seen it and I sat through it again. It was really good, so I didn't mind. The stage show started at 6:30 tonight, and the movie didn't end until just now.... (about midnight!)." With his letter that night, Harvey included an article about the stage show:

Bedtime Stories
by S/Sgt. Willis K. Jones

G.I. Life has, at last, been touched with glamour, mystery and music too, right in the 314th Bomb Wing's new all G.I. show, Bedtime Stories, (FOR ADULTS), which is now touring the 20th Air Force.

This zestful and delightfully rowdy musical, with its extravagant sets and clever skits, brings a touch of Broadway and Never Never Land to the Rock, but we wonder how many soldiers will recognize their favorite fairy tales in these highly contemporary and hotted-up versions.

Pfc. Blaine Berner of New York, writer, and producer, was assisted by Cpl. Jack Kunin, Philadelphia, and Pvt. Max Ackerman, New York. Sgt. Eugene Klavan, Baltimore, wrote the new lyrics and the narration.

After a rousing opening chorus, "Eagers, American Eagers", things really got going when Klavan, a contented latrine orderly, who is intent on improving his mind, starts reading "Bedtime Stories" on duty in his stream-lined latrine.

The article then goes on to describe some of the show's scenes: "Army Camp," about Master Sergeant, "an eight-striper with luxurious military quarters"; an adagio dance about the girl on the VD poster whose partner doesn't seem to pay attention to the warnings; and "Snow White" where Dopey is the only one of the dwarves to avoid the draft. The intermission featured the 314th Band with GI vocalists, supplemented by Sgt. Francis Nogle on the piano. The finale was a "Scheherazade"-themed ballet number.

Just after supper on Tuesday, the camp was rocked by a huge explosion, which shook buildings all over the area. "I jumped in my jeep and went out to see it, and sure enough, a dynamite storage dump about a mile from our area had blown sky high. There were three huge warehouses housing somewhere in the neighborhood of ten tons of T.N.T. and dynamite, and now there is hardly a trace of any of them. The concussion was terrific!! First we saw this blinding flash, and then a huge cloud of smoke, a lot like those photos you've seen of atomic bomb explosions, and then about ten seconds later, that awful blast. Two guards haven't been found yet. There will probably be an item about it in one of our papers tomorrow, so I'll clip it out for you."

That night, Harvey and his buddies were back at the theater, and he saw another movie he had seen before, *Those Endearing Young Charms*. "And surprisingly, it was good the second time, too! I guess it's because there were lots of little things about it that reminded me of you."

With his next letter, Harvey enclosed the article about the explosion, along with another one describing an attack that weekend by a group of Japanese soldiers still hiding on the island. Clearly, Guam was still a dangerous place, even as the Americans were gradually being sent home:

Two Missing as Dynamite Explosion at Northwest Field Rocks Island

A giant explosion rocked Guam last night when a dynamite dump at the Northwest end of the island blew up. At least two men are known to be missing.

The explosion occurred at 18:15 at the 927th Engineer Battalion area, which is near Northwest Field. The blast was heard as far away as Orote peninsula and a sheet of flame 1,000 feet high was seen.

Cause of the explosion is as yet undetermined, but a party under the direction of Major James H. Holtenroth, USA, 1869 Engineer Battalion commander, is conducting an investigation of the accident.

Six dynamite sheds, filled with high explosives, were demolished. One shed exploded and completely levelled the others. They were 50 feet by 18 feet and set five feet above the ground.

Sticks of dynamite and containers were strewn over 1,000 square yards, and the area for a quarter of a mile around the dump was completely devastated.

Two guard tents were blown away by the concussion and trees were uprooted. For safety reasons, the dynamite area was located at a considerable distance from the rest of the camp. No other casualties have been reported.

A careful search for the two guards posted in the dynamite area was made last night with the aid of a battery of mobile searchlights."

Special Marine, Guam Police Patrols Sweep Island in Widespread Jap Hunt

Special reconnaissance patrols have been scouring the Asan Point area for Japanese renegades who shot down a four-man Marine patrol on Saturday, Col. Howard N. Stent, USMC, Island Command Intelligence Officer, announced yesterday.

Units of the 3rd Marine Division still based on Guam and the 9th Marine Anti-Aircraft Artillery Battalion are expected to take up the hunt to sweep the area for the remaining Japanese.

Continuous small reconnaissance patrols must be used at present to ferret out the renegades because the Japanese quickly go into hiding when they encounter large searching parties. "These Japs are the few obnoxious ones left on the island," authorities said. "They will be treated as desperadoes and shot down at sight if they attempt to resist when they are apprehended. There are numerous other Japanese on the island, but for the most part, they only constitute a minor annoyance, stealing small quantities of food and clothing.

Supplementing Marine activities, the Guam Police department's combat patrol has been combing the area. 1st Lt. Joseph F. Anderson, police chief, said that those causing the present disturbances are part of a group the combat patrol contacted August 10 when the Japanese opened fire on the patrol near Piti. The patrol killed two and wounded the third.

The all-Guamanian police patrol is led by S/Sgt. Juan U. Aguon, former Lt. colonel in the local militia. Most of the members acted as guides for the 3rd Marine Division and the 177th Army Division during the war. To date, they have accounted for 117 Japanese dead and have taken five prisoners.

The unit has been enlarged to fifteen men since Saturday's incident and is now operating in the form of two patrols which work together and coordinate their tactics so as to achieve a minor scale pincers movement on their objective. "These men are all picked scouts who are unsurpassed in hunting down Japanese in their jungle habitat," said Lt. Anderson.

Helen Hunt's husband, Jack, and his friend Sgt. Anderson visited Harvey at Northwest Field, and they spend an entire afternoon visiting and chatting about Betty and Helen. "We took a short ride around the field so they could get a look at things here, and then we went down to the office and sat until after four thirty. He thinks he's probably got about two more months or so to go before he can start sweating out his discharge, and he thinks that before then he may be shipped to Manilla. He shouldn't worry too much about that because his eligibility for discharge won't change, although I understand that transportation there is a little more critical. Maybe you shouldn't mention his move to Helen because I don't know whether or not he told her about it."

Harvey had been part of the team from the Utilities Section that had worked on the Red Cross Building. The group was asked to the new facility for an informal get-together, and Harvey went along. "That night was their official opening, so we got more or less a sneak preview. They had coffee, doughnuts, and ice cream for us in large quantities. I ate as much as I could, since it was the first opportunity I'd ever had to make use of a Red Cross Service. It is strictly an enlisted man's club, so we officers stayed in the background as much as possible. The movie tonight was an Olsen and Johnson show which everyone said was terrible, so I didn't bother going." Olsen and Johnson (Ole Olsen and Chic Johnson) were a slapstick comedy team who starred on radio and in a series of movies in the 1930s and 1940s. The picture that Harvey skipped that night was probably *See My Lawyer*, which Universal had released earlier that year.

He received a package from Betty on Thursday and, along with other items, it contained a pair of slippers. "I'm not going to wear them now but will save them for the trip home which I'm almost positive will be by boat. By that time my moccasins will be just about gone, so I'll change into the slippers on shipboard. Now I'm going to tell you something, but I don't want you to count on it at all because there are so many chances for it to fall through. There is a chance that I may get to leave here on the 20th of this month. An outfit is leaving here then, and it is expected to hit the States about the 5th of January. I have a small chance of going along with them, and I'm using all my energy in that direction. I'll keep you posted on my progress along that line. Mac and Sol Mayer may be on that boat, too."

On the 14th, since he hadn't heard anything to the contrary, Harvey was still hoping to leave Guam on the 20th, only a week from the time he was writing his next letter. "The thing we are worried about is the fact that MacArthur, who is now in command of Air Force units in the Pacific, is against men leaving for the States before they actually become eligible. Men with 48 months service won't be eligible to go before January 1st, but the 20th Air Force has been doing their very best to send men out so they will be in the States when they become due for discharge. Don't know why MacArthur wants to change the system, but it's got all of us sweating. So far, I'm due to leave the 20th, but it anything changes, I'll let you know. Bill Zierenberg is leaving here on Sunday. I sure hate to lose him, but I wouldn't hold him here even if I could. Without a doubt, he's the best all-around soldier I ever saw. Bar none. His work was the selling point that got me my captaincy. And through our whole tour of duty together in the 75th, there wasn't a thing I could do to get him a promotion. But at least he knows I really tried. I'm O.D. (officer of the day) tomorrow and have to get up earlier than usual, so I'll knock off now and try to write a longer letter tomorrow."

On the 15th, Harvey was still sorting out his property account. "The whole property set-up in the Wing is so screwed up that it's hard to make heads or tails of anything. I'm thanking my lucky stars that I started so soon to clear my account. If I had waited until I found out how close I was to going home, I never would have made it. I still haven't got definite word I'll leave here on the 20th, but the situation still looks favorable. Jimmy Ray left this morning, and the ship he is on should reach the States in about two weeks. That should put him in L.A. harbor around New Year's Day. I hope I get a break and land there, too. When I finally get to the States, I don't know where they will send me for discharge, but it shouldn't be too far from Los Angeles since I've got your house listed as my home address."

Harvey was finally allowing himself to start making plans with Betty for AFTER his discharge. "What sort of tentative plans have you got in mind for us after I get home? I've been thinking about it quite a bit, and all I can picture in my mind is spending all the time possible alone with you. As far as going back East is concerned, I haven't given much thought to it at all. I doubt very much whether you'll be able to write me about any of this since I hope to have left before a return letter can get back, but I do want you to think about what you would like us to do. And, whatever you think we ought to do is exactly what we will do! I'm just hoping and praying that I can find a job that will let me spend 24 hours a day with you. Maybe one of those rich uncles (which I don't have) will leave me a million or two? Think I'll get in touch with a couple of those uncles (which I still don't have!)."

There wasn't much going on in camp on Sunday. Harvey slept in, and after supper went to the movie and saw *Main Street After Dark* with Edward Arnold. "I used to think his pictures were all pretty good, but the last ones have been strictly 'Class B'. Still nothing on our leaving here as yet. I should know in the next day or two. Usually, the officers don't find out they are leaving until the day before, so when I give you the word, I won't be here much longer."

The ups and downs of discharge plans was tough on all the officers, and there was more bad news for Mac on Monday. "This morning he got a call from the personnel section that there was an opening for five officers on a B-24 leaving tomorrow morning and that Mac was in the top five on the list. He started to finish packing right away and was in a lather all day trying to make it in time. Finally, at supper time he was just about finished and was having sweet visions of being in the States by Christmas, when "personnel" called again to say a mistake had been made and only one officer could go.... Mac's morale just plopped to the bottom. He's a nervous character anyway, and this just about put the finishing touches to him. There has been a mix-up on the boat that leaves on the 20th, too, so I don't know just where I stand either. But I'm all set to go as soon as they give me a "go" sign.

"We went to the show tonight to see 'Mildred Pierce' with Joan Crawford, and the jokers changed programs on us by showing 'Out of this World', which I had already seen. Such a business."

Finally, on Tuesday, December 18th, Harvey got the news he had been waiting for, and this time it appeared to be more than just a rumor. "Orders are coming out tomorrow for Mac and I and seven other officers to leave. We take off from here on a boat bound for Saipan on Friday, the 21st. We'll probably stay there a couple of days until they get a full boatload arranged, and then we'll leave for the States. I have no idea which boat it will be or what port it will enter when it comes in, or even when it will get there, but I'll try to let you know ahead of time if I can. We should get to Saipan on Friday afternoon, and maybe will get out of there that weekend. I sure hope so, anyway. Unless we have an awfully slow boat, or we have to wait in Saipan longer than I think, we should dock in the States before the 15th of January. Golly, doesn't it sound wonderful!

"I've got my footlocker all packed up with clothes and stuff, and it's too heavy to send by Parcel Post, so I guess I'll have to send it via the quartermaster service which will probably take from three to six weeks. But I'm not too particular, just as long as it gets there eventually. I'm glad we got this length of time to get ready because now I'll have everything all cleaned up before I leave here. Some of these guys have been leaving on such short notice that they have hardly had time to pack their clothes. We go through a processing line tomorrow morning at nine o'clock where all our records will be checked, etc. Then we'll have some free time until the boat leaves on Friday. I've got a few people I want to see before I leave, so I'll spend that time running around the island (Jack, Bob Anthony, and a few more.) Maybe I'm putting the cart before the horse on this since something could still go wrong, but frankly, this looks like 'D-day' for me. (D meaning discharge!!) I got hold of a Japanese rifle today which I'm going to send home, so if a long, thin box arrives, you'll see it's not an umbrella. That's the only Japanese article I've been able to get so far, unless I have a little luck before I leave.

"I hung my B-4 bag out to air today so it wouldn't be quite so musty smelling when I pack it. Wouldn't you know it would rain! Now, I've got to sweat out getting it dry. One thing for sure – it's well aired!! The rain has come down, on and off, for the last week or so, and it begins to look as if the island is in for another rainy season. Four of the nine who are shipping are bridge players, and I'll bet we have some rare games on the way back. It will probably be a casual shipment, and we shouldn't have anything to do but rest and enjoy the ride.

"I'll write to you from Saipan, darling, and try to let you know as much as possible about our schedule and route from there on. This is the news I've been waiting nine months to tell you, and now that it's here, I can hardly believe it. Oh, Happy Day!"

With his letter, Harvey enclosed an article about another 23 more Japanese soldiers who had recently come out of the jungle after learning of the surrender:

23 Japanese Read of War's End, Give Up Here

Twenty-two (Japanese) soldiers and an 18-year-old Geisha girl came out of the wilds of Guam and gave themselves up yesterday after reading in a magazine that Japan had surrendered.

Despite an extensive campaign which has brought in 445 other Japanese since Aug. 15, the group claimed that they did not learn of the war's end until they saw a picture in a magazine of the Tokyo surrender ceremony.

They told Colonel Howard N. Stent, USMC, of Warner Springs, Calif., and island Command G-2 officer, they suspected things were going badly for Japan upon reading an earlier issue of the magazine that the war was over. But when the issue containing the surrender pictures came, they were convinced the first story was not mere propaganda. After conferring with his buddies and the girl friend, the English-speaking member of the holdouts sat down and penned this note, possibly to the periodical's editor:

"The War ends! Comes peace in the World! We are join! We had been lived in this Jangle from last year, but now we known by this book that the war end - now we comes from this jangle. Please give me answer of next word. No. 1 When came ship we ride on from Japan? No. 2 Where we go from this land?"

The note was tacked onto a coconut tree beside a path. When no one had found their message eight days later, the group became impatient, ripped their note from the tree and rushed to the nearest highway, where they flagged down the first passing truck to surrender to the startled driver.

The expected orders did, indeed, come out Wednesday, finalizing the first stage of homeward travel plans for Harvey, Mac, and their seven fellow officers from the 75th. Harvey sent a copy of the orders to Betty, warning her that it was written in military shorthand. Harvey and Mac were listed among the officers released from duty in Guam: "Capt. John H. Brown, Venice, California," and "1st Lt. Arthur W. McKinney, St. Louis, MO."

R-E-S-T-R-I-C-T-E-D

HEADQUARTERS
315TH BOMBARDMENT WING

SPECIAL ORDER NUMBER 228
18 DECEMBER 1945

[A rough translation from the "military shorthand."]
The following named Officers are released from assignment and duty as indicated and attached unassigned on or about December 21, 1945, to WPEC Personnel Center & Casual Depot, APO 244 (Saipan), for further processing under current readjustment regulations under authority indicated below. The CO of Officers will ensure that all pertinent records are checked and forwarded. Officers will advise correspondents of a non-military address.

"So, everything seems to be all set for us to leave on or about Friday. Mac and I are all finished here. We didn't have a thing to do but wait for the boat to leave. We've finished all of our packing, and I'm ready to send my footlocker(s) home in the morning. I decided I'd try to send mine by parcel post, and since it weighed too much I got hold of two small boxes. I think the two of them will get under the line. I got rid of as much clothing as possible, trying to save what I might use a little later on. There's a possibility we may leave here tomorrow some time, so if you don't get a letter tomorrow night, you'll know what happened. Incidentally, your mail hasn't been coming through, and I haven't had a letter for four days...I hope my mail isn't being delayed on your end.

"We thought we'd go to the movies one last time. We saw 'Junior Miss' tonight and I think it's the best I've seen in a long time. I thought Mac and Herrick and I would die laughing! ... don't miss it."

Harvey wrote his last letter from Guam after midnight on Thursday, December 20th. He had been on the island for over seven months, and it seemed unreal that he would finally be leaving in the morning. "We leave the area here at 7:15 tomorrow morning, so I won't write at length. I got three of your letters today – the last mail I'll get from you, because I'll be enroute from now on. I finally decided to pack your letters, and they'll be in my foot lockers when they finally get home. Don't know why I even thought about throwing them away in the first place!! *[My note: I'm glad you didn't!!]* A bunch of the boys from the 75th had a little get-together tonight, so the nine of us went to the show and saw 'Anchors Aweigh' with Sinatra, Gene Kelly, and Kathryn Grayson. Not too good. Kelly's dancing was swell, Sinatra's singing was mediocre, and Kathryn Grayson's claims to fame seem to be a fair voice and a well-filled sweater. After the show, we had two tables of bridge for a couple of rubbers while we had a few drinks and a couple of cheese sandwiches. Had a great time! (Remind me to tell you about the deer we hit with our jeep.) Here's a big, extra-long, kiss until I see you in person! That shouldn't be more than three weeks from now, unless things go haywire on Saipan. I'll write from there to let you know how we make out."

30

ONE LAST LETTER

TO GUAM

On Saturday night (December 1, 1945), Betty and Helen Hunt represented their Culver City Bethel at a Job's Daughter's Installation in Hollywood. "We were late getting there because we got tied up in traffic. Imagine having the Masonic Temple on Hollywood Blvd. right across from the Grauman's Chinese Theater! We parked in a little auto park about 5 blocks away so we wouldn't get mixed up in the traffic on the boulevard (Alfred Hitchcock's 'Spellbound' was playing at Grauman's!). Can't you see us dashing all that way down Hollywood Blvd. in our formals?" Strangely, it was the next day that Harvey met Helen's husband Jack in Guam.

That afternoon, Betty's dad had been to the Los Angeles Coliseum to see USC play UCLA. He enjoyed the game, which the Trojans won 26-15. "And how about that Army – Navy game? Pretty good! I imagine you all heard that one over there...by the way, did we make any money on bets?" (Army won 32-13, and President Truman was at the game in Philadelphia.)

Rod also wrote to Harvey on December 1 and filled him in on the beginnings of his military career. "Five of us left L.A. on October 30 and arrived here in Aberdeen on Nov. 4. On the way, we stopped in Chicago for a day. It's quite a city. I remembered a little from our previous visits. We also had about four hours in Washington, D.C., and it is really beautiful. I want to go back and see more of the town though. We've finished our third week of basic training now. It's not too bad, but the cold really gets me. We go to the rifle range next week. I've been appointed platoon sergeant because of the shortage of 'cadies' (graduates of Special Cadet School). In about two weeks I have a chance to go to Cadet School and come out a Corporal and stay here to train new men. What do you think of it? Maybe I can get transferred to a camp in California! We have rain here too, but it never stops. Always wet, and the cold wind doesn't help. We march, practice bayonet and everything right in the rain. I'm planning to go to Baltimore tomorrow and look the town over!"

On Monday night, Betty and several of her friends went to the movies at the Strand Theater in San Pedro to see *Hurricane*. "That old one with Jon Hall and Dottie Lamour. I still liked it even though we'd seen it years ago. Did you see it? There was some terrific photography in it and a couple of torrid love scenes – wow! The second feature was something about radio stars with Frances Langford and Skinnay Ennis, etc. Very clever, and I think you would have liked that one too." *(Note: the second film was Radio Stars on Parade.)*

Both Betty and Harvey wrote letters on Friday. Betty chatted about her Christmas shopping, about some family news, and about how much she missed Harvey. Harvey focused on his bridge games, on the ongoing rumors about discharge plans, and on how much he missed Betty. Interestingly, that Friday was December 7th, the fourth anniversary of the attack on Pearl Harbor, and neither of them mentioned it in their letters! During the war, the date had been a rallying point for the country, but all that changed with the end of hostilities. Like everyone else, Harvey and Betty were now more focused on getting back together. The only person to mention the date was Harvey's mother in Pittsburgh. "Pearl Harbor Day is here and gone again. How the world has changed in the last four years."

A special collection of records came into Stella's, and Betty sent them on to Harvey in Guam. "Here are the 'G.I.' records I got such a kick out of. I'm sending the folder along in another package so you can put the records back in them. They were made by G.I.'s who were professional musicians before the war and all proceeds from the sale of the records go to some fund or other. The tree with the album is for the officers club!"

Betty wrote one last brief letter to Harvey in Guam on Thursday, December 13, 1945. At least it is the last of her letters to be passed down over the years. She had just received a note from him, dated the 8th, saying he might be flying home rather than being sent by troop ship, and it's likely she doubted any further letters would reach him before he left. There were a couple of "I wonder where you are now" letters that she sent to the Army in hopes he might get them eventually, but this letter of the 13th was the last directed to him in Guam.

USS CLERMONT BOUND

FOR LOS ANGELES

Harvey and the others boarded a ship at the Navy base on Guam at 7:30 in the morning on Thursday, December 20, 1945, and by mid-afternoon they were in Saipan. They were there for a week, spending Christmas waiting for transport back to the States.

On Saturday, December 22nd, Betty wrote to Harvey, knowing he had left Guam and probably wouldn't receive the letter until he got home. The letter was returned to Venice! "Gosh, by now you may be two days out! It doesn't seem real! I got two letters from you in the afternoon mail, finally - the first since Monday, and they were written on the 13th and the 15th. I hope the deal about your leaving on the 20th went through OK. That would mean you'd be home in two weeks!! I'm the happiest girl in the world! Poor Mac, he really should be home by now, shouldn't he? I'll bet Dottie is disgusted with the whole deal. That's grand that Jimmy Ray is landing here in L.A., but I doubt he will be able to leave the ship. Thousands of boys who are on the ships are being held aboard because there is no transportation available. Only boys who live in California are getting off. Maybe if he'd give our address it would help? We'd be glad to let him stay here if it would make it easier for him. Boy, it would be no fun sitting looking at the docks and not be able to get off the ship. You'll probably get your discharge in Mac Arthur (San Pedro). That is where Rod went in. They are sending transfers through there, too.

"As far as what we are going to do - that will work itself out nicely, I'm sure. As long as we are together, that's all that really matters. I do feel it is only fair that we go back East to see your folks and spend some time there. You have a job waiting for you there, and if it is still what you want to do – fine. You may even want to go back in the Army when you see what a mess everything is in over here in civilian life! Eventually, I'd like for us to have our home in California. With some land, even a couple of lots – for our children to grow strong and healthy. But time will tell. We'll live wherever we are supposed to live, and we'll be happy!"

On Sunday, the 23rd, Betty tried to find a news program from Guam on the radio but didn't have any luck. The worst storm of the season had hit Southern California, and heavy rain and mud slides had damaged homes and blocked highways. She sent a clipping about the storm with her brief letter.

On the day after Christmas, orders were issued for Harvey's trip home, and he wrote a letter to Betty. "Well, honey, orders came out for us today, and we leave here tomorrow aboard the USS Clermont bound for Los Angeles! We will debark at San Pedro and should be there around the 10th or 12th of January, if things go as planned. I'm sure they will.

"We have a baggage inspection at 9:00 in the morning and we board the ship about noon or so. If the loading isn't too slow, we'll be able to get out of the harbor here before six in the morning. The boat is one that is known as an A.P.A. and was used during the war to carry large numbers of troops to beach heads etc. It's not a bad boat and should be fairly comfortable. We'll have about 2000 enlisted men with us and around 25 officers. That's a capacity load for this tub 'cause the Navy isn't wasting any space at all!!

"I saw Mac and the rest off this morning. It was kind of hard to see them go, but before they got away, our shipment was announced so we didn't feel too bad about it. It would have been much nicer if we could have all gone together, but that's the Army for you. I can hardly sit still, just waiting for this old boat to bring me back to you. After all these months of waiting, I can just barely bring myself to realize that at last I'm really on my way <u>home</u>!! I'm not even conscious of what I'm doing or what is going on around me. And I'll bet I don't come out of it until I finally see you again. I hope they don't hold me too long at the separation center, because it'll be tough knowing I'm in the same country with you and not actually with you. But a couple of days should see it finished. I love you so much."

Betty wrote a quick note to Harvey on Sunday, the 30th. "I'm listening to the radio, and they are playing 'I'll be Walkin' with My Honey Down Honeymoon Lane (Soon, Soon, Soon)'...how true!! I wonder where you are now? Maybe at Pearl Harbor? Hope you get a good look around the Islands if you have any kind of layover there. Funny – here I am talking to you, and you'll probably read the letter when you come back and are parked here close to me!" The Army sent her letter back a week later. It was the last letter either one of them ever needed to send to the other!

Harvey wasn't able to write again before the *Clermont* left Saipan on December 27th, but the following notice appeared in many US newspapers on Friday, January 11th:

25,000 COMING TO U.S. TODAY

20 Ships Due to Dock at Various East and West Ports
By United Press

Twenty ships were due to dock at east and west coast ports today with more that 25,000 servicemen.

[Among the ships listed was:]
Due at Wilmington, California:
U.S.S. Clermont from Saipan - 2049 undesignated personnel

ACKNOWLEDGMENTS

When I first thought about writing this book, I had my doubts. Writing was what other people did, not me. With the support and encouragement of family and friends, I took the plunge and, over the next two years, *900 Letters* slowly took shape. I occasionally sent "snippets" of the project to family and friends, and their support reassured me that this story was interesting and worth telling.

Thank you to everyone who helped so much during the writing of *900 Letters*. I can't possibly mention everyone who helped me, but please know that your support has been appreciated. You know who you are.

Thank you to my entire family for your support. I want to especially thank Elizabeth and our daughters, Maggie and Sophie, whose affection and encouragement keep me going. I love you.

Thank you to all of my friends—from Hastings Ranch (Bob, Peter, Dave, Storm, Craig, Charlie, and Gary); from Vassar and the Ramblers; from Pomona, Colgate, and Cornell; from Hawaii and Scandinavia; from Scandinavian Seminar and Elderhostel. You, too, know who you are, and you know how much your support means.

Special thanks go to Gregg Bachman for his advice and guidance throughout the writing process; to Dave Greenlee, who was writing his first book as I was writing *900 Letters*, and whose thoughtful feedback was always on point; and to Gard Holby for sharing his own family's experiences on Guam during the war.

Additionally, I want to thank Matt Seelinger, Chief Historian at The National Museum of the United States Army, and Archangelo DiFante and

Tammy T. Horton at the Air Force Archives-Maxwell AFB, for their help in securing access to the official history of the 75th Air Service Group.

I also want to thank Dory and Colin at Epigraph Publishing for their professional and caring advice to this first-time author.

Finally, and most importantly, I want to thank my parents, Betty and Harvey Brown, for sharing their story with the family and now with readers of this book. It has been more than seventy-five years since you wrote these letters, and you have given us an amazing peek at what life was like during those war years. Thank you, Mom and Dad. We love you, and we miss you.

—DB Brown

Appendix A

MOVIES MENTIONED

IN 900 LETTERS

CHAPTER 4 - *Fort Belvoir to Patterson to Middletown*

For Me and My Gal (MGM, 1942)
Gene Kelly/Judy Garland/George Murphy
Filmed at MGM Studios, Culver City, CA.

Johnny Doughboy (Republic, 1943)
Jane Withers/Henry Wilcoxon
Filmed at Republic Studios, North Hollywood, CA.

Stand By for Action (MGM, 1942)
Robert Taylor/Brian Donlevy/Charles Laughton
Filmed at MGM Studios, Culver City, CA.

CHAPTER 5 - *Camouflage*

Bataan (MGM, 1943)
Robert Taylor/George Murphy/Lloyd Nolan
Filmed at Hollywood, CA; MGM Studios, Culver City, CA.

Coney Island (Twentieth Century Fox, 1943)
Betty Grable/George Montgomery
Filmed at Twentieth Century Fox Studios, Century City, CA.

Crash Dive (Twentieth Century Fox, 1943)
Tyrone Power/Anne Baxter/Dana Andrews
Filmed at U.S. Submarine Base in New London, CT; Twentieth Century Fox Studios,
Century City, CA.

Early to Bed (Paramount, 1936)
Mary Boland/Charles Ruggles
Filmed at Paramount Studios, Hollywood, CA.

Guadalcanal Diary (Twentieth Century Fox, 1943)
Preston Foster/Lloyd Nolan
Filmed at Camp Pendleton, CA; Catalina Island, CA; Twentieth Century Fox Studios,
Century City, CA.

Hit Parade of 1943 (Republic, 1943
John Carroll/Susan Hayward
Filmed at Republic Studios, Encino, CA.

Orchestra Wives (Twentieth Century Fox, 1942)
George Montgomery/Ann Rutherford
Filmed at Twentieth Century Fox Studios, Century City, CA.

Saludos Amigos (Walt Disney Productions, 1942)
Filmed at Lake Titicaca, Bolivia; Rio de Janeiro, Brazil; Walt Disney Feature
Animation, Burbank, CA.

Sweet Rosie O'Grady (Twentieth Century Fox, 1943)
Betty Grable/Robert Young
Filmed at Twentieth Century Fox Studios. Century City, CA.

The Iron Major (RKO, 1943)
Pat O'Brien/Robert Ryan
Filmed at Boston College, MA; Boston University School of Law, MA; Dartmouth
College, NH; College
of the Holy Cross University, MA; University of Cincinnati, OH; RKO Studios,
Hollywood, CA.

The Purple Heart (Twentieth Century Fox, 1944)
Dana Andrews/Richard Conte
Filmed in Washington, D.C.; Twentieth Century Fox Studios, Century City, CA.

Top Man (Universal, 1943)
Donald O'Connor, Suzanne Foster, Peggy Ryan
Filmed at Universal Studios, Studio City, CA.

CHAPTER 8 - *Bivouac*

Dragon Seed (MGM, 1944)
Katherine Hepburn/Walter Huston
Filmed at Chinatown, Los Angeles, CA; John Show Ranch, Woodland Hills, CA;
Calabasas, CA; MGM Studios, Culver City, CA.

CHAPTER 10 - *Landing Strip in Mississippi*

Arsenic and Old Lace (Warner Bros., 1944)
Cary Grant/Priscilla Lane
Filmed on Stages 6,9,19, Warner Bros. Studios, Burbank, CA.

Casanova Brown (International Pictures, 1944)
Gary Cooper/Teresa Wright
Filmed in Hurricane, UT; Cedars of Lebanon Hospital, Hollywood, CA.

San Diego, I Love You (Universal, 1944)
Jon Hall/Louise Allbritton
Filmed in San Diego, CA; Universal Studios, Studio City, CA.

The Merry Monahans (Universal, 1944)
Donald O'Connor/Peggy Ryan
Filmed at Universal Studios, Studio City, CA.

CHAPTER 11 - *Secret Letters*

The Woman in the Window (Christie Corp., 1944)
Edward G. Robinson/Joan Bennett
Filmed in New York City, NY; Samuel Goldwyn Studios, West Hollywood, CA;
Paramount Studios, Hollywood, CA; RKO Studios, Los Angeles, CA; Selznick
Studios, New York City, NY; PRC Studios, West Hollywood, CA.

CHAPTER 12 - *President Stricken*

I'll Remember April (Universal, 1945)

Gloria Jean
Filmed at Universal Studios, Universal City, CA.

Let's Go Steady (Columbia, 1945)
Jackie Moran/June Preisser/Pat Parrish

Sudan (Universal, 1945)
Maria Montez/Jon Hall
Filmed in Gallup, NM; backlot of Universal Studios, Studio City, CA.

Tonight and Every Night (Columbia, 1945)
Rita Hayworth/Lee Bowman/Janet Blair
Filmed in London, England.

CHAPTER 13 – *The Kota Baroe*

Fashion Model (Monogram, 1945)
Robert Lowery/Marjorie Weaver

Here Come the Co-eds (Universal, 1945)
Bud Abbott/Lou Costello
Filmed at UCLA, Westwood, CA; North Hollywood Park, Hollywood, CA; Universal
Studios, Studio City, CA.

Hi Diddle Diddle (Andrew L. Stone Productions, United Artists, 1943)
Adolphe Menjou/Martha Scott

It's a Pleasure (International, 1945)
Sonja Henie/Michael O'Shea
Filmed at Tropical Ice Garden, Westwood, CA; the Hollywood Polar Palace,
Hollywood, CA.

The Lives of a Bengal Lancer (Paramount, 1935)
Gary Cooper/Franchot Tone
Filmed at Alabama Hills, CA; Lone Pine/Iverson Ranch, Chatsworth, CA; Paramount
Ranch,
Agoura, CA; Red Rock Canyon State Park, CA; the Buttes, Palmdale, CA; Buffalo
Flats, Malibu, CA;
Paramount Studios, Hollywood, CA.

Roughly Speaking (Warner Bros., 1945)
Rosalind Russell/Jack Carson
Filmed at Terminal Island, Wilmington, CA; Warner Bros. Studios, Burbank, CA.

San Francisco, (MGM, 1936)
Clark Gable/Jeanette McDonald/Spencer Tracy
Filmed at MGM studios, Culver City, CA; background footage from San Francisco, CA.

South of the Border (Republic, 1939)
Gene Autry/Smiley Burnette
Filmed at Republic Movie Ranch, Soledad Canyon, CA; Republic Studios, Encino, CA.

CHAPTER 15 - *26 Days, 5700 Miles*

A Song to Remember (Columbia, 1945)
Paul Muni/Merle Oberon/Cornel Wilde

After the Thin Man (MGM, 1936)
William Powell/Myrna Loy
Filmed at MGM studios, Culver City, CA.

Gentle Annie (MGM, 1944)
James Craig/Donna Reed
Filmed in Agoura, CA; MGM studios, Culver City, CA.

Jezebel (Warner Bros., 1938)
Bette Davis/Henry Fonda
Filmed in LA; Chatsworth, CA; Stages 1,4,11,20,21,24,26, Warner Studios, Burbank, CA.

CHAPTER 16 - *Salesmen from Capitol and Decca*

A Royal Scandal (Twentieth Century Fox, 1945)
Charles Coburn/Tallulah Bankhead
Filmed at Twentieth Century Fox Studios, Century City, CA.

Brewster's Millions (Universal, 1945)
Dennis O'Keefe/Helen Walker
Filmed at Universal Studios, Universal City, CA.

Bring on the Girls (Paramount, 1945)
Veronica Lake/Sonny Tufts/Eddy Bracken
Filmed at Paramount Studios, Hollywood, CA.

Dark Waters (Benedict Bogeaus, 1944)
Franchot Tone/Merle Oberon
Filmed at General Service Studios, Hollywood, CA.

Rough, Tough and Ready (Columbia, 1945)
Chester Morris/Jean Rogers/Victor McLaglen

The Horn Blows at Midnight (Warner Bros, 1945)
Jack Benny/Alexis Smith
Filmed at Warner Bros. Studios in Burbank, CA.

The Keys of the Kingdom (Twentieth Century Fox, 1944)
Gregory Peck/Thomas Mitchell
Filmed in Laguna, CA; Malibu, CA; Stage 9, Twentieth Century Studios, Century City, CA.

The Three Caballeros (Walt Disney, 1944)
Aurora Miranda/Carmen Molina
Filmed in Acapulco, Mexico; Veracruz, Mexico; Pátzcuaro, Mexico; Walt Disney Studios, Burbank, CA.

CHAPTER 17 - *"El Gecko" Theater*

Between Two Women (MGM, 1945)
Van Johnson/Lionel Barrymore/Gloria DeHaven
Filmed at MGM Studios, Culver City, CA.

Dark Waters (see Chapter 16)

Enter Arsene Lupin (Universal, 1944)
Ella Raines/Charles Korvin
Filmed at Universal Studios, Universal City, CA.

Gambler's Choice (Paramount, 1944)
Chester Morris/Nancy Kelly

Filmed at Paramount Studios, Hollywood, CA.

Girl Crazy (MGM, 1943)
Mickey Rooney/Judy Garland/Gil Stratton
Filmed near Palm Springs, CA; MGM Studios, Culver City, CA.

Ladies of Washington (Twentieth Century Fox, 1944)
Trudy Marshall/Ronald Graham/Anthony Quinn
Filmed at Twentieth Century Fox Studios, Century City, CA.

Mrs. Miniver (MGM, 1942)
Greer Garson/Walter Pidgeon
Filmed at MGM Studios, Culver City, CA.

Saratoga Trunk (Warner Bros., 1945)
Gary Cooper/Ingrid Bergman
Filmed at Warner Bros. Studios, Burbank, CA.

The Keys of the Kingdom (see Chapter 16)

The Story of Louis Pasteur (Warner Bros., 1936)
Paul Muni/Josephine Hutchinson
Filmed at Stages 12,18,22 Warner Bros. Studios, Burbank, CA.

The Woman in the Window (see Chapter 11)

Tonight and Every Night (see Chapter 12)

True to the Army (Paramount, 1942)
Allan Jones/Judy Canova/Ann Miller
Filmed at Paramount Studios, Hollywood, CA.

CHAPTER 18 - ***Sneak Preview of Anchors Aweigh***

Anchors Aweigh (MGM, 1945)
Kathryn Grayson/José Iturbi/Frank Sinatra/Gene Kelly
Filmed at Hollywood Bowl, Hollywood, CA; MGM Studios, Culver City, CA.

Earl Carroll Vanities (Republic, 1945)
Dennis O'Keefe/Constance Moore/Eve Arden

Filmed at Republic Studios, North Hollywood, CA.

Flame of Barbary Coast (Republic, 1945)
John Wayne/Ann Dvorak
Filmed at Republic Studios, North Hollywood, CA.

Patrick the Great (Universal, 1944)
Donald O'Connor/Peggy Ryan
Filmed at Universal Studios, Universal City, CA.

Strange Illusion (PRC,1945)
Jimmy Lydon/Sally Eilers

They Were Expendable (MGM,1945)
John Wayne/Robert Montgomery/Donna Reed
Filmed in Key Biscayne, FL; Florida Keys, FL; Miami, FL; Melville, RI; MGM Studios, Culver City, CA.

Two Girls and a Sailor (MGM, 1944)
Van Johnson/Gloria DeHaven/June Allyson
Filmed at MGM Studios, Culver City, CA.

Without Love (MGM, 1945)
Spencer Tracy/Katherine Hepburn
Filmed at MGM Studios, Culver City, CA.

CHAPTER 19 – **Out of the Jungle to Surrender**

Can't Help Singing (Universal, 1944)
Deanna Durbin/Robert Paige
Filmed in Duck Creek, UT; Navaho Lake, UT; Cedar Breaks National Monument, UT; Cedar City, UT; Lake Arrowhead, CA; Big Bear Lake, CA; Universal Studios, Universal City, CA.

Carolina Blues (Columbia, 1944)
Kay Kyser/Ann Miller

Christmas in Connecticut (Warner Bros., 1945)
Barbara Stanwyck/Dennis Morgan
Filmed at Warner Bros. Studios, Burbank, CA.

Destination Tokyo (Warner Bros.,1943)
Cary Grant, John Garfield/Alan Hale
Filmed in Portuguese Bend, CA; U.S. Naval Station, Mare Island, CA; Warner Bros. Studios, Burbank, CA.

Flame of Barbary Coast (see Chapter 18)

Having Wonderful Crime (RKO, 1945)
Pat O'Brien/George Murphy/Carole Landis
Filmed in Carmel, CA; Malibu Lake, CA; Del Monte, CA; Lakeside Country Club, Burbank, CA; RKO Studios, Hollywood, CA.

Lake Placid Serenade (Republic, 1944)
Vera Hruba Ralston/Eugene Pallette
Filmed at Republic Studios, North Hollywood, CA.

Meet Me in St. Louis (MGM, 1944)
Judy Garland/Margaret O'Brien
Filmed at La Grande railway station (corner of Santa Fe and Second Street), Los Angeles, CA; MGM Studios, Culver City, CA.

Music in Manhattan (RKO, 1944)
Anne Shirley/Dennis Day
Filmed at RKO Studios, Hollywood, CA.

Rhapsody in Blue (Warner Bros., 1945)
Robert Alda/Joan Leslie
Filmed at Warner Bros. Studios, Burbank, CA.

The Suspect (Universal, 1944)
Charles Laughton/Ella Raines
Filmed at Universal Studios, Universal City, CA.

The Women (MGM, 1939)
Norma Shearer/Joan Crawford/Rosalind Russell/Mary Boland/Paulette Goddard/ Joan Fontaine/Marjorie Main
Filmed at Los Angeles County Arboretum & Botanic Garden, Arcadia, CA; MGM Studios, Culver City, CA.

CHAPTER 20 – *Boris Karloff on Selznick Set*

Bedlam (RKO, 1946)
Boris Karloff
Filmed at RKO Studios, Hollywood, CA.

Escape in the Desert (Warner Bros., 1945)
Jean Sullivan/Philip Dorn
Filmed at Death Valley National Park, CA; Warner Bros. Studios, Burbank, CA.

Murder, He Says (Paramount, 1945)
Fred MacMurray/Helen Walker
Filmed at Paramount Studios, Hollywood, CA.

Out of This World (Paramount, 1945)
Eddie Bracken/Veronica Lake
Filmed at Paramount Studios, Hollywood, CA.

The Valley of Decision (MGM, 1945)
Greer Garson/Gregory Peck
Filmed in Pittsburgh, PA; MGM Studios, Culver City, CA.

This Love of Ours (Universal, 1945)
Merle Oberon/Charles Korvin
Filmed at Universal Studios, Universal City, CA.

Thrill of a Romance (MGM, 1945)
Van Johnson/Esther Williams
Filmed at Yosemite National Park, CA; Big Bear Lake, CA; Lake Arrowhead, CA; Arrowhead Springs Hotel, San Bernardino, CA; MGM Studios, Culver City, CA.

CHAPTER 21 – *Celebration*

A Royal Scandal (see Chapter 16)

A Tree Grows in Brooklyn (Twentieth Century Fox, 1945)
Dorothy Maguire/Joan Blondell
Filmed at Stage 5, Twentieth Century Fox Studios, Century City, CA.

Bring On the Girls (Paramount, 1945)

Veronica Lake/Sonny Tuft/Eddy Bracken
Filmed at Paramount Studios, Hollywood, CA.

Cobra Woman (Universal, 1944)
Maria Montez/Jon Hall
Filmed at Los Angeles County Arboretum & Botanic Garden, Arcadia, CA; Universal Studios, Universal City, Ca.

Crime, Inc. (Madison PRC, 1945)
Leo Carillo/Martha Tilton/Tom Neal
USA.

Dangerous Passage (Pine-Thomas, 1944)
Robert Lowery/Phyllis Brooks

For Whom the Bell Tolls (Paramount, 1943)
Gary Cooper/Ingrid Bergman
Filmed in Sacramento, CA; Sierra Nevada mountains, CA; Blue Canyon, CA; Kennedy Meadows, CA; Relief Canyon, CA; Sonora Pass,CA; NV; Paramount Studios, Hollywood, CA.

Keep Your Powder Dry (MGM, 1945)
Lana Turner/Susan Peters/Laraine Day
Filmed at Des Moines, IA; Fort Oglethorpe, GA; MGM Studios, Culver City, CA.

Mister Big (Universal, 1943)
Donald O'Connor/Gloria Jean/Peggy Ryan
Filmed at Universal Studios, Universal City, CA..

Music for Millions (MGM,1944)
Margaret O'Brien/José Iturbi/Jimmy Durante/June Allyson
Filmed at MGM Studios, Culver City, CA.

My Reputation (Warner Bros., 1946)
Barbara Stanwyck/George Brent
Filmed at Wrightwood, CA; Warner Bros. Studios, Burbank, CA.

Sahara (Columbia, 1943)
Humphrey Bogart/Bruce Bennett
Filmed in Eagle Pass, CA; Brawley, CA; Zzyzx, CA; Palm Springs, CA; Anza- Borego

Desert State Park, CA; Iverson Ranch, Chatsworth, CA; Yuma, AZ; Mojave Desert, AZ.

The Heavenly Body (MGM, 1944)
Hedy Lamarr/William Powell
Filmed at MGM Studios, Culver City, CA.

This is the Army (Warner Bros., 1943)
George Murphy/Ronald Reagan/Joan Leslie
Filmed on Stages 1,4,5,7,8,11,19,20,22,24,26,27,27A,28,28A, Warner Bros. Studios, Burbank, CA.

CHAPTER 22 – **Movie Stars Served in "Fum-Poo"**

Anchors Aweigh (see Chapter 18)

Christmas in Connecticut (see Chapter 19)

The Corn is Green (Warner Bros., 1945)
Bette Davis/John Dall/Nigel Bruce/Rhys Williams
Filmed at Warner Bros. Studios, Burbank, CA.

Keep Your Powder Dry (see Chapter 21)

Main Street After Dark (MGM, 1945)
Edward Arnold/Selena Royle
Filmed at MGM Studios, Culver City, CA.

Son of Lassie (MGM, 1945)
Peter Lawford/Donald Crisp/June Lockhart
Filmed in Jackson Hole, WY; Banff National Park, Alberta, Canada; Brentwood Bay and Patricia Bay, British Columbia, Canada.

That's the Spirit (Universal, 1945)
Peggy Ryan/Jack Oakie
Filmed at Universal Studios, Universal City, CA.

The Clock (MGM, 1945)
Judy Garland/Robert Walker

Filmed in Hollywood, CA; MGM Studios, Culver City, CA; Stage 27, Sony Pictures Studios, Culver City, CA.

The Naughty Nineties (Universal, 1945)
Bud Abbott/Lou Costello
Filmed at Universal Studios, Universal City, CA.

A Thousand and One Nights (Columbia, 1945)
Evelyn Keyes/Phil Silvers
Filmed in Vazquez Rocks Natural Area Park, CA; Santa Clarita, CA; Iverson Ranch, Chatsworth, CA; El Segundo, CA.

CHAPTER 23 – *Jeep Ride to the Southern End of the Island*

Boom Town (MGM, 1940)
Clark Gable/Spencer Tracy/Claudette Colbert/Hedy Lamarr
Filmed in Bakersfield, CA; Taft, CA; MGM Studios, Culver City, CA.

Circumstantial Evidence (Twentieth Century Fox, 1945)
Michael O'Shea/Lloyd Nolan
Filmed at Twentieth Century Fox Studios, Century City, CA.

Destry Rides Again (Universal, 1939)
(Marlene Dietrich/James Stewart
Filmed in Kernville, CA; Universal Studios, Universal City, CA.

Devotion (Warner Bros., 1946)
Ida Lupino/Olivia de Havilland
Filmed at Warner Bros. Studios, Burbank, CA.

God is My Co-Pilot (Warner Bros., 1945)
Dennis Morgan/Raymond Massey/Dane Clark
Filmed at Luke Field, AZ; Iverson Ranch, Chatsworth, CA;) Warner Bros. Studios, Burbank, CA.

Great Stagecoach Robbery (Republic, 1945)
Bill Elliot/Robert Blake
Filmed at Cudia City Studios, Phoenix, AZ.

Hangover Square (Twentieth Century Fox, 1945)

Laird Cregar/Linda Darnell/George Sanders
Filmed at Twentieth Century Fox Studios, Century City, CA.

Leave it to Blondie (Columbia, 1945)
Penny Singleton/Arthur Lake

National Velvet (MGM, 1944)
Mickey Rooney/Elizabeth Taylor
Filmed at Pebble Beach, CA; Monterey, CA; Midwick Country Club, Alhambra, CA;
Uplifters Club, Santa Monica, CA; Alhambra, CA; MGM Studios, Culver City, CA.

Show Business (RKO, 1944)
Eddie Cantor/Joan Davis/George Murphy
Filmed at RKO Studios, Hollywood, CA.

The Adventures of Robin Hood (Warner Bros., 1938)
Errol Flynn/Olivia de Havilland/Basil Rathbone
Filmed in Hooker Oak Tree, Chico, CA; Big Chico Creek, Chico Canyon, Bidwell Park,
Chico, CA; Warner Ranch, Calabasas, CA; Busch Gardens, Pasadena, CA; Sherwood
Forest, CA; Lake Sherwood, CA; Midwick Country Club, Alhambra, CA; Ray Corrigan
Ranch, Simi Valley, CA; Jungleland, Thousand Oaks, CA; Stages 4,5,11,12,18,25 and
Dijon Street, Warner Bros. Studios, Burbank, CA.

The Clock (MGM, 1945)
Judy Garland/Robert Walker
Filmed in Hollywood, CA; MGM Studios, Culver City, CA; Stage 27, Sony Pictures
Studios, Culver City, CA.

The Great Mike (PRC, 1944)
Carl "Alfalfa" Switzer/Stuart Erwin/Robert "Buzz" Henry

The Impatient Years (Columbia, 1944)
Jean Arthur/Lee Bowman/Charles Coburn
Filmed in Sonoma, CA.

The Song of Bernadette (Twentieth Century Fox, 1943)
Jennifer Jones/Charles Bickford/William Eythe
Filmed in Cherry Valley, CA; Twentieth Century Fox Ranch, Malibu Creek State Park,
Calabasas, CA; Twentieth Century Fox Studios, Century City, CA.

The Unseen (Paramount, 1945)
Joel McCrea/Gail Russell
Filmed at Paramount Studios, Hollywood, CA.

The Valley of Decision (see Chapter 20)

What a Blonde (RKO, 1945)
Leon Errol/Richard Lane
Filmed at RKO Studios, Hollywood, CA.

CHAPTER 24 – *Studio Audience for Burns and Allen*

A Bell for Adano (Twentieth Century Fox, 1945)
Gene Tierney/John Hodiak/William Bendix
Filmed in Malibu, CA; Twentieth Century Fox Studios, Century City, CA.

Conflict (Warner Bros., 1945)
Humphrey Bogart/Alexis Smith/Sydney Greenstreet
Filmed at Angeles Crest Highway, Angeles National Forest, CA; Warner Bros. Studios, Burbank, CA.

For Whom the Bell Tolls (see Chapter 21)

Guest Wife (Greentree, 1945)
Don Ameche/Claudette Colbert

Hangover Square (see Chapter 23)

Incendiary Blonde (Paramount, 1945)
Betty Hutton/Arturo de Córdova
Filmed in Tucson, AZ; Paramount Studios, Hollywood, CA.

Midnight Manhunt (Pine-Thomas, 1945)
William Gargan/Ann Savage

Million Dollar Legs (Paramount, 1939)
Betty Grable/John Hartley/Donald O'Connor
Filmed at Paramount Studios, Hollywood, CA.

Pan-Americana (RKO, 1945)

Phillip Terry/Audrey Long/Robert Benchley
Filmed at RKO Studios, Hollywood, CA.

Pride of the Marines (Warner Bros., 1945)
John Garfield/Eleanor Parker
Filmed at San Diego Naval Hospital, San Diego, CA; Philadelphia Naval Yard, St. Leo's Church, 30th Street Station, Hellerman Street, Cottman Avenue, Tulip Street, Fillmore Street, Philadelphia, PA; Warner Bros. Studios, Burbank, CA.

Spellbound (Selznick, 1945)
Ingrid Bergman/Gregory Peck
Filmed at Alta Lodge, Alta, UT; Cooper Ranch, Northridge, CA; Penn Station, New York City, NY; Grand Central Station, NY.

The Great John L. (Bing Crosby, 1945)
Linda Darnell/Barbara Britton/Greg McClure
Filmed at General Service Studios, Hollywood, CA.

The Palm Beach Story (Paramount, 1942)
Claudette Colbert/Joel McCrea
Filmed at Penn Station, New York City, NY; Paramount Studios, Hollywood, CA.

A Thousand and One Nights (see Chapter 22)

CHAPTER 25 – ***Opening Night at the Officers Club***

A Medal for Benny (Paramount, 1945)
Dorothy Lamour/Arturo de Cordova
Filmed at Paramount Studios, Hollywood, CA.

Escape in the Desert (Warner Bros., 1945)
Jean Sullivan/Philip Dorn
Filmed at Death Valley National Park, CA; Warner Bros. Studios, Burbank, CA.

Hitchhike to Happiness (Republic, 1945)
Al Pearce/Dale Evans
Filmed at Republic Studios, North Hollywood, CA.

Northwest Mounted Police (Paramount, 1940)
Gary Cooper/Madeleine Carroll/Paulette Goddard

Filmed at Big Bear Lake, San Bernardino National Forest, CA; Big Bear Valley, San Bernardino National Forest, CA; Shay Ranch, San Bernardino National Forest, CA; Paramount Studios, Hollywood, CA.

Pillow to Post (Warner Bros., 1945)
Ida Lupino/Sydney Greenstreet
Filmed at intersection Wilshire Boulevard and South Alvarado Street, Los Angeles, CA; Warner Bros. Studios, Burbank, CA.

The Corn is Green (see Chapter 22)

The Cowboy and The Lady (Samuel Goldwyn, 1938)
Gary Cooper/Merle Oberon
Filmed at Russell Ranch, New Cuyama, CA; Iverson Ranch, Chatsworth, CA; Agoura, CA; Malibu Lake, CA; Bishop, CA; Triunfo, CA; Samuel Goldwyn Studios, West Hollywood, CA.

Utah (Republic, 1945)
Roy Rogers/Dale Evans/Trigger
Filmed in Agoura Ranch,Agoura, CA; Alabama Hills,Lone Pine, CA; Iverson Ranch, Chatsworth, CA.

CHAPTER 26 – **Los Angeles Parade for Admiral Halsey**

Duffy's Tavern (Paramount, 1945)
Bing Crosby/Betty Hutton/Ed Gardner
Filmed at Paramount Studios, Hollywood, CA.

Guest Wife (Greentree, 1945)
Claudette Colbert/Don Ameche

Her Highness and the Bellboy (MGM, 1945)
Hedy Lamarr/Robert Walker/June Allyson
Filmed at MGM Studios, Culver City, CA.

Kiss and Tell (Columbia, 1945)
Shirley Temple/Jerome Courtland

Love Letters (Hal Wallis, 1945)
Jennifer Jones/Joseph Cotten,

Filmed at Paramount Studios, Hollywood, CA.

Mildred Pierce (Warner Bros., 1945)
Joan Crawford/Jack Carson
Filmed at Malibu, CA; Carl's Sunspot, Los Angeles, CA; Glendale, CA; Los Angeles City Hall, Los Angeles, CA; Hollywood Boulevard, Hollywood, CA; Stages 1,4,5,11,12 ,14,15,17,18,22,24,26,27,27A, Warner Bros. Studios, Burbank, CA.

Our Vines Have Tender Grapes (MGM, 1945)
Edward G. Robinson/Margaret O'Brien
Filmed at Rowland V. Lee Ranch, Canoga Park, CA; MGM Studios, Culver City, CA.

Week-End at the Waldorf (MGM, 1945)
Ginger Rogers/Lana Turner/Walter Pidgeon/Van Johnson
Filmed at Waldorf-Astoria Hotel, New York City, NY; Park Avenue, multiple locations, New York City, NY; MGM Studios, Culver City, CA.

Wonder Man (Samuel Goldwyn,1945)
Danny Kaye/Virginia Mayo
Filmed at Samuel Goldwyn Studios, West Hollywood, CA.

CHAPTER 27 – *Point System for Discharge*

A Bell for Adano (see Chapter 24)

Along Came Jones (International Pictures, 1945)
Gary Cooper/Loretta Young/William Demarest
Filmed in Tucson, AZ; Nogales, AZ; Sasabe, AZ; Iverson Ranch, Chatsworth, CA.

Christmas in Connecticut (see Chapter 19)

Dangerous Partners (MGM, 1945)
James Craig/Signe Hasso
Filmed in Pennylvania Station, New York City, NY; MGM Studios, Culver City, CA.

Her Highness and the Bellboy (see Chapter 26)

Murder, He Says (Paramount, 1945)
Fred MacMurray/Helen Walker
Filmed at Paramount Studios, Hollywood, CA.

Nob Hill (Twentieth Century Fox, 1945)
George Raft/Joan Bennett
Filmed at Twentieth Century Studios, Century City, CA.

Of Human Bondage (Warner Bros., 1946)
Paul Henreid/Eleanor Parker/Alexis Smith
Filmed at Warner Bros. Studios, Burbank, CA.

Of Human Bondage (RKO, 1934)
Bette Davis/Leslie Howard
Filmed at RKO Studios, Hollywood, CA.

Over 21 (Columbia, 1945)
Irene Dunn/Alexander Knox/Charles Coburn

Out of This World (see Chapter 20)

Patrick the Great (see Chapter 18)

Salome, Where She Danced (Walter Wanger, 1945)
Yvonne De Carlo/Rod Cameron/David Bruce
Filmed in Lone Pine, CA; Universal Studios, Universal City, CA.

The Fighting Guardsman (Columbia, 1946)
Anita Louise/Willard Parker

The Gang's All Here (Twentieth Century Fox, 1943)
Alice Faye/Carmen Miranda/Phil Baker/Benny Goodman
Filmed on Stage 16, Twentieth Century Studios, Century City, CA.

The House of Fear (Universal, 1945)
Basil Rathbone/Nigel Bruce
Filmed at Universal Studios, Universal City, CA.

Week-End at the Waldorf (see Chapter 26)

Wonder Man (see Chapter 26)

CHAPTER 28 – *Selling Records at the Meralta Theatre*

Duel in the Sun (Selznick International, 1946)
Jennifer Jones/Joseph Cotten/Gregory Peck
Filmed at Tucson Mountain Park, Tucson, AZ; Triangle T Guest Ranch, Dragoon
Mountains, AZ; Texas Canyon, AZ; Saguaro National Park, AZ; Empire Ranch,
Senoia, AZ; Las Cienegas National Conservation Area, AZ; Circle Z Ranch, Patagonia,
AZ; Ray Corrigan Ranch, Simi Valley, CA; Sierra Railroad, Jamestown, CA; Lasky
Mesa, Los Angeles, CA; Selznick International Studios, Culver City, CA.

Love Letters (Hal Wallis, 1945)
Jennifer Jones/Joseph Cotten,
Filmed at Paramount Studios, Hollywood, CA.

Mama Loves Papa (RKO, 1945)
Leon Errol/Elisabeth Risdon
RKO Studios, Hollywood, CA.

Our Vines Have Tender Grapes (see Chapter 26)

Rhapsody in Blue (see Chapter 19)

The Falcon in San Francisco (RKO, 1945)
Tom Conway/Rita Corday
Filmed at Palace of Fine Arts, San Francisco Ferry Building, Chinatown, Legion of
Honor Museum, Colt Tower, California Street, San Francisco, CA; RKO Studios,
Hollywood, CA.

Yolanda and the Thief (MGM, 1945)
Fred Astaire/Lucille Bremer
Filmed at MGM Studios, Culver City, CA.

CHAPTER 29– *Dynamite Explosion at Northwest Field Rocks Island*

Anchors Aweigh (see Chapter 18).

Blood on the Sun (William Cagney, 1945)
James Cagney/Sylvia Sidney
Filmed at General Service Studios, Hollywood, CA.

Four Jills in a Jeep (Twentieth Century Fox, 1944)
Carole Landis/Kay Francis/Martha Raye/Mitzi Mayfair/Jimmy Dorsey
Filmed at Los Angeles Metropolitan Airport, Van Nuys, CA; Twentieth Century
Studios, Century City, CA.

Junior Miss (Twentieth Century Fox, 1945)
Peggy Ann Garner/Stephen Dunne
Filmed at Twentieth Century Studios, Century City, CA.

Main Street After Dark (see Chapter 22)

Mildred Pierce (see Chapter 26)

Out of This World (see Chapter 20)

See My Lawyer (Universal, 1945)
Ole Olsen/Chic Johnson
Filmed at Universal Studios, Universal City, CA.

The Big Sleep (Warner Bros., 1946)
Humphrey Bogart/Lauren Bacall
Filmed on Stages 7,8,15,16,19,20,20,24,28A,Warner Bros. Studios, Burbank, CA;
Warner Bros. Studios, Burbank, CA.

The Hidden Eye (MGM, 1945)
Edward Arnold/Frances Rafferty
Filmed at MGM Studios, Culver City, CA.

The Thin Man (Cosmolitan, MGM, 1934)
William Powell/Myrna Loy, Maureen O'Sullivan
Filmed at Southern Pacific Railway, Mojave, CA; MGM Studios, Culver City, CA.

Those Endearing Young Charms (RKO, 1945)
Robert Young/Laraine Day
RKO Studios, Hollywood, CA.

Week-End at the Waldorf (see Chapter 26)

CHAPTER 30– *One Last Letter to Guam*

Radio Stars on Parade (RKO, 1945)
Wally Brown/Frances Langford/Alan Carney/Ralph Edwards
Filmed at RKO Studios, Hollywood, CA.

The Hurricane (Samuel Goldwyn, 1934)
Dorothy Lamour/Jon Hall
Filmed in Pago Pago and Tutuila Island, American Samoa; Santa Catalina Island,
Channel Islands, CA; Point Magu, CA; Samuel Goldwyn Studios, West Hollywood,
CA.

Appendix B

MAJOR MOTION
PICTURE STUDIOS IN
THE 1940S

Hal Roach Studios
8822 Washington Boulevard
Culver City, CA
(Three long blocks/.7-mile down Washington Boulevard from Stella's Music Store.)

During World War II, leased to U.S. Army for production of training/propaganda films ("Fort Roach").

MGM (Metro-Goldwyn-Mayer) Studios
10202 W. Washington Boulevard
Culver City, CA
(.8-mile from Stella's Music Store, and 2.5 miles from Betty's home on Caswell Avenue, Culver City.)

Metro-Goldwyn-Mayer Studios opened in 1915 as Triangle Pictures and became MGM Studios in 1924. President Calvin Coolidge and Will Rogers were both present for the Grand Opening. MGM was the most powerful studio in Hollywood, and Louis B. Mayer had many of the era's biggest stars under contract. In 1939, MGM released both *The Wizard of Oz* and *Gone with the Wind*. Although most of both pictures were filmed in the MGM studios, the Atlanta fire scene in *GWTW* was created by burning down abandoned back lots of nearby Culver Studio, owned by RKO. Betty and her family could see the smoke and flames from their Caswell Avenue home.

MGM was sold in 1969, and thirty-eight acres of the studio's back lots were sold to housing developers. In 1990, the studio was purchased by SONY International, and is now the home of SONY's Columbia Pictures and TriStar Pictures.

Paramount Studios
5555 Melrose Avenue
Los Angeles, CA
(7.2 miles from Stella's Music Store, and 10.5 miles from Betty's home on Caswell Avenue.)

A studio was built in 1916 on the Melrose Avenue property for Robert Brunton Studios. Cecil B. DeMille, one of the founders of the Jesse Lasky Company, produced films there, including *The Squaw Man* in 1917. Part of the lot became the home of United Pictures and was used for Rudolph Valentino's productions. United owned this portion of the lot until 1926, when the Famous Players-Lasky Corporation took over. The following year, the company was renamed Paramount-Famous Lasky Corporation, and eventually became Paramount Pictures, Inc. in 1936.

RKO Studios (Culver Studios)
9336 W. Washington Boulevard
Culver City, CA
(.2-mile from Stella's Music Store, and 3.4 miles from Betty's home on Caswell Avenue.)

The RKO studio, also known as "Forty Acres," was used by Selznick International Pictures until 1943, when the company was dissolved. David O. Selznick then formed Vanguard Films to complete the Selznick pictures already in production, including *Spellbound*. The Vanguard pictures were distributed by United Artists.

Twentieth Century Fox
10201 W. Pico Boulevard
Century City, CA
(Formerly Tom Mix ranch; 2.5 miles from Stella's Music Store, and 7.5 miles from Betty's home on Caswell Avenue.)

In 1936, TCFFC (Twentieth Century Fox Film Corp.) purchased a ninety-seven-acre portion of a golf course in West Los Angeles. It stretched between Pico Boulevard and the future Olympic Boulevard in what is now Century City. In 1946, Twentieth Century Fox purchased the remaining ninety acres of the golf course, extending from Olympic Boulevard North to Santa Monica Boulevard. A few months later, the company sold six acres of the property to the City of Beverly Hills as a site for Beverly Hills High School.

NOTES

(Most of the material in *900 Letters* is based on personal correspondence (1942 – 1946). In order to simplify the NOTES section, I'll use the following abbreviations when referencing personal letters. Since most of the correspondence is between Harvey and Betty, for those letters I'll simply indicate which of them wrote it, where it was sent from, and the date. For multiples on the same page, I'll give range of dates: (H = Harvey, B = Betty, AP = Harvey's Aunt Peggy, E = Harvey's mother, M = Betty's mother, R = Betty's brother, Rod, AA = Harvey's Aunt Agnes, AAL = Harvey's Aunt Alice, JH = Harvey's father, F = Betty's father)

page

Chapter 1: The Dance

1 **"the Doolittle raid..."** "Japs Fear Bombing of Four Cities Start of Huge Air Offensive," *Los Angeles Times*, Apr. 19, 1942.

1 **"involved with various USO..."** B, Venice, CA, Jul. 26, 1945.

1 **"Post's clubhouse..."** *Beverly Hills (CA) City Directory*, 1938, p.7; www.ancestry. com.

Chapter 2: Harvey

3 **"Lee Harvey Brown..."** conversation with AP, (Lee Harvey Brown's daughter), Jun. 24, 1978.

3 **"most devastating outbreak..."** Delfavero, Dina, "Spanish flu epidemic: The worst health catastrophe," May 9, 2012 "Spanish Flu," https://archive.triblive. com/news/spanish-flu-epidemic-the-worst-health-catastrophe'.

3 **"In Philadelphia…"** HHO, Public Health Report, "The 1918-1919 Influenza Pandemic in the United States".

3 **"In Pittsburgh…"** Thomas A. Garrett, "Pandemic Economics: The 1918 Influenza and it's Modern Day Implications".

3 **"gathered in large celebrations…"** D. Harvey Brown, *A Brief Family History*, (Poughkeepsie, 2011).

4 **"enlisted in the Army"** J. Harvey Brown's 210 military personnel records, 1943.

4 **"New Cumberland Army Depot…"** Leslie Przybelek, "Regards…to all my Friends…", 2015.

5 **"facade was such a success…"** "Douglas' Dream Took Wing in Santa Monica," *Los Angeles Times*, Aug. 4, 2002.

5 **"I didn't see much…"** H, Hershey, PA, Feb. 20, 1944.

Chapter 3: Betty

8 **"Job's Daughters Dance party…"** Lois Child, Santa Monica, CA, Nov. 4, 1941.

Chapter 4: Fort Belvoir to Patterson to Middletown

9 **"into the sunshine…"** H, Guam, Oct. 21, 1945.

10 **"looking forward to Sunday…"** H, Santa Ana, CA, Apr. 21, 1942.

10 **"dances in Beverly Hills…"** H, Hershey, PA, Feb. 20, 1944.

10 **"Casa Mañana.** Christopher Popa, "Jan Savitt: The Swing Happy Years," BigBandLibrary.com, 2007.

10 **"I'm almost at the end…"** H, Pensacola, FL, May 20, 1942.

11 **"keep 'em jumpin'…"** H, Savannah, GA, May 29, 1942.

12 **"more darn planes…"** H, Savannah, GA, Jun. 14 to Jul. 9, 1942.

13 **"Those records you wrote about…"** H, Savannah, GA, Jul. 24-27, 1942.

14 **"George Mason Hotel…"** H, Alexandria, VA, Aug. 5, 1942.

14 **"finally settled here…"** H, Fort Belvoir, VA, Aug. 9, 1942.

14 **"third week here at Fort Belvoir…"** H, Fort Belvoir, VA, Aug. 21 to Sep. 7, 1942.

16 **"over nine months now…"** H, Fort Belvoir, VA, Sep. 25, 1942.

16 **"1941 Chevrolet…"** H, Spokane, WA, Jul. 16, 1944.

16 **"We graduate on the 28th…"** H, Fort Belvoir, VA, Oct. 22-24, 1942.

17 **"I wish you could have seen…"** H, Patterson Field, OH, Nov. 21, 1942.

17 **"912th Engineering Air Force Headquarters"** J. Harvey Brown's 210 military personnel records, Apr. 22, 1943.

17   **"Osborn is a little town..."** H, Osborn, OH, Nov. 13-21, 1942.

19   **"For Me and My Gal..."** H, Dayton, OH, Jan. 1 to Feb. 27, 1943.

20   **"piano concert by Robin Tureck..."** "Pianist of Amazing Gifts Plays for Music Club," *Journal Herald* (Dayton), Feb. 5, 1943.

21   **"I was offered a chance..."** H, Patterson Field, OH, Apr. 1-23, 1943.

22   **"I'm in Tobyhanna..."** H, Tobyhanna, PA, May 10, 1943.

Chapter 5: Camouflage

23   **"Do you realize..."** H, Middletown, PA, May 30 to Jun. 6, 1943.

24   **"managed to see 'Orchestra Wives'..."** H, Middletown, PA, Jun. 23 to Jul. 8, 1943.

25   **"headed to Fort Dix..."** "28th Service Gr." CBI Lineages and History, Air Service Groups, http://www.cbi-history.com/part_iii_asg.html.

26   **"Harry James and Betty Grable..."** H, Middletown, PA, Jul. 8, 1943.

26   **"I was in New York last night..."** H, Fort Dix, NJ, Jul. 12, 1943.

26   **"the little pin and the bar..."** H, New York City, NY, Jul. 18, 1943.

27   **"there ought to be a song title..."** H, Fort Dix, NJ, Jul. 21-28, 1943.

28   **"Roosevelt gave a progress report..."** "Fireside Chat 25: On the Fall of Mussolini," Presidential Speeches, Miller Center, University of Virginia.

28   **"Metropolitan Hotel..."** H, Asbury Park, NJ, Aug. 1, 1943.

29   **"Lt. Mass and I went to New York..."** H, Fort Dix, NJ, Aug. 16, 1943.

29   **"Subject: Camouflage Classes..."** Report on camouflage courses , Fort Dix, NJ, Aug. 1943.

30   **"The Commander of the 10th sent..."** Report by Lt. Col Charles Maxwell, Fort Dix, NJ, Aug. 27, 1943.

30   **"well organized and interesting..."** Report by Lt. Col Charles Maxwell, Fort Dix, NJ, Aug. 27, 1943.

31   **"He visited a fortune teller..."** H, Fort Dix, NJ, Sep. 1, 1943.

31   **"We came in from Fort Dix..."** H, Middletown, PA, Sep. 16, 1943.

31   **"wants me to come to the wedding..."** H, Middletown, PA, Sep. 16-28, 1943.

31   **"only a short time together..."** H, New York City, NY, Oct. 10, 1943.

32   **"Hotel Dixie on 43rd St..."** H, Fort Dix, NJ, Oct. 12-18, 1943.

32   **"base theater last night..."** H, Fort Dix, NJ, Oct. 20-26, 1943.

33   **"SILVER BARS REPLACE THE GOLD..."** H, Middletown, PA, Oct. 28-30, 1943.

34   **"my old stomping grounds..."** H, Middletown, PA, Oct. 30 to Nov. 3, 1943.

35   **"still at Middletown..."** H, Middletown, PA, Nov. 8 to Dec. 4, 1943.

36   **"in conjunction with our Farm Shaw Bldg..."** H, Middletown, PA, Nov. 26, 1943.

Chapter 6: Train Commander

Chapter 7: Engaged on the Fourth of July

51 **"heading to the train station..."** B, Venice, CA, Jul. 1, 1944.

51 **"had arrived in Portland..."** B, Portland, OR, Jul. 3, 1944.

51 **"Harvey met her at the station..."** H, Robins Field, GA, Aug. 18, 1944.

51 **"both sent letters to their parents..."** B and H to M, Spokane, WA, Jul. 6, 1944.

52 **"what her parents' reaction to the news had been"** B to R, Spokane, WA, Jul. 6, 1944.

52 **"Henry King Orchestra at Riverfront Park..."** William F. Lee, _American Big Bands_, Hal Leonard Publishing, 2006.

52 **"Every day we go someplace..."** B to M, Spokane, WA, Jul.10, 1945.

52 **"we packed our swimsuits and took a bus to Idaho..."** B to M, Spokane, WA, Jul. 10, 1945.

53 **"three airmen from local area...severely wounded in air attack..."** E to B and H, Wilkinsburg, PA, Jul. 17, 1944.

53 **"the picnic for enlisted personnel..."** H, Spokane, WA, Jul. 16-19, 1944.

54 **"would leave Spokane Sunday morning..."** H, Spokane, WA, Jul. 20, 1944.

54 **"By 10:30, they were in Minot..."** H, Minot, ND, Jul. 24, 1944.

54 **"103 degrees in the Montana plains..."** H, aboard troop train, Jul. 23-24, 1944.

54 **"allowed his men to 'see the town'..."** H, Minneapolis, MN, Jul. 25, 1944.

55 **"brief stop near Albert Lea..."** H, Albert Lea, MN, Jul. 25, 1944.

55 **"dinner at the Canton Café here in town..."** H, aboard troop train, Jul. 25, 1944.

55 **"through Iowa and Missouri..."** H, St. Louis, MO, Jul. 26, 1944.

55 **"through Evansville..."** H, Evansville, IN, Jul. 26, 1944.

55 **"Nashville, and Atlanta..."** H, Atlanta, GA, Jul. 26, 1944.

55 **"reaching Robins Field..."** H, Warner Robins, GA, Jul. 26, 1944.

55 **"they learned that the 75ᵗʰ would be attached..."** Al Seeloff, "History of the 75th Air Service Corp".

Chapter 8: Bivouac

56 **"leave Georgia for the 'Mid West'..."** H, Warner Robins, GA, Aug. 2-11, 1944.

57 **"there was a bivouac planned..."** H, Warner Robins, GA, Aug. 11-18, 1944.

59 **"I was covered in it tonight..."** H, Warner Robins, GA, Aug. 18-25, 1944.

60 **"Dragon Seed, with Katherine Hepburn..."** H, Warner Robins, GA, Aug. 25-31, 1944.

Chapter 9: Landing Strip in Mississippi

61 **"1ˢᵗ of September had come and gone…"** H, Robins Field, GA, Sep. 1-5, 1944.

62 **"father and son…"** "Son, Father Exchange Notes on Two Wars," *Los Angeles Herald-Express*, Sep. 7, 1944.

62 **"World War in 1918…"** "Son and Father Exchange Notes on Two Wars," Los Angeles Herald-Express, Sep. 7, 1944.

63 **"well situated at Herbert Smart Airport…"** H, Macon, GA, Sep. 9, 1944.

63 **"would be leaving on about October 1ˢᵗ…"** H, Macon, GA, Sep. 9-17, 1944.

64 **"first parade here at Herbert Smart…"** H, Macon, GA, Sep. 17-20, 1944.

66 **"Mississippi Ordnance Plant…"** "Mississippi Ordnance Plant", RG 156, Records, Office of the Chief of Ordnance (1940-1966), National Archives at Atlanta.

66 **"heavy machinery and maintenance…"** https://wikivisually.com/wiki/Flora,_Mississippi#Mississippi_Ordnance_Plant.

66 **"received his orders to go to Mississippi…"** H, Macon, GA, Sep. 21-22, 1944.

67 **"checked into the Heidelberg…"** H, Flora, MS, Sep. 25, 1944.

67 **"not a tough job…"** H, Flora, MS, Sep. 25, 1944.

67 **"On Saturday…"** H, Macon, GA, Sep. 30 to Oct. 1, 1944.

67 **"Pullman reservations for the men…"** H, Flora, MS, Oct. 6-8, 1944.

68 **"finished job will be 1700' by 60'…"** H, Flora, MS, Oct. 11-14, 1944.

69 **"pretty proud of my little outfit…"** H, Macon, GA, Oct. 17, 1944.

71 **"mom described the gift…"** E to B, Wilkinsburg, PA, Oct. 19, 1944.

71 **"several wires come through from Patterson…"** H, Macon, GA, Oct. 25, 1944.

72 **"the radio is KDKA from Pittsburgh…"** H, Macon, GA, Oct. 25, 1944.

72 **"enclosed a handout…"** "Navy Day 1944," Navy Day Committee, Pittsburgh Chamber of Commerce, Oct. 28, 1944.

73 **"assigned to the Asia-Pacific Theater…"** "LST-831," Naval History and Heritage Command, https://www.history.navy.mil/research/histories/ship-histories/danfs/l/lst-831.html.

73 **"on the firing range at Herbert Smart…"** H, Macon, GA, Nov. 1, 1944.

73 **"The next day, he was issued his M-1 rifle…"** H, Macon, GA, Nov. 1-2, 1944.

74 **"boarded a troop train…1000-mile trip to Tinker Field…"** Al Seeloff, "History of the 75th Air Service Corp".

Chapter 10: Malibu Honeymoon

75 **"finally settled here at Tinker Field…"** H, Oklahoma City, OK, Nov. 9-14, 1944.

76 **"could catch a train the rest of the way..."** H, Oklahoma City, OK, Nov. 14-18, 1944.

76 **"Will Rogers Highway..."** "Route 66 Timeline," Legends of America, https://www.legendsofamerica.com/66-timeline/, 2003.

76 **"A year later in Guam, Harvey would think back..."** H, Guam, Nov. 11, 1945.

77 **"scheduling had been tight..."** B, Venice, CA, Nov. 15, 1944.

77 **"honeymooned...Las Tunas Isle Motel..."** B, Venice, CA, Nov. 1, 1945.

77 **"1930's hideaway spot..."** Brochure of the Las Tunas Isle Motel, circa 1960's.

77 **"Harvey's parents weren't able to come..."** E to H and B, Wilkinsburg, PA, Nov. 27, 1944.

77 **"minister of family's Episcopal church..."** Rev. H. Boyd Edwards to H, Pittsburgh, PA, Nov. 24, 1944.

78 **"340 miles in a truck convoy..."** Al Seeloff, "History of the 75th Air Service Corp".

78 **"Lt. Cain had received new orders..."** Lt. Cain to H, Hillsboro, OR, Dec. 13, 1944.

78 **"ordered to spend a week in Omaha..."** J. Harvey Brown's military personnel records, May 9, 1944.

Chapter 11: Secret Letters

80 **"knew he would soon be going overseas..."** H, Guam, Jun. 9, 1945.

80 **"forwarded to the Squadron Headquarters..."** Change of Address Form, Feb. 2, 1945.

81 **"Lt. Col. Joe Neyer...asking them to write letters..."** Al Seeloff, "History of the 75th Air Service Corp".

81 **"asked him to remember everything he saw and did..."** B, Hays, KS, Mar. 24, 1945.

81 **"when you cross the equator, they say they dunk you..."** E to H, Wilkinsburg, PA, Apr. 13, 1945.

81 **"clearly worried about him..."** E to H, Wilkinsburg, PA, Mar. 24 to Apr. 13, 1945.

81 **"clerk at the Veteran's Hospital in Pittsburgh..."** AP, to H, Pittsburgh, PA, Mar. 24, 1945.

81 **"keep a scrapbook...to share one day with children and grandchildren..."** AG, to H, Butler, PA, Mar. 27, 1945.

81 **"experiences with the food rationing system..."** AAL, to H, Pittsburgh, PA, Mar. 24, 1945.

82 **"sweet gesture...to have letters for you men on the way**..." M to H, Venice, CA, Mar. 29, 1945.

Chapter 12: President Stricken

83 **"$1.55...plus 22 cents tax..."** Pullman train ticket (Oakley, KS to Denver, CO), Apr. 2, 1945.

83 **"snowing heavily..."** B, on train in Colorado, Apr. 2, 1945.

84 **"already awaiting his return from overseas..."** B, Denver, CO, Apr. 2, 1945.

84 **"snow-capped Rockies and the Great Salt Lake..."** B, on train in Utah, Apr. 3, 1945.

84 **"she had arrived safely..."** B, Los Angeles, CA, Apr. 4, 1945.

84 **"troop train with part of Harvey's unit..."** Al Seeloff, "History of the 75th Air Service Corp".

84 **"hard to watch her train pull away..."** H, Hays, KS, Apr. 2-4, 1945.

84 **"Joe E. Brown donated baseball...equipment..."** Al Seeloff, "History of the 75th Air Service Corp".

84 **"his men were 'really on edge'..."** H, Hays, KS, Apr. 5, 1945.

85 **"forwarded until after he left the country..."** H, from troop train, Apr. 8, 1945.

85 **"continued writing.. .after he left Hays..."** B, Venice, CA, Apr. 5, 1945.

85 **"Where Hollywood Movies are Made..."** Culver City (CA) City Directory, 1937, p. 13, Ancestry.com.

85 **"Majestic Theater near the beach..."**Majestic Brought Culture to Santa Monica in 1911," *Hollywood Reporter*, Aug. 10, 2019.

85 **"Betty saw 'Tonight and Every Night'..."** B, Venice, CA, Apr. 7, 1945.

85 **"arrived at Fort Lawton..."** H , Seattle, WA, Apr. 10-11, 1945.

86 **"later found the pass and sent it to California..."** H, Guam, Jul. 12, 1945.

86 **"'ROOSEVELT PASSES'"** "Roosevelt Passes,' *Spokane Daily Chronicle* (Spokane, WA), Apr. 12, 1945.

86 **"'PRESIDENT STRICKEN...'"** "President Stricken," *Daily Chronicle* (Centralia, WA), Apr. 12, 1945.

86 **"Too bad he couldn't have lived to see..."** H, Seattle, WA, Apr. 12, 1945.

86 **"both kidded about writing a book about their experiences..."** B, Venice, CA, Apr. 12, 1945.

86 **"could be sent to servicemen with messages..."** "Personna is the Blade to Buy," *Life Magazine*, May 22, 1944.

86 **"Betty's family...each enclosed a note..."** Lundin family, Venice, CA, Apr. 13, 1945.

87 **"talking to you for last time in probably a very long time..."** H, Seattle, WA, Apr. 13, 1945.

87 **"couldn't control her tears..."** B, Venice, CA, Apr. 13, 1945.

87 **"one of the iconic 'music palaces'..."** "Carthay Circle Theatre" https://en.wikipedia.org/wiki/Carthay_Circle_Theatre.

Chapter 13: The Kota Baroe

88 **"75th boarded their troop ship docked at Pier #42..."** Al Seeloff, "History of the 75th Air Service Corp".

88 **"it wasn't a bad send off at all..."** H, on board the "Kota Baroe", Apr. 28, 1945.

88 **"censors missed...receipt noted 'Seattle, WA' as the point of origin..."** H, Seattle, WA, Apr. 15, 1945.

88 **"given to staff before the ship left..."** author unknown, "The Good Ship Kota Baroe," given to the 75th, Apr. 1945.

90 **"If you are a land lubber..."** author unknown, "The Good Ship Kota Baroe,", given to the 75th, Apr. 1945.

91 **"the ship pulled away..."** H, on board the "Kota Baroe", Apr. 15, 1945.

91 **"on a (this word was censored) vessel..."** H, on board the "Kota Baroe", Apr. 15-19, 1945.

92 **"pier #28 in Honolulu's Hawaii Harbor..."** Al Seeloff, "History of the 75th Air Service Corp"

92 **"clues to his whereabouts were there between the lines..."** H, Honolulu, HI, Apr. 24, 1945.

92 **"a little table he had set up on the bridge..."** H, on board the "Kota Baroe", Apr. 28, 1945.

93 **"the films on board were 'pretty old and decrepit'..."** H, on board the "Kota Baroe", Apr. 28, 1945.

93 **"broke down...between Honolulu and Micronesia..."** Al Seeloff, "History of the 75th Air Service Corp".

93 **"gathered around a piano in the mess hall..."** H, on board the "Kota Baroe", Apr. 29, 1945.

Chapter 14: Back at the Record Store

94 **"continued writing to his A.P.O. address..."** B, Venice, CA, Apr. 16-20, 1945.

94 **"Manning's Coffee Shop..."** Santa Monica (CA) City Directory, 1940. www.ancestry.com.

94 **"all American ships at sea would hold services for Roosevelt..."** E to H, Wilkinsburg, PA, Apr. 17, 1945.

95 **"news about the United Nations Founding Conference..."** "San Francisco Conference", historycentral.com.

95 **"The purpose of the meeting..."** B, Venice, CA, Apr. 21-8, 1945.

95 **"pair of silly cartoons..."** *Los Angeles Evening Herald and Express*, Apr. 21, 1945.

95 **"enclosed more cartoons..."** Dave Breger, "Private Breger Abroad,"*Los Angeles Evening Herald and Express*, Apr. 23, 1945.

96 **"guessed that Harvey was headed to Okinawa..."** E to H, Wilkinsburg, PA, Apr. 25, 1945.

96 **"Dome Theater..."** Jeffrey Stanton, "Ocean Park Pier (1926 to 1956)", https://www.westland.net/venicehistory/articles/oceanparkpier.html.

96 **"servicemen's wives club..."** B, Venice, CA, Apr. 30, 1945.

97 **"an exclusive girls' college upside down..."** "Comics Go Collegiate," *Los Angeles Times*, Apr. 23, 1945, p. 12.

97 **"her growing worry about Harvey..."** E to H, Wilkinsburg, PA, Apr. 29, 1945.

Chapter 15: 26 Days, 5,700 miles

98 **"Censors cut the date..."** H, aboard the Kota Baroe, May 2-9, 1945.

99 **"this was where they would be stationed..."** H, Guam, May 10-12, 1945.

100 **"the generators were still not set up..."** H, Guam, May 14-19, 1945.

101 **"Harvey's unit was the exception..."**H, Guam, May 19-25, 1945.

103 **"plans were underway for a coordinated blitz..."** Brad Lendon, "Hiroshima after 75 Years," CNN.com, Aug. 6, 2020.

103 **"B29's involved in the bombing runs took off from Guam..."** H, Guam, May 26-30, 1945.

104 **"the Post Engineer at Bruning Army Air Field..."** Lt. R.B. Haver to H, Bruning, NE, May 29, 1945.

104 **"the proposed Officer's Club..."** H, Guam, May 29-31, 1945.

Chapter 16: Salesmen from Capitol and Decca

105 **"back to work at the music store..."** B, Venice, CA, May 1-3, 1945.

106 **"an island that had been retaken..."** E to H, Wilkinsburg, PA, May 2 to Jun. 20, 1945.

106 **"V-mail"** Edward Wells, "Mailshot – a history, Forces Postal Services," Defense Postal and Courier Services, London, 1987.

107 **"rationing of meat in the city..."** AP to B, Pittsburgh, PA, May 5, 1945.

107 **"Westwood Village"** "Village Theatre", Los Angeles Conservancy, www.laconservancy.org/locations/village-theatre.

107 **"Saturday afternoon at the music store..."** B, Venice, CA, May 5-7, 1945.

107 **"Everyone I saw was rather on the quiet, sober side…"** B, Venice, CA, May 7-11, 1945.

108 **"U.S.O. Canteen in South Park…"** E to H, Wilkinsburg, PA, May 9, 1945.

108 **"Harvey's father didn't write often, but…"** JH to H, Wilkinsburg, PA, May 11, 1945.

109 **"becoming frustrated with the V-Mail process…"** B, Venice, CA, May 12-21, 1945.

109 **"frustrated with repeat announcements of VE Day…"** Dick Whitfield to H, Pittsburgh, PA, May 12, 1945.

109 **"Do you suppose the end of the war will be in my lifetime…"** E to B, Wilkinsburg, PA, May 16-20, 1945.

110 **"newly reopened Meralta Theatre…"** Marc Wanamaker, "Culver City's Meralta Theatre", Dec. 1, 2008.

110 **"she listened to the Lucky Lager radio program…"** B, Venice, CA, May 22-26, 1945.

110 **"reported casualty numbers in the Pacific Theatre…"** E to H, Wilkinsburg, PA, May 22-26, 1945.

111 **"Grauman's Chinese Theatre…"** Genie Davis, "Hollywood History: TCL Chinese Theatre," Hollywood Partnership, Apr. 28, 2017.

111 **"'Diamond Horseshoe'…"** B, Venice, CA, May 27-30, 1945.

111 **"Bing Crosby winning Best Actor…"** https://www.oscars.org/oscars/ceremonies/1945/G?qt-honorees=1#block-quicktabs-honorees.

111 **"Pacific Electric Short Line Train…"** "Venice Short Line," Electric Railway Historical Assoc. of So. Calif., www.erha.org.

112 **"going practically every night…"** "Regency Bruin Theatre" Cinema Treasures, www.cinematreasures.org.

112 **"becoming increasingly worried…"** E to H, Wilkinsburg, PA, May 29, 1945.

112 **"Ten cartons of records arrived at the store…"** B, Venice, CA, May 31, 1945.

Chapter 17: "Gecko" Theater

113 **"sat in our jeep to watch the movies…"** H, Guam, Jun. 1-7 and Jul. 15, 1945.

114 **"heavy equipment unit worked hard all morning…"** H, Guam, Jun. 3-5, 1945.

115 **"heads are five or six inches off the road…"** H, Guam, Jun. 5-13, 1945.

117 **"they have a pretty hot team…"** H, Guam, Jun. 9-11, 1945.

117 **"Christie Film Company…"** Marc Wanamaker, *Westwood*, Arcadia Publishing, 2010, p. 115.

118 **"starring Greer Garson and Walter Pidgeon…"** *Mrs. Miniver*, Internet Movie Database, IMdb.com.

118 **"Marilyn Maxwell came on the screen..."** H, Guam, Jun. 11-15, 1945.

120 **"at the PX they had Fort Pitt beer..."** H, Guam, Jun. 15-17, 1945.

121 **"rocky, coral cliff fell away almost straight down..."** H, Guam, Jun. 17-20, 1945.

122 **"didn't have a single experienced administrative man..."** H, Guam, Jun. 9, 1945 and Jun. 20-23, 1945.

123 **"thinking about their life after the war"** CPI Inflation Calculator, www.in2013dollars.com.

124 **"a G.I. band from another part of the island..."** H, Guam, Jun. 23-25 and Jul. 27, 1945.

125 **"thriving souvenir-for-liquor barter operation..."** H, Guam, Jun. 25-29, 1945.

126 **"129th Airborne Engineering Battalion, stationed Auxerre..."** Howard Sperber to H, Auxerre, France, June 11, 1945.

126 **"Art ...was, shall we call it lucky, to get out..."** Howard Sperber to H, Auxerre, France, Jun. 11, 1945.

126 **"who had graduated with Harvey from Fort Belvoir..."** Ralph Haver to H, Salina, KS, Jun. 18, 1945.

127 **"Another Pittsburgh friend..."** Jean Robinson Dietz to H, Ligonier, PA, Jun. 12, 1945.

128 **"she knew that her husband's plane had gone down..."** Jean Robinson Dietz to H, Pittsburgh, PA, Jul. 5, 1945.

127 **"remains of a US Serviceman..."** "Airman Missing in Action from World War II Identified (Dietz), Defense POW/MIA Accounting Agency, Apr. 6, 2011.

128 **"awarded a Purple Heart..."** "2LT Regis Elmer Edward Dietz", National Cemetery, Alleghenies (findagrave.com/memorial/68370437).

128 **"predicted rains had finally arrived..."** H, Guam, Jun. 25-30, 1945.

128 **"were listening to a weekly radio program..."** E to H, Wilkinsburg, PA, Jun. 30, 1945.

Chapter 18: Sneak Preview of *Anchors Aweigh*

129 **"Stacks of records came in..."** B, Venice, CA, Jun. 1-6, 1945.

130 **"The Wilshire had opened in 1930..."** "Wilshire Theatre," Santa Monica Conservancy, www.smconservancy.org.

130 **"she missed him terribly..."** B, Venice, Ca, Jun. 6-11, 1945.

130 **"appointed Assistant Finance Officer..."** AP to H, Pittsburgh, PA, Jun. 10, 1945.

131 **"George Patton and Jimmy Doolittle came home..."** Walter Cochane, *Los Angeles Times*, Jun. 10, 1945.

131 **"shut off General Patton's microphone because of his profanity..."** B, Venice, CA, Jun. 11-16, 1945.

132 **"150 B-29 Superfortresses from India..."**"L.A. man puts big B-29 fleet...," *Los Angeles Times*, Jun. 13, 1945.

132 **"plane went down over the English Channel..."** "Glenn Miller," Biography (on-line newsletter), www.biography.com.

132 **"upcoming wedding of Judy Garland..."** "Judy Garland, Donna Reed, Become Brides," *Los Angeles Times*, Jun. 16, 1945.

133 **"Symphonies under the Stars series at the Hollywood Bowl..."** B to H, Venice, CA, Jun. 16-23, 1945.

133 **"jazz adaptation of Bizet's opera, *Carmen*..."** "Bizet Music Gets Jazz Treatment", *Los Angeles Times*, Jun. 5, 1945.

133 **"Harvey was concerned that his foot locker would soon overflow..."** H, Guam, Jun. 21, 1945.

134 **"quite a parade in Pittsburgh tomorrow..."** AP to H, Pittsburgh, PA, Jun. 24, 1945.

134 **"Three huge, four-engined Army transports...."** "Record Crowd to Cheer Heroes," *Pittsburgh Press*, Jun. 24, 1945.

134 **"Similar celebrations featuring Gen. Eisenhower..."** AP to H, Pittsburgh, PA, Jun. 24, 1945.

134 **"headaches related to dynamite blasting..."** B, Venice, CA, Jun. 28-29 and Aug. 28, 1945.

135 **"1,498 American casualties in the battle..."** M. Hamlin Cannon, "Leyte, The Return to the Philippines," ,U.S. Army Center of Military History, 1954, https://history.army.mil/catalog/pubs/5/5-9.html.

135 **"northern entrance to the Ormoc Valley..."** http://www.32nd-division.org/history/ww2/32ww2.

Chapter 19: Out of the Jungle to Surrender

136 **"Dick Jurgens was an American orchestra leader..."** "Dick Jurgens/La Veda Libby Collection (M1987)", Dept. of Special Collections and University Archives, Stanford University Archives, Stanford, CA.

136 **"we had the big stage show we had been waiting for..."** H, Guam, July 1, 1945.

137 **"'One O'clock Jump'..."** H, Guam, July 1-4, 1945.

139 **" I saw the Japanese Zero..."** H, Guam, July 4-8, 1945.

140 **"he was killed here and I'd like to find his grave..."** H, Guam, July 8-9, 1945.

140 **"Eddie Bracken and Bob Hope took..."** " The USO Boosts Morale," Victory in the Pacific: The End to a Ferocious Conflict, *TIME-LIFE*, Sep. 16, 2016.

140 **"Bracken's Troup3... sponsored by the Navy..."** Obituary, Shirley Gallagher, Rogers Family Mortuary, Alamosa, CO, Aug. 13, 2020.

141 **"show was always the same..."** Ellen Sussman, "1945 USO show: She remembers it like it was yesterday," *Green Valley News*, Mar. 7, 2013.

141 **"Bracken later told a story..."** Faires, Robert, "Miracle Man," *The Austin Chronicle*, Feb. 18, 2000.

141 **"despite the big build up..."** H, Guam, July 10, 1945.

142 **"this particular letter had been opened by a censor..."** H, Guam, July 10-14, 1945.

143 **"sent Harvey...a list of updates..."** Ralph Horner to H, Pittsburgh, PA, July 11, 1945.

143 **"Ensign Bob Jarvis..."** Ralph Horner to H, Pittsburgh, PA, July 11, 1945.

144 **"had been bombed March 19th..."** Joseph A. Springer, *Inferno: The Epic Life and Death Struggle of the USS Franklin in World War II*, Fisher Press, 2004.

145 **"Seaman 1/c J.D. Hutchinson..."** Ralph Horner to H, Pittsburgh, PA, July 11,1945.

146 **"picture-taking regulations were relaxed..."** H, Guam, July 12, 1945.

146 **"I'm sitting here on an angle..."** H, Guam, July 13-15, 1945.

147 **"Japanese coming out of the jungles..."** "Come With Us," *TIME MAGAZINE*, July 2, 1945.

148 **"U.S. soldiers were beginning to detect some response..."** "Come With Us," *TIME MAGAZINE*, July 2, 1945.

148 **"Another show at El Gecko on Tuesday..."** H, Guam, July 17-19, 1945.

149 **"we can now say we are part of the 315th Bombardment Wing..."** H, Guam, July 20-21, 1945.

149 **"concentrated their attacks on Japanese oil refineries..."** Al Seeloff, "History of the 75th Air Service Corp".

150 **"An 'oldie', Destination Tokyo was our movie tonight..."** H, Guam, July 21-25, 1945.

151 **"Hank (Lt. Milleville" and I had a tough day today..."** H, Guam, July 25-27, 1945.

153 **"a pair of clippings his mother had sent..."** H, Guam, July 27-28, 1945.

153 **"Lieutenant Killed..."** "Four District Men Killed in action: Another Loses Life in Jeep Accident", *Pittsburgh Press*, July 12, 1945.

153 **"Captain Dougall..."** "Lt. William Ziegler Price, Jr., Killed in Jeep Accident," *Pittsburgh Sun-Telegraph*, July 12, 1945.

154 **"it ducked between his legs and got away..."** H, Guam, July 28-30, 1945.

155 **"Bandit Chief..."** "U.S. At War: Bandit Chief," *TIME MAGAZINE*, July 16, 1945.

155 **"WARTIME LIVING..."** "Home Sweet Home," War Time Living, *TIME MAGAZINE*, July 16, 1945.

156 **"As July ended..."** H, Guam, July 31, 1945.

Chapter 20: Boris Karloff on Selznick Lot

157 **"I'd go over to Guam to meet you..."** B, Venice, CA, Jul. 2-3, 1945.

159 **"I listened to a 4ᵗʰ of July program on the radio..."** B, Venice, CA, Jul. 4-6, 1945.

159 **"an article... on home-buying..."** Sidney Margolius"The Boom in Homes," *Collier's Magazine*, Jul. 7, 1945.

159 **"Virjeane was ushering at the theater..."** B, Venice, CA, Jul. 6-9, 1945.

160 **"Eddie Bracken played the lead, with Bing supplying his voice..."** Bosley Crowther, *New York Times*, Jul. 7, 1945.

160 **"a new airplane the government was building..."** E to H, Wilkinsburg, PA, Jul. 8, 1945.

160 **"21st Air Force Fighter Group..."** Maurer, Maurer, "Air Force Combat Units of World War II", Office of Air Force History, Washington D.C., 1983, https://media.defense.gov.

161 **"C-47 was essentially a modification..."** Dana T. Parker, *Building Victory: Aircraft Manufacturing in the Los Angeles Area in World War II*, Cypress, CA, 2013.

161 **"During the War, it was mainly used for transport of troops..."** Dana T. Parker, *Building Victory: Aircraft Manufacturing in the Los Angeles Area in World War II*, Cypress, CA, 2013.

161 **"Betty met Mary Alice at the R.K.O. Studio..."** B, Venice, CA, Jul. 10-11, 1945.

161 **"That raid on Tokyo last night..."** E to H, Wilkinsburg, PA, Jul. 10-11, 1945.

162 **"took the Pico bus to Ocean Park..."** B, Venice, CA, Jul. 11-13, 1945.

163 **"TYPHOON RIPS U.S. FLEET..."** Leif Ericson, "Damage to 21 Vessels of 3ʳᵈ Fleet in Raging Typhoon", *Sacramento Bee*, Jul. 13, 1945.

163 **"thunderstorm ripped off 104 feet..."** Leif Ericson, "Damage to 21 Vessels of 3ʳᵈ Fleet in Raging Typhoon", *Sacramento Bee*, Jul. 13, 1945.

164 **"plan to meet the boys at the port..."** Dottie McKinney to B, St. Louis, MO, Jul. 13, 1945.

164 **"the Gershwin Memorial..."** B, Venice, CA, Jul. 14, 1945.

164 **"Leopold Stokowski..."** "'Every Type Music' for Hollywood Bowl," *The Capitol: News from Hollywood*, Jul. 1945.

165 **"Tuesday nights will feature symphonic..."** "'Every Type Music' for Hollywood Bowl," *The Capitol: News from.Hollywood, Jul. 1945.

165 **"news from the Pacific was non-stop..."** B, Venice, CA, Jul. 15-17, 1945.

166 **"Hughes Aircraft's 'Hercules'..."** "Howard Hughes Sky Leviathan Found Amazing" *Los Angeles Times*, Jul. 17, 1945.

166 "a B-29...could be placed under each wing..." "Howard Hughes Sky Leviathan Found Amazing" *Los Angeles Times*, Jul. 17, 1945.

166 "while on the lot, I saw Boris Karloff..." B, Venice, CA, Jul. 19-24, 1945.

166 "Oberon was filming 'This Love of Ours'..." "Merle Oberon," Internet Movie Database (IMdb.com).

167 "he just about fell through the hedge..." B, Venice, CA, Jul. 24-28, 1945.

168 "the scenes were supposed to be in Pittsburgh..." E to H, Wilkinsburg, PA, Jul. 28, 1945.

168 "Army plane hits 79ᵗʰ floor..." "13 Killed, 25 Hurt as Plane Hits Empire State Building," *Los Angeles Times*, Jul. 28, 1945.

169 "zoomed down fashionable Fifth Avenue..." "13 Killed, 25 Hurt as Plane Hits Empire State Building," *Los Angeles Times*, Jul. 28, 1945.

169 "I went to SC to find out about the scholarship..." R to H, Venice, CA, Jul. 29, 1945.

Chapter 21: Celebration

170 "the same briefing being given to combat bomber crews..." H, Guam, Aug. 1, 1945.

170 "attacking with propaganda..." Joe Fisher, "Psychological Warfare Does the Job Guns Can't," *Stars and Stripes*, Jul. 1945.

171 "Gene Autry, now playing Tinian..." "Show Troupes Heading West," *Stars and Stripes*, Jul. 1945.

171 "Live Shows (Pacific)..." "Live Shows (PACIFIC)," *Stars and Stripes*, Jul. 1945.

171 "described his life on Guam..." H to R, Guam, Aug. 2, 1945.

172 "one package was a tin of records..." H, Guam, Aug. 2-5, 1945.

174 "a pretty fair idea what life is like on an island in the Pacific..." H, Guam, Aug. 5-7, 1945.

175 "watching a test explosion with binoculars..." H, Guam, Aug. 7-8, 1945.

175 "Robinson Crusoe, U.S.N..." Blake Clark, *Robinson Crusoe, U.S.N.*, McGraw-Hill, 1945.

175 "Tweed, with the permission of his commanding officer..." W.G. Rogers, "Robinson Crusoe, U.S.N.", *The Freeport Journal-Standard*, Freeport, IL, Apr. 17, 1945.

176 "four years in the Army on the 17th of December..." H, Guam, Aug. 8-10, 1945.

177 "so far, all of them are shooting in the air..." H, Guam, Aug. 10-11, 1945.

178 "headed for the Pacific..." Ralph Haver to H, from aboard ship, Aug. 11, 1945.

179 "possible our opinions are flavored with a strong desire to get home..." H, Guam, Aug. 11-13, 1945.

180 **"everyone is holding their breath…"** H, Guam, Aug. 13-15, 1945.

181 **"there wasn't any great show of jubilation here…"** H, Guam, Aug. 15-17, 1945.

181 **"I can't see why they'll want to keep us over here…"** H, Guam, Aug. 14-16, 1945.

183 **"look on Tallulah Bankhead's face…"** H, Guam, Aug. 17-19, 1945.

184 **"they asked him to say a few words…"** H, Guam, Aug. 19-20, 1945.

185 **"Irving Berlin's 'This is the Army'…"** Sheldon Winkler, "*This is the Army*, Irving Berlin's War," The Warfare History Network, https://warfarehistorynetwork.com.

185 **"Harvey and his unit saw the production…"** H, Guam, Aug. 21, 1945.

186 **"This is the Army…"** official program of *This is the Army*, handed out in Guam, Aug. 21, 1945.

187 **"in which you tell all about the peace celebration…"** H, Guam, Aug. 22, 1945.

187 **"we are so glad this mess is all over…"** E to H, Wilkinsburg, PA, Aug. 22, 1945.

188 **"enclosed a clipping…"** H, Guam, Aug. 23, 1945.

188 **"saved the life of an American Naval Officer…"** Katherine Scarborough, "Mother of Baltimorean Is 'First Lady of Guam'," *Baltimore Sun*, Jul. 15, 1945.

188 **"Advanced Service Rating Scoring System…"** "What is a U.S. Army ASR Score?," Mar. 11, 2021, https://work.chron.com/army-asr-score--22134.

188 **"points were awarded for time in service…"** "Army Reveals Discharge Plan," *Stars and Stripes*, May 11, 1945.

188 **"don't have much of a chance to be sent home very soon…"** H, Guam, Aug. 24-25, 1945.

189 **"asked about the typhoon in the Pacific…"** E to H, Wilkinsburg, PA, Aug. 25, 1945.

189 **"whose husband had been shot down in 1943…"** Jean Dietz to H, Pittsburgh, PA, Aug. 29, 1945.

189 **"traveled over quite a few of the main roads…"** .H, Guam, Aug. 26-27, 1945.

190 **"coral pit was shut down because of an Act of God…"** H, Guam, Aug. 27-29, 1945.

192 **"so mushy that dump trucks have a hard time…"** H, Guam, Aug. 29, 1945.

193 **"laughed at the most serious scenes, booed the villains…"** H, Guam, Aug. 30-31, 1945.

194 **"Sterno, an inexpensive alcohol-based gel…"** Mike Rugel, "Drinking Canned Heat and Jake," *Uncensored History of the Blues, Show 5*, Oct. 2, 2005, http://uncensoredhistoryoftheblues.purplebeech.com.

Chapter 22: Movie Stars Served in "Fum-Poo"

195 "Betty and Mary Alyce went to Selznick Studios..." B, Venice, CA, Aug. 1-3, 1945.

195 "an estimated 10,500 CSU workers went on strike..." "The War for Warner Bros." IATSE Local 728, https://www.iatse728.org/about-us/history/the-war-for-warner-brothers.

196 "dinner at Carter's Restaurant in front of the Cathay Circle Theater..." B, Venice, CA, Aug. 3-4, 1945.

197 "a number of Hollywood stars..." "Film Notables at Bowl Tonight," *The Los Angeles Times*, Aug. 4, 1945.

197 "Japanese ship captured in the East Indies..." "Yanks Capture Fake Japanese Hospital Ship," *The Pasadena Independent*, Aug. 5, 1945.

197 "Tokio Rose Asks..." "Tokio Rose Asks New Records For Program So Yanks Supply Them", *Sacramento Bee*, Aug. 4, 1945.

197 "parents were closely following the news from Guam..." E to H, Wilkinsburg, PA, Aug. 4, 1945.

198 "planes leaving Guam loaded with 3 million leaflets..." E to H, Wilkinsburg, PA, Aug. 4, 1945.

198 "first time I've been in the station...since we left for Hays..." B, Venice, CA, Aug. 5-7, 1945.

199 "Major Richard Bong..." "Jet Plane Explosion Kills Major Bong", *Los Angeles Times*, Aug. 7, 1945.

199 "on Thursday, the telephone rang in the music store..." B, Venice, CA, Aug. 8-10, 1945.

200 "news spread like wildfire over Guam..." "Guam Tars Nearly Tear Off Roof," *International News Service*, Aug. 10, 1945.

200 "Harvey's mother sent Pittsburgh reactions to the week's news.." E to H, Wilkinsburg, PA, Aug. 11, 1945.

201 "Yehudi Menuhin was soloist for the night..." B, Venice, CA, Aug. 11, 1945,

201 "for two days they've pumped fresh water into the ships..." B, Venice, CA, Aug. 11-14, 1945.

203 "we listened to the news hit the different cities..." B, Venice, CA, Aug. 14-15, 1945.

203 "described the scene in Pittsburgh...." E to H, Wilkinsburg, PA, Aug. 15, 1945.

204 "had taken Harvey, then 10 months old, to downtown Pittsburgh..." E to B, Wilkinsburg, PA, Aug. 20, 1945.

204 "you should have seen the cars lined up to get gas..." B, Venice, CA, Aug. 16-18, 1945.

204 **"nationwide 35 mile an hour speed limit was lifted..."** "Gas and Canned Goods Rationing Comes to End," *Los Angeles Times*, Aug. 16, 1945.

205 **"here comes another of my rare letters..."** JH to H, Wilkinsburg, PA, Aug. 18, 1945.

205 **"looking at everyone's faces, you could tell Peace had come..."** B, Venice, CA, Aug. 18-23, 1945.

206 **"wedding of Shirley Temple..."** "Shirley Temple Picks Out Her Wedding Dress," *Los Angeles Times*, Sep. 11, 1945.

206 **"the window displays at Stella's..."** B, Venice, CA, Aug. 24-28, 1945.

207 **"F.M.P.U. (or 'fum-poo')..."** G.E. Nordell, "First Motion Picture Unit", Magic Lantern Video & Book Store, https://www.genordell.com/stores/lantern/FMPU. htm#story.

208 **"a chorus of 1000 voices would perform tonight..."** B, Venice, CA, Aug. 29-31, 1945.

Chapter 23: Jeep Ride to Southern End of the Island

209 **"September didn't start out well..."** H, Guam, Sep. 1, 1945.

210 **"their ship was rolling so badly..."** Earl Sexton to H, Saipan, Sep. 13, 1945.

210 **"the peace agreement had finally been signed..."** H, Guam, Sep. 2-3, 1945.

211 **"the sooner it stops, the better..."** H, Guam, Sep. 3-7, 1945.

212 **"Commander of the Strategic Air Forces..."** "General Carl A. Spaatz," U.S. Air Force website https://www.af.mil/about-US/Biographies/Display/Article/105528/general-carl-a-spaatz.

212 **"*Devotion* with Olivia de Havilland..."** *Devotion*, Internet Movie Database, IMdb.com.

213 **"one large group, consisting of three large Squadrons..."** H, Guam, Sep. 7, 1945.

214 **"already acquired two Quonset huts for the project..."** H, Guam, Sep. 9-13, 1945.

215 **"had found a document..."** author unknown, "The Good Ship Kota Baroe,"... evidently given to the 75th, Apr., 1945.

215 **"arrangements at the camp..."** H, Guam, Sep.13-16, 1945.

216 **"Harvey's favorite journalists was Bill Henry..."** Bill Henry, "By the Way," *The Los Angeles Times*, Sep. 7, 1945.

216 **"musical was closed down..."** Robert Sylvester, "A Veteran Comedian Comes Home...", *New York Daily News*, Apr. 23, 1946.

216 **"several natives villages here and there..."** H, Guam, Sep. 15-16, 1945.

218 **"he will be stationed in the Nagasaki area..."** H, Guam, Sep. 15-18, 1945.

218 "we stopped at Pearl Harbor for one week..." Ralph Haver to H, Okinawa, Sep. 17, 1945.

219 "we have inspectors that come around periodically..." H, Guam, Sep. 18-19, 1945.

221 "servicemen had been producing their own little newspaper..." H, Guam, Sep. 19-20, 1945.

221 "General MacArthur announces..." "Occupation to Require Small Force," *Pacific Courant*, Guam, Sep. 19, 1945.

222 "Pop Bristow left for home." H, Guam, Sep. 20, 1945.

222 "P.R.C. Pictures..." Sean McLachlan, "Vintage Trash: Producers Releasing Corporation, the Poorest of Hollywood's Poverty Row," blackgate.com, May 11, 2016.

222 "Utilities Section was putting up a Red Cross building..." H, Guam, Sep. 21-22, 1945.

223 "Another night at the 'Gecko' theater..." H, Guam, Sep. 24-25, 1945.

224 "article about Mickey Scrima caught his eye..." "Vine Street Gab," *Capitol Magazine*, Sep. 1945.

224 "He and Frank Sinatra..." Mickey Scrima obituary, *Dallas Morning News*, Apr. 5, 2009.

225 "cross between Frankie Sinatra and Morton Downey..." "Jan Garber's Services in LA," *Billboard*, Oct. 15, 1977.

225 "because the film we had was a reprint..." H, Guam, Sep. 25-28, 1945.

226 "organize our Officer club..." H, Guam, Sep. 28-30, 1945.

227 "Betty received the letter describing this incident..." B, Venice, CA, Oct. 5, 1945.

227 "All in all, not too bad..." H, Guam, Sep. 30, 1945.

Chapter 24: Studio Audience for Burns and Allen

228 "last night of the Hollywood Bowl season..." B, Venice, CA, Sep. 1-3, 1945.

229 "Santa Fe's eastbound California Limited derailed..." "Rail Wreck at Santa Anita Injures 50," *Los Angeles Times*, Sep. 5, 1945.

229 " I found some more little Penguin books for you..." B, Venice, CA, Sep. 6-8, 1945.

230 "Meat rationing will end Oct 1..." "No date set to end meat rationing," *Daily News*, Los Angeles, Sep. 10, 1945.

231 "the point system is the means..." "Releases by July 1.," *Los Angeles Herald-Express*, Sep. 12, 1945.

231 "I helped Mr. Stella put a new head on a banjo..." B, Venice, CA, Sep. 14-16, 1945.

232 **"George Burns and Gracie Allen show at NBC..."** B, Venice, CA, Sep. 17-20, 1945.

232 **"another about Truman's plans to end draft..."** "Truman Sees Draft End Sooner," *Los Angeles Herald-Express*, Sep. 18, 1945.

232 **"Pasadena pastor...predicting that the world would end..."** "Explains World End Prediction," *Los Angeles Herald-Express*, Sep. 18, 1945.

233 **"husband-and-wife comedy team..."** "Maxwell House Coffee Time, Starring Burns and Allen," THE PALEY CENTER FOR MEDIA, New York, NY, Sep. 20, 1945, paleycenter.org.

234 **"Gen. George C. Marshall..."** "CUT ARMY PTS. TO 70 ON OCT.1", *Los Angeles Herald-Express*, Sep. 20, 1945.

234 **"Rod played his first JV football game for SC..."** B, Venice, CA, Sep. 21-25, 1945.

235 **"heard on the radio that Guam was definitely Navy..."** B, Venice, CA, Sep. 25-29, 1945.

236 **"mother wrote to the Lundins expressing her sympathy..."** E to M, Wilkinsburg, PA, Sep. 26, 1945.

236 **"L.A.'s radio station, WMPC..."** "Fred Haney," *KMPC Program Guide*, Sep. 1945.

237 **"with a gleam in her eye..."** B, Venice, CA, Sep. 29, 1945.

Chapter 25: Opening Night at the Officers Club

238 **"Harvey and his fellow officers..."** H, Guam, Oct. 1-2, 1945.

239 **"'the forgotten men of this war...'"** H, Guam, Oct. 2-5, 1945.

240 **"should be good for football games..."** H, Guam, Oct. 5-9, 1945.

241 **"Young Man with a Horn..."** "Book for the Jitterbugs," *The Brooklyn Daily Eagle*, Jun. 5, 1938.

242 **"Irving Berlin and all those other guys..."** H, Guam, Oct. 9-10, 1945.

243 **"with the fighting over..."** H, Guam, Oct. 10-12, 1945.

244 **"Lt. Leonard's sudden departure was ironic..."** H, Guam, Oct. 12-13, 1945.

245 **"Ring Lardner's only novel..."** Colin Fleming, "The Greatest Baseball Novel Ever Written: 'You Know Me, Al'", *The Atlantic*, Aug. 28, 2013.

245 **"typhoon that had hit Okinawa..."** E to H, Wilkinsburg, PA, Oct. 13, 1945.

246 **"*Young Jefferson (The Statesman Scholar)*..."** E to H, Wilkinsburg, PA, Oct. 13, 1945.

246 **"dozen officers, including Harvey, worked all day on their club..."** H, Guam, Oct. 14-15, 1945.

247 **"There should be a crowd of more than 500..."** H, Guam, Oct. 15-17, 1945.

248 **"a new Wing regulation was announced..."** H, Guam, Oct. 17-18, 1945.

263 **"he was enlisting in the regular army..."** B, Venice, CA, Oct. 16-19, 1945.

263 **"the Navy's Third Fleet was in Los Angeles..."** "Los Angeles Gives Halsey Hero Greeting," *Los Angeles Times*, Oct. 18, 1945.

264 **"reminded me of Major Bennett..."** B, Venice, CA, Oct. 19-20, 1945.

265 **"Gibson had been the intermission pianist for Fats Waller**..." "Harry 'The Hipster' Gibson" hyzercreek.com.

265 **"Louis played there, Billie Holiday, all the big names..."** Joe Darensbourg, *Telling It Like It Is*, Macmillan Popular Music Series, 1987.

266 **"*Guest Wife*, with Claudette Colbert..."** B, Venice, CA, Oct. 20-23, 1945.

267 **"I wish I could write something here to make you feel a lot better..."** H, Guam, Oct. 23,1945.

267 **"urged universal military training..."** "The President's Training Plea," *The Los Angeles Times*, Oct. 24, 1945.

267 **"Betty thinking of going back for further education..."** B, Venice, CA, Oct. 23-25, 1945.

268 **"tentative plans call for an end of shoe rationing..."** "Shoe Ration Near End", *Los Angeles Herald-Express*, Oct. 24, 1945.

268 **"the telephone rang, and it was Rod..."** B, Venice, CA, Oct. 25-26, 1945.

268 **"This is my first day here at Fort MacArthur..."** R to H, Fort MacArthur, CA, Oct. 25, 1945.

269 **"understand just what you are going through..."** E to B, Wilkinsburg, PA, Oct. 26, 1945.

270 **"saw 'Mildred Pierce' at the Wiltern..."** B, Venice, CA, Oct. 26-27, 1945.

270 **"three Academy Awards..."** *Mildred Pierce*, Internet Movie Database, IMdb. com.

270 **"parade through downtown Los Angeles..."** "500,000 Cheer Great Navy Day Parade," *Los Angeles Herald-Express*, Oct. 27, 1945.

271 **"address by President Truman in Central Park**..." "Truman Reveals Foreign Policies,"*Los Angeles Herald-Express*, Oct. 27, 1945.

271 **"and then we left for Fort Mac Arthur..."** B, Venice, CA, Oct. 28-31, 1945.

272 **"a man on Attu Island in the Aleutians..."** "Willie's Afraid to Go Home," *Los Angeles Herald-Express*, Oct. 2, 1945.

272 **"dolled up in a clown suit..."** B, Venice, CA, Oct. 31, 1945.

Chapter 27: Point System for Discharge

273 **"Harvey had been on Guam for almost six months..."** H, Guam, Nov. 1-2, 1945.

274 **"Bernie Armstrong..."** Duquesne Light Company Newsletter, Oct. 1945.

274 **"guys got started on stories about their college days..."** H, Guam, Nov. 2-4, 1945.

275 **"envelope was marked : <u>Inter Island</u>..."** Ralph Havers to H, Okinawa, Nov. 5, 1945.

276 **"C-Rations were developed in 1938..."** David Vergun, "C-Rats Fueled Troops During and After World War II," U.S. Dept. of Defense, Aug. 13, 2019.

277 **"soldiers complained about the taste..."** David Vergun, "C-Rats Fueled Troops During and After World War II," U.S. Dept. Defense, Aug. 13, 2019.

277 **"I thought...there wouldn't be any re-enlistments..."** H, Guam, Nov. 6, 1945.

277 **"family in Pittsburgh was also reading about the re-enlistment..."** E to H, Wilkinsburg, PA, Nov. 6, 1945.

277 **"Aberdeen Training Grounds in Maryland..."** R to H, Aberdeen, MD, Nov. 6, 1945.

278 **"the last two evenings now, we've played volleyball..."** H, Guam, Nov. 6-8, 1945.

279 **"guys that sign up for the regular army..."** H, Guam, Nov. 8-10, 1945.

281 **"the time off won't really do me any good..."** H, Guam, Nov. 10-14, 1945.

282 **"he still had a scar on his arm from the 'mustard gas' shot..."** H, Guam, Nov. 13-14, 1945.

282 **"the actress in the film wasn't Faye Emerson..."** *The Fighting Guardsman*, Internet Movie Database, IMdb.com.

283 **"in the theater the other night it got away and raced back and forth..."** H, Guam, Nov. 13-16, 1945.

285 **"they hoped the new space would provide relief from the heat..."** H, Guam, Nov. 16-18, 1945.

286 **"there hasn't been anything posted..."** H, Guam, Nov. 18-21, 1945.

287 **"the movie tonight was 'Blonde from Brooklyn'..."** H, Guam, Nov. 20-22, 1945.

288 **"only anniversary you and Betty will ever have to spend apart..."** E to H, Wilkinsburg, PA, Nov. 24, 1945.

288 **"It'll be on the Hit Parade, or I miss my guess..."** H, Guam, Nov. 22-26, 1945.

288 **"stationed in Saga, north of Nagasaki..."** Earl Sexton to H, Saga, Japan, Nov. 23, 1945.

290 **"American military's newspaper..."** Lt. J.G. Humphries, Army, "Lifetime Cast System," *Stars and Stripes*, Nov. 24, 1945.

291 **"Lt. J.G. Humphries..."** Lt. J.G. Humphries, Army, "Lifetime Cast System," *Stars and Stripes*, Nov. 24, 1945.

291 **"Went to the show again at the Agaña Bowl..."** H, Guam, Nov. 27-29, 1945.

292 **"based on the 1915 novel..."** W. Somerset Maugham, *Of Human Bondage*, George H. Doran Co., New York, 1915.

292 **"special showing for the military..."** Philip Scheuer, "Hollywood Tries Repeat With 'Of Human Bondage,' *Los Angeles Times*, July 20, 1946.

292 **"seems to sneak into every picture..."** H, Guam, Nov. 29, 1945.

Chapter 28: Selling Records at the Meralta Theatre

293 **"I played records in the lobby of the Meralta Theater..."** B, Venice, CA, Nov. 1-3, 1945.

293 **"promptly sent overseas to entertain the troops..."** *Rhapsody in Blue*, Internet Movie Database, IMdb.com.

294 **"school kids who visited the battleship..."** "USS Missouri 'Wreck' After Kids' Visit," *Los Angeles Herald-Express*, Nov. 3, 1945.

295 **"she and Harvey Sr. had gone to see the Ice Capades..."** E to H, Wilkinsburg, PA, Nov. 3, 1945.

295 **"Sonja Henje to skate..."** Mike Mackin, "Let's Talk About: the Ice Capades," *Pittsburgh Post-Gazette*, Dec. 31, 2009.

295 **"for the benefit of hospitalized servicemen..."** "Ice Capades for Vets Sept. 15," *Pittsburgh Sun-Telegraph*, Sep. 2, 1945.

295 **"received a long letter from Rod..."** B, Venice, CA, Nov. 5-7, 1945.

296 **"vocalist with Count Basie..."** Tony Russell, *The Blues: From Robert Johnson to Robert Cray*, Carlton Books, London, England, 1997.

296 **"to buy five thousand records from a juke box dealer..."** B, Venice, CA, Nov. 8-9, 1945.

296 **"large hotels on the boardwalk have been turned into hospitals..."** AP to B, Pittsburgh, PA, Nov. 9, 1945.

297 **"hospitals will be turned over to the Veteran's Administration..."** AP to H, Pittsburgh, PA, Nov. 9, 1945.

298 **"one of the country's first super models..."** "Anita Colby," Internet Movie Database, IMdb.com.

298 **"working for David O. Selznick..."** Otto Friedrich, *City of Nets: A Portrait of Hollywood in the 1940's*, Harper & Row, New York, 1987.

298 **"drove up to Sunset Blvd...."** B. Venice, CA, Nov. 11-15, 1945.

300 **"roses and beautiful ones too..."** M to H, Venice, CA, Nov. 19, 1945.

300 **"first husband...had been killed in India..."** B, Venice, CA, Nov. 19-23, 1945.

300 **"Ebell of Los Angeles..."** "The Ebell Club History," ebellofla.com/club/about/history.

301 **"South American explorer, and cinematographer..."** Edwin Schallert, "Betty Caulfield Sought for Picture with Joan," Drama and Film Section, *Los Angeles Times*, Nov. 21, 1945.

302 **"I liked the series on Peru better"** B, Venice, CA, Nov. 23-30, 1945.

Chapter 29: Dynamite Explosion at Northwest Field Rocks Island

304 **"Harvey's unit had an inspection..."** H, Guam, Dec. 1-3, 1945.

304 **"Four Jills in a Jeep**..." "Carole Landis" Glamor Girls of the Silver Screen, http://www.glamourgirlsofthesilverscreen.com/show/154/Carole+Landis.

305 **"to the other end of the island..."** H, Guam, Dec. 3-5, 1945.

305 **"Betty and Helen had been running down Hollywood Blvd..."** B, Venice, CA, Dec. 2, 1945.

306 **"Bogart played his usual good part..."** H, Guam, Dec. 5-8, 1945.

308 **"if I come by plane it will either be Mather Field (Sacramento)..."** H, Guam, Dec. 8, 1945.

308 **"12 Units Slated..."** J.D. Cross, "12 Units Slated for Movement by First of Year," 20th Air Force publication, Dec. 1945.

309 **"as men become become eligible..."** J.D. Cross, "12 Units Slated for Movement by First of Year," 20th Air Force publication, Dec. 1945.

309 **"getting close to the time when I'll see you..."** H, Guam, Dec. 9-10, 1945.

310 **"314th Bomb Wing's new all G.I. show..."** Sgt.Willis Jones, "Bedtime Stories" 20th Air Force publication, Dec. 1945.

310 **"a dynamite storage dump about a mile from our area..."** H, Guam, Oct. 11, 1945.

311 **"a giant explosion rocked Guam**..." "Two Missing as Dynamite Explosion at Northwest Field Rocks Island," 20th Air Force publication, Dec. 12, 1945.

312 **"Guam Police Patrols Sweep Island..."** "Special Marine, Guam Police Patrols Sweep Island in Widespread Hunt", 20th Air Force publication, 12/12/45

312 **"we took a short ride around the field..."** H, Guam, Dec. 12-14, 1945.

314 **"I'm O.D. (officer of the Day) tomorrow..."** H, Guam, Dec. 14-17, 1945.

315 **"We take off from here on a boat for Saipan..."** H, Guam, Dec. 18, 1945.

316 **"Japanese Read of War's End..."** "23 (Japanese) Read of War's End, Give Up Here", 20th Air Force publication, Nov. 6, 1945.

317 **"the expected orders did, indeed, come out Wednesday..."** Release orders, Headquarters, 315th Bombardment Wing, Guam, Nov. 18, 1945.

317 **"all set for us to leave on or about Friday..."**H, Guam, Dec. 19, 1945.

318 **"we may leave here tomorrow..."** H, Guam, Dec. 19-20, 1945.

Chapter 30: One Last Letter to Guam

319 **"Alfred Hitchcock's 'Spellbound'..."** B, Venice, CA, Dec. 1-3, 1945.

319 **"Betty's dad had been to the Los Angeles Coliseum..."** "Troy Clinches Rose Bowl Bid, 26 – 15." *Los Angeles Times*, Dec. 2, 1945.

319 **"I imagine you heard that one over there..."** "Army's Mighty Men Defeat Navy Team," *Los Angeles Times*, Dec. 2, 1945.

319 **"the beginnings of his military career..."** R to H, Aberdeen, MD, Dec. 1, 1945.

320 **"How the world has changed in the last four years..."** E to H, Wilkinsburg, PA, Dec. 8, 1945.

320 **"Here are the 'G.I.' records..."** B, Venice, CA, Dec. 10-13, 1945.

Chapter 31: U.S.S. Clermont Bound for Los Angeles

321 **"wouldn't receive the letter until he got home..."** B, Venice, CA, Dec. 22-23, 1945.

322 **"we leave here tomorrow aboard the USS Clermont..."** H, Saipan, Dec. 26, 1945.

322 **"I wonder where you are now. Maybe at Pearl Harbor?..."** B, Venice, CA, Dec. 30, 1945.

323 **"U.S.S. Clermont from Saipan-2049 undesignated personnel..."** "25,000 COMING TO U.S. TODAY: 20 Ships Due to Dock at Various East and West Ports" *Fremont News-Messenger*, OH, Jan. 11, 1946.

ABOUT THE AUTHOR

David Harvey "DB" Brown, born in Pittsburgh and raised in Pasadena, California, holds a BA in English Literature from Pomona College, an MA from Colgate University, and a PhD from Cornell University. DB retired from Vassar College after working there for thirty-eight years, the last twenty-four as Dean of Students. He does family history research (https://www.storiesinyourtree.com/); has led Elderhostel/Road Scholar tours to Scandinavia, Iceland, and the United Kingdom; hosts a folk/Americana radio podcast, *The Hudson Valley Rag Shop*; and regularly performs with a folk group, the Roundabout Ramblers. DB lives in Poughkeepsie, New York.